The
Red
Heifer

Endorsements

Anthony Cardinale has combined his success as an award-winning journalist and playwright to dramatically share his passion for Israel. Based on years of interviews with Orthodox rabbis, secular Israelis, Palestinian Arabs and believers, Cardinale has produced an innovative blend of fact and story for the reader. This book will cast new light on the current Arab-Israeli stalemate, challenging popular views while solidifying believers' love for the Jews.

— Terri Gillespie, chief operating officer of MJAA, author of *Making Eye Contact with God,* and ongoing writer of the "Restoration of Israel Minute" heard on international radio.

The Red Heifer is an extraordinary piece of literature, well researched, and extremely timely. I found it to be well worth reading and I highly recommend it!

— Rabbi Michael Wolf of Congregation Beth Messiah in Cincinnati, author of *The Upper Zoo,* and national treasurer of MJAA

Anthony Cardinale paints a beautiful portrait of the red heifer, as it was from the time of Moses, and as it may be in our time. In his fictional chapters, he develops the theme that the final days are upon us, and that God is sifting His people for a crucial decision—who is this Lamb without blemish? Be prepared to be challenged, provoked and informed about the red heifer, and what it means to *you!*

— Barri Cae Mallin, PhD of biblical studies, author of *The Name HaShem,* and founder of the humanitarian organization Maasay Yahdav (the Works of His Hands) in Israel

The Red Heifer

A Jewish Cry for Messiah

Anthony Cardinale

Lederer Books
A division of
Messianic Jewish Publishers
Clarksville, MD 21029

Unless otherwise indicated, all scripture quotations are taken from the New King James Version.

2015   4

Library of Congress Control Number: 2012941579

ISBN: 9781936716470

Printed in the United States of America

Copyright © 2012 by

Anthony Cardinale

Published by

Lederer Books

A division of

Messianic Jewish Publishers

6120 Day Long Lane

Clarksville, Maryland 21029

Distributed by

Messianic Jewish Resources Int'l.

www.messianicjewish.net

Individual and Trade Order line: 800-410-7367

Email: lederer@messianicjewish.net

She stares out at the world through dewy eyes, stumbling on awkward legs, dipping into her trough with abandon, oblivious to the soaring hopes and apocalyptic fears that have spread with the news of her birth. Watched over by an armed guard in a skullcap and visited by rabbis and other seekers of meaning, this rust-colored six-month-old heifer is hailed as a sign of the coming Messiah and decried as a walking atom bomb. Of a variety believed extinct for centuries, the red heifer is seen by some as the missing link needed for religious Jews to rebuild their ancient Temple in Jerusalem. Sacrificing the animal in its third year and using its ashes in a purification rite would allow Jews to return 2,000 years later to the Temple site, a spot holy both to Jews and Muslims . . . Many fear that the calf's arrival could create an explosive situation.

— *The Boston Globe*, April 6, 1997

DEDICATION

To the memory of Eric Mahr,
a true modern-day Maccabee

Contents

Author's Preface

The Red Heifer: A Jewish Cry for Messiah takes us
to present-day Israel and explores the ongoing search
for a red heifer by certain religious Jews who intend
to rebuild the Temple. They may be few in number—
easily dismissed even by fellow religious Jews—but if
you listen carefully to all sides of the conversation, you
will hear the loudest shofar cry *ever* of Jews longing for
Messiah to come in our time, for God is turning their
hearts Himself.

"If the trumpet makes an uncertain sound, who will get ready for
battle?" Rabbi Sha'ul of Tarsus once asked. Indeed, the message
is uncertain, unclear and even misleading if we listen only to the voices
of these ultra-Orthodox radicals, who would risk a regional war over
the Temple Mount, where the Muslim Dome of the Rock now stands.

But the trumpeting that I have been hearing is a blend of the voices
of *everyone* who has a stake in the quest for the red heifer. This book
is based on interviews from my five sojourns thus far in Israel, going
back to 1981 (as well as my interviews with Palestinian refugees in
Jordan). As unpopular as the red heifer movement is, I have found it
a great conversational icebreaker with religious Jews in Israel. After
they dismiss the very subject, they proceed to open up to me about the
related issues of the red heifer: Obedience to God's Word. Repentance.
Forgiveness. Sanctification. Salvation. The imminent coming of the
Messiah. And God's command to Zionists of every generation to grant
"justice to the stranger in your midst." All of these issues reveal Jewish
longings for Messiah to come and make all things right.

The Red Heifer: A Jewish Cry for Messiah is written primarily for Jews and Gentiles who believe that Yeshua of Nazareth is the Messiah of Israel. But for traditional Jews, it will serve as a detailed, heartfelt explanation of what's really behind the dedication that Christian Zionists like me have for Israel—with a special salute to Jews who have returned to their faith after the miraculous recovery of Jerusalem in the Six Day War. For it was during the mid-1960s that rabbis began searching for fallen-away Jews to invite to their home for "just one Sabbath," and then for another and another, with no strings attached. In the decades since then, multitudes of Jews have responded and become Orthodox as part of this *baal t'shuvah* (master of return) renewal.

In the Christian world, that miraculous decade saw the Holy Spirit enter the hearts of thousands like myself through the charismatic movement. It was also the decade that birthed the Jesus movement and the born-again movement. Surely, the Ruach ha-Kodesh of old is at work again, building a people for the final days.

Now, this book has two parallel story lines: One is a factual account of the red heifer and its related issues. The other is a fable.

The numbered chapters of this book recreate the drama of my recorded interviews with religious and secular Jews and Palestinian Arabs. Each chapter is a self-contained, scenic episode, allowing us to eavesdrop on Israelis and Palestinian Arabs in their daily routine, and giving us a slice of life as it is being lived today in their profoundly divided society.

Between these factual chapters, I have inserted the unfolding episodes of a tale I have spun—titled, simply, *The Red Heifer*—about what might happen if a Bedouin nomad from the desert were to mysteriously appear in Jerusalem with a genuine red heifer (the fable is based on my award-winning play script of the same title). *The Red Heifer* could stand alone as a short novel and, in fact, its plot gives the entire book an emotional continuity. My dramatic little fable—laced with comedy and romance as well as biblical solemnity—presents the personal conflicts we can expect to see exploding after a baby red cow is suddenly placed in the midst of religious Jews, secular Jews, and Arabs who are otherwise trying to live together peacefully in modern-day western Palestine.

Some of the people I was interviewing as a journalist were aware of the fiction plot that I was also writing—and they actually commented on the characters and the wisdom of their actions, as you will see . . .

So, what is the red heifer?

Certain ultra-Orthodox Jews in Israel have been planning the reconstruction of the ancient Temple and are now searching for a perfect heifer—all reddish-brown, with no white or black hairs—whose ashes are needed to purify the priests (Book of Numbers, Chapter 19). There were nine red heifers from the time of Moses until the Romans destroyed the Temple in 70 AD. The Talmud predicts that the tenth red heifer will herald the Messiah.

An authentic red heifer has not been seen in Israel in two thousand years. The search is on, and surely one will be found. Regardless of when that will happen, the issues that gave rise to the search are accelerating at a rapid rate, as Israeli society becomes more and more widely polarized between religious and secular Jews.

Virtually all religious Jews pray three times a day for Messiah to come and rebuild (or bring) the Temple himself. But the Book of Revelation indicates that the Temple will already be in place when Yeshua of Nazareth returns to begin His reign as Messiah. No matter how it eventually unfolds, the ramifications of the red heifer will affect everybody who loves Israel and who cares about the issues of repentance, salvation and the nature and role of Messiah. Not to mention justice to Palestinian Arabs and world peace.

Much of my research was done during my residency at Mishkenot Sha'ananim, Jerusalem's guesthouse for visiting writers and artists. This beautiful campus, with its red-tiled roofs and signature windmill, is within sight of the walled Old City, where most of the little tale takes place. For over thirty years I have been interviewing Israelis, both Jew and Gentile, and consulting many learned rabbis. I have walked the familiar paths of the city with my wife, Shirah. We have grown to love it as our spiritual home.

Most of my major Jewish sources in Israel are rabbis who were raised in liberal American homes but became Orthodox Jews after the Six Day War of 1967, when the Old City was recovered for the first time in two thousand years. The Talmud says that a repentant Jew is like a 'new creation.' When Yeshua urged Nicodemus of the Sanhedrin to be 'born again,' He was referring to a spiritual phenomenon that Nicodemus, "a teacher of Israel," should have known from the Old Testament. In the Book of Ezekiel, God promises to replace stony hearts with hearts of flesh. In the Book of Jeremiah, God says, "I will put My Torah within them and write it on their hearts," so that they would no longer have to strive in the flesh to follow the Law.

In my interviews with these prospectively 'newborn' rabbis, I pressed them for some insight into how far rabbinic Judaism has come from what Christians would call 'biblical Judaism,' which was once based solely on the Old Testament. The Orthodox, by the way, are the only surviving sect of First Century Judaism—the Pharisees. And their oral commentaries on the Scriptures (printed as the Talmud) have come to supersede the Scriptures. But the power of the Holy Spirit is in the Scriptures, not in man-made commentaries on Scripture!

To make matters even more disconcerting to Christians like myself, when Orthodox Jews refer to the 'Torah,' they usually mean only the Pentateuch (the first five books of the Old Testament containing *the Law*). They give considerably less attention—and authority—to the rest of the Old Testament, including the Prophets. How can modern-day Jews follow the advice that Nicodemus received from Yeshua—that they must be born again—if such Prophets as Ezekiel and Jeremiah are overshadowed by the books of the Law?

I have asked the Orthodox: What is it about your Talmudic teachings that cause religious Jews to cling so closely to the letter of *the Law*—even prompting a few radical Jews to risk a religious war by struggling to obey the Bible's mysterious ordinances of the red heifer?

Rabbinic Judaism was born a generation after the birth, in the mid-30s AD, of the so-called 'early church,' which in reality was a Jewish messianic congregation, whose members met in a private home and continued to visit the Temple daily. After the temple was leveled in 70 AD, Rabbi Akiva and his cohorts who formulated post-Temple Judaism steered as far away as possible from the direction being taken by those controversial messianic Jews, starting with the rabbis' denial that the Messiah would be divine. Fifty days after Yeshua's resurrection, during the feast of Shavuot (Pentecost), the early believers received the Holy Spirit, which would empower them to spread the Word throughout Palestine and to the Gentiles across the Mediterranean. The signs and miracles of the Old Testament continued in the New Testament.

But rabbinic Judaism doesn't give miracles, or the Ruach ha-Kodesh, this prominent role. And so I have asked: Does rabbinic Judaism still see itself as a supernatural religion, carrying on with the power given Jews in biblical times? It may sound like I'm begging the question, fishing for negative replies; but I've been looking for *positive* answers. And I found many—although they were limited to the miracle of modern-day Israel and the *baal t'shuvah* neo-Orthodox revival, based on the testimony that many devout Jews give of the power of God in their lives since their return from the secular world. I must add that, after visiting Orthodox synagogues in Israel and America for over thirty years, my spirit is discerning a greater and greater sense that the Holy Spirit is starting to come to these worshipers.

No one can have the Holy Spirit *within* him or her without the Messiah, but Ezekiel and other Old Testament prophets had it *on* them (Ezek 3:14). While the Holy Spirit empowers Christians to follow moral laws cheerfully—rather than out of fear of divine punishment—observant Jews seem to have been left to struggle in the flesh to follow the Law. To the typical Christian mind, the ultimate absurdity of 'slavishly following the Law' is being played out by this band of radical latter-day Pharisees who, in obedience to Numbers 19, are searching diligently for a young female cow, unblemished, with a rusty brown coat. However, I don't find it absurd: These Jews truly recognize that we are entering into the end times. And their blind faith puts me as a Christian to shame, because Orthodox Jews don't follow the kosher and Sabbath laws to gain *personal* salvation—they're doing it all out of obedience to God, working toward the *collective* salvation of the Jewish people.

Many Evangelicals will frown on the idea of secular Jews returning to 'the slavery of *the Law*' and might ask why my book treats this neo-Orthodox movement with such respect and approval. I must answer that First Century Jews who rejected the Son still believed in God the Father. But for more than a century now, the secularization of the Jewish world has resulted in assimilation and a generation of Jews who even doubt the existence of the Father—the Holy One of Israel. Looking back in church history, the first Christians were Jews who continued to follow the Law—but who nonetheless *had* come to believe in Yeshua of Nazareth as the Messiah. (And whenever any of them tended to treat the Law as a mandatory component of their salvation, Rabbi Sha'ul reminded them again and again that faith in Yeshua was the *sole* source of their salvation.) So I would ask: If God was able to instill a belief in the Son among Jews still living under the Law in the First Century, why can't He do it again in our century, as we approach the final days? When the time finally comes for the scales to fall from their eyes, will it be more likely to happen to secular Jews who have no faith—or to Jews who are faithfully following the religion handed down, as they see it, from the Holy One of Israel?

Overzealous Christians who ambush Jews with the New Testament forget that only God can remove the scales from their eyes, since He blinded them in the first place so that the rest of the world would have the opportunity to accept salvation. It is natural for Christian missionizers to reach for the low-hanging fruit—the secular Jews who don't share rabbinic Judaism's uncompromising rejection of Christianity. But the fruit on the highest branches is turning out to be the ripest, for the Orthodox are increasingly eager for Messiah to come in our time and

God will turn their hearts, not Christian missionaries. These are the Jews who will ultimately close the circle that was left open by their ancestors during the time of Christ (see Chapter 9, "The Pharisees' Unfinished Business"). God alone can make this happen, while the church's role must be to defend and encourage the Jewish people as they return to their faith after the twin nightmares of the Holocaust and assimilation by secular society.

And yet, this critical problem remains: Without the Holy Spirit, how can modern-day Jews' spiritual eyes be opened to the biblical path that God has laid out for them—so that they can survive the coming times of Jacob's Trouble and herald the coming of Messiah to the world? That is a central issue of my book.

As religious Israelis grow closer to God, and as secular Israelis wander farther into apostasy, a profound polarization is taking place in Israeli society. I believe that this sifting of the Jews (as well as Gentiles) is part of God's plan for the end times, when everyone will be forced to take sides in a final showdown between good and evil. In this final harvest, God is separating the wheat from the weeds that were sown into the field by an enemy.

But as this sifting of God's people goes on, the growing distance between religious and secular Jews is heartbreaking to witness.

The greatest disappointment I have felt during my most recent visits to Jerusalem has been the gradual unraveling of the patriotic joy I had seen among Israelis back in June 1981 (a few days after Israel bombed the Iraqi nuclear reactor). It was common for passengers to break out in applause, tears, and peals of "Havenu Shalom Aleichem" as the first view of Tel Aviv broke through the clouds. On buses somebody would start a patriotic song and everybody Jewish would join in. And on Israel's Memorial Day, all traffic stopped for a minute of silence for the nation's fallen fighters, and all the passengers who were Jewish would stand (except for certain anti-Zionist Orthodox Jews who insisted that the Talmud doesn't mandate this secular holiday).

I may be mistaken, but I believe I even saw a few of Israel's Arab citizens associating with Israeli Jews, playing board games at sidewalk cafes and frequenting one another's business. At Munir MaTouk's falafel stand inside Jaffa Gate, I had lengthy discussions with Palestinians about prospects of peace in return for land, with friendly IDF soldiers wandering by for some refreshment. But now that all seems a thing of the past. The turning point for me was during the celebration of the 50th birthday of the State of Israel in 1998.

The festivities were dampened by rumblings of a nasty cultural war between religious and secular Jews.

In addition, Israel's lifelong Arab citizens, now numbering 1.5 million, have been growing even farther apart from their Jewish neighbors, because of the mounting violence between Israel and radical Palestinian factions in the "occupied territories."

One of the burning issues of this book is the network of Jewish settlements that have sprung up in the territories captured by Israel in 1967. The settlements are related to the red heifer because they go to the heart of how Israel, in receiving the land, was commanded to "neither wrong nor oppress a foreigner living among you." Until this is fully obeyed, the Zionist dream will continue to falter.

Between 250,000 and 300,000 Israelis have moved into the captured 'West Bank' (Samaria and Judea) to expand the Zionist dream. The best of them now feel trapped in the unwanted role of 'occupiers' of territory now inhabited by 2.5 million Arabs. Even worse, a growing minority of settlers have bitterly harassed Arabs living on the West Bank—and now are vandalizing the property of *Arab citizens living in Israel*. They even have taken up guerrilla warfare against the Jewish state, with their 'price tag' attacks in retaliation for the military's enforcement of the frequent court rulings meant to protect the rights of Israel's Arab citizens.

But I must stress that most Orthodox Jews living in Israel proper are nonviolent, in obedience to the Law, and wish only to practice their rabbinic Judaism in peace.

If the emergence of the State of Palestine should someday require Jewish settlers to evacuate the West Bank, Israel faces either a bloody civil war or, more likely, the poisoning of Israeli society as a quarter of a million resentful settlers return to Israel proper with their anti-Arab activism. Unlike Palestinian schools, which teach little children hatred for the Zionists, Israel's 'progressive' schools today downplay Zionism and the Holocaust and recognize Palestinians as victims—but what if thousands of ultra-Orthodox Jews start spreading vitriolic hatred in Israeli neighborhoods where Jews and Arabs already live, at best, in tentative peace?

Meanwhile, a popular conflagration has been ignited within the Arab world. The Arab Spring in 2011 will go down in history either as a harbinger of a new, democratic order in Arab society, or as an omen of extended chaos in the nations surrounding Israel/Palestine. Neither scenario seems promising for an Arab-Israeli peace breakthrough to take place in our time.

And any eventual peace will undoubtedly tear at the heart of Jerusalem. After recovering the Old City in 1967, Israel's leaders decided to placate the outraged Muslims by granting them continued guardianship over the Temple Mount. No Jew may openly move his lips in prayer in the vicinity of the ancient Temple—an irony that would have flabbergasted and infuriated King David, who purchased Mount Moriah, and his son, Solomon, who built the first Temple there a thousand years before Christ.

Many religious Jews now ask this question: If the Temple is to be rebuilt *before* the Messiah comes, how can this happen while the Muslim Dome of the Rock stands on the holy foundations?

Israeli society is divided over whether Jews should ever resume their historical place on the Temple Mount. One survey conducted by the Israel Religious Action Center found that 64 percent of traditional Israelis favored rebuilding the Temple. Among the ultra-Orthodox, it was a whopping 87 percent. Yet, overall, 55 percent of all Israeli Jews said that, for the time being, the Temple Mount should remain off-limits to Jews wishing to pray there.

Religious and secular Jews continue to move farther and farther apart today, as a bitter struggle over the ultimate meaning of the Zionist dream unfolds before our eyes. I was reminded that the reason given in the Talmud for the destruction of the Temple in 70 AD—prophesied by Yeshua of Nazareth around 33 AD—was actually God's displeasure with the Jewish people for not loving one another enough.

"According to Rabbi Shmuel (Schneersohn of Lubavitch), on Rosh Hashana the angels listen expectantly, waiting to hear a Jew speak well of another, because the angels know that there is nothing that God desires more than to hear the praise of His children for each other," writes Rabbi Alona Lisitsa (she is on the faculty of Hebrew Union College in Jerusalem).

And so, this book carries two themes: First, the desire of religious Jews and religious Christians to hasten the coming of the Messiah, who alone can bring peace between Israel and her enemies from *without*. And second, the ongoing struggle to bring peace among the factions that are eroding Israel from *within*.

Along the way, I hope and pray that my book will instill in Christians a deeper love for Israel and a deeper respect for the Jewish religion—and remind them that the role of the church is to encourage fallen-away Jews to return to their God and our God, and to soften all Jewish hearts, for such a time as this.

A Personal Note

The earliest origins of this book were seeded one morning in June of 1981, on the shore of the Sea of Galilee. I was standing by myself, gazing into the waters where Yeshua of Nazareth had once recruited many of his apostles, and where he later walked on water and performed many other miracles. This was also one of the last places where he appeared to his apostles after his resurrection and before departing this world, to return in the final days.

I had spent the previous week in Jerusalem, covering the historic World Gathering of Jewish Holocaust Survivors and telephoning daily dispatches to my newspaper, *The Buffalo News*. As these aging Jews searched for long-lost relatives and friends, I wept with those who wept and rejoiced with those who rejoiced.

Now I was touring the country on my own and pondering the next step in my journalism career, which was at a critical crossroads. I had just gained national recognition for a series of articles on the military's experimentation with drugs on healthy recruits, many of whom had died. Our series had prompted the Servicemen's Medical Protection Act of 1980 to be drafted in Congress. And my colleague Modesto Argenio and I had won a national award from the Investigative Reporters and Editors, second only to the Pulitzer Prize.

But "The Bitter Pill" series had left a bitter taste in my mouth. When the new Congress reconvened in January 1981, our bill was no longer on the agenda. It never even made it to the floor. Now, in June, I stood in my swim trunks on a beach at Ganei Hammet and tried to visualize what my next step should be as a writer. I'd done other investigations that were nominated for a Pulitzer Prize. But the thought of diving into a new project and spending the next several months searching and scratching for a worthy cause—only to see it dashed again by powers beyond my control—did not appeal to me. In fact, I sensed that I was coming to the end of my rope as a secular writer.

Now, as I prayed for guidance, I heard myself asking the Lord to take my writing career and do with it as he pleased. Then I stepped into the water and ducked under the waves until I was immersed. When I ran out of breath and stood up in the water, I was holding in my hand a flat little stone that I had clutched from the bottom of the Sea of Galilee. It was shaped like a heart. Or the continent of Africa.

I don't remember hearing church chimes (or the shofar) as I rested in the sun, but I do recall volunteering to the Lord that I would accept the position of religion reporter that was about to open at *The News*. I say "volunteer," because in those days no rising young journalist would aspire to cover only religion. Not until a few years later, when the law makers and the judges had usurped religious issues and turned them into political issues, did the religion beat come to life in American journalism. Today it's one of the most coveted positions in the media.

The Red Heifer was conceived in my heart that day, but I wouldn't even become aware of the subject until 1997, when I heard that a heifer named Melody had been born on a religious kibbutz near Haifa and was rumored to be a genuine red heifer. After becoming a news sensation, Melody was disqualified by the Orthodox rabbis (descendants of the punctilious Pharisees) on the basis of the white hairs that had since appeared in her tail.

Back home in Buffalo, on the night before I was to return to work, I got a call from my city editor, Ed Cuddihy. He said that I had been assigned as the new "rewrite man," starting in the morning. This is an indoor reporter who sits all day long next to the city editor—at the newsroom's bustling 'action central'—talking by phone to reporters in the field and news sources of his own, in order to piece together developing stories, under deadline pressure, from one edition to the next. Only the sharpest researchers and quickest writers could qualify for this key position, and I guess I should have been flattered. But in fact the rewrite man doesn't originate story ideas, and seldom gets to see his by-line on a story that is entirely his own. So I immediately told Cuddihy I didn't want this job. I was greatly relieved when he backed down.

It didn't occur to me until years later that the Lord was immediately taking me up on my bold offer at the Sea of Galilee, and testing me in the waters of humility.

I was already a Christian believer the day I gave my writing career to the Lord at the Sea of Galilee, but I had no idea that I would have to die as a star newspaper reporter in order to become a born-again writer. Little did I know that I would spend the next two decades on the night shift, covering routine meetings for the paper. Cuddihy told me, as kindly as he could, that he thought I was burned out, because the only story ideas I was turning in after returning from Israel in 1981 were about Jews, Israel, Palestinian Arabs, and how Christians were deepening their personal worship in order to come closer to God. But to his credit, Cuddihy let me spend one or two months every year on the Sunday magazine (circulation 300,000), where I made my own hours and wrote more than 100 cover stories, most of them on in-depth topics of my choice that were too lengthy or too introspective for the daily news pages. Even on the night shift, I turned in articles on Jewish subjects between my routine assignments, and they usually got into the paper.

But what really destroyed my chances of becoming the full-time religion reporter was a magazine article I wrote in 1984 about a messianic congregation of Jews who believed in Yeshua (Jesus) but still considered themselves fully Jewish. My religious scoop had blind-sided the Editor and the Publisher, both of them Jews, who had to face the Jewish establishment about having publicized *approvingly* this controversial Jewish-Christian movement. A blitzkrieg of angry comments appeared on our editorial page from five rabbis (including my landlord, Rabbi Yaacov Haber). However, what most pained me personally was a phone call from Rubin Literman, organizer of the Buffalo delegation of Jewish Holocaust survivors that I had accompanied to Jerusalem just three years earlier. A survivor of Buchenwald and Theresienstadt—who had lost his entire family in the Holocaust—Rubin had insisted that I be credentialed as a member of the Buffalo delegation I was covering, even though I wasn't a Holocaust survivor and (as far as we all knew at the time) didn't have a drop of Jewish blood. On the phone now, Rubin sounded bewildered by my article, which all the aging Holocaust survivors saw as a Christian assault on their traditional Judaism. "Tony," he said sadly, "why would you take this from us?"

All of this fallout spurred me to begin writing articles about traditional Jews and rabbinic Judaism, almost in reparation for what I had allegedly done to them. And it ended up drawing me closer and closer to the Jewish community, and cementing my calling to write articles about their history and their destiny—and eventually to write *The Red Heifer*.

Now, here is how my calling to the Jewish people began. Back in the 1970s I had left the church and had wandered in the secular wilderness for seven years. One night I found myself at a charismatic prayer meeting. As they read from the Bible and prayed for each other's needs, I was transfixed by the spectacle of men and women praying openly—some of them in tears, without shame—amid a rising cacophony of voices and melodies and tongues that reached a crescendo as they all rose to their feet, arms in the air, engulfed by the presence of the Holy Spirit. These charismatics had learned that religion is about more than ethics; even atheists have ethics. *It's about worship!*

I began reading the Bible. I had listened to Bible readings in church from my childhood, but the Old Testament was new and absolutely absorbed me. I found myself deeply moved by the story of the Hebrew people who would fashion the backbone of modern-day Judaism and Christianity. I felt personally touched by them and didn't know exactly why. (Thirty years would pass before I would discover the Jewish bloodlines I had inherited through my Sicilian grandparents.) I studied Hebrew and began reading the Psalms every day in both English and Hebrew. I even learned from an Israeli-born tutor how to sing some of the Hebrew prayers that are sung by cantors.

Then, one night in 1980, I had two dreams in a row, each consisting solely of the spoken words, "*born-again Jew.*" The following year I went to Israel for the first time, and soon I was collecting factual material for what would eventually become this book—and collecting characters for the tale that appears between chapters.

The first character I encountered was Munir MaTouk at his falafel stand, just inside Jaffa Gate in the Old City of Jerusalem. On the day that I stopped there, I had just purchased something at a shop run by Chabad in the Jewish Quarter of the Old City. And I didn't want anybody to know what I was carrying in this shopping bag . . .

And let them make Me a sanctuary,
that I may dwell among them.

  Exodus 25:8

From the day the Temple was destroyed,
the Gates of Prayer were locked . . .
but the Gates of Tears remained
unlocked.

  Talmud (Berachos 32b)

Don't you know that you yourselves
are God's temple, and that God's Spirit
lives in you?

  1 Corinthians 3:16 (NIV)

I saw no Temple in the city, for *Adonai*,
God of heaven's armies,
is its Temple,
as is the Lamb.

  Revelation 21:22 (CJB)

Chapter 1

'When Will There Be Peace?'

JERUSALEM

The black-clad Chasidic man with dense beard and side curls had wrapped my precious purchase in tissue paper and laid it limp in the bottom of a plastic bag with carrying loops. As I walked through the Old City, I fancied that everyone in the marketplace could guess what was in the low-slung bag suspended from my fingertips. Leaving the Jewish Quarter, I climbed the familiar hill to Zion Gate, where I paused to turn around and gaze over the Old City walls toward the Mount of Olives in the distance. Then I bypassed Zion Gate and followed the inside of the city wall as the street curved with it to the right and headed north, through the Armenian Quarter. Past David's Citadel, the street came to an end at David Street, where a cluster of Arab eating-places runs into a cluster of jewelry shops and money changers.

To my left stood Jaffa Gate and the way back to the apartment where we were staying. To my right was the Suq El-Bazaar, which takes tourists down an endless progression of stone steps through a crowded tunnel buzzing with merchants and confident men and young boys who attach themselves to visitors and beg for a donation, a purchase, or a tour guide's fee.

At the corner where I had stopped was Munir's falafel stand, shaded from the sun by a tin roof and colorfully decorated with cans and bottles of American soft drinks with their names in Hebrew and Arabic. The wooden shanty and counter projected from the stone block building that housed the kitchen and, as I learned later, some back rooms.

1

The man cooking in the kitchen was the owner's nephew, Younis. He came over to the counter, and we got into a conversation.

"When will there be peace?" Younis repeated my question. "I get up in the morning, have some coffee, open the newspaper and turn on the radio—and then I feel bad: Iran-Iraq war, Lebanon war. I have a son who has a good chance of being hurt or dying in a war." He paused. "When we sit on the floor to eat, instead of at a table with spoons; when we ride on horses instead of cars, *then* there will be peace."

Younis went back to his cooking, and I took out my notebook and began writing. The falafel stand had a meaty odor to it, for he was cooking *shwarma* on a vertical spit. On the radio inside the shanty, the muezzin was calling the time of prayer.

That was when Munir came out. An affable little man in a brown V-neck sweater, Munir struck up a conversation with me as I sipped on a Coke and clutched my plastic bag at the counter. Munir said his family had lived in Jerusalem since 1880.

"God wants us to be one—but God is all alone now," Munir said, his irony tinged with an edge of comedy in his voice. "I had a house in 1948; we run away."

Munir said he had owned this falafel stand since before the 1948 Jewish War of Independence. The walled Old City, where the family now lived as well as worked, was under Jordanian control from 1948 until the Six Day War of June 1967. Now that Jerusalem was annexed to Israel and was again the capital of Israel, Munir and his family had Israeli citizenship—but he didn't mention this to me at the time.

"We are forced by the Jews to pay income tax and customs," he said. "We are paying by force. And we are refugee. We had three houses—now occupied by Jews. We live in the Old City, seven of us in two rooms."

"Isn't that the best place to live?" I asked, "being the Old City? The history . . ."

"Yes," Munir replied, "but it's not good—no fresh air."

"Small w.c.," Younis interjected, then laughed about the water closet (bathroom).

"We are living now, not too rich, not too low," Munir went on. "Some of our family are in Lebanon and Jordan. We can live in peace with the Jews—if we have our rights. We have a good business because of the tourists . . . I'm going to pray now."

The Muslim disappeared inside for a minute and emerged wearing a black-and-white checked kaffiyeh on his head and a sport coat over his

V-neck sweater. My fingers silently tightened around the loops of the plastic bag that hung by my side. After Munir had left for the mosque, I paid Younis and left . . .

I walked out Jaffa Gate and headed down Mamilla to King David Street, my thoughts deeply engaged. Then I walked down Agron Street, passing Independence Garden, and crossed King George Street at the Kings Hotel and took Gaza Road down to the Rochavia section of Jerusalem. I passed the familiar patio of the Resto Bar, across the street from the fortified residence of the Prime Minister of Israel. At last I reached the apartment house on Metudela Street. Inside, I took off my jacket and opened my plastic bag. I unwrapped the tissue paper and felt the rich, heavy folds of linen in my hands. Standing in front of the mirror, I opened the prayer shawl and placed it over my shoulders for the first time. I looked like a bearded Jew. Now I could *really* pray like one.

Isaac's Dream

Dusk was falling on Jerusalem. The slanting rays of the late afternoon sun struck the sandstone blocks of the Old City walls, giving them a mystical golden hue and casting stark shadows in the market places within. The vendors squinted in the low sun as they hurried to close their stalls, to gather in their unsold fruits and vegetables, their fish and meats, their jewelry and leather and baskets and olive wood, and to seal up their bursting sacks of beans and berries, grains and spices, mints and sweets, leaving behind their pungent co-mingled aromas.

From the Mount of Olives, rising just east of the Old City and the Temple Mount, the view of the ancient panorama was undergoing a magnificent transformation. Soon the Muslim Dome of the Rock—standing where the Jewish Temple once stood—would disappear in the deepening twilight, and the silhouette of the 3,500-year-old city would blend in with the tall buildings of modern Jerusalem behind it until darkness was complete . . .

In his bed tonight, young Isaac Cohen was having a dream. First he was standing in his favorite place on all the Earth—in front of the Wailing Wall. Then he was walking out of the Old City through the Dung Gate and was heading up the road toward the Mount of Olives overlooking Jerusalem.

"Abba," he was praying, "send us your Messiah *now!* Send Messiah now! Messiah now!—*Moshiach achshuv!*"

Suddenly the sun broke brilliantly through the clouds and shone on Isaac. He could feel its heat on his face. He heard a voice addressing him . . . and he answered: "You call me—'friend'?" Isaac heard himself say. "You called *Abraham* your friend. Thank you, Lord!—*Toda raba, Adonai.* Come now, Messiah Redeemer—come to those who truly love you. Yes—*Baruch haba b'shem Adonai!*—Blessed is he who comes in the name of the Lord!"

Now Isaac, in his dream, had a quick glimpse of the parting of the Red Sea.

"And You also spoke to *Moses* face to face, as a friend!" Isaac heard himself say. "Then Moses told the people at the Red Sea, 'Stand still

4

and see the salvation of the Lord.' *Ooh-roo et yeshuat Adonai! Yeshuat Adonai!*"

From somewhere in the distance now, Isaac heard the wail of the shofar—"**Ta-RUUUU-ahhhh!**"

Now Isaac saw a white cloud arise over the Temple Mount, above the Wailing Wall, engulfing everything. As the cloud slowly dispersed in the gentle breeze, he saw a woman standing on top of the Temple Mount. She looked like a Bedouin nomad. And on her shoulders she carried a small animal, its feet and its head visible on opposite shoulders.

Isaac could hear heavenly flute music.

"Here we are, at last, little one!" the nomad was saying as she craned her neck to look at the animal's head. "Take a good look—the New Jerusalem! Oh—you're fast asleep! Just as well," she said, tenderly removing the Red Heifer from her shoulders and placing it on the floor of the Temple Mount. She petted its head. "It isn't really the New Jerusalem—not yet. But soon, my little one, you're going to play a wonderful role in making it all happen. For now, sleep, after our long journey."

Then the Bedouin nomad set up a surveyor's transit on its tripod. She peered through its scope, looking upon the Old City of Jerusalem below the Temple Mount.

"I can see it all now," she said, then straightened up again. "Little one, you and Noor must soon part. But don't fret! Noor will be with you every step of the way!" She snuggled and kissed the little creature. "Trust Noor!"

Noor fiddled with the transit, looking through the telescope again.

"I'm very much interested in the land," she said. "Some people might think it's strange that a nomad, who has no home but moves from place to place with her flock, should be interested in land and boundary lines. Well, Bedouin nomads know a great deal about land—we even see things that cannot be seen by people who have their own piece of land to live on . . ."

Moving closer to the edge of the Wall that supports the ancient Temple Mount, she looked down and began to compose a story.

"Once upon a time," Noor began, "in a land where it all began—and where they say it will all end—there was a Palestinian woman by the name of Samira. . . . And she had two Jewish friends . . ."

When Isaac Cohen awoke from the dream, he felt energized and happy, but he couldn't remember anything that he had seen or heard. For, a divine spell had been cast over Jerusalem.

Chapter 2

'Why Doesn't He Just Come?'

JERUSALEM

One day, while writing on the porch of a hotel off Emek Refaim Street, I was suddenly overrun by 36 teenagers from the Epstein School in Atlanta, Georgia. They had virtually taken over the Little House in the Colony and turned it into a youth hostel. The American youths had just come back from a bus tour of Masada and the Dead Sea.

Standing on a tiny side street in one of Jerusalem's modern neighborhoods (once known as the German Colony), the Little House in the Colony is a modest hotel with an attached movie house and restaurant/bar—named Lev Smdar—that we will visit later.

As I sat upstairs in the large enclosed porch that serves as the lunchroom, the American teens were busy calling their parents from the pay phone. As some of the youths stood around, talking, one of them asked me what I was doing in Jerusalem. I told him and the others that I was researching the red heifer.

"You can't even go up to the Temple Mount to plan a new Temple unless you have the ashes to purify you," said John. He called out to Charlie, who was doing his term paper on the *Para Aduma*. Charlie came over to me and readily chanted like a cantor, from memory, the

7

instructions from the Book of Numbers: *Para aduma, t'meemah, asher ayn-bah moom, asher lo-alah aleyha nol.*

"Red heifer . . . perfect . . . on which there is no blemish . . . which has never had a yoke on her."

Thirty-five centuries after the writing of the Book of Numbers a Jewish youngster was reciting the Hebrew command concerning the red heifer, whose ashes were required to purify those about to enter the Tabernacle in the wilderness. Moses and his generation would have been astounded to flash-forward to modern-day Jerusalem and witness their descendants, coping with the trials of life in a hostile world, and still waiting for the Messiah.

A short walk from the Old City, Emek Refaim Street is the spine of a bustling secular Jewish neighborhood, with a string of shops, restaurants, grocery stores, fruit and vegetable stalls. It also has its own post office, a copy shop, a bicycle shop, a shoe-repair kiosk, a pet food store, and even a camera shop with a dog in the window. Outside the spreading lawn of the Hasdna Conservatory of Music, one of the children had left a crust of bread on the low stone wall for the birds.

As the young Americans mingled around me, a tiny girl named Lauren came over and asked what will happen when Messiah comes.

"Will all the people be good before he comes?" she asked. "Why doesn't he just come?"

Arrival of the Red Heifer

In the darkness that evening, the Bedouin woman from the desert was now walking down the steps from the Temple Mount. When she reached the plaza at the bottom, she walked through the winding streets of the Old City until she reached an Arab falafel stand. It was late at night, and the stand was about to close. Drawing her outer garment around her like a tired traveler, she leaned wearily on the counter and spoke to the father and daughter. She told them she needed a place to stay while she spent a few days, surveying some property in Jerusalem.

"We have a little corner of our dwelling that you can rent," Samira told Noor. "My mother's sewing room is idle. Our home is modest, but you should be comfortable."

"I have no money for the rent," Noor said, looking at the woman's father, Munir. "But my family has many cattle, and I'm sure you could pick out the very best one and have meat to serve at your stand for many weeks."

In the darkness, the Bedouin woman led Munir and Samira outside the Old City to the hill where she had left her goats and cows. It was above Herod's Gate, near the cemetery.

*

Next morning Isaac, the yeshiva boy, went to the Western Wall. To the left was an opening to a cave, and immediately inside its arched doorway was a Jewish prayer and study room. This was where Isaac and Rabbi Abram could usually be found.

Now, Isaac Cohen, being of the priestly line, was a brilliant yeshiva boy and had attracted the attention of the yeshiva's dean. This Rabbi was the leader of a small, ultra-Orthodox sect that was intent upon hastening the coming of the Messiah. In fact, Rabbi Abram and his group were making preliminary plans for rebuilding the Temple. *And* he had singled out Isaac as a prime candidate for the priesthood. But the tiny cult that had gathered around Rabbi Abram had run into a major obstacle. They had already completed the blueprints for rebuilding the

Temple, taking the specifications out of the Hebrew Scriptures. And they had identified the type of stone needed for the Temple, where to find it, and the utensils to be used in the Temple sacrifice.

"Yitzak!" Rabbi Abram called out to Isaac, speaking his name in Hebrew. "I have been reading again in the Book of Numbers."

"Oh, Rabbi, not again," replied Isaac, who was sitting across from the Rabbi at a study table cluttered with books in the prayer room.

"Yitzy," the Rabbi said. "It has been two thousand years since the Temple was destroyed, and our people were thrown out of the Land of Israel. But, even though we have been back in our homeland for more than a generation, the Messiah still has not come, to bring us redemption—and to bring peace to the world."

Isaac, who had heard all of this before, stood up and walked out of the study room into the sunlight.

Rabbi Abram followed him. "Could it *really* be," the Rabbi called after him, "that the Messiah is waiting for the Jewish people to rebuild the Temple?"

Isaac was walking along the Western Wall, toward its other end, where a curved stone stairway leads up to the Temple Mount. The Rabbi slowly followed him.

"Surely," Isaac replied, "when the Messiah comes, he can find a way for the Jews and the Arabs to live together in peace."

"Of course, Itzak," the Rabbi replied. "But the real question is: Can the Messiah find a way for all the *Jews* to live together in peace?!" He smiled and shrugged.

Laughing at this remark, Isaac walked over to the steps and began to climb them.

The Rabbi stopped near the foot of the stairs. "Uht-uht!" he warned.

But Isaac took the first two or three steps before stopping. "The Messiah can do things that even Moses couldn't do," he said, turning to climb the next step. "Things that even wise King Solomon couldn't do. Solomon built the First Temple, and the Holy One dwelt in it for a time. But then the Holy One departed, never to return."

The Rabbi raised a finger toward Isaac and said: "Solomon's father, King David, had purchased Mount Moriah, where Abraham had once gone to sacrifice his son, Yitzak. And this is where David's son, Solomon, built the Temple, three thousand years ago. Here in Zion!"

"For the Lord has chosen Zion," Isaac shouted joyfully, quoting from the Psalms of the Bible and taking another step up the stairway.

"He has desired it for His habitation. And the Lord says: This will be My resting place forever."

"Yitzak! No further!" the Rabbi shouted

But Isaac continued to climb the steps till he was near the top of the Western Wall and could see the Mughrabi Gate, which leads to the Temple Mount . . . "Here I will dwell, for I have desired it," Isaac said, prayerfully speaking the words of the Lord from the Psalm. "I will clothe her priests with salvation, and her saints shall shout aloud for joy!"

"Yitzy!" the Rabbi shouted from the bottom step. "The Temple Mount is holy ground, and you have not been purified yet!"

"Here, I will prepare a lamp for my Anointed—the Messiah!" Isaac said.

"Yitzak Cohen!" the Rabbi shouted hysterically. "Come down now!"

Slowly, Isaac began his return down the steps and returned with the Rabbi to the study room.

"Yitzy," the Rabbi gently reminded Isaac, "no one is pure enough, even to approach the Temple Mount, much less stand there and rebuild the Temple! But in the Book of Numbers, the Lord spoke to Moses, saying, 'Speak to the children of Israel and have them bring you a red heifer.' And the Lord listed four specifications. And what are they?"

First looking reluctant, then turning more and more eager, Isaac began to sing the four specifications in Hebrew, from the Book of Numbers, Chapter 19—

"Para aduma [which means red heifer], t'meemah [perfect], asher ayn-bah moom [on which there is no blemish], asher lo-alah aleyha ol [which never came on her a yoke]."

"Precisely!" cried the Rabbi. "Then it says—'And you shall give her to Eleazar the priest, and he shall have it brought outside the camp. And she shall be slaughtered in his presence. . . . And the heifer shall be burned.' For a blood sacrifice is necessary to atone for serious sin."

"Ah-main!" the yeshiva boy cried, meaning Amen. "And a man that is clean," Isaac said, continuing the quotation from the Bible, "shall gather up the ashes of the heifer, and lay them outside the camp in a clean place. And it shall be used by the children of Israel for the water of sprinkling. It is a purification offering."

"And there is this warning, Itzak," the Rabbi said—"'But that man that shall be unclean, and shall not purify himself'—and dare go near the Holy of Holies, where the Temple was and will be again—'that soul shall be cut off from among the congregation, because he has

11

defiled the sanctuary of the Lord—the water of sprinkling has not been sprinkled upon him, he is unclean.'"

*

"You have quite a flock here, my Bedouin friend," Munir said as they stood outside the Old City walls.

"Take your pick, my brother," Noor said.

"Oh, Father," Samira said, "can I pick out my favorite?"

"No, my child. I must select the animal that will give us the largest quantity of choice meat for our falafel stand."

"This one, Father!" Samira said.

"But he is so small, my child!"

"*She*, Father! It's a *she*. And isn't she sweet? Oh, Father! . . ."

"Oh, Samira . . ."

Noor told them that this little heifer was too young to tether with a leash. And so, as they were returning from Jaffa Gate, the lights of the Old City revealed Munir pulling a wooden cart up to the side of his falafel stand.

"Oh, Father, isn't she the most beautiful baby cow you have ever seen?" Samira said, cuddling the head of the Red Heifer.

"Now, Samira, don't you get too attached to this critter."

"What shall we name her?"

"Enough!" her father shouted. "The animal will not be given a name! She—*it*—won't be around that long."

"But Father! . . . What do you intend to do with her?"

"What indeed?" Noor said to herself with a smile.

*

Next morning, Samira got up early and hurried down to the Wailing Wall, more formally known as the Western Wall. She loved the way the sun played on the honey-colored blocks of limestone, whose cracks cuddled the nests of house sparrows, doves and swift black swallows.

The wall sprouted a variety of plants, particularly the golden henbane, with its large leaves and purple-throated yellow flowers. The historian Josephus likened this flower to the High Priest's headdress. However, its Hebrew name, *shikaron*, suggests the intoxicating (and poisonous) sedative made from it.

Also on the Wall, Samira saw thorny capers stretching out their long shoots bearing oval leaves with distorted thorns at their sides. Their flower buds produce white flowers that morph into tiny cucumber-like fruits every day—in fact, the Mishnah (Shabbat 30 b) quotes a rabbi citing this plant when predicting that trees will bear fruit every day when Messiah comes. The flower bud is edible as flavoring or garnish, after it is pickled or salted.

Here the wind scatters the seeds of rock phagnalons, whose white stalks grow skulls of tiny flowers; the seeds of yellow-flowered Sicilian snapdragons, which Yeshua of Nazareth saw growing wild on the rocks of the Upper Galilee. Pale blue and white flowers of the Syrian podosnoma are shielded in dense, sticky bristles. And hanging from the left-center of the Wall are long-shooted horsetail knotgrass bearing clusters of tiny white-pink flowers, which are cited in the Mishnah as an antidote for snakebites.

Here, too, between the cracks of this Wall of Lamentations and Tears, the wind plays with the daily infestation of crumpled notes bearing the prayers, fears and exultations of visitors from every corner of the earth.

And this was where Samira loved to stand—sometimes at a distance—and watch the Jews pray, the men on the left, and the women on the right. Bobbing and bent in prayer, they seemed to her like a historical resurrection, a precious cavalcade of children whose parents and grandparents had survived the Holocaust, re-opening the curtain of history that the enemies of God had tried to close.

Suddenly Samira noticed that a new soldier was guarding the Wall, and a flash of recognition crossed her face.

But the soldier ignored her eyes and turned away.

Now, Samira was a devout student of religion. She had been raised as a Muslim, but a couple years ago, after her mother's death, she had converted to Christianity—very unusual in the Muslim world. This did not please her father. Furthermore, Samira had been studying the Bible to discover the roots of her Christian religion, and her studies always led her back to Judaism—most unusual in the Christian world. So unusual, in fact, that were it not for Christians like Samira, the Red Heifer would not have come to Jerusalem at this time . . .

Munir had once been a fairly large landholder here in the region called Palestine, until 1948, when thousands of Palestinian Arabs fled their homes during the Jewish War of Independence. With the establishment of the State of Israel, Munir lost his wife's family homestead and his own land, just outside the walls of the Old City. But he did manage to hold onto his falafel stand—just inside the Old City, which had come under Jordanian occupation in 1948. He and his daughter ran the business and lived in the back of the tiny building near Jaffa Gate. When Israel captured the Old City from the Jordanians in the Six Day War of 1967, it was reunited with modern-day West Jerusalem, and its Arab inhabitants became Israeli citizens. But Munir still couldn't reclaim his wife's lost property outside the Old City, in Israel proper.

Today, many years later, two of Samira's old classmates from public school lived nearby. But they had lost touch with one another. One of them was Simon—the soldier Samira saw guarding the Western Wall this morning. Simon had remained a secular Jew after finishing school. Since he was an ardent Zionist, he entered the Israeli Defense Forces and was making it his career.

The other was Isaac Cohen. After finishing public school, he had held down various jobs until, in his late twenties, he entered an Orthodox yeshiva, studying to become a rabbi. Isaac was one of thousands of secular Jews who became swept up in the Jewish revival that followed the recovery of Jerusalem to Jewish hands after the Six Day War. He was called a *baal t'shuvah*, meaning a "master of return"— return to the Jewish faith.

Chapter 3

Remembering Akiva ben Joseph at the Jerusalem Christian Embassy

JERUSALEM

It was quiet for me now in the Little House in the Colony after the 36 American teens packed their bags and left for home. From here, I took a short walk down Emek Refaim, then several blocks down Rachel Imeinu Street, until I reached the International Christian Embassy in Jerusalem. Attorney David Parsons, the information officer, told me his Bible-based organization would like to encourage the rebuilding of the Temple. But first, he said, it is fighting for freedom for Christians and Jews to pray on the Temple Mount, which is controlled by the Muslims.

In due time, he said, the Jews will rebuild the Temple, hoping that this will bring the Messiah.

"They'll be disappointed when the Temple is rebuilt and nothing happens," said Parsons, who as a Christian believes that Messiah has already come, and has shed His blood for the sins of the world.

In the New Testament, the writer of the Letter to the Hebrews declares: "For if sprinkling ceremonially unclean persons with the blood of goats and bulls and the ashes of a heifer restores their outward purity, then how much more the blood of the Messiah—who through the eternal Spirit offered himself to God as a sacrifice without blemish—will purify our conscience from works that lead to death, so that we can serve the living God!" (Hebrews 9:13, CJB).

15

As for blood sacrifices on the altar, Parsons reminded me, Judaism took a drastic turn after the destruction of the Temple by the Romans and the expulsion of the Jews from Jerusalem. A few years later, rabbinical Judaism was born at Yavne, where the leading Pharisee thinkers regrouped after the catastrophe.

"Rabbi Akiva ended the idea of vicarious suffering for sins—and substituted Torah study," Parsons recalled. "The system replaced the Temple as the center of Jewish life—and sacrifice in the Temple was replaced by study."

So, who was Rabbi Akiva ben Joseph?

Born two or three decades before the Romans destroyed the Temple, Akiva was an illiterate shepherd who had never studied the Hebrew Scriptures. Legend has it that one day, at the age of 40, while gazing into a bubbling brook, Akiva was amazed that the water—so soft to the touch—was able to wear the rough rocks smooth over time. This convinced him that even his mind could still be penetrated by the Torah.

By then, the Jews had been banished from Jerusalem, and the Roman Emperor Vespasian had given Rabbi Johanan ben Zakkai permission to open an academy at Yavne, near the Mediterranean coast. The Sanhedrin moved to Yavne, and here the Pharisees labored to reshape Judaism so that it could function without the Temple sacrifices.

Ben Zakkai once said this about the mystery of the Red Heifer to a pagan idolater who accused the Jews of practicing sorcery by this rite: "By your life! The dead does not have the power by itself to defile, nor does the mixture of ash and water have the power by itself to cleanse! It is a decree of the Holy One, blessed be He, who declared: 'I have set it down as a statute, I have issued it as a decree which you are not to question.'"

It was their obedience in following this mysterious command—not the ashes—that purified them to come into God's presence in the Tabernacle.

Akiva studied at Yavne and excelled so greatly that he would go down in history, along with Rabbi Johanan ben Zakkai, as a father of *rabbinic* Judaism. Until then, Torah scholars were not given the title *rabbi* (which doesn't appear in the Hebrew Scriptures). After Akiva, the authority of the rabbis would supersede the authority of the Scriptures. The rabbis' pronouncements became the Oral Law, which was later written in the Talmud.

"It is a Rabbinical ordinance, and the Scriptural verse is merely a support," the rabbis later wrote in the Talmud (*Avodah Zarah 38a*).

Akiva was so successful in reshaping the Jewish religion that his first teacher, Eliezer ben Hyrcanus, scolded him for ignoring Scripture.

"Akiva!" he exclaimed. "You would erase what is written in the Torah!" (*Pesachim 66a*).

Under Akiva, the rabbis no longer predicted that the coming Messiah would be divine. Rather, he would be a great king, like David, and would bring peace to the world by purely human means. Nor would the Messiah suffer and die as an atonement for the sins of the nation. The very idea of blood sacrifices no longer seemed relevant, in the absence of the Temple. After Akiva, the suffering servant in the Book of Isaiah, who was "crushed because of our iniquities," was not the Messiah but the entire Jewish nation.

Yet, before the time of Yeshua, Jews expected the coming Messiah to provide a blood atonement by taking the place of all sinners, who face the death penalty under the Law. The earliest Jewish interpretations of Scripture, such as the *Targum Jonathan* and the *Jerusalem Targum,* held this view. This position was later rejected by the Rabbis, according to the Talmud, because of "the sages of the Nazarenes, who apply it to that man whom they hanged in Jerusalem towards the close of the second Temple, and who, according to their opinion, was the Son of the Most Blessed, and had taken human nature in the womb of the Virgin."

And so, rabbis no longer taught that a divine Messiah with a human body had been foreshadowed in Genesis, where, for example, the Lord appeared as one of three men outside Abraham's tent in Mamre to announce that Sara would have a son. More than a thousand years after Akiva, Maimonides laid down the Thirteen Articles of Faith, including this one: "I believe with complete faith that God does not have a body. Physical concepts do not apply to Him. There is nothing whatsoever that resembles Him at all."

This, despite the statement in Genesis that God created man in His own image and likeness . . . and that the Lord *walked* in the garden in the cool of the day.

Still, the rabbis looked forward to the return of the Jews to their homeland someday, the rebuilding of the Temple, and the coming of Messiah. And for this to be completed, they would need the ashes of a red heifer.

The Deal Is Done

Now Noor, who had been walking along the Western Wall and listening to the Rabbi and his yeshiva boy, stopped to talk to Isaac outside the study room.

"Young man," Noor said, "I couldn't help overhearing you and your Rabbi talking about a certain breed of animal that you haven't been able to find."

"A red heifer?" Isaac replied.

"Yes. I happen to know someone nearby who has one!" Noor said. "It's Munir, who has the falafel stand inside Jaffa Gate!" Then, smiling again, she walked away.

Isaac ran back into the prayer room and called the Rabbi. Soon the two came out, with Isaac leading the Rabbi by the sleeve through the cobbled alleys of the Old City. Catching their breath and straightening out their black coats and hats, they approached the falafel stand.

When Munir heard what they were looking for, he pulled the wagon from behind the counter to display the animal. Rabbi Abram knelt down and examined the animal with care, then rose and nodded his head.

"It's kosher!" he shouted to Isaac, but then quickly composed himself and turned to Munir.

"How much for this heifer?" he asked.

For the next several minutes they haggled over the price, as is commonly done in the Middle East. As the Rabbi made his bids, and the Arab made his counter offers, their loud shouts attracted the attention of several people in the vicinity of Jaffa Gate.

A middle-aged Muslim in a sport coat had been sitting against the storefront of a souvenir shop, his brass shoeshine stand at his side. He immediately rose to his feet and sauntered over to the falafel stand. An Israeli soldier with a beard was eating an ice cream cone, his rifle slung over a shoulder and his cap cocked over his sunglasses. He, too, paused to take in the spectacle. The shouts of Munir and the Rabbi also drew several Arab men from a smoky café where they had been playing cards and drinking strong black tea out of tiny glasses. A couple of tourists also joined the crowd.

18

"Five thousand shekels!" Rabbi Abram said at last. "That is my final offer!"

"Accepted!" cried Munir. "It's a deal!"

Many of the on-lookers clapped their hands and cheered before moving on their way.

Munir shook hands with the Rabbi, who then counted out the money, while Samira served a round of hot tea in little glasses. They all silently toasted and drank up. Then Isaac and the Rabbi pulled the cart away.

"Take good care of her!" Samira called after them. But a few moments later she found herself following them, with Noor by her side, to the Rabbi's study room next to the Western Wall.

After letting the Red Heifer out of the cart and nudging her into the stall that had been prepared for such a day as this, Isaac and the Rabbi returned to the Wall and celebrated by singing from the Hebrew Scriptures.

Rabbi Abram began singing from the First Book of Kings: "And Solomon said, upon dedicating the Temple—'But will God indeed dwell on the earth? Behold, the highest heaven cannot contain You! How much less this house that I have built? Yet give attention to Your servant's prayer.'"

Isaac drew open the curtain along the wall of their prayer room and took out the sacred Torah scroll, which he hoisted in the air, dancing for joy in the plaza before the Wailing Wall.

All the excitement caused the birds that make their nests in the cracks of the Wall to swirl around and around the plaza, as the Rabbi and his yeshiva boy celebrated with dance and song.

"But the Glory of the Lord filled His Temple as a cloud," Isaac sang from the same text, which he too knew by heart. He added, "It was the same Shekinah Glory that had led the Israelites as a pillar of cloud in the desert."

"He who scattered Israel now gathers him together and keeps him as a shepherd keeps his flock," the Rabbi sang from the Book of the Prophet Jeremiah.

"Where is the house that you shall build Me?" Isaac sang, from the Prophet Isaiah, still dancing with the Torah.

"Rebuild the walls of Jerusalem!" the Rabbi sang from Psalm 51. "Then You will be pleased with the sacrifices of righteousness . . . Then they shall offer bulls on the altar of Your Temple."

*

After listening to all of this, Samira and Noor returned to the falafel stand. Gesturing with her flute as if it were a Yiddish violin, Noor laughed and said, "Ah, listen to them! *Fiddler on the Hoof!*"

But Samira didn't laugh.

"Noor, "she said, "what a beautiful religion they have! Such— unrestrained joy! Islam was never like this. And now, even Christianity could learn something from it."

"How do you mean?" Noor asked.

"Well," Samira said, "on the one hand, their rules and regulations are an almost comical chain-reaction that never ends. For instance, in the Book of Exodus they are commanded, 'Do not cook a young goat in its mother's milk.' Fine. So they don't cook *any* kid—a goat or a lamb or a baby heifer—in milk from its mother—or in milk from any *other* mother. Just to be safe."

Noor was smiling to herself.

"Then," Samira continued, "to make absolutely sure that nobody violates the original command, the rabbis say you are not to consume milk—*or any other dairy product*—with meat! So a meal must be either all meat or all dairy. I mean, talk about obsessive compulsive! Then they go a step further—their cooking utensils and serving dishes must be designated either for meat only or for dairy only. I mean, if you make a mistake and pour coffee and cream into a cup that you once used for soup with meat in it, the cup becomes useless for dining. It can only become a flower pot."

Noor laughed out loud.

"Eventually," Samira said, "the Pharisees end up with two sinks in their kitchen—one for meat meals, one for dairy meals. All because God said—for reasons known only to Him—not to cook a kid in its mother's milk!"

"Well," Noor told her, "the original purpose of that simple command was to prevent God's people from imitating an ancient pagan fertility cult in which a kid was boiled in its mother's milk to appease the gods. So I wouldn't make fun of what the rabbis have done to avoid any semblance of that evil practice."

"Nooo!" Samira said. "I'm not making fun of all this."

Noor put on her mischievous smile: "Still," she confided, "my favorite overkill is when I see the owner standing in front of his restaurant, blow-torching the insides of all his pots and pans for everyone to see that he's super-kosher for Passover!"

Samira laughed, then got serious. "In fact," she told Noor, "I find all of it awesome—even terrifying at times, when I think about it. Because, in the end, I truly admire the Orthodox for their strict, unquestioning obedience to God, even when He doesn't offer them an explanation. That's real faith. It takes real courage to live like this every day, in the face of cruel persecution by their fellow Jews. And most of all, I adore their tenderhearted devotion to God—and their unrestrained joy for life! We Christians can learn a great deal from religious Jews."

"I'll let you in on a little secret," Noor told her.

"What?"

"Samira, the Pharisees are the only Jewish sect that has come down to us—in an unbroken line—from the time of Yeshua of Nazareth. The Zealots, who rose up against Rome and brought about the destruction of the Temple, are gone. You could say that their descendants are the Zionists of today, who succeeded in gaining independence but whose religion is Zionism, not God. The Sadducees, who didn't believe in life after death, are all dead. In their place are the multitudes of secular Jews who don't even believe in their God anymore."

Samira thought about this. "You know," she said, "the Pharisees were the only ones Yeshua even bothered with. Do you suppose He identified with them by His training in the Temple as a youth?"

Noor looked at Samira for a long moment.

"Two thousand years after His sacrifice," Noor asked, "what has Yeshua got to show for it today on the face of the earth? Gentiles who believe in Him. More and more Jews who *finally* believe in Him. And the Pharisees—who must also turn to Him—if history is to come full circle for the Messiah's final return."

"How I love them," Samira said. "And how they long for Messiah to come."

"Yes, the Father still loves them," Noor said. "As His chosen people, they are still dear to God, if only for the sake of their forefathers. For God's calling to His people is irrevocable."

"So," Samira said, "what's that 'secret' you mentioned?"

Noor looked intently into Samira's eyes.

"Because Christians like you love them so," Noor replied, "the Red Heifer has come back into the world, in your generation."

Chapter 4

Rabbi Yaakov Fogelman's Lesson on the Red Heifer

JERUSALEM

Immediately after Israel's stunning victory in the Six Day War, reports circulated that a red heifer had been found at Kibbutz Chefetz Chaim. It was perfectly reddish-brown, but later was disqualified by the Pharisees.

Is it possible that God allowed that red heifer in 1967 to become unkosher because—within days of the miraculous recovery of Jerusalem—Israel's political leaders foolishly gave the Temple Mount back to Muslim supervision in order to appease the Muslim nations that rejected the Jewish state?

Nonetheless, the nations will be satisfied when Israel builds the Third Temple, says Rabbi Yaakov Fogelman, quoting the 12th Century Torah scholar Maimonides, known as the Rambam.

"Remember," Rabbi Fogelman says, "the Rambam said nobody is going to fight over the third Bait HaMikdash. The Arabs will agree. The Christians will agree. In my opinion, this can happen only if all the Jews shape up and the nations see that we are a holy people, doing our job as the Kingdom priests, and a holy nation. They won't object. They will be very glad that we're doing this for them—bringing everyone back to the Garden of Eden, bringing everyone back to themselves!"

In the heart of the Jewish Quarter of the Old City, Rabbi Yaakov Fogelman once operated his Jerusalem Jewish Information Center and Reading Rooms on Chabad Road. A promoter of the *baal t'shuvah* revival, Fogelman walks down to the Wailing Wall daily to seek fallen-away Jews and invites them to his home for "just one Shabbos," and then perhaps another Sabbath, and then another . . . Eventually, the person will agree to take classes on the Torah (the first five books of the Bible) and, one day, become a fully observant Jew.

Many rabbis agree that this revival has been the first of its kind in Jewish history. Never before, they say, has a fallen-away Jew been invited to return to the faith one step at a time—instead of confessing that he had been unfaithful and agreeing immediately to become Orthodox and follow all the kosher and Sabbath rules and other laws of the Talmud. A Jew who does eventually become Orthodox is known as a *baal t'shuvah*, a "master of return" to the faith.

At the time I first met Rabbi Fogelman, his reading room was inside a 900-year-old Crusader church building at 46 Chabad Road. In addition to the hundreds of books on his shelves, Fogelman had a television set on which he played, for those interested, a videotape of his research on the Red Heifer.

A graduate of Yeshiva University and Harvard Law School, the rabbi left his real estate career in 1974 to make aliyah to Israel, where he opened his Torah outreach center in the Jewish Quarter of the Old City. The father of eight children and progenitor of some three dozen grandchildren and great-grandchildren, he has thousands of on-line subscribers to his Torah sheet, providing his insights into the week's Torah readings.

During today's live lecture, the Rabbi turns to the Torah (using his translation of Numbers 19:2) and points out where God tells Moses: "Tell the Israelites to bring you a red heifer, perfect, without blemish and that has never been under a yoke."

Rabbi Fogelman then asks his students about the unusual introduction to the Red Heifer in the preceding sentence: "This is the law of the Torah which God commanded." What's unusual, he says, is that those exact words occur nowhere else in the Torah—except in Numbers 31:21. There, the Israelites have just defeated the Midianites and are about to divide the spoils. But they are commanded by God to purify everything that had belonged to those idolaters, especially cooking and serving utensils. "Gold, silver, bronze, iron, tin, lead and anything else that can withstand fire must be put through the fire, and then it will be clean," the Torah says. "But it must also be purified with the water of cleansing. And whatever cannot withstand fire must be put through the water" (NIV).

In both verses the Torah is talking about a very basic law of purification, Fogelman tells his listeners. This kind of law is called a *chukah*, because its purpose is a mystery.

Fogelman is fascinated by what the 11th Century biblical commentator Solomon Yitzhaki. (known as Rashi) had to say about the law governing the Red Heifer. "Rashi says the word *chukah* means a law of God which is virtually arbitrary, which we can't understand the reason for," Fogelman explains. "Still, Rashi gives a reason for this law, and he quotes Moses—'After the sin of the golden calf, let a law come and make up for the calf.'"

Fogelman tells his students about another problem in Numbers 19:2. There seems to be a redundancy, he says, in which the Torah requires a red heifer that is *t'meemah*—meaning perfect—and "without blemish." But didn't "perfect" and "without blemish" mean the same thing? The answer, he says, is that the word *t'meemah* doesn't refer to the heifer but refers to its color: "*perfectly* red."

The significance of red, Fogelman says, is discovered by asking yourself what all these requirements have in common—red, without blemish, and never yoked. Red signifies life and vitality, he says, and in fact all three requirements suggest life, for the sacrificed animal was never restrained, and its spirit was never killed.

There were nine red heifers throughout early Jewish history, the Rabbi says, and there was no need for a tenth one because the Temple was destroyed in 70 AD. But he added, "There is one more to come—at the time of Moshiach—and it will make a minyan, ten."

Despite the return to the land, Rabbi Fogelman says, Judaism is still incomplete because, without the Temple and its altar of sacrifice, many of the 613 commandments in the Talmud still cannot be followed. But for now, the Arab nations are violently set against the rebuilding of the Temple.

In the 1980s a group of Israelis were arrested for plotting to blow up the Dome of the Rock. Yehuda Etzion was identified as the ringleader. Then, in 1996, Etzion was present at Kfar Chasidim during the inspection of a red heifer named Melody. She had been born of a black-and-white cow and a brownish-gray bull.

"We have been waiting 2,000 years for a sign from God," Etzion exclaimed, "and now He has provided us with a red heifer." But not long after that, Melody was disqualified for growing white hairs in her tail.

Back in June 1967, Gershon Salomon—a sixth-generation resident of Jerusalem—had been present when the Old City was recovered by Israel's military, the IDF. In his opinion, God was reasserting His continued relationship with the Chosen People and was about to fulfill His plans for the final days. In 1998 Salomon organized a demonstration in which a cornerstone for the new Temple was carried into the Old City. His Temple Mount and Land of Israel Faithful organization carried it toward the Mughrabi Gate, where they were stopped by the IDF because of opposition by Muslims (who had rioted in 1990, throwing stones and molotov cocktail bombs down from the Temple Mount). And so the Temple Faithful carried their cornerstone around the walls of the Old City seven times. The ceremony has been repeated annually. After it was stolen, it was replaced by a 6.5-ton cornerstone, which is kept on display on a busy traffic circle outside Damascus Gate.

Made of stone from the Negev Desert to replicate the original material, the cornerstone would have been placed either in the plaza north of the Dome or in the open area south of it. Most Jews believe the Dome is on the very spot where the Temple stood. But physicist Asher Kaufman places the site about 330 feet north of the Dome. And architect Tuvia Sagiv has concluded that the Temple was to the south, between the Dome and the Al-Aqsa Mosque.

Whatever the case, Gershon Salomon has vowed to remove all Muslim structures from the Temple Mount when the time comes to rebuild the Temple.

"We are sure that no one can stop the prophetic march of history in these end-times," says Salomon, who refers to the Dome of the Rock as "the Islamic abomination on the Temple Mount."

Picking up on this, Christian Zionists have quoted Yeshua's warning of the coming "abomination that causes desolation" standing in the "holy place." The desecration of the holy place will be the final sign of a cataclysmic battle between good and evil, in the Kidron Valley below the Old City, climaxed by the second coming of Messiah. The Prophet Joel referred to the Kidron as the Valley of Jehoshaphat, where all the nations will be gathered for judgment.

Young Friends, Now Enemies

Simon, the soldier who had recently been assigned to guard the Western Wall, couldn't help eavesdropping on Rabbi Abram and Isaac Cohen as he patrolled the base of the Wall.

"Itzy!" the Rabbi exclaimed. "To think that we will be privileged to raise the Red Heifer for the noble purpose of bringing in the Messiah!" Then he added, "*Baruch Hashem!*"

"Yes!" said Isaac. "*Praise His name!*"

"Itzy," the Rabbi said as they stood outside their prayer room to the left of the Wall. "Let me hear you chant it again—the requirements for the Red Heifer, from the Book of Numbers."

"*Para aduma,*" Isaac began, chanting to an ancient melody.

"Red heifer," Simon mumbled to himself as he listened.

". . . *t'meemah* . . ." Isaac continued.

". . . perfect . . ." Simon translated.

". . . *asher ayn-bah moom.* . . ." Isaac went on.

". . . on which there is no blemish. . ." the soldier said slowly.

. . . *asher lo-alah aleyha ol,*" Isaac said in conclusion.

". . . which—has never had a yoke on her?" Simon said, unsure of the meaning.

"Excellent!" Rabbi Abram said. "Come, Itzak," and the two of them disappeared inside the cave that served as their study and prayer room and closed the door.

As Simon continued patrolling the wall, Noor came walking along and approached the soldier. Turning her head toward the study room, she said, as if to herself, "So *that's* where that animal wound up."

"What animal?" the soldier asked, doing a cursory security check on her.

"Why, that heifer," Noor said, pointing toward the cave. "That red heifer."

"What are you talking about?" Simon demanded.

"You didn't see the animal with that Rabbi who just walked by a little while ago?" she said. "Everybody else did!"

Simon turned away in disgust, muttering, "Another crazy Bedouin."

"Sir," Noor said. "I'm a shepherd of the desert. I know livestock. What I just saw was a red heifer if there ever was one!"

Simon turned back to face her. "*Para Aduma*," he said in Hebrew. "Red heifer. So what?"

"The last red heifer that was born in this land was sacrificed outside the city gate," Noor replied, "and its ashes were used for the water of purification for the Temple priests—2,000 years ago."

"I know about the *Para Aduma*," Simon told her. "I don't need a Bible lesson from a Bedouin nomad from the desert." He started to walk away again.

"My dear Sir," Noor called after him, "you can learn much from a stranger like me."

"There are too many strangers in my country," the soldier said without looking back. "Especially here in *Yerushalayim*."

"Remember, Sir," Noor said, "that your dreams of world peace, as an Israeli, cannot come true until the Jewish people follow their own religion. And this includes dealing justly with the strangers living in your midst."

"Scram!" Simon shouted and began patrolling the Wall.

"*For you were strangers in the land of Egypt*," Noor said, quoting from the Hebrew Scriptures.

Simon ignored her and continued his patrol. When he reached the far end of the Wall, he turned and marched back toward this end.

Noor was still there, waiting for him.

"I wonder what that Rabbi and his student are up to . . ." she said, almost to herself. "Do you know them?"

The soldier stopped and looked at her. "Sure," he said. "The yeshiva boy is Itzak Cohen. I went to school with him."

"So you *do* know him!" Noor said. "But I didn't see you greet each other."

"We're not exactly on speaking terms these days," he said.

"How so?"

Simon laughed. "Just look at him—wearing that black hat and hanging around with that super-religious Rabbi. They're more Orthodox than the *Orthodox* are!"

"And you?"

"Me?" Simon said with a shrug. "I'm a soldier of Israel. I defend Mount Zion. That's *my* religion—Zionism."

"Well," said Noor, "Zionism isn't the religion of Rabbi Abram."

"I don't imagine so," he said. "Do you know him?'

"I know of him," Noor said. "He's the founder of that movement."

"Yes—'Messiah Now,'" Simon said. "Ah, yes, and they're going to rebuild the Temple." He gestured toward the Wall. "Right up there, where that Muslim mosque is. Then we'll have World War III."

"You're awfully pessimistic, for a Zionist," Noor told him.

"*You* tell *me,*" the soldier replied. "Would the Muslim nations stand still if we went up there and claimed our Temple Mount as our own?"

Noor pursed her lips and said nothing.

"Not that it's going to happen in *my* time!" Simon continued. "The Rabbis are too superstitious to even walk up there." He turned to leave. "See you around."

"Don't be so sure," Noor said.

Simon turned and scoffed. "Where did they get that animal, anyway?"

"From Munir," she said. "He runs the falafel stand at Jaffa Gate." Turning to leave, and smiling slyly, she said, "See *you* around."

Simon stood by himself at the Wall for a long moment. Then, getting an idea, he adjusted the Uzi machine gun strap on his shoulder and hurried through the streets of the Old City until he reached Munir's falafel stand.

*

Munir looked up, saw that it was an Israeli soldier, and quickly turned away. So Simon leaned his elbows on the counter of the falafel stand and spoke quietly to the Muslim in Arabic. Munir stopped what he was doing and listened.

Suddenly Munir exploded.

"They *what?!*" he shouted. "What did you say they're going to do with that animal?"

Simon turned and pointed proudly into the distance. Then he walked off, smiling smugly to himself.

"I have been had!" Munir shouted. "The scoundrels! Samira! Samira!"

His daughter emerged from the back of the falafel stand. "What is it, Father?"

"That rabbi!" he exclaimed. "He bought the heifer from us! Guess what he's going to do with it!"

"What, Father?"

"He's going to tear down the Dome of the Rock so they can rebuild their Temple!" he said, pointing toward the Western Wall. "Up there, on the *Haram al-Sharif* . . . ! On the holy spot where Mohamed departed on his night journey to paradise!"

"What nonsense!" she said. "Who told you that?"

"Over there! That soldier with the scar on his face!"

Samira sucked in her breath and said nothing. Wrapping her garment more tightly around her shoulders, she walked quickly through the cobbled streets of the Old City and, within ten minutes, was outside the Wall. Taking her stand on one spot, she stared intently at the soldier. But Simon ignored her as he patrolled the Wall. So she began to follow him, as a cat after a mouse, until Simon finally halted and looked at her.

"*Shalom!*" she sang, flirting with her eyes.

Simon forced a smile and greeted her in Arabic: "*A salaam aleikum*, pretty face. Shouldn't you be on the women's end of the Wall?"

"Sir," Samira told him, "you got my father all upset by something you said at our falafel stand."

"Is he your father?" he replied.

"Of course." Now she gave him a good, hard look. "Hey—don't you remember me, Simon?"

"How do you know my name?" he demanded.

"Simon," she said impatiently. "I'm Samira . . . !"

"Samira . . ."

"I haven't seen you in so long!" Samira said. "You look—different!" Now she stared at the scar on his face. "Oh, Simon," she said and touched her own face.

"Well, I—I've been away," Simon said. "Assigned to the Golan Heights—until recently."

"What did you tell my father?"

"That crazy rabbi who bought that animal from your father is going to use it to fulfill a requirement in the Bible! They think they'll be able to use its ashes to purify themselves—so they can go up to the Temple Mount and rebuild the Temple."

"They're going to burn my little heifer?!" Samira exclaimed.

Simon drew a finger across his throat. "First they'll slaughter it, kosher style. The critter won't feel a thing."

"They must be crazy!" Samira said.

"And guess who's going along with it? One of our old friends."

"Who?"

"Itzak!" he said. "Itzak Cohen. He's become religious—and now he's become the crazy Rabbi's right-hand yeshiva boy. They're going to raise the cow till it's old enough to slaughter."

"We've got to do something about it!" Samira said.

"They're all crazy," Simon said. "That heifer should be shot! It should be ground up into hamburger and cast into the sea! Because if they retrieve even a *shank* from its leg, they'll burn it and use the ashes for their superstitious games." He glanced up toward the Dome of the Rock. "And bring about the war to end all wars."

Now Munir arrived and joined them. "Sir!" he begged. "You've got to help us!"

"Why should I help *you?*" the Israeli soldier told the Arab.

"I've got to get that heifer back!" Munir pleaded. "I'll give him back all his money." Munir took out the wad of money and waved it in the air.

"Father!" Samira said, eyeing the large wad.

"*Oy vey!*" said the soldier. "How much did he pay you for it?"

"Five thousand shekels!" Munir said. "But I don't want their money. You've got to help me buy it back!"

Simon sighed. "All right. Let's go talk to him."

They walked to the prayer room and the soldier knocked on the door. After a moment Rabbi Abram came out.

"You Zionist mad man!" Munir shouted. "How *dare* you think you can build a Jewish Temple up there!"

"And how dare *you* build that mosque on the mountain where our Father Abraham was about to sacrifice his son, *Itzak!*" the Rabbi shouted back at him.

"It was his son *Ishmael*" Munir said. "And that happened on the mountain in Mecca!"

"It was here on Mount Moriah," the Rabbi said, "and it was his son *Itzak!*"

"*Ishmael*" the Muslim insisted.

"*Itzak!*" the Rabbi persisted.

"It was **Ishmael**!"

"It was **Itzak!**"

Samira broke in. "Rabbi," she said, "your Old Testament says that God doesn't want a Jewish Temple up there anymore."

"Where does it say that?" Rabbi Abram demanded.

"In the Book of Isaiah, the Lord said that He had grown tired of your animal sacrifices," she said. "And in Psalm 50, the Lord says He owns every beast of the forest and the cattle on a thousand hills—and *'If I were hungry I would not tell you.'*

"Let me explain something to you about our ancient animal sacrifices in the Temple," the Rabbi said. "A blood sacrifice is required, to remove sin. Everyone in the Holy Land should welcome a return to this ritual. Because only *then* will there be peace in the land."

Isaac added: "That's right. In the Book of Leviticus, the Lord says— 'The life of a creature is in the blood, and I have given it to you on the altar to make atonement for yourselves—for it is the blood that makes atonement.'"

"Blood sacrifice! Huh!" Munir shouted. "Your old pagan blood sacrifice has *already* gone too far—at the expense of innocent Palestinian Arabs!"

Simon turned to face Munir. "*You're* the ones who are killing Israeli children in the name of your god! You're as crazy as the rabbis."

"I am a citizen of this country, just like you!" Munir shouted at Simon. "There are a million of us Arab citizens of Israel."

"I am talking about your brothers elsewhere who wish to invade our country, Israel, and take it over by force," Simon said. "They're like the Canaanites who sacrificed their babies to demons. Now they sacrifice their children as suicide bombers."

"So why have you allowed my Palestinian brothers to remain in refugee camps for all these years?" Munir demanded.

"The Arab nations put them there, by refusing to take them in," Simon retorted. "So much for brotherly love."

"Our Palestinian brothers will fight with every ounce of their blood until you return their land!" Munir shouted. "Even if it takes a thousand years!"

"What about *two* thousand years?" the soldier countered. "That's how long *we* waited to return to our land. Was *that* too long an absence to allow our return?"

"Our brave fighters will outlast yours," the Muslim snarled.

"Sure," Simon said. "They have plenty of 'brave' murderers to kill Jewish children, but not a single one of them has even *risked* his life to rid his people of their corrupt Palestinian leaders. Maybe they enjoy living in poverty."

The soldier then returned to patrolling the Wall.

Samira turned again to Rabbi Abram. "Rabbi," she said, "it says in the Psalms—'O Lord, You don't take pleasure in burnt offerings. My sacrifice to God is a broken spirit. God, You won't spurn a broken, chastened heart.'"

The Rabbi shook his head sadly. "You don't think I have a broken heart?" he told Samira. "It is said that from the day the Temple was destroyed, the Gates of Prayer were locked . . . but the Gates of Tears remain unlocked." And with that the Rabbi walked into the study room and slammed the door.

Now the sound of the muezzin began calling the hour for Muslim prayers. Hearing it, Munir straightened the checkered *kheffiyah* on his head and took out his prayer beads, then turned and began climbing the stone steps to the top of the Temple Mount, where he could pray in the Dome of the Rock. Outside the door he removed his shoes, then disappeared in the shrine, which has been turned into a mosque in recent years. Inside, he made his way to the center and thrust his hand into an opening—and touched the ancient Rock. Squinting his eyes with sheer pleasure, he felt his hand running along the indentation that had been left in the Rock by Muhammed's foot as he mounted his winged steed, Buraq, and sprang into the sky for his Night Journey to heavenly places.

*

Down at the foot of the Wall, Munir's daughter Samira was still talking to the yeshiva boy.

"Samira," Isaac said, "please try to understand how I feel about the teachings of the Torah, now that I'm religious. It commands us Jews to sacrifice an animal on the altar of the Temple. We transfer the guilt of our sins to the animal, and it pays the price by dying in our place. But I wouldn't expect a Muslim like you to understand."

"Itzak," she replied, "I became a Christian—two years ago, after my Christian mother died. I needed to have the same assurance that *she* had of life after death. So . . . I believe that I shall arise from the dead because Yeshua of Nazareth—Jesus—made the only Blood Sacrifice necessary to atone for sin."

"Sin, sin, sin!" Isaac snapped. "That's all you Christians ever talk about! We Jews don't accept your concept of 'original sin'—we are not a 'fallen' people."

"Oh, no?" she retorted. "So tell me why Job said, 'How can one born of woman be cleared of guilt?' And why do Jews work for *tikkun olam*—to repair the world—if the world is not fallen in sin? And what

33

about all of nature? Isn't nature fallen? Why else does Isaiah say that the wolf will lie down with the lamb, in peace, when Messiah comes?"

"Never mind Job and never mind the animals," Isaac said. "We have *not* inherited Adam and Eve's sin in the Garden of Eden. We are all born with the evil inclination as well as the good inclination."

"So you're blaming God for creating Adam and Eve with an evil inclination," Samira replied. "In that way, you avoid having to ask God for His Holy Spirit to help you avoid sin."

"But He also gave us the inclination for good—and that's what we focus on, doing mitzvahs," Isaac said.

"So how do you avoid the evil inclination?" she asked. "We're going to be saddled with it until the day we go to heaven."

"By Torah study," Isaac said. "And as Rabbi Hirsch says, 'Judaism guarantees us that it is possible to attain such a blessed state on earth as well (as in heaven), if only we sanctify every aspect of our lives.'"

Samira stepped closer to the yeshiva boy and thought for a moment.

"Itzak," she said quietly, "I think we've now come closer to the heart of the matter. You don't believe that *we are all a fallen race*, even though our first parents fell to temptation from the devil in the Garden of Eden. Therefore, you don't recognize the role of Satan and his demons in leading us to sin today. And you also don't recognize the need for us—*as a fallen people*—to die and be banished forever from heaven because of our sinful lives." She took a deep breath. "And so, in spite of what the Hebrew Scriptures say, today's followers of rabbinic Judaism reject the need for the Messiah to die in our place—and the need for Him to be the divine Son of God so that He can take away the power of the devil—and arise from the dead, triumphant!"

Isaac looked confused.

"Look, Samira," he said. "I want Messiah to come as much as you do. *Moshiach achshuv!* Messiah now! And so, rebuilding the Temple will invite the Messiah to come in our time. And it will invite God's Cloud of Glory to return to Jerusalem and live among us again."

"So we're back at that?" Samira said. "God asks the Jews in Psalm 50—'*Do I eat the flesh of bulls? Offer thanksgiving as your sacrifice to God.*'" Then Samira added—quoting from the New Testament—"Offer *yourselves* as a sacrifice, living and set apart to God."

"We are commanded to build a house for God!" Isaac said. "He says in <u>Exodus</u>, 'They are to make Me a sanctuary, so that I may live among them.' We are simply following His wishes."

"But then He asks in the Book of <u>Isaiah</u>, 'What kind of house could you build for Me? . . . Didn't I Myself make all these things?'—heaven and earth?"

"Samira," Isaac cried, "how can we praise God without a Temple—where He once was kind enough to place His Shekinah Glory? We want His Presence to return!"

"Don't you know that we are supposed to become the Temple of God—all of us walking around with God inside of us?" Samira said.

"What blasphemy!" Isaac exclaimed. "There was only one Temple of the Lord, even if it was a house of stone. In fact, your Yeshua from Nazareth referred to it as his Father's house! Would you contradict him?"

Stunned, Samira turned silent.

"Speaking of blasphemy," Isaac went on, "how can your messiah have the audacity to go and heal someone on the Sabbath, when no work is permitted?"

"Oh, give me a break?" she shot back. "Don't you pray in your synagogue for the health of your family—on the Sabbath? Is prayer suddenly work?"

Now Isaac let his embarrassment and rage rise up inside him, and his face turned red.

"There are times when I resent all Christians, including you, Samira," he said. "And I especially resent evangelical Christian tourists who come to my country and claim to love Israel. Their real agenda is to convert us to Christianity and to hasten the coming of their so-called Messiah—and to bring on us the final days and Jacob's Trouble."

After a long moment, Samira folded her arms and said: "Isaac, I have a riddle for you from the Bible. Solomon's Riddle! Look up <u>Proverbs 30</u>, verse <u>4</u>—'Who established all the ends of the earth? What is His name, *and what is His Son's name?* Surely you know!'" She paused. "Isaac? Don't you know who the Prophet was talking about?"

Isaac said nothing.

Chapter 5

Polarization of the Jews in Israel

Bound together by their common relationship to God and to His Law, the righteous gather into one united group, lest the desirable elements in the body of God's nation be choked off by the less desirable growths and . . . the entire nation would be lost.

— Rabbi Samson Raphael Hirsch's commentary on Psalm 50:5 - "Gather for Me My devoted ones, who uphold My covenant."

JERUSALEM

In Romema, in northwest Jerusalem, Shalamis Frankel was standing on her front porch one day when she saw two Israeli motorists stopped, facing each other on her narrow street. Turning to her screen door, she called for me to come outside and see a spectacle.

One driver was Orthodox and wore a kippa on his head. The bareheaded driver was a secular Jew from the same neighborhood. Neither was willing to back up and let the other pass. After about twenty minutes, one of the drivers pointedly steered his car behind a parked car—without backing up—and let the other driver pass.

"I've seen some drivers sit out there for two hours, waiting for one another to move," Mrs. Frankel told me.

I returned to the back yard of their modest home in Romema (which means 'lifted up'), where the Frankels and their eleven children have been able to look across an expansive valley and see in the distance two Israeli towns. Both towns were once Jordanian strongholds for shelling Israel, until they were recovered in the Six Day War of 1967. To my left, on one distant hill, I saw Har Nof, To my right, on another hill, I saw Ramot, whose red-roofed houses stood transfixed in the deepening dusk. As the sun lowered in the west, shining gently through a mist, the shadows lengthened across the green, gray hillside terraced with trees, shrubs and rocks. Evergreen trees grow in lush stands on these hills, which are crisscrossed by narrow dirt paths just begging to be explored.

The valleys between the two towns, at this hour, had a bluish-gray mist cut by the lowering sun. Surely, I thought to myself, these must be the same Judean hills that the Prophets saw in ancient times.

Now and then I saw coming into view a bird whose neck and head resembled a mourning dove, but whose tail feathers revealed white as the bird fluttered about, low to the ground, then returned to a roof top.

The Frankels' back yard drops sharply, and as I looked down I could see cars and trucks silently passing along a quiet road, where a lone jogger named Zerach could barely be picked out.

That night Rabbi Yaakov Frankel returned home from the nearby yeshiva where he teaches. His oldest son was living on his own, but still living at home were the other ten children, including the 12-year-old twins and the Frankels' youngest daughter, just two months old.

As Shalamis prepared dinner for us all, I mentioned the research I was doing at Mishkenot Sha'ananim on the Red Heifer. Rabbi Frankel said he had been somewhat disappointed a year earlier when he learned that the heifer named Melody had been disqualified. He told me he hoped that her story would end on a note of hope—perhaps Melody could be bred, he mused, and give birth to a kosher red heifer.

Then our conversation turned to the spectacle that I had witnessed earlier—the two Israeli motorists in front of his house—an Orthodox Jew and a secular Jew fighting over the right of way.

"There is a polarization going on," Rabbi Frankel said at last. "But this must happen before Messiah comes."

Rabbi Frankel told me that the Talmud hints that the Messiah will finally come when God has nothing further to gain by his delay. This might happen when the entire world has become totally wicked, and no one is left who might still repent. Then Messiah would come and bring judgment. Or it might happen when the world has become totally righteous, with no one left to repent. Then Messiah would come with his reward.

I asked Rabbi Frankel whether there might be a third possibility—if someday the whole world is divided between those fully righteous and those fully wicked, with nobody sitting on the fence and waiting to change their mind.

That, too, he said, would bring the Messiah, who will reign for a thousand years of justice and peace among all the peoples of the earth.

*

Three years later, it was Shavuot (Pentecost), and I was returning to the Frankel home with my wife, Shirah, whom they had never met. Because of the Jewish holiday, when Jews are not to drive, we had to find an Arab cabbie. Our driver, however, stopped his cab on Ha Mem Gimel, a couple blocks short of this Orthodox neighborhood, and apologized for having to let us out here: He was afraid of having his cab stoned by angry Orthodox residents who don't drive on Shavuot.

As we walked toward Ma'ane Simcha, we happened to pass a house where two young Chasidic men in black were sitting on the front porch. "Chag Sameach!" they called out, wishing us a joyful holiday. We returned their greeting. Shirah and I felt honored to be greeted by the ultra-Orthodox, who are known for shunning non-Jews and even Reform Jews. I was wearing a kippa, and my wife was wearing a dress from shoulders to ankles and had her head wrapped like a Jewess. They thought we were Orthodox (and Shirah's dark skin might have marked her as an Ethiopian Jew). But to us, the real reason they greeted us was because we had made a covenant with the Jewish people, and our anointing had made us one with them.

Zerach, the lone hitchhiker, was already at the Frankels'. In fact, this is where Zerach stays whenever he's in Jerusalem; he keeps his clothing and toiletries in his own closet in the basement.

Before dinner, we all went into the kitchen to ritually wash our hands with a two-handled cup.

Two German guests had arrived unexpectedly, a common occurrence in the Frankel home. They had come to visit their young relative, Svee, who was also at the table. Svee had met Zerach in Frankfort the previous year and was now studying here at Rabbi Frankel's yeshiva.

Shalamis started the meal by serving pumpkin soup. It was so delicious that Zerach left the table and disappeared in the kitchen, where he spooned and devoured the rest from the bottom of the pot. A skimpy eater, he barely ate anything else that afternoon. (Years earlier, I had seen Zerach subsist on kosher crackers and jam out of his suitcase during the entire week we spent together on assignment in Jordan; see Chapter 18). Our hostess had also put out olives, hummus, and a hot red sauce dish called *madbooka*. Then she brought out roast chicken. Then came the roast beef, and the kugel, followed by a non-dairy ice cream and chocolate cake. After that, she poured a vanilla extract into our soda water, and the aroma lifted us up to the heavens.

During dinner, I asked Rabbi Frankel if it was true that Jews have always expected something spiritual to happen on Shavuot, which comes 50 days after Passover. The New Testament indicates that the Jewish believers had gathered for Shavuot 50 days after the Resurrection, expecting something special—and behold, the Holy Spirit came down on them, prompting them to speak in different languages. Originating as a harvest festival when the first fruits were offered in the Temple, Shavuot is also associated with the giving of the Law on Mount Sinai during the wandering in the desert.

Rabbi Frankel replied that not only Shavuot but all Jewish festivals have an opportunity for special blessings. My heart sank, for I am always looking for Jewish expectations that have been fulfilled in the New Testament. Also sinking by now was the late afternoon sun, which was shining so brightly over the distant hills that I got up to adjust the blinds; but they were broken. Zerach joined me, and we took a blanket and fashioned what I jokingly trumpeted as a *mechitsah*, to protect the guests' eyes from the bright glare. Meanwhile, the Rabbi was telling stories about the Chafetz Chaim, the Lithuanian scholar who majored in writing about the laws of slander. Slander has been cited as a cause of the loss of the Temple.

Nearly 900 years before Christ, God had appeared to King Solomon after the dedication of the Temple and warned him what would happen if he or his sons ever fell fall away and served other gods: "Then I will cut off Israel from the land which I have given them; and this house which I have sanctified for My name I will cast out of My sight" (1 Kings 9:7).

The first Temple was indeed destroyed by the Babylonians some 500 years before Christ. Around 33 AD, Yeshua of Nazareth prophesied that the second Temple would be destroyed because of His rejection by His people. In fact, during Yeshua's time, Rabban Yochanan ben Zakkia predicted its destruction. It all came to pass when the Romans razed the Temple in 70 AD. Today, rabbinic Judaism teaches that the God of Israel permitted this to happen because Jews were slandering each other.

Sundown arrived, and it was time Shirah and me to depart. Now that the holiday was over, we were permitted to call a cab—even a Jewish one—for the ride back to our hotel. Rabbi Frankel escorted us down the street, and as we were reaching the circle where our cab would be waiting, he blessed us and said: "May the Shekinah be over your house."

Standing alone on the circle now, we began to witness one of the most overpowering royal pageants ever to unfold before our eyes, as the feast of Shavuot came to an end for the Jews of Mea She'arim. And it swelled like a symphony as we watched it from the windows of our cab in the passing night. It was like the final panoramic scene of an epic motion picture, the recollection of which would never fail to send shivers down my spine—for we were witnessing a veritable vision of God's holy people marching out of history—*past the Holocaust and done with it!*—as hundreds of black-clad men, women and children poured out of synagogue after synagogue along our route through Mea She'arim. They walked, they mingled, they called out to each other, they rejoiced, and some of them even danced in the street!

I will never forget this foretaste of heaven as long as I live.

The Song of Solomon

Up on the Temple Mount, Munir was coming out of the Dome of the Rock after prayer. The 7th century octagon-shaped building, with its blue and white tiles and golden dome, shone brilliantly in the late afternoon sun. After putting on his shoes, Munir looked up and noticed Noor. She was gazing down toward Samira and the soldier who were talking below, at the foot of the Wall.

Shrugging innocently, Noor told Munir: "I've heard of one mad cow causing a national panic, but what's all this fuss over one little heifer!" She looked quizzically at Munir. "In this land, you never know *what* they're going to fight about next!"

Munir paused to talk to her. "You would never believe that those kids used to be bosom buddies," he said.

"Who?"

"My daughter and those two Jewish boys," Munir said.

"Oh, really?"

"They were all in high school together, and Samira became fast friends with those boys when they ran into each other at a 'Peace Now' rally. Thousands of people came together and demanded an end to the fighting. They felt that it was time for the killing to stop and for both sides to make peace—at whatever the cost."

"Did that peace movement bring Jews and Arabs together?" Noor asked.

"Yes . . . But it didn't make many *lasting* friendships. Soon the two Jewish boys parted and went their separate ways. One went away to the Army and the other went to study to become a rabbi someday."

"And Samira?" Noor asked. "How did she lose touch with her old buddies?"

"Well," Munir said, "Itzak Cohen doesn't associate with a woman unless she is also a religious Jew." He smiled. "But *Simon*—I think Samira wanted to keep in touch with *him!*" Munir shook his head in amusement. "They were kind of sweet on each other."

"Really!"

"Oh yes!" Munir said. "One night the three of them were at a rally, and all the peaceniks were singing their peace songs and holding hands. And when it was over and all the people starting going home, Samira and Simon were still holding hands."

"Ooooooh!" Noor said and chuckled.

Munir turned serious. "That's exactly what I said," he said. "So I thank Allah that the Israeli boy entered the Army and was soon transferred somewhere else—and was never seen again—until recently, when he started guarding the Wall."

"But, now that he's back in Jerusalem, maybe he can help you get back your red heifer," Noor said.

"Why should he?" Munir said with a shrug. "I'm a Palestinian Arab and he's an Israeli soldier."

"Well," Noor said, "in the wrong hands, one little red heifer could cause a lot of trouble for an Army man like Simon. I should think he'd be on your side!"

Munir's eyes narrowed. "I wonder how Isaac Cohen and his Rabbi heard that I had that animal . . ."

"Ma salamah!" Noor said abruptly and walked away.

Munir looked down at the city and said to himself, after a pause, "It certainly didn't take them long to learn about it . . ."

As he looked down, Munir saw that Samira and Simon were alone at the foot of the Wall, still talking. He couldn't hear what they were saying, but it was obvious to him that his daughter and this Israeli soldier were renewing their old friendship.

Now they were sitting together against the Wall.

"Simon," Samira was saying to the soldier. "Simon the Zealot! You can help my father."

"What can *I* do?" he asked.

Samira leaned on his shoulder and said: "Simon, tell me more about this red heifer business. Is there any way that this calf can be made un-kosher? What do the rabbis say?"

"They're *all* a bunch of mad cows," Simon replied.

Twilight was falling on the city and the couple was sitting closer, head to head.

Atop the Temple Mount, Munir grimly recited a passage from the Qur'an: "Men should lower their gaze and guard their modesty . . . Women should lower their gaze and guard their modesty—that they should not display their beauty . . . except to their husband and their father."

*

That night Munir tossed and turned in his bed and had an unpleasant dream. He was standing on the Temple Mount (known to him as the *Haram al-Sharif*, the Noble Sanctuary), facing the Mount of Olives. Looking in the distance, he saw his daughter Samira and that Israeli soldier, coming up from the Kidron Valley.

"I am dark tan but lovely, you daughters of Jerusalem," Samira was saying. "Don't stare at me because I am dark—it's the sun that tanned me. My mother's sons were angry with me and made me look after the vineyard. But I haven't cared for my own vineyard" (CJB).

Turning to the soldier, Samira said, "Tell me, my love, where you pasture your flock."

"If you do not know, you most beautiful of women," the Israeli soldier replied, "follow the footsteps of *the heifer.*" Simon continued, "My love, I compare you with my mare, pulling one of Pharaoh's chariots—your cheeks are lovely with ornaments, your neck with its strings of beads. . . . Your eyes are doves."

Then Munir heard his daughter cry out, "Look at you! So handsome, so pleasing, my darling! . . . I am but a rose from the Sharon," she added, caressing the cross on her necklace, "just a lily in the valleys."

Suddenly the Israeli soldier looked up at Munir and blurted, "Like a lily among *thorns*, is my darling among the other women!"

Taking an apple from her pocket—an apple that she had taken earlier from the falafel stand—Samira said, "Like an apple tree among the other trees in the forest is my darling among the other men. I love to sit in his shadow; his fruit is sweet to my taste."

Then, in disbelief, Munir heard his daughter cry out, "Refresh me with *apples*, for I am sick with love!"

"Come, my darling, let's go out to the country," the solider said, "and spend the nights in the villages!"

"The voice of the man I love!" Samira said, and her eyes lit up. "Here he comes, bounding over the mountains, skipping over the hills. There he is, standing outside our wall, looking in through the windows."

"Get up, my love, my beauty," Simon told her. "Come away!"

Munir could no longer contain his anger. "Catch the foxes for us," he heard his voice roar, "yes, the little foxes! They are ruining the vineyards when our vineyards are in bloom!"

But Samira looked at her father, up on the Haram all-Sharif, and boldly declared, "My darling is mine, and I am his! . . . When I found the man I love, I took hold of him and would not let him go until I had brought him into my mother's house, to the bedroom of the woman who conceived me."

Turning away, Samira cried out into the night, "I warn you, daughters of Jerusalem, that if you find the man I love, what are you to tell him? That I am sick with love!"

Munir could hardly believe what was happening before his eyes.

Simon was calling out to Samira, "You are as beautiful as Samaria, my love, as lovely as Jerusalem—but formidable as an army marching under banners! Turn your eyes away from me, because they overwhelm me. Your hair is like a flock of goats streaming down Gil'ad. Your teeth are like a flock of sheep that have just come up from being washed . . . My dove, my perfect one is unique, her mother's only child, the darling of the one who bore her."

Samira replied, "I belong to my darling, and his desire is for me . . . If I met you outdoors, I could kiss you, and no one would look down on me. I would lead you and bring you to my mother's house."

Watching them approach the walls of the Old City, Munir demanded in a loud voice, "Who is this, coming up from the desert, leaning on her 'darling'? . . . Under the apple tree!?—it was there that your mother conceived you!"

Samira glared at her father and insisted, "No amount of water can quench love, torrents cannot drown it!" Then, turning to Simon and placing her hand in his, she said, "Flee, my darling! . . . "

Then they disappeared, walking hand in hand. When Munir awoke from his dream, he rushed into Samira's bedroom. There she was, sleeping peacefully in the night.

Chapter 6

Remembering the Words of Rabbi Meir Kahane

BUFFALO, NEW YORK

Rabbi Meir Kahane spent nine months in a maximum-security prison in Israel in 1980 for plotting to blow up the Muslim Dome of the Rock on the Temple Mount. Following his release, he began a series of lectures on Jewish intermarriage and assimilation, and on the need to turn Israel into a more religious Jewish state.

When I first met Kahane in 1981, he was preaching that Israel's Jewish character could only be preserved by moving the Arab residents from the "occupied territories" to other countries—mainly to neighboring Jordan, where Palestinian Arabs were already in the majority. This made him a lightening rod for Arab protesters wherever he spoke.

One night in November 1981 at Buffalo State College, Rabbi Kahane had spoken for only twenty minutes when Eric Mahr and his team of bodyguards from the Jewish Defense League almost came to blows with protesting Palestinian Arab students.

"Long live Palestine!" chanted the Arab students.

"There *is* no 'Palestine'!" the bearded rabbi shouted back at them, insisting that Palestine was never a country or a people, only a regional term assigned by the Romans after exiling the Jews.

"Long live Palestine!" they chanted.

As the Arabs and the JDL men lunged for each other, security guards whisked Kahane out of the building and into the night. Kahane's last words were, "There *is* no 'Palestine'!"

Six months later, the scrappy little rabbi returned to Buffalo State College, mounted the stage and began: "As I was saying, there *is* no

47

'Palestine'!" More than 120 students clamored in the student union this night, but this time he finished his speech.

Kahane even challenged Jewish students who were joining in the heckling. It was May 1982 and Israel was about to invade Lebanon to drive PLO forces and their Katyusha rockets away from the border with Israel. Palestinian refugees in Lebanon, he told them, "come from Jaffa and Haifa. That's where they want to come back, foolish Jewish dupes, not the West Bank."

"Throw him off the stage!" one of the protestors shouted.

"You want to try it, mister?" the rabbi snarled back, gesturing toward Eric Mahr and the dozen Jewish Defense League men standing behind him on stage, their arms folded. "Try it!"

A native of Brooklyn and a law school graduate, Kahane had established the JDL in 1968 and moved to Israel in 1971, gaining dual citizenship. He traveled back and forth between the two countries, leading often violent demonstrations against the Soviet Union for refusing to allow Jews to immigrate to Israel. After the terrorist massacre of Israeli athletes at the 1972 Olympic games in Munich, Kahane plotted with an old Irgun leader to sabotage the Libyan embassy in Brussels; it failed.

In 1984 he formed the radical Kach party, later winning a seat in the Knesset. The Kach party called for removing Palestinian Arabs from the West Bank (which he called by its biblical names, Judea and Samaria) and from Gaza, either by force or by paying Arab families restitution for their property. This would allow Israel to settle Jewish families on those lands, which had been promised to Israel by God.

"For God will give salvation to Zion and build the cities of Judah," the Psalmist prophesied. "They shall abide there and shall take possession of it once more."

As for the 1.5 million Arab citizens of Israel whose families had never left in 1948, Kahane said they could remain in Israel proper and elect their own village and city officials. But they should be stripped of their voting rights in national elections, so that their swelling population could never take over the democratic government and turn Israel into a non-Jewish state.

Arabs already have a Palestinian state, one that should have been named *Palestine* when it was created in 1947, according to Kahane. That country is Jordan, which occupies all of traditional eastern Palestine. (Israel was left with less than half of western Palestine when it gained independence a year later, in 1948.) About 70 percent of Jordan's citizens are Palestinian Arabs, whose families fled western Palestine in 1948 and 1967.

As many as 700,000 Arabs fled western Palestine when Israel declared its independence in May 1948 and the neighboring Arab countries attacked the Jewish state. Many of the Arab residents were driven out by Jewish fighters, but many others left voluntarily—with the encouragement of the Arab world—thinking they could return when the Jews had been defeated. But that wasn't the outcome.

In its issue of Feb. 19, 1949, the Jordanian daily newspaper *Falastin* published this statement:

> The Arab states which had encouraged the Palestine Arabs to leave their homes temporarily, in order to be out of the way of the Arab invasion armies, have failed to keep their promise to help these refugees.

Back in 1947, the United Nations had offered the Arabs and the Jews of Palestine the opportunity to carve two countries out of western Palestine. The Jews reluctantly accepted; the Arab nations, speaking on behalf of the Palestinians, refused. Then they attacked the Jews in May 1948 and tried to take all the land for the Palestinian Arabs.

Of all the Arab countries that rejected the two-state solution and invaded the land, only Jordan offered citizenship for fleeing Palestinians. Yet even today, many Palestinians still live in refugee camps in Jordan; I visited one of them in 1985 and interviewed Palestinians about the "land for peace" proposal that had just been launched (see Chapter 18).

The other Arab nations that attacked Israel in 1948 have refused to welcome Palestinian refugees, preferring to use them as pawns against Israel. Meanwhile, about 800,000 Jews fled to Israel after being forced from their longtime homes in Arab countries—because the Muslim world, comprising 22 countries, would never forgive Jews for forming their own tiny state in the Middle East.

In 1964 the Arab League established the Palestine Liberation Organization, and Yasser Arafat later became its president. At no time did Arafat or the PLO seek to establish a Palestinian state in Gaza, which Egypt occupied, or on the West Bank, which Jordan occupied. Rather, its goal was to eliminate the Jewish state by terrorism and "liberate" all of western Palestinian for the Arabs.

Then, in June 1967, Egypt, Jordan and Syria (backed up by Iraq) amassed their armies on the borders of Israel and prepared to attack and "liberate" all the rest of western Palestine for the Palestinian refugees. With 250,000 enemy troops and 2,000 tanks on its borders, Israel struck first and not only pushed back the Arab armies but "liberated" the West Bank from Jordan—and Gaza and the Sinai Desert from Egypt (as well as the Golan Heights from Syria). In 1980 Israel annexed the Old City of Jerusalem as its capital, as it had been in the days of King David.

After Anwar Sadat's visit in 1977, Israel returned the Sinai to Egypt in exchange for peace. And Israel evacuated Gaza and turned it over to Palestinian control in 2005.

None of the territory occupied by Israel after the Six Day War was taken from a sovereign Palestinian state; there had never been such a state in all history.

"We do not see it as an occupied territory," said Justice Elyakim Rubenstein of the Israeli Supreme Court, "because there was no recognized sovereignty there before 1948."

And now, for the first time in nearly 2,000 years, Israel again had control over all of western Palestine, including the Old City of Jerusalem, which was reunited with modern-day Jerusalem as the capital of Israel—and as the site of the ancient Temple.

Since then, Israel has established 150 Jewish settlements on the West Bank, housing nearly 300,000 Jews. And the Arabs, who number 2.5 million on the West Bank, have added 260 settlements since 1967. The lingering question is how to grant a measure of local autonomy to Arab communities on the West Bank without creating a sovereign Palestinian state that still refuses to accept Israel as a Jewish state.

In later years the Arab nations that had rejected the UN's partition plan of 1947 turned around and began to promote a "two-state solution." One state, to be named Palestine, would take over the "occupied territories" and become entirely Arabic—in other words, *Judenrein*. The other state, known until now as Israel, would grant millions of Arab Palestinians the Right of Return, which would gradually transform it into an Arab-dominated state. The two states would eventually merge as Palestine, where the remaining Jews would be permitted to live as a minority under Muslim rule, until the end of time.

Kahane would have added that, in all of history, there was never a Palestinian state before Jordan came into being in 1947. As for the *Palestinians*, Kahane would have added, the term *Palestinian* was always an adjective—never a noun. There were Palestinian Jews, Palestinian Christians, and Palestinian Arabs—until the Palestine Liberation Organization began using it as a noun in the 1960s. Suddenly, a *Palestinian* was a native (always Arab) of Palestine (always western Palestine). The media picked up the term, and a nationality was born in a day.

To people like Kahane, the Swedes might just as well have declared themselves the only true "Scandinavians," vowing to drive the Norwegians into the sea.

*

Meir Kahane was back in Buffalo, New York, in 1982 on a national speaking tour while running for a seat in the Knesset, the parliament of Israel. This time his topic was the tragedy of Jewish intermarriage and assimilation, and the added threat of Christian missionaries, both here and in Israel. After speaking at an Orthodox synagogue, Kahane went to the home of his host, Eric Mahr, who headed Kahane's Jewish Defense League in Buffalo.

Here, the rabbi agreed to be interviewed by me with my tape recorder. In contrast to his bombastic speeches, Kahane now spoke softly, intimately, at times almost inaudibly.

First, I asked Kahane whether there was ever a time in history when the Jews lived in the region now called Palestine without any non-Jewish neighbors.

"Why, certainly," he said, "in Judea and Samaria thousands of years ago. There weren't any Arabs then."

There weren't Samaritans or other non-Jews living in Samaria?

"I don't know," he said, "but it was a Jewish state. In the days of the first Temple."

But there were foreigners living there, right?

"I would say there were foreigners living there," Kahane admitted, "but they certainly were not voting citizens."

I asked him how the Hebrew Scriptures command the Jewish people to treat the foreigner living in their midst.

"First of all," Kahane said, "when it speaks of that, it uses the Hebrew word *ger*, which is translated as stranger, but *ger* means convert, it never means stranger. Now, obviously, someone who's not Jewish, certainly we should not oppress or persecute. But there's a tremendous gap, a gulf, between not persecuting someone and making him a citizen."

Doesn't the *Gamara Ketubot* in the Talmud say that the Jews may not cast out other people from Israel until the Messiah comes?

"It doesn't say that at all," Kahane replied. "It says on Page 110 that God gave two oaths to the Jews, and one to the nations. The two oaths to the Jews basically were that they should not rise up in force against the world nations. The oath that the nations gave was that they should not persecute the Jews while the Jews are in exile. All the rabbis say that when the nations broke their oath, of course we were free from our oaths."

Two wrongs make a right?

"It isn't a question of whether we were wrong," he said. "God certainly didn't want Jews to be placed in a position of having to go into gas chambers and not doing anything about it. So God said to the nations, 'Don't make gas chambers,' and to the Jews, 'You sit quietly.' They wanted to go to Palestine in the 1930s, and they were told to stay in Europe and die. And those who went lived."

Didn't the Jews establish Israel as a democracy in 1948, and doesn't Judaism require the Jewish state to give equal rights to non-Jews living in its borders?

Kahane replied that 'democracy' and the 'state' are secular concepts that arose long after Judaism, so they cannot take precedence over what the Torah has taught about Jews and Gentiles living together over the centuries. He was upset over all the secular Jews who have, in effect, adopted democracy as their religion.

"The Jews are the last of the ancient Hebrews," Kahane said. "Many Jews today—including Orthodox Jews—are assimilated Jews. They have assimilated non-Jewish concepts. . . . We have Orthodox Jews here who are influenced by Thomas Jefferson. Judaism is Judaism! And the Jewish nation faces tragedy because it doesn't want to be Jewish."

I then asked Kahane about the theory of some archeologists that the Temple once stood either north or south of the spot now occupied by the Muslim Dome of the Rock. Is there room on the Temple Mount for both the Dome of the Rock and a future, third Jewish Temple?

"I don't need an archeologist to tell me," Kahane angrily replied. "We know, everyone knows, that on the Temple Mount, on that area on that site, stood both holy Temples. That's the holiest site in all of Judaism. The outrage is not only that Moslems came on our holiest site and built two mosques, but that the Israeli government, in its fear and panic and lack of any kind of Jewishness and Jewish faith, is so terrified that it leaves them there and orders Jews not to pray there. I want a Moslem ban, I want the mosques removed, and I want—"

"—Isn't that World War III?" I interjected. *"Wouldn't that cause all the countries that are Islamic to rise up as one and declare a holy war against Israel?"*

Kahane said something low, inaudible, as if whispering to himself.

"Hmmm?" I asked.

Speaking ever so softly, Kahane repeated: "It would bring the Messiah."

Sabotage of the Red Heifer

Simon the soldier knocked on the wooden door of Rabbi Abram's prayer and study room door and waited. Soon Isaac the yeshiva boy opened the door and looked out at him.

"I guess you've heard about all the commotion," Simon told him.

Isaac just stared back at him in the doorway. "Who are you?" he replied at last. "What are you talking about?"

"Come on, Yitzak," the soldier chided. "You remember me."

"Should I?" the yeshiva boy said.

"I'm Simon!" the soldier shouted. "Remember? 'Peace Now'?"

Isaac adjusted the black hat on his head and said, "What do you want?"

Simon looked at him with disgust. "Since I came back from the Golan, I've guarded the Wall, and you've seen me," he told Isaac. "Not once did you meet my eyes."

Isaac looked away. "I know," he said quietly. "These are different times."

"They certainly *are*," the soldier said, looking past Isaac into the prayer room. As the soldier stepped through the doorway, the yeshiva boy moved aside and closed the door. Simon picked up a book from the table and scowled at the title. "Religion, religion, religion," he said.

"Religion?" the yeshiva boy replied. "What a strange word, coming from a fallen-away Jew."

Simon slammed the book on the table and turned to Isaac. "I've fought your battles for you—while you've spent all these years in your yeshiva, studying *religion*!" he shouted. "Did you learn anything *useful* for the defense of the State of Israel?"

"As a matter of fact I did, Shimon," Isaac shot back, calling him by his Hebrew name. "I discovered that in the entire Hebrew Bible, not once will you find a word for *religion*."

The soldier squeezed his eyes shut and shook his head. "Impossible," he said.

"Do the birds have a word for *air*?" Isaac asked. "Do the fish have a word for *water?*"

Shrugging, the soldier paced the room, then stopped and looked directly at the yeshiva boy.

"Listen, Yitzak," he said. "There's something I have to tell you."

"But first tell *me* something," Isaac said. "All right, so I knew who you were. I was avoiding you. But why were *you* avoiding *Samira?*"

"What?!"

"And then you pretended not to *remember* her—when her father wanted the Red Heifer back from us. "*A salaam aleikum,* pretty face!"— like you were flirting with a *stranger!*"

Simon thought a moment.

"I wasn't pretending, Yitzak," he said. "Since I got hurt, some of my memory has been a bit fuzzy." He paused and rubbed the scar on his face. "What are you getting at, anyway?"

"Shimon," Isaac said, "I know why you were transferred out of Jerusalem two years ago."

"You *what?*" the soldier said, blinking his eyes.

"And it wasn't pretty, was it?"

Simon stepped toward Isaac. "Who else knows?" he demanded.

"Like Samira and her father?" Isaac said. "Don't worry, Simon. They haven't got a clue."

Simon looked very agitated. "Yitzak—you wouldn't—"

"Don't worry, Shimon," Isaac taunted him. "Your secret is safe with me."

Simon thought a moment and sighed.

"Listen, Yitzak," he said. "I came to tell you about something."

"Well?"

"Well, it's about all that commotion that I mentioned." Simon paused. "Yitzak, I know that no one is supposed to go near that heifer. But—"

"But what?" Now Isaac looked alarmed.

"Well, Samira wanted to see her heifer again and—"

"Why?"

"She missed her little heifer. And I was curious about the little critter myself—I mean, I'd never even gotten a look at it."

"And?" Now Isaac's face was turning red. "And?"

"And so," the soldier said, "I stood guard for her when no one was around, while she went into the pen to pet the heifer."

"Did she touch it?"

"I—I didn't actually see it happen."

"What happened?" Isaac demanded, turning more red in his face.

"I couldn't even see—I was standing by the door, looking out for her."

"Shimon!" Isaac shouted. "What happened?!"

"Well, Samira came running out, and I went with her back to the falafel stand."

Isaac raised his hands in exasperation, and the black hat began to slide on the back of his head. "Are you going to tell me what happened?!" the yeshiva boy cried.

"Well," Simon said, speaking slowly now, "she said she wanted to pet the heifer . . . so she bent down and . . . she was hugging it in the pen, and . . . she kind of slipped in the slop and fell down—on top of the heifer."

"She *what!?*" Isaac cried out in the prayer room.

"But it wasn't hurt," Simon said quickly.

"Are you sure?" Isaac implored him. "She fell *on top of* the heifer?"

"Just for a moment," Simon assured him.

"She, *the woman,* she fell to the ground?"

"Yes."

"And, and the heifer was under her?"

"Yes—well, sort of. I think."

"Shimon, think carefully—did the heifer fall down too?"

"But it got right back up! It's all right now!"

"Answer me!" the yeshiva boy screamed. He was trembling. "Did it fall *under the woman's weight?*"

"Well . . . yes . . ." Now the soldier went on the offensive: "All right, enough of this cross-examination! I've told you all I know."

After a dizzy pause, as he pivoted in a little circle, Isaac turned to Simon and shouted: "Tell no one else! Do you hear me, Simon? *Tell no one about this—for Samira's sake!*"

"All right!" Simon said, turning to go. Then he added a sarcastic "Shalom!" and left.

Alone now, Isaac frantically paced the prayer room—stopped—opened the curtain containing the Torah scroll—touched it—then resumed his frantic pacing.

The door opened again and Rabbi Abram entered the prayer room, humming to himself. "Yitzak Cohen!" the Rabbi said. "I have been talking to the other rabbis about the priesthood, and about you—why Yitzy! You look so sad!"

"Oh—I'm just a bit tired, Rabbi," Isaac replied.

"Well, my boy, it's almost dinner time! Come—we'll sit down with the others and sing the blessing and have dinner. We have much to discuss."

"Discuss *what*, Rabbi?" Isaac said as they left the prayer room and walked toward the dining room.

"The Red Heifer, of course!" the Rabbi said. "Now, the final examination of the red cow will take place when she is three years old. If it still is pure red, and if it still has no blemish, then it will be led outside the gate, up to the Mount of Olives, for the ritual sacrifice." Rabbi Abram drew a finger across his throat. "Then the fire will be lit, and—"

"Rabbi, you forgot the third condition," the yeshiva boy said, and they both stopped walking.

"I did?"

"Yes," Isaac said. "In addition to being pure red, and without blemish—it must never have carried a yoke," Isaac said, wrapping hands around his own neck,

"Yes! Yes!" the Rabbi said. "It must never have pulled a plow or been *ridden* by anyone."

"Rabbi?" Isaac said, and they began walking again. "Suppose a child were to sit on its back? Would that disqualify it?"

"Oh, yes, I believe it would!"

"Now, suppose someone were to lean on it?"

"How hard?"

"Enough to push it out of the pen?"

"No problem," Rabbi Abram said. "We do that all the time."

Isaac stopped walking again. "What if it were pushed—enough to bring it to its knees?"

"Not so good. But I don't believe—"

"—What if it was pushed to the ground?"

"Under a person's weight? As if under a yoke?" Rabbi Abram said. "No! That would instantly disqualify the Para Aduma! Instantly! God forbid! That's why it is guarded day and night . . ."

"I see," the yeshiva boy said, his heart pounding, and they headed for the dining hall.

Chapter 7

The Pharisees Are
Taking Over Jerusalem

NEVE YAAKOV

U p in northern Jerusalem, Eric Mahr is cooking a barbecue for his wife, Jody, and their children out on the upstairs balcony of their apartment. In the distance, Mahr points to two Arab towns in the shimmering desert of Samaria (part of the 'West Bank').

Only a mile from Ramallah, Neve Yaakov is considered by some to be part of the "occupied territory" of the West Bank. Actually, it pre-existed the State of Israel and was one of the little Jewish settlements that were given up after much fighting in 1948. Israel recaptured Neve Yaakov in 1967 and incorporated it into Jerusalem.

A native of Buffalo, New York, Mahr identifies himself as a *baal t'shuvah*, a Jew who chose to become Orthodox during the religious revival that swept the Jewish world after the recovery of Jerusalem after the Six Day War of June 1967.

Based on his radical background back in Buffalo, Mahr might have been expected to become part of the movement to find a red heifer and rebuild the Temple. After all, he had often hosted Rabbi Meir Kahane, founder of the Jewish Defense League, in his home and in fact was president of the Buffalo chapter of the JDL. Mahr's JDL men used to patrol Jewish cemeteries on Halloween and on Jewish holidays and would beat up vandals attempting to damage or desecrate the headstones with swastikas.

Rabbi Kahane later moved to Israel and formed a radical political party, Kach, whose platform included removing Palestinian Arabs from

57

the West Bank and Gaza. He was called a racist, and his Kach Party was outlawed in Israel in 1988.

But he was willing to fight to the death for the survival of his people—quoting from the Talmud, "If your enemy comes to slay you, slay him first!"

Kahane was assassinated by an Arab in 1990. A few years later Kahane's son, Benjamin, was shot to death with his wife in a highway ambush.

"He never wanted his son Benjamin to do what *he* was doing," Mahr recalls. "And he got killed."

Kahane used to funnel charity money to the poor, Mahr recalls, from his office on Ussishkin Street. The street was named after Menachem M. Ussishkin, the Russian Zionist who from 1923 headed the Jewish National Fund, purchasing large tracts of land for lease to Jewish settlers.

"Those of us who were closest to him—I don't want to say I'm sorry, but we've moved on with our lives," Mahr says now. "The ones who were left after he died were the farthest from his teachings. When we first came to Israel, some guys were trying to give a weekly class on Rabbi Kahane's teachings. They had no clue what they were talking about. He came to his teachings by long years of studying the Torah. All these guys did was take the fluff around the outside—they didn't penetrate the core."

Asked why he isn't interested in the search for a kosher red heifer, Mahr says, "The Third Temple will fall from heaven and crush whatever is on the Temple Mount—or it will be built by us when the time is right."

His wife interjects: "When all the Jews are holy enough, then the Shekinah will be able to come down to the Temple."

When will that be?

"The Talmud says that if the Jews will all be worthy, God will hurry the Redemption," Mahr replies. "If they do not, then every prophecy in the Bible will come true, and there will be wars and rumors of wars."

Oddly enough, Mahr has somehow picked up Yeshua's phrase "wars and rumors of wars" from the New Testament.

A decade later, in 2007, I visited the Mahrs again. They were still living in this northern Jerusalem desert suburb, and his neighbors were seeing their children marrying and starting their own Orthodox families. Mahr's oldest son, Benny, said the country was becoming more religious because of the *baal t'shuvah* religious revival, which was continuing to gather momentum since Israel's recovery of the Old City.

"Everything revolves around weddings nowadays," says Benny, who also will marry in a few months. "All the music is made for wedding dances. This is because the first generation of *baal t'shuvah* children are getting married now. A whole generation of fresh Jewish blood."

In fact, secular Jews are moving out of Jerusalem at a quickening pace, as the city becomes more religious. In a single year, more than 17,000 residents left the city, to be replaced by 11,000 newcomers, most of them Orthodox Jews or Arab citizens of Israel.

The seriousness of this polarization between Orthodox and secular Israelis was underlined in the *Israel Religion and State Index* for 2011, which found that 64 percent of Jews in Israel consider this to be the first or second most acute domestic conflict in Israel. Only 30 percent consider the gap between rich and poor to be the No. 1 cause of domestic conflict. Eighty percent of the public believes that the Orthodox should be required to perform military or national service; that subsidies to students in yeshivas should be reduced, to encourage these men to join the work force; and that core curriculum courses related to modern-day life should be required in religious schools, as they are in public schools.

With the rise of Orthodoxy, secular Israelis are finding themselves deserted by their own secular world system, says Eric Mahr, as one political solution after another fails to bring peace with the Palestinians. His prime example was Israel's unilateral withdrawal from Gaza.

"The radical leftists, secularists, are completely ignorant of anything regarding Judaism," Mahr says. "Suddenly, secular Zionists are completely disillusioned. Because everything they stood for, all their principles, turned out to be a house of cards."

Mahr says that every major tragedy in Israel has brought Jews closer to God. After the assassination of Prime Minister Yitzhak Rabin in 2005, he recalled, a high school principal in a secular neighborhood of Tel Aviv began to notice some of his students attempting to pray. And the traumatic removal of Jewish settlers from Gaza—and the failure of an autonomous Palestinian Gaza to bring peace—left Peace Now activists without a cause. Many secular Jews turned to God.

The Talmud also predicts, Mahr adds, that when the Messiah comes, an earthquake will strike near the Mount of Olives and will swallow the cemetery, which the Muslims have since extended to the city walls in a vain attempt to keep this Jewish holy man from entering Jerusalem by the Golden Gate.

"There will be no red heifer until after the Messiah comes," Mahr says. "If a red heifer came first, then the Messiah wouldn't need an ᴄe to swallow the cemetery—the Messiah would then be purified of the cemetery by the ashes of the red heifer. But the Talmud says it's the earthquake that will make it all possible for Messiah to enter the Golden Gate."

A daily prayer once known as the Eighteen Benedictions—going back to the First Temple, a thousand years before Christ—gives some clues to Biblical Judaism's traditional expectation of the order of events preceding the final days. The Tenth Benediction asks God for the ingathering of the Jews from exile to their ancestral homeland—fulfilled, for the last time, in the years before and after 1948. The Fourteenth prays for the restoration of Old Jerusalem—fulfilled in 1967. The Fifteenth seeks the coming of Messiah. The Seventeenth asks for the rebuilding of the Temple and restoration of the blood sacrifices on the altar.

A Nineteenth Benediction denouncing heretics was added, around 85 AD, to pressure Jewish believers in Yeshua to leave the synagogue and go their separate way as Jews. Which they eventually did, with the greatest reluctance. These ostracized Jews established their own synagogues and invited Gentiles to join them. However, the Jewish authorities had actually initiated the rift half a century earlier, when they sent Sha'ul of Tarsus to Damascus to arrest and bring back in chains Jewish believers in Yeshua. On the road to Damascus, Saul had a vision of Messiah Yeshua, who appointed him to bring the message of salvation to the Gentiles—who later took over the church.

Fighting Over the Land

Back at Munir's falafel stand, Simon was talking to Samira about his encounter with Isaac in the prayer and study room.

"You told Itzak that I went to see the heifer?" Samira exclaimed.

"Of course!" he replied.

"How could you? Your only job was to be my lookout!"

"He had to be told," Simon said, and he smirked. "Now he doesn't know *what* to do!"

Samira was angry. "You made this decision yourself!" she said. "I thought we were working together to get the heifer back—and I was just going to check out the security."

"This had to be done," Simon told her.

"Now they're going to come after *me*!" she said. "Those crazy rabbis are dangerous!"

Simon put an arm around Samira. "I'll take care of you Samira. I'm your soldier boy."

Samira pushed him away. "Sure!" she snapped. "You're Simon the Zealot—the soldier of Israel—you don't have to consult anybody else who might be affected by it, do you? Especially if she's a second-class citizen—an Arab!"

"Samira, please," he said. "This isn't about that."

"Isn't it?" she said, glaring at him. "Isn't everything about the land? The land your people took from mine?"

"Samira," Simon pleaded, "we weren't going to let this come between us. Remember?"

"But it *is* between us, Shimon! As the soldier of an occupying force, you actually think you have some God-given right to make decisions that affect all of us!"

"But—"

"But, oh, I misspoke!" Samira said sarcastically. "I shouldn't say 'God-given.' You don't even believe in God!"

"No," Simon said slowly. "Not really . . ."

"So, my dear Israeli friend," she said, " if it wasn't God who gave you all of the Land of Palestine, thousands of years ago, then who *was* it?"

"We were just—here! Period."

"But you drove out the nations that were here before there were any Jews or Arabs living here."

"We drove out the pagan nations that had polluted the land by sacrificing their babies to demons," Simon said. "Before there were ever any Arabs living here. And we needed a safe place to live after we escaped from persecution in Egypt."

"So, tell me," Samira demanded, "on *whose authority* did the Israelites take over this land after wandering in the desert for forty years?"

Simon raised his hands helplessly. "This is pointless," he said. "Why are we fighting? You've got to hide yourself—now!—in case someone should come after you."

"Go hide yourself, Shimon," Samira said. "I'm a Palestinian Arab—I don't *have* a place to run and hide."

Pounding his fist on the counter, Simon adjusted his belt holster and left the falafel stand.

Now Noor came from a back room of the falafel stand, where she was staying while in Jerusalem. "Trouble in paradise?" she said, smiling.

"Oh, Noor, what am I going to do?" Samira said. "I think I've always loved him! But he's always turning against me!"

"Sounded to me like he was the one being 'turned against,'" said Noor.

"Things were going so well between us!" Samira told her. "We were working together to get back the Red Heifer. But now something's come between us."

Noor sat Samira down at a table behind the counter in the falafel stand and looked at her intently.

"Samira," she said, "if you are serious about your love for Simon, you must remember the New Testament's prohibition against marrying a non-believer in Messiah."

"I know," Samira replied. "But I hope to bring him to Yeshua beforehand. I just don't know how to help him believe in the Messiah."

"Let me explain something to you about the word *believe*," Noor told her. "In modern society, we *believe* something only if we are satisfied it is true, based on the limited evidence available. But when Yeshua said you must *believe* in Him, He was talking about a conscious decision that is made, based on faith."

"Noor," Samira said, "I've been through all of this with my father! And he keeps asking me, 'How can God expect me to *believe* in someone when that person may be false?'"

Noor smiled. "I'll tell you a secret. When a person decides to *believe* in Yeshua as the Messiah, it means that the Holy Spirit has touched that person with an anointing. You see, God knows our hearts and when we are ready or not ready for this challenge."

"So . . . what can I do in the meantime?"

"In the meantime," Noor said, rising from her seat, "you must be Yeshua to this man. Your actions and behavior as a Christian should bring him to see that you have something special—something that he wants too!"

"Well," Samira said, rising, "first let's see if he ever speaks to me again, after our argument today."

"You want Simon to come to you?" Noor said, taking Samira's hands in hers. "Well, there is an old saying—'If the mountain won't come to Mohamed, then Mohamed will have to go to the mountain.'"

"What do you mean?!" Samira asked.

"You'll see," the Bedouin replied with a wink. "Just trust Noor."

Chapter 8

Arabs Discuss Peace Outside Munir MaTouk's Falafel Stand

JERUSALEM

Yes, the late Munir MaTouk's falafel stand still stands just inside Jaffa Gate, and I visit his family whenever I'm in town. Today a Palestinian Arab named Norman is asked what he thinks of the basic idea of "land for peace" that was recently proposed by the Palestine Liberation Organization. The year is 1985.

"Well, good solution," he tells me. "But after West Bank they give us Gaza. We need more. Jerusalem—this is Palestine!"

"But Jerusalem isn't even mentioned in the Qur'an," I note.

"Who said that?" Norman demands "Mohammed was taken up from the Haram al-Sharif on his horse and he went up to heaven."

"Before Mohammed, there were Jews in Jerusalem," I reply.

"They were the Prophets of God," Norman retorts. "Prophets who appear in the Qur'an."

A man named Ali, with a shock of white in his black hair, drops by the falafel stand and quickly joins in our conversation.

"I was born near the mosque," Ali says, gesturing toward the Temple Mount, where the sprawling, silver-domed Al Aqsa Mosque stands, not far from the golden Dome of the Rock.

Now Norman, who happens to own a store nearby, turns to me and says, only half in jest, "Come in my shop and let me rip you off!"

Ignoring him, I unfold a map on the counter of the falafel stand and point to the Temple Mount. "Do you see this empty spot, between the Dome of the Rock and the Muslim Quarter?" I ask. They bend over and follow my finger on the map. "Some rabbis want to built the Temple there," I tell them.

Norman looks at me in disbelief. "I think if they do it, a great big war will happen," he says.

"Suppose this concession were made to the Israelis," I suggest to him, "as part of a larger agreement that might succeed in trading land for peace?"

"It would be hard to make agreement," Norman replies. "No agreement. Nobody is sure what is the best thing. The Temple is nothing. It's destroyed. But what can't be denied—Dome of the Rock!"

"When the Israelis gained control of Jerusalem in 1967," I persist, "they allowed Muslims to remain in charge of the Temple Mount."

"Yes," Norman says. "And we never take something not for us. It was very fair."

*

Not far from the falafel stand is a Palestinian Arab with an entirely different view of the relationship between Muslims and non-Muslims. He has even come up with a non-violent solution to the Arab-Israeli conflict.

Ismael Obydat is well known in Israel for his persistent attempts to bring people together. In fact, the City of Jerusalem has invited him to take part in the annual Jerusalem Day ceremonies as a representative of the country's Arab Palestinian citizens.

An engineer, architect and inventor, Ismael has his office just inside Jaffa Gate. The narrow room is thirteen feet long and only five and a half feet wide. But he has been here for years, and from his second-floor window he can look down at Munir's falafel stand and see the shops surrounding it, as well as David's Citadel, Christ Church and other landmarks inside the walls of the Old City.

A middle-aged man with a full mustache and bushy head of hair—and a quizzical smile on his face—Ismael has no sympathy for the red heifer. As an Arab citizen of Israel, he wouldn't approve of building a Jewish Temple on or near the spot where the Dome of the Rock has stood for the past fourteen centuries. But he has his own project for making peace between the next generation of Jews and Arabs.

For many years, Ismael has been perfecting and promoting his new version of football. He calls it Fireball. In this game, there is no physical contact between players on the two opposing teams. Each player is assigned a large square of grass to protect, and if the ball falls there the referee cries, "Fireball!"

"The object," Ismael explains, "is to keep the ball from touching the ground. Imagine a ball of fire that must not set the field aflame."

Hanging on his wall are a street map of Jerusalem and color drawings of the layout of his game, which is to be played on a grassy field measuring seventy-five meters square. Each player must defend a fifteen-meter square.

"Your ground is hay," Ismael says. "Football is fire, and hay burns."

Munir's nephew, Aduin, who is thirteen years old, has walked up the stairs and is at the open door. He comes in, sits on the floor and plunks on a lute that was lying in a corner.

A bird begins chirping in a cage.

The boy stops plunking on the lute and looks up at the birdcage.

I turn to look at the bird too.

"I'm a sensitive man," Ismael says by way of explanation.

I return my attention to the chart on the wall.

"Yes, Fireball is a little bit hard to learn," Ismael continues. "You play it with people. It's not a table game. It's on the ground, but it's not dangerous."

How did he come to invent this game?

"One day I was playing football and I have an ache in my foot. So from that day I think of a safety playing football."

The game itself is a combination of human and scientific discoveries.

"I study sociology and architecture," he says. "I want to go to the United States to discuss my invention with the American people—and the whole world, in addition to the Palestinian people. And I hope it will be a message between the Palestinians and the whole world—the Jews, too. A sport is a sport."

Before leaving, I remark to Ismael that the rules of his game seem a bit complicated. Smiling understandingly, he explains, "One captain is in the center square, the other is thrown out. Captain A and Captain B are either in or out of the game. The player—or team—is either in or out. You have two teams."

"Or two peoples," I observe.

"Or two peoples," Ismael agrees without hesitation, still smiling.

I still think about Ismael's game. It's almost a perfect parable about the Arabs and the Jews fighting over the land, right down to flying objects landing in your territory and burning. I did try to steer our conversation toward a clearer acknowledgment of this, but Ismael slipped away, leaving an air of mystery . . .

Years later, when I visited him again, Ismael Obydat gave me this
poem:

> I mounted the wind
> with the migratory fowl;
> with longing I traveled to you.
> I have left behind my homeland,
> There . . . behind the ocean,
> There . . . before the seas.
> My longing for you is fastening me,
> tossing me as a hurricane
> to you, Jerusalem,
> Jerusalem, O Bride,
> dressed in a snowy garment
> for your lovers everywhere,
> . . . to you, Jerusalem,
> the way of the prophets,
> the candle of Jesus.
>
> I am whispering my love
> to every lamp along your lanes;
> my love embraces the children on the swings.
> I lean to every lemon tree on your hills,
> and whisper to your olive trees in the swards.
> I confer closely with the palm trees
> drawn near to your walls,
> asking after . . . secrets:
> Who are the builders? From where are the stones?
>
> By your love I live,
> and for your love I live,
> by your love my stature lengthens.
> . . . With a branch of your olives,
> and the flower of your lemons,
> the sun sows a crown around my forehead.

*

There is yet another Arab approach to the puzzle of Palestine.
This one goes to the true heart of the Qu'ran and the Muslim religion.
Prof. Abdul Hadi Palazzi, who was an imam for the Italian Islamic

community, holds a doctorate in Islamic sciences by decree of the Grand Mufti of Saudi Arabia. In July 1996, during an international seminar in Jerusalem, he delivered the following scholarly observations:

"Considering Jewish immigration to Israel as a western 'invasion' and Zionists as new 'colonizers' is very recent and has no relation to the basic features of the Islamic faith. According to the Qu'ran, no person, people or religious community can claim a permanent right of possession over a certain territory, since the earth belongs exclusively to God, who is free to entrust sovereign right to everyone He likes and for as long as He likes:

> Say: O God, King of the kingdom, Thou givest the kingdom to whom Thou pleasest, and Thou strippest off the kingdom from whom Thou pleasest. — Sura 3:26

"Sometimes He gives a land to a people, and sometimes He takes His possession back and gives it to another people . . .

"The idea of Islam as a factor that prevents Arabs from recognizing any sovereign right of Jews over Palestine is quite recent and can by no means be found in Islamic classical sources. To see anti-Zionism as a direct consequence of Islam is a form of explicit misunderstanding . . . This was originally done by the late Mufti of Jerusalem, Amin al-Husseini, who was responsible for most of the Arab defeats, and during World War II collaborated with Adolf Hitler.

"Both Qu'ran and Torah indicate quite clearly that the link between the Children of Israel and the Land of Canaan does not depend on any kind of colonization project—but directly on the will of God Almighty. The Qu'ran cites the exact words in which Moses ordered the Israelites to conquer the Land: *O My people, enter the Holy Land which God has assigned unto you.* — Sura 5:23.

"Moreover . . . the Holy Qu'ran quite openly refers to the reinstatement of the Jews in the Land before the Last Judgment, where it says:

> And thereafter We said to the Children of Israel: Dwell securely in the Promised land. And when the last warning will come to pass, We will gather you together in a mingled crowd. — Sura 17:104.

"The most common argument against Islamic acknowledgment of Israeli sovereignty over Jerusalem is that, since al-Quds is a holy place for Moslems, they cannot accept its being ruled by non-Moslems . . . The definition of Jerusalem as an Islamic holy place depends on *al-Mi'raj*, the ascension of the prophet Muhammad to heaven, which began from the Holy Rock. We must admit that there is no real link between *al-Mi'raj* and sovereignty rights over Jerusalem, since when *al-Mi'raj* took place the city was not under Islamic but under Byzantine administration.

"Moreover, the Qu'ran expressly recognizes that Jerusalem plays the same role for Jews that Mecca has for Moslems . . . As no one wishes to deny Moslems complete sovereignty over Mecca, from an Islamic point of view there is no sound theological reason to deny the Jews the same right over Jerusalem . . . Roman Catholics consider Rome their own capital, and the fact that city has the largest mosque in Europe and an ancient Jewish community does not alter its role as the center of Catholicism.

"We cannot even think of creating another Berlin [Wall] in the heart of the Middle East. The idea of 'two Jerusalems,' if ever realized, will by no means be a solution, but a source of new troubles and conflicts. There are special officials in the area whose task is to insure that Jewish visitors on the Temple Mount are not moving their lips in prayer. To my mind, this is clearly opposed to Islamic prescriptions and rules. What kind of religion can let us interfere in the relationship between the Creator and His creature? On this point the Qu'ran says: *I answer the prayer of every suppliant who calleth on Me.* — Sura 22:186."

The Chase

Samira was running down the streets of the Old City, turning up alleyways to get away. Behind her, above the sound of her panting breath, she could hear him running, now and then shouting at her whenever she came into his view.

Yeshua! she prayed. *Where can I hide?* Suddenly she knew.

Isaac heard loud pounding on the prayer room door and opened it.

"Samira?" he said. "What in the world?"

Samira rushed inside and pulled the door shut, fumbling to bolt the lock. "Rabbi Abram is chasing me," she said, trying to catch her breath. "He has a knife! He's going to kill me!"

Isaac quickly opened the curtain of the ark, picked up the Torah scroll and gestured for her to step inside. He handed her the Torah scroll, which she clutched to her breast, and then he drew the curtain shut. "Stay here till I tell you it's safe!" he said. "Don't even *move!*"

There was heavy pounding on the door. Isaac unbolted the door, and Rabbi Abram burst into the prayer room, holding a knife in the air.

"Where is she? Is she here?" he demanded, all out of breath.

"Rabbi! Who? Who?"

"That Arab woman!" the Rabbi said, and he coughed and paused before he went on. "The one who wants the Red Heifer back! Earlier today, someone saw her lurking near it! We've been looking for her ever since—and just now I saw her and she ran in this direction!"

"Rabbi Abram!" Isaac said. "What are you doing with that knife?"

The Rabbi stared at the knife in his hand, as if he were surprised to see it, then slid it into a sheath under his garment. "It was for," he began. "Just in case." He paused. "She knows the soldier who guards the Wall—in case they were armed—"

"Rabbi, you wouldn't have harmed *her,* would you?" Isaac asked.

Rabbi Abram had caught his breath now and was coming back to reality. "I—I was going to question her," he said. "And God forbid, if anyone has done any harm to the Para Aduma, someone will pay!"

"But how do you know she was up to anything?" Isaac said. "Maybe she just wanted to pet the heifer."

"She is in cahoots with the soldier who guards the Wall," the Rabbi said, scowling. "Look at him! He's a Jew who does not keep the Sabbath. I've even seen him eating at their falafel stand! Drinking tea is one thing, but eating meat from a Gentile table?"

"Rabbi, I'm sure she meant no harm to the heifer," Isaac said. "She just misses her little pet."

"She is an Arab, Yitzy."

"Even so, she isn't even Muslim anymore," Isaac replied. "She's Christian."

The Rabbi looked into Isaac's eyes. "How do you know so much about that girl?"

"Her family has run that falafel stand for ages," Isaac said. "Do you remember when that girl's mother died? Her mother was the one killed when that grenade went off—during that Arab uprising near the Temple Mount—two years ago?"

"They are *all* trouble for us," the Rabbi said with a wave of his hand. "The Christians don't want us to rebuild the Temple either! And she was seen conspiring with this soldier."

"But Rabbi—"

"And then today," the Rabbi said, "one of the guards said the woman was trying to get past him, and when he approached her and asked her about it, she immediately ran away. So something was definitely up."

They stood in silence for a long moment.

"Well," Isaac said at last, "as long as she didn't touch the Red Heifer."

"The others are now checking the animal to see . . . And if it has been harmed in any way, to make it unkosher—somebody will pay a terrible price!"

"Rabbi Abram," Isaac said, "why don't we take a walk and see for ourselves—I'm sure the Red Heifer is just fine." He gently nudged the Rabbi toward the door. "Come on, let's take a little walk . . ."

The Rabbi turned and walked out the door.

Isaac stepped near the curtain and whispered: "*Stay put!*" and then followed Rabbi Abram to the pen. There, the Rabbi opened the gate and stepped into the pen, then bent down and closely examined the Red Heifer.

"There!" Isaac said. "See?"

"She looks all right!" the Rabbi said, standing up in the pen. "They told me she looked all right, but I . . . I still want to question the woman about what exactly happened. Because only she can give us a clue if the Red Heifer has been disqualified . . ."

Isaac had followed the Rabbi into the pen. He could feel his heart beating faster as he stepped closer to the Red Heifer. "Let me pet her ears," Isaac heard himself say, and his voice sounded different, like that of a frightened young boy.

"Oh, Yitzy!" the Rabbi said affectionately. "You are like a little boy with his pet!"

Isaac's heart was racing, and he felt out of breath as he leaned over the heifer, placing both hands on her, and then slipped, losing his balance, and fell on top of the Red Heifer. The animal fell to the ground.

"Ohhh, nooooo!" Rabbi Abram cried out in anguish. **"Nooooo! Noooooo . . ."**

"I'm sorry! I'm sorry! Rabbi!" Isaac cried. "What have I done? Did she really fall under me? **Oh no!"**

Rabbi Abram helped Isaac to his feet, and they watched as the Red Heifer struggled to her feet, shook herself, and looked around, as if bewildered.

Both the Rabbi and his yeshiva boy were in tears, groaning. Suddenly the Rabbi reached up to his collar, grabbed the cloth of his garment in both hands and tore it with a loud groan.

Without another word, they walked back to the prayer room and went inside. They were standing in the middle of the room, sobbing, when a thud was heard from behind the curtain of the ark.

Samira had dropped the Torah scroll from her hands.

"What was that?" the Rabbi said.

"Nothing," said Isaac.

Rabbi Abram stepped closer to the ark and opened the curtain, revealing Samira. Now she picked up the Torah scroll, thrust it into the Rabbi's arms and ran out of the room.

"What?" the Rabbi said. "What?" He stood with the Torah scroll frozen in his arms. "What was this all about?"

"Rabbi," Isaac said, " I . . ."

There is a long silence.

Then Rabbi Abram took in a deep breath. "Ah, Itzak," he said. "Itzak . . . Now I understand what has happened."

"Do you . . . ?" the yeshiva boy said in a barely audible voice.

The Rabbi returned the Torah scroll to its place and closed the curtain. Then he turned to Isaac. "Itzak Cohen!" he shouted. "You were chosen to be the first priest to serve in the new Temple. You are my brilliant yeshiva student—everybody knows this. But now, for the rest of your life, you shall be known as the brilliant yeshiva boy who made one fateful mistake—and disqualified the Red Heifer! Think of the consequences for our time! No ashes! No purification! No Temple! *No Messiah coming in our time!*

Rabbi Abram reached out and slapped Isaac behind the head.

"I know, Rabbi," Isaac said, and he again was weeping. "I wish I were the Red Heifer—and that someone would be kind enough to slit my throat!"

"But Itzak," the Rabbi continued, placing hands on Isaac's shoulders and looking at him kindly. "On that great and glorious day of Redemption! Itzak! You shall be known for evermore as the yeshiva boy who sacrificed his own good name—to save a life!" Now he embraced Isaac. "The Torah says that he who saves one life, it is as if he saved the whole world!" He kissed Isaac's head. "That is what the Redemption is all about . . . Temple or no Temple in our time . . ."

Now the door was pushed open and Munir burst into the prayer room. "Rabbi Abram!" he shouted. "My daughter Samira tells me that you had some unpleasant business with her today."

The Rabbi looked at him for a moment. "Well," he replied, "that was a misunderstanding. I no longer need to talk with her."

Stepping closer, Munir shouted into the Rabbi's face, "If you have anything to discuss with my daughter, you can take it up with me. Her Father!"

"Certainly, Munir!"

Munir turned and was about to leave but stopped. "Rabbi Abram," he said, "whatever has possessed your mind to think that you can get away with tearing down our Dome of the Rock to rebuild your Temple?"

"Why, Munir," the Rabbi replied, "I've never had any such intention. I know many rabbis may disagree with this, but I believe the Temple stood quite some distance north of the Dome—in that empty plaza. In that spot, the Temple was in direct line with the Golden Gate, which your people have blocked up. We'd rebuild the Temple *there.*"

Munir thought about this for a moment, then asked, "Wouldn't Jews feel uncomfortable, praying in a Temple with a Muslim mosque so close?"

"In fact, Munir," the Rabbi replied, "that mosque of yours is right where the Court of the Gentiles used to be. It could serve that purpose again—with Muslim Gentiles welcome at all times."

Munir seemed pleased with this, but then he had another question. "Even so," he said, "if the Jews were suddenly seen up on the Haram al-Sharif preparing to construct something—wouldn't it provoke all the Arab nations to send their armies to Jerusalem? Doesn't that trouble you?

"Nooooo . . ." the Rabbi murmured.

"No?" Munir cried. "Why?"

The Rabbi answered softly, in a awe-struck whisper: "It would bring the Messiah."

"Now I *know* you are mad!" Munir shouted. "And I'll tell you one more thing, Rabbi."

"What?"

Pulling his butcher knife out, Munir said: "I say this, most solemnly, to the man who dared to wield the sword at my daughter! I will have my red heifer back! Dead or alive!"

"I do beg your forgiveness!" the Rabbi said.

"My *daughter* is the one whose forgiveness you should beg!" Munir said and, turning away, stalked out of the prayer room.

*

An hour later, Rabbi Abram left the study room and began walking home by himself. He was walking down one of the narrow alleys of the Old City when he saw that Bedouin woman walking toward him. As they came closer, the Rabbi attempted to move to the right, then to the left, in order to walk around her—without touching her—but she stopped and stood right in front of him, blocking his path.

She wasn't smiling.

"Excuse me," he told her. "I need to be somewhere."

"Shouldn't you be right here?" she asked him.

"What—what do you mean? You're blocking my path."

"I saw what you did to Samira this morning," she told him. "You need to do t'shuvah—big time!"

"But how—how did you hear about it?" the Rabbi stammered. "Who are you, anyway?"

"Don't you know me?" she asked. "I'm the one who brought the Red Heifer to Jerusalem."

The Rabbi stared at her for a long moment. "Well," he said at last, "we don't have a kosher red heifer anymore."

"I know you don't," she said, barely concealing her anger. "It serves you right!"

75

Rabbi Abram again attempted to walk past her, but she wouldn't budge.

"What do you want?" he asked her. "Can't you see that I am trying desperately to serve the Lord and bring the Redemption?"

"Yes," she said. "We have seen all this. But there is no need for such desperation—chasing a godly woman with a knife in your hand. It shows that you don't really have faith that God is fully in charge."

"Why, of course He is!" Rabbi Abram said. "But we have failed to do our part. It has been two thousand years since the Temple was destroyed, and—"

"—It's better to spend one day in the courts of the Lord than a thousand days elsewhere," she told him. "Why are you always elsewhere?"

"I beg your pardon?"

"Yes, you have fear of the Lord, and that's the beginning of wisdom," she went on. "But I have watched you davening—"

"—You *what?* How did you watch me davening?" the Rabbi demanded.

Ignoring his question, she went on: "You look like you are in pain when you pray! You Pharisees cry out begging for intimacy with God, and you daven for hours on end, but I wonder how close this is bringing you to the Lord. Do you even *know* what you're begging for? Have you never experienced it?"

Rabbi Abram just stared at her, speechless.

"Rabbi," she said, "the other day Samira told you that God is more impressed by someone with a broken, contrite heart, than with animal sacrifices. And do you remember what you told her?"

"You don't think I have a broken heart?" he said, again.

"Right," she said. "Now that the Temple is gone, I believe that the Lord wants you to present yourself to Him—in prayer—as a living sacrifice. No more animal sacrifices! And in order to make yourself an acceptable sacrifice—you must become like the Red Heifer, without blemish—and you must be transformed by the renewing of your mind."

"Madam," he said to her, "we devote our minds every day to studying the Torah. This is a very serious undertaking."

"But where is the *joy?*" she exclaimed. "Rabbi, Sir, we admire and respect you for what you are trying to do for our people. But we would be so thrilled if we could just see you dancing before the Lord, as David did—filled with unfettered joy!"

"Didn't you see Yitzak and me dancing for joy with the Tora when we found the Red Heifer?" he said.

"Yes," she said. "*That's* what I'm talking about! You celebrated a moment of triumph. But you should be waking up *every morning*, feeling the assurance that the Holy One of Israel is at your side, every step of your way! What's come over you lately, Rabbi?"

"Nothing has come over me!" he cried.

"Was it the Red Heifer?" she asked. "Did the Red Heifer harden your heart, Rabbi?"

Rabbi Abram just stared at her, unable to fathom the meaning of her question. "You have a lot of chutzpah to be scolding *me!*" he roared. "The Messiah is supposed to bring *peace*—so where is *your* Messiah's peace?

"The Messiah atoned for our sins and brought *inner* peace to those who will accept him."

"We have inner peace by strictly following the Law that we were given by God," the Rabbi said. "We alone have been obedient to his Law."

"You know the letter of the Law," she replied—"and you've even added a few! But do you know the *spirit* of the Law? The reasons *behind* the Law? The Lord told Ezekiel to tell the people, 'I will give you a new heart and put a new spirit inside you. I will take the stony heart out of your flesh and give you a heart of flesh.'"

"What stony heart?" the Rabbi demanded.

"Does a true man of God carry a knife around—and wave it at a woman?" she exclaimed.

"I must do *t'shuvah* about that. You are right. But what does Ezekiel have to do with the spirit of the Law? He simply says, 'I will sprinkle clean water on you'—water containing the ashes of a red heifer!—'to cleanse you from all your idols.'"

"The Lord also said, 'I will put My Spirit inside you and cause you to live by My laws,'" she went on. "You need the Holy Spirit—the *Ruach ha Kodesh*—to energize you to do the right thing! Instead, you think you have to struggle for it in the flesh. You tie yourself to a daily existence of navigating through a minefield of nebulous, conflicting requirements. It must be exhausting for you! Thank God that you have Shabbat, for a full day of rest!"

"We live for Shabbos!" the Rabbi cried out.

"And that's the only time you seem to be truly happy," she said, "on Shabbat, and on all the holidays. But still, you live in such fear of being caught by someone when you make a little mistake. God doesn't want you to live in slavery."

"We are not slaves!" Rabbi Abram shouted. "We are children of Abraham, free at last from our dispersion, and working to hasten the coming of the Redemption!"

"Judaism was once a *supernatural* religion!" she said. "Remember the miracles in your Bible? And what about the miracles of Yeshua—healing the sick?"

"Your Yeshu!" the Rabbi shouted.

"It's Yeshua, if you don't mind," she retorted.

"This Yeshu of yours," the Rabbi said. "A man asks to be healed, and instead of healing him, this Yeshu declares that his sins are forgiven! What blasphemy!"

Noor smiled broadly, in spite of herself. "Rabbi Abram," she said, "may I direct you to the Talmud—it's at *Nedarim 41a*, I believe—where it says that all physical illness stems from blemishes and sins of the soul—so that a person cannot recover from illness until all of his sins are forgiven. As David says in Psalm 103—'Who forgives all your sins, Who heals all your ailments.' So, David first asks God to free his soul by forgiving his sins—and only then can his body be healed."

"You have read *Imros Tehoros*?!" the Rabbi exclaimed. "What are you, an agent provocateur from some foreign power?"

"Not some *foreign* power, Rabbi," Noor replied. "You, a teacher of Israel, should know the things of which I speak."

The Rabbi pointed his finger at Noor: "And another thing. This Yeshu of yours—in the end, he abandoned all pretense to being the son of God when he cried out, '*Eli! Eli! Lama sabachthani!* My God! My God! Why have Your forsaken me?'"

"Can't you figure that one out?" Noor said. "From the day He was conceived, Yeshua was one with the Father. Only death could separate Him from the Father. It wasn't Yeshua's spirit that cried out—it was his flesh, in its death throes!"

"So he died like an ordinary man!" the Rabbi shouted.

"Not exactly," Noor replied. "Just before He died, the last thing He said—speaking in the spirit, not in the flesh—was, 'Father, into Your hands I commend My spirit.' And at the moment of His death, the 60-foot curtain to the Holy of Holies was torn in two, from the ceiling to the floor of the Temple. Thus, Yeshua's atoning death opened the Holy of Holies to all who would repent."

"What Christian nonsense!" the Rabbi said, and he spat on the ground.

"Nonsense?" Noor replied. "Just look in the Talmud, Rabbi. Yeshua died forty years before the Temple was destroyed. Go back to *Nedarim*—where it says that forty years before the Temple was destroyed, the doors of the sanctuary opened of their own accord."

Rabbi Abram turned his back on her but, thinking better of it, faced her again. "Do you know what I hate most about Christians?" he seethed. "I've also read your Book of Revelations."

"Revelation," she corrected him.

"Whatever," he said. "You Christians can't wait for a blood bath to cover the Holy Land in the final days! You're so impatient for your phony Messiah to return—you're willing to use Jews as pawns for your so-called prophecies to come true."

Rabbi Abram angrily turned and headed for home another way.

Noor gazed after him in utter sorrow. "Oh, my dear Rabbi," she whispered with a sigh, "without the Holy Spirit, you don't even know how to read your own Scriptures—*or* your Talmud."

Chapter 9

The Pharisees' Unfinished Business

JERUSALEM

Rabbi Abram is a product of the oldest Jewish sect that has come down to us from ancient times, the Pharisees (meaning 'separate'), now known as the Orthodox. There is something about the Orthodox that seems to have evaded the minds of Christians who see the restoration of the State of Israel and the recovery of Jerusalem as signs of the final days and the return of the Messiah. There is ample evidence to suggest that the Orthodox will still have an important role in the fulfillment of human history. Their interest in the red heifer is only one of many signs that God is working on them and intends again to work *through* them.

This group traces its history back to the Maccabees, who saved the Jewish religion from destruction in 164 BC. The Syrian invaders had set up a pagan statue in the Temple—a foreshadowing of the future "abomination of desolation"—and forbade the practice of Judaism. The Maccabees drove off the Syrians and restored the desecrated Temple—giving birth to the story of Hanukkah.

After the Romans destroyed the Temple in 70 AD and banished the Jews from Jerusalem, it was the Pharisees who emerged as the dominant group that gathered with the Sanhedrin at Yavne to work out a form of Judaism that could function without the Temple sacrifices. What emerged was rabbinic Judaism, which is based on the rabbis' oral commentaries on the Scriptures. Known as the Oral Law, it was finally codified many centuries later in the written Talmud. By then the Pharisees had disappeared as an identifiable sect, but their legacy and the mission continues with the Orthodox.

81

Now, let us go back forty years before the destruction of the Temple, when Christianity was born as a Jewish sect that followed Yeshua of Nazareth as Messiah. Yeshua had interacted extensively with the Pharisees, while virtually ignoring the Sadducees and the Zealots. But although most of His followers were sympathetic to the Pharisee sect, and continued to worship at the Temple, they were never fully accepted after His death. In fact, they were persecuted as a controversial cult. Over the next several decades, this Jewish sect attracted more and more Gentiles, especially as it rapidly spread in the Diaspora, until its Jewish followers were greatly outnumbered. Eventually the church shed most of its Jewish trappings and even turned against the Jews for continuing to reject Yeshua as the risen Messiah.

Moving up to modern times, the Orthodox flourished in Eastern Europe, despite anti-Semitism, and gave rise to the Chasidic movement in the 18th Century. These were Orthodox Jews who went beyond the study of the Torah and gave themselves lovingly and wholeheartedly to God, with unrestrained affection, after the manner of David, who danced before the Lord.

During the 19th Century, perhaps the most influential defender of Orthodoxy during the rise of the Reform movement in Germany was Rabbi Samson Raphael Hirsch. Regarded as the founder of neo-Orthodoxy, Rabbi Hirsch published brilliant commentaries on the Torah and the Psalms. His insights and spiritual perspectives, in my opinion, read like the writings of a Spirit-filled Christian man of God, fervently looking forward to the ingathering of Jews back to the land and the coming of Messiah.

After the Holocaust, when multitudes of disillusioned Jewish survivors succumbed to assimilation, it was the Orthodox who did the most to save Judaism from absorption into the secular world. Then, in 1967, following Israel's miraculous recovery of Old Jerusalem in the Six Day War, the Orthodox—sensing the coming of the messianic age—stepped up their efforts to stem the tide of secularism.

Orthodox rabbis began roaming the streets of Jerusalem, looking for Jews who had fallen away from the faith and inviting them for a Sabbath meal and a lesson or two, without requiring any commitment to come back again. Within a few years, the *baal t'shuvah* (master of return) revival, as it came to be known, saw hundreds of thousands of secular Jews across the globe embracing Orthodox Judaism.

It is a revival of monumental proportions, unprecedented in all of Jewish history.

Evangelicals who fume against the very idea of Jews returning to 'the slavery of the Law' might consider the following dichotomy: Rabbi Sha'ul fought ferociously to defend the Pharisees' version of Judaism against the rise of messianic Judaism in the First Century—but ended up accepting Yeshua as Messiah and writing much of the New Testament. Today, *baal t'shuvah* Jews are trying to preserve Orthodoxy in the face of secularism—but we know from the Book of Revelation that 144,000 Jewish evangelists will herald the coming of Messiah in the final days. How can secular Jews possibly fill that role? Yes, Christian missionaries seek out secular Jews as the 'low-hanging fruit' to pluck for conversion. But the Pharisees were the only sect of Judaism that Yeshua considered authentic enough for Him to persistently challenge about the role of Messiah. The Orthodox today are the living remnants of the Pharisees, the only sect to survive the passage of time. They must take up the role that God chose for them and that they abandoned in favor of the creation of rabbinic Judaism after the destruction of the Temple. And today the Orthodox show the greatest yearning of all the Jews for the restoration of the Temple and the coming of Moshiach.

*

I once interviewed the late Rabbi Noach Weinberg, founder of Aish HaTorah Yeshiva, across the plaza from the Western Wall, who was generally credited with having started the revival. (However, the Chasidic Jews, particularly the Lubavitchers, had been quietly doing the same for many years.) Rav Weinberg was 56 years old and had 12 children at the time I met him. As he sat at his desk he held an unlit Kent cigarette in his hand. It was three weeks before Passover, and on his desk were three oranges, a bottle with ' Pardis' on its label, a coffee cup and a *shalach manos* gift basket from the recent Purim holiday.

"When I started the first yeshiva in '66," he recalled, "people thought I was out of my mind—'You can't take a secular man and get him to come to the Jewish religion.' See, the Jewish religion is a little more difficult than getting somebody to be 'born again.' It's got to be an intellectual commitment." He chuckled warmly as he looked at me. "Emotions you can turn on; you can get somebody to feel that he's missing something, and he can make a commitment of the moment."

He was obviously referring to Christian services where, upon invitation, people suddenly step forward to surrender their lives to Jesus and become 'born again.' I wanted to give him my Christian response, but I wasn't here for that; I was here to interview a historic figure about how the modern *baal t'shuvah* revival got its start.

"At that time," Rav Weinberg recalled, "people didn't believe it could happen. Because in Judaism you take on a lot of obligations, you've got to study a lot, you have to know a lot, and you have to come (to a yeshiva) with recognition; it just hadn't been done before."

As I sat listening, with my notebook and tape recorder, I realized that I was in the presence of one of the most warm-hearted Orthodox rabbis I had ever met. This man who had started yeshivas for *baalei t'shuva* across the United States and in Toronto was calling me Tony and was thoroughly enjoying our conversation.

"The first school that I had," and he interrupted himself to laugh in his husky voice, "I had to introduce them (teachers) to the students to show them that they're normal guys. It was called Mevaseret Yerushalayim— the Harbinger of Jerusalem. It comes from the prophet, 'Tell them that the Messiah has come'" (Isaiah 40:9).

The telephone bleeped and he answered it. I studied the rabbi as he spoke. He had a white beard and wore a black skullcap and a dark suit with a striped gray tie. He also had put on a blue sweater vest against the early spring chill of Jerusalem. Now he invited the person on the telephone to come into his office.

Rav Weinberg apologized to me for the interruption as a member of his staff came in and stood before his desk. For some reason I didn't turn off my tape recorder.

"Okay," the soft-spoken aide began. "This boy is very intelligent; he seems like he's good material. But he comes—he's a Russian, he's been in America for ten years, and he's *kura* Chabad (made religious through the Chabad Chasidic movement). He's been *frum* (religiously observant) for around three years, but he doesn't know basics. On the one hand, his Chabad background makes me a little bit hesitant; on the other hand, I feel that he's good material. And because of his experiences, the way that he got out of Russia—"

"Russia," the rabbi repeated.

"—and became a *baal t'shuvah* . . ."

"He speaks English well?"

"Yes, he speaks English very well."

"How old is he?"

"Twenty-two."

"Twenty-two," the rabbi repeated.

"Twenty-two."

"The only thing that you question is his allegiance to Chabad?" the rabbi asked.

Now, the Chabad schools run by the competing Lubavitcher chasidic sect poses problems for straight Orthodox rabbis, not only because the chasidim refuse to fully recognized the validity of other Orthodox groups, but also because the *baal t'shuvah* revival in Israel has its historic roots in the Mitnaggedim, the original "opponents" of the 18th century chasidic movement in Lithuania. As indicated by Weinberg's train of thought throughout our taped interview, his movement's approach is a "rationalist" one that seeks to reach out and challenge secular society, which he ruefully refers to as "the so-called intellectuals."

"I don't even know if it's Chabad so much," the man was saying to the rabbi. "That's half of it. And the other half of it is that I see in him a certain stiffness, a certain stress of character, which, I don't know to what degree he's open."

"Uh-huh," the rabbi said, nodding and thinking.

"It's a slight emotional thing," the man went on. "I can only see it to a very, very slight degree."

"So do you want to take him into the intermediate program or the beginner's program?"

"The intermediate program."

"The intermediate program . . ."

"The intermediate program," the man said. "My only question is, could we do it on a trial basis, let's say two months?"

"Well, see if he's able to fit in," the rabbi said. "Did he live in Morristown?" Chabad has a yeshiva in Morristown, New Jersey.

"Yes, he's lived in Morristown."

"Does he know anything about Talmud?"

"No," the man said. "He commuted for an hour a day, and he also worked. He does not have a penny to his name."

"Tell him to come in for a couple of days," the rabbi said. "Let's get acquainted."

"Okay," and the man left.

I asked Rav Weinberg whether there was ever a time in Jewish history that saw such a mass voluntary departure from Orthodoxy.

"No," he said. "No other time. See, this is a breakdown in the educational system. Basically, we had a monopoly on education. You know what happens when you have a monopoly? You become complacent . . . We failed in giving them an environment, and being told about love, and about the love of God, and God loves you, simple Jewish consciousness which happened at home."

The Jewish monopoly over Jewish education broke down as secular society taught Jewish children that the Hebrew scriptures had been superseded by a modern carnal world ruled by Gentiles.

"We have to show the power that is in our heritage," Rav Weinberg said. "And the word of God. After all, the Almighty spoke; and what do you think, Tony, do you think He was talking mundane things? I mean, you've got to learn how to listen."

He sounded so much like a born-again pastor, teaching the Word of God.

During that same decade of the 1960s, when Rav Weinberg and others were leading secular Jews back to Judaism, the charismatic revival within the Church was also taking place, bringing fallen-away Christians like myself back to the faith. Like the Chasidics, we charismatics also joyfully danced before the Lord with unbridled affection. It was as if the Holy Spirit was starting fires on many fronts, following the recovery of Jerusalem after two thousand years . . . preparing the way for Messiah to come and bring peace to the world.

Both Jews and Christians seem to fear the growing threat of "polarization," as religious and secular people grow farther and farther apart, to the point of verbal and even physical conflict. But this must happen in order for human history to come full circle and confront itself and its Creator. In fact, a case can be made that this world polarization of good against evil will bring religious Jews and Christians together to fight their common enemy—this 'new world order' intent on remaking man in his own image and likeness.

The red heifer is the perfect metaphor for all of this. Only among the Orthodox—the descendants of the Pharisees who rescued Judaism from fading away—do we find a few Jews who remain zealous enough to take seriously the mysterious command in the Book of Numbers: To slaughter a red heifer, burn it, and sprinkle its ashes in spring water in order to purify the priests for the resumption of Temple sacrifices. These Jews are truly longing for Messiah to come.

It is interesting to listen to the voices of *baal t'shuvah* Jews in Israel who have strong feelings about the search for a red heifer. Most of them disapprove of it. Yet all of them are deeply committed to the related issues of obedience to God, purification, repentance, salvation and the coming of Messiah. And, like most Bible-believing Christians, they are convinced that the Holy One of Israel is about to physically step back into human history and manifest Himself in the holiest place on the face of the earth—on the Temple Mount, where it all began with Abraham and Isaac . . . and where the Prophets say it will all end.

The Rabbi's Nightmare

Not until bedtime did Rabbi Abram allow himself to ponder, alone in his room, the enormity of the day's events. Now he could think about the loss of the Red Heifer without letting young Itzak see just how devastated he felt.

As he drifted off to sleep, the Rabbi recalled the first day he had met young Itzak. The Sabbath was about to fall on Jerusalem, and Rabbi Abram was standing in front of the Wailing Wall, watching and listening as the boys from a nearby yeshiva came onto the scene. Dancing arm in arm, the yeshiva boys chanted songs to welcome the Sabbath as they made their way to the Wall. There, they separated and prayed at the Wall.

One of them stood out from the others. Rabbi Abram couldn't put his finger on it, but he knew that this yeshiva boy was destined to behold the Messiah. When he learned that Itzak Cohen was from the priestly line, the Rabbi instantly knew that this would be the man he would train as a priest for the restored Temple.

Now, deep in sleep, the Rabbi heard a voice speaking in Hebrew from Psalm 74.

"Why have You rejected us forever, God," the voice pleaded, "with Your anger smoldering against the sheep You once pastured? Remember Your community, which You acquired long ago, the tribe of Your redeemed to be Your very own. Remember Mount Tziyon, where You came to live!" (CJB).

Suddenly the ancient Temple came into view, above the Western Wall. It was engulfed in smoke!

"Hurry your steps to these endless ruins," the voice was saying, "to the sanctuary devastated by the enemy!"

Then he saw the flames shooting out of the Temple. And he heard the loud sound of banging from afar.

"The roar of Your foes filled the meeting place!" the voice wailed. "The place seemed like a thicket of trees where lumbermen hack away with their axes! With hatchet and hammer they banged away, smashing all the carved woodwork! They set Your sanctuary on fire, tore down and profaned the abode of Your name!"

Smoke now covered the entire scene.

And when the smoke cleared, he could see the Muslim Dome of the Rock emerging near the spot where the Temple had stood. It was shocking to the eyes.

Rabbi Abram cried out: "God has been my king from earliest times, acting to save throughout the earth! . . . Look to the covenant, for the land's dark places are full of the haunts of violence. Arise, God, and defend Your cause!"

Now he heard the sound of the muezzin calling prayer in Arabic from somewhere near the Dome of the Rock.

"Lord!" the Rabbi cried out with all his might. *"Don't forget what Your foes are saying, the ever-rising uproar of Your adversaries!"*

Then there was silence and darkness. Rabbi Abram must have slept a long time before he had another dream. He saw Itzak Cohen chanting and dancing by himself on his way to the Wailing Wall. There, Itzak looked up and saw the Red Heifer dancing on top of the Wall. And there was that Bedouin woman from the desert, playing her flute.

Itzak headed for the steps leading up to the Temple Mount. But the Rabbi called a warning after him, and he stopped. Now the Red Heifer was on the ground in front of the Wall, standing upright and full grown. And Itzak was embracing her. And then—they began to dance!

But wait! What was the music they were dancing to on the plaza before the Wall? It was the "Mazel Tov" song that was played at weddings, with its rising "Hamentaschen" refrain! Itzak and the Red Heifer whirled around the plaza, dancing happily. Now and then the Red Heifer would break away from Itzak and literally fly around in a circle, beaming with joy.

Suddenly thunder broke out, and all was darkness.

Gradually the darkness dispersed, and a heavy, ominous song was being played. As the Red Heifer came into view, Rabbi Abram strained to see her face, but all he could see was her back. Then she slowly turned—and he saw her teeth bared in rage! And now she was chasing Itzak Cohen around in circles in the plaza before the Wailing Wall. As the growling animal got closer and closer to him, Itzak headed for the steps and climbed up to the Temple Mount. At the top, he looked back quickly, then fled for his life through the Maghrabi Gate, the Red Heifer in close pursuit.

Chapter 10

The Temple Institute of Jerusalem

The Jewish state fell because its inhabitants were content to act simply in accordance with the strict letter of the law.

— *Baba Metzi'a 30b*

JERUSALEM

While Isaac Cohen was bitterly lamenting the loss of the Temple, people at the Temple Institute a few blocks away were talking about rebuilding it. Directly across Chabad Road from Rabbi Fogelman's old reading room, the Temple Institute of Jerusalem is a museum displaying all of the materials and utensils and vestments and dyes necessary for rebuilding the Temple and resuming the animal sacrifices. Officials downplay any serious plans for doing so in the near future, but their sentiments are very clear.

"In our times, the commandment of the red heifer takes on more and more significance," says Rabbi Chaim Richman, author of *The Mystery of the Red Heifer*, who has been associated with the Temple Institute for many years. "For without it, the Divine service of the Holy Temple cannot be resumed. There is a spiritual renaissance today in Israel; after almost 2,000 years, Israel is clearly moving towards the time when the Holy Temple on Mount Moriah—the prophesied Third Temple—will be rebuilt.

"More and more Jews are returning to the Torah, to the God of Israel and the ways of the fathers. And more and more are beginning to realize that the Holy Temple is the only solution for achieving the elusive peace we all desire to see."

Richman, who was raised in Massachusetts and became a *baal t'shuvah*, does not believe, as many rabbis do, that the Temple will descend from heaven when Messiah comes.

"When the Messiah arrives," he says, "he will stand atop the roof of the Holy Temple and cry out: 'Humble ones! The time of your redemption has arrived!' Thus: the Temple will be built *before* the Messiah arrives."

Rabbi Richman appreciates the support of Christian evangelicals for rebuilding of the Temple, and at one time he even entered into a contract with a Pentecostal rancher in Mississippi to breed cattle in Israel in hopes of producing a red heifer. But Richman also is deeply offended by radical Christians who care more about hastening the end times than they care about the welfare and lives of Jews living in Israel.

"Basically, we're a doormat for them to get to their own eschatological culmination," he told *The New Yorker* in July 1998, about a year after a red cow named Melody was born in Israel and soon disqualified. "It's a pretty scary thing, because the whole rapture thing that is popular in some evangelical circles—which calls for a fulfillment [of New Testament prophecies] by the hard times for Jacob—is essentially an invitation to genocide."

Rabbi Abram and Isaac Cohen are among those who believe that the Temple was located either north or south of where the Dome of the Rock now stands. Recent archeological discoveries have given rise to the theory that the Temple was to the north, its front perfectly lined up with the Golden Gate, through which the Messiah is to enter Jerusalem.

So the question arises: If the Temple is rebuilt on that nearly vacant spot, could the Dome of the Rock remain standing and serve as the Court of the Gentiles, which once stood there?

"There were various opinions about how the Temple was situated on the Temple Mount," I was told by Raphaella Tabak, education director of the Temple Institute. "No one knows for sure."

"Different opinions were passed down through history, and sometimes it's changed a little bit," added Chaim Jutkowitz, the development director. "It's like a passing train."

I asked: Does the Talmud say that someday there will no longer be a need for a Temple made of stone for God to dwell in—because God will prefer to dwell within the hearts of men and women?

"They are to make Me a sanctuary, so that I may live among them," Raphaella replied, quoting from the Book of Exodus.

Jutkowitz explained: "It's our obligation in today's world to prepare ourselves for the future. As the Talmud states, in every community it's a man's responsibility to govern his own *beit knesset*—his own household—and his next obligation is to build our own *Beit HaKnesset*—synagogue. So people have to be prepared to come together. People have to come to terms with themselves until that happens."

I mentioned the Talmudic rabbi who said he would keep on hoeing out in the field if he learned that Messiah had come.

"That's it," Jutkowitz said.

"The ultra-Orthodox who are raising a red heifer," Raphaella said, "their whole goal is to fulfill a commandment that's in the Bible."

During a tour of the museum, Raphaella showed drawings and paintings of the red heifer in various stages of the ritual of the red heifer, whose ashes are to be mixed in the waters of purification.

"To rebuild the Second Temple (from 538 to 515 BC) they needed a pure person to purify all the others," she said. "How did they do this? They raised children in an elevated courtyard—like a house on stilts—not touching the ground for fear that somewhere underneath there may be a grave. The children were elevated so they wouldn't become impure. When the right time came, they traveled on huge oxen—and they were sitting on these wooden boards—because there was air separating them from the ground. They filled their containers with natural spring water. They took the red heifer on the bridge that stretched from the Eastern (Golden) Gate of the Temple Mount—over the Kidron Valley—until they reached the Mount of Olives. Here, in sight of the Temple, the red heifer would be prepared. They were standing on elevated platforms. The red heifer was slaughtered by one of the *cohanim*, and he sprinkled the blood seven times in sight of the Temple. Then they burned the red heifer and threw in three items—some cedar wood, hyssop and scarlet wool. Then they took the ashes and divided them into three stone baskets. One contained ashes to purify the people and the *cohanim*. Another had ashes for the Israelites, particularly those arriving in Jerusalem on pilgrimage. The third basket was kept in the Temple for safe keeping."

It is believed that the ashes of the last red heifer were taken away and saved before the destruction of the Temple in 70 AD, and that Jews continued to use them for ordinary purification purposes until as late as the third century. Archeologists have been trying to find where they might have been hidden since then.

"It would be preferable to find the ashes of a previous red heifer," Raphaella said. "Those ashes kept in the Temple for safe keeping were mixed with the new ashes—as a precaution, if the new red heifer were invalid." Then she added, "The red heifer law is a mystery. Even though we don't understand it, we do it. That's what God wants."

During his interview with *The New Yorker* in 1998, Rabbi Richman added: "The Holy Temple in Judaism is so important and primary that it can really be said that Judaism as it is practiced today is not the vehicle that God intended it to be. The Temple is actually the device through which God manifests his presence to mankind."

*

A group of Chassidic Jews has quietly set up a secured compound in a settlement somewhere outside Jerusalem, where candidates for the priesthood can be raised from infancy to bar mitzvah age without becoming ritually impure. Rabbi Yosef Elboim's Movement for Establishment of the Temple is raising boys in a compound on solid bedrock, insulating them from the soil.

Mothers who are married to *cohanim*—Jewish men like Isaac Cohen who are descended in the priestly line from Aaron—will arrive at the camp to give birth in a building that is elevated from the ground. The babies will be raised there, insulated from any possibility of coming into contact with the dead or with anything that touched the dead in the ground. When they come of age—and when a female red heifer turns three years old and is still fully red, without blemish and never yoked—the men will be carefully transported to the Mount of Olives, where the red heifer will be sacrificed and its ashes mixed in rain water. This water of purification will be sprinkled on Jews who are to enter the Temple Mount, rebuild the Temple, and take up the blood sacrifices that ceased two thousand years ago. For, while the heifer's ashes are applied for routine instances of impurity, blood sacrifices are necessary as an atonement for serious sin.

Meanwhile, Rabbi Elboim, a leader of the Belzer Chassidic sect in Jerusalem, is determined to maintain a Jewish presence on the Temple Mount, where he conducts weekly walking tours with his black-clad followers and any other Jews wishing to join in. The visits are in violation of rabbinic orders going back to 1967, banning Jews from entering the former Temple precincts where they might risk walking over the place where the Holy of Holiest once stood. Police thoroughly search the rabbi and his followers at the Mughrabi Gate, at the top of the Wall, to make sure they aren't carrying prayer books, prayer shawls or phylacteries.

"A sheikh can call for worldwide Muslim rule from the Temple Mount," Rabbi Elboim declares, "but if a Jew whispers Yibeaeh

HaMikdash [a prayer to rebuild the Temple], they immediately take him away for questioning and restrict him from visiting the site again. Where are we living?"

One of his recent walking tours was taped and appeared on the Internet, showing the rabbi speaking in Hebrew as he led his followers along the southern promenade paved with ancient stones on the Temple Mount. As they returned to the Mughrabi Gate, Rabbi Elboim suddenly turned north and began walking toward the Dome of the Rock. One of his followers could be heard exclaiming that the rabbi had never ventured that close before. When he reached the stone steps, however, the rabbi lingered for a while, then turned and led his people away.

Excommunication orders have been issued against Rabbi Elboim, purporting to bar him from being counted for a minyan. Ultra-Orthodox Jews have torn the mezuzahs off the doorpost outside his house and set fire to his front door. In response, his followers protested outside the home of the rabbi of that ultra-Orthodox neighborhood, and the harassment stopped.

*

There is nothing new about violent disagreements among the religious leaders of Israel. In ancient times a controversy arose between the Pharisees and the Sadducees over one particular detail of the red heifer ritual. The Sadducees controlled the priesthood and the Temple, but the Pharisees were the teachers and wielded great influence with the people. Rabbi Louis Finkelstein, who was 89 when I visited his apartment in New York in 1984, explained the disagreement—and the bizarre measures taken by the Pharisees in order to have their way—in his two-volume work, *The Pharisees*, first published in 1938:

"The law required that the priest who prepared the red heifer be Levitically pure," he wrote, "but what was meant by 'pure'? If a man touched the carcass of a dead animal, he was, according to Leviticus 11:28, 'unclean until the evening.' The verse says nothing about the necessity of bathing, [but Jewish practice] seems to have required a ritual bath for all manner of impurity that lasted 'till evening.'"

The Sadducees insisted that a man who had 'bathed from his impurity' could sacrifice the red heifer, but only after evening had come. The Pharisees, however, insisted that the bath merely served to lessen the impurity, and that in any case it was permissible to perform the ritual before sundown. If the sacrifice was being performed in the Temple, the Pharisees certainly would have insisted on priestly purity—but the red heifer was to be sacrificed outside the city gates, on the Mount of Olives.

So the only reason the Sadducees would insist on ritual purity was to discredit the Pharisee point of view.

"It would seem that the controversy centers around a matter of unimportant ritual detail," Finkelstein wrote, "but for the Pharisees it was apparently of great consequence. So insistent were they on the correctness of their views that they would compel the High Priest who was about to perform the ceremony to enter into a state of *impurity*, so that he might have to bathe, and then, by performing the sacrifice *before* the setting of the sun, testify to his acceptance of *their* interpretation.

"Commentators on the Mishna find some difficulty in explaining the strange perversity of the Pharisees," Finkelstein continued. "For what could possibly be gained by rendering impure a priest who was pure? . . . This astonishing obstinacy is hardly in keeping with the urbanity for which Josephus praises them."

Two anecdotes recounted in *The Pharisees* serve to demonstrate the extraordinary lengths that they would take to prove how right they were—and how wrong the Sadducees were—about the ritual of the red heifer.

"A certain High Priest, Ishmael ben Phiabi, accidentally prepared the red heifer in a state of *complete purity*," Finkelstein recalled. "The Pharisees, who had neglected to make him impure, insisted that the ashes, prepared with such diligence and at such cost, be strewn and wasted and that another heifer be prepared . . .

"And then there is the story of Rabbi Johanan ben Zakkai, the man of peace and quiet, disciple of the great compromiser Hillel, who nevertheless lost all his usual tolerance when he found that the High Priest of his day was preparing to sacrifice the red heifer without previous defilement."

(Now, Rabbi Jonahan had headed the Sanhedrin at the time of the Roman siege of Jerusalem in 70 AD, and had escaped by having his disciples carry him out of the city in a coffin. The commander, Vespasian, recognizing that this rabbi had striven for peace and mediation with the Romans, gave him permission to establish the academy at Yavne after the Temple was destroyed.)

Rabbi Jonahan corrected the High Priest and sent him off to defile himself and then to bathe before sacrificing the red heifer.

"As the priest returned," Finkelstein recounted, "Rabbi Johanan, still dissatisfied, approached him and nipped his ear in such a way as to make him a man with a 'physical blemish' and unfit to perform *any* priestly service."

Samira's Shopping Spree

The next morning, Samira slipped out of the falafel stand and, walking past the Petra Hotel, headed down David Street into the cavernous "Chain"—the *suq el-bazaar* leading to the Moslem Quarter of the Old City. As she made her way through the crowded corridors, and down the 28 steps, she was confronted right and left by Arab shopkeepers chattering at her about their merchandise. Some of them—young men attracted by her beauty—came out of their little stalls and tried to follow her, pestering her in Arabic to come and buy jewelry, clothing, sandals, basket ware.

Steadfastly ignoring them—and resolving not to walk this way again—Samira came out into the Moslem Quarter, veined with winding, narrow lanes, stone steps and green doors. She headed north on El-Wad Road, making her way in the direction of Damascus Gate. Inside the gate, a much more courteous breed of merchants operated in the light of the open air. Gone was the persistent shouting of hucksters in the Chain, but in its place was a dull rumble of outdoor commerce that was comforting to Samira.

At the two crossings of the Via Dolorosa, she remembered attending Good Friday processions that traced the supposed route of Yeshua of Nazareth toward Golgotha. It wasn't his true route (which was actually somewhere outside the city gates), but Samira felt that the Via Dolorosa had been sanctified by pilgrims who had walked over its cobblestones and wept over their martyred Messiah all these centuries.

Yeshua, the Beloved, she murmured to herself.

Samira had to walk carefully to avoid stepping on the women who sat on the street with their fruits and vegetables spread out around them. A shopkeeper weighed a bunch of bananas in an old scale for a customer. Money changers sat in the doorways of their shops, their eyes peeled for tourists in need of Israeli shekels. A young Arab boy carried a large wooden tray brimming with oval-shaped rings of sesame-seeded bagels, called *ka'ak*, whose aroma was so inviting but whose taste never fully satisfied her; the best thing about this bread was that it could be left on the kitchen table for days without spoiling.

95

In the midst of this crowded Moslem marketplace, a bearded Orthodox yeshiva boy dressed in black patiently walked his bicycle up the stone steps toward Damascus Gate. His expression was totally impassive, but she suspected that he was less than calm underneath his black coat and hat. The Arabs seemed to barely notice him; but the Moslem Quarter had lately become a dangerous place for Jews. At special risk were the Orthodox, who had somehow managed to purchase a building in the Muslim Quarter for their new yeshiva, rousing much distress in the city and warfare in the courts. One night a yeshiva boy was stabbed to death on the street.

Lord, protect Your people from our bloodthirsty brothers, she prayed.

Outside the Damascus Gate, flanked by turreted walls with archers' slits, the plaza resembled the open drawbridge of a medieval castle. Here more street merchants were selling their wares. On top of a barrel sat a steaming-hot metal platter of brown "broad beans," covered with a layer of sliced lemons and sprinkled with mint leaves. Down the street, two Arab boys had set up a small green tent festooned with bottles of perfume of every color. One of the boys was sucking on the hose of a water pipe.

Regretting that she had come all this way and not seen what she was looking for today, Samira turned left on Sultan Suleiman Street and headed toward West Jerusalem, the modern city that the Jews had built up during the British occupation before 1948. Passing Notre Dame on her right, she walked past the New Gate and reached Jaffa Road, where the wall around the Old City came to a corner.

Lord, why are You taking me this way?

Instead of turning left and walking the short distance to Jaffa Gate and home, Samira felt her spirit making a bold decision and headed down Jaffa Road toward the busy commercial district of Jewish Jerusalem. She passed City Hall on her right and the Central Post Office on her left. Then she passed the site of the old Fefferberg's restaurant, which used to serve delicious roast chicken dinners. It also used to offer *patcha* (calf's foot jelly), *pupiks* (chicken stomachs), stuffed *miltz* (spleen), and lungs in gravy. And you could top it off with a shot of a strong Arab drink called *karak*.

Samira had walked this street many times over the years, always filled with the sense that she was an outsider here, even though she was one of more than a million Arab citizens of Israel whose families hadn't fled during the 1948 war. Something bold was stirring inside her today—something downright rebellious!—and as the plot became more clear to her, she could feel her heart beating faster.

Should I do it today, Lord? May I please . . . ?

At the Ben Yehuda Mall, she stepped into a women's shop and poked around the dresses. The Israeli clerk glanced at her, then turned away. Choosing an outfit that seemed to be her size, Samira asked if she could try the clothes on. The woman stared at her for a moment, then pointed to the dressing room.

A few minutes later, Samira emerged from the shop dressed as an Israeli Jew. In the shopping bag hanging from her arm were the clothes she had put on this morning. As she strolled down Jaffa Road, she made eye contact with everyone she could. But something was missing. Stopping at a jewelry shop, she picked out a necklace with the Star of David and purchased it.

Today raba, Adonai! she prayed, thanking God.

Back on the street, Samira marched confidently, even attempting to hum "Havenu Shalom Alechem" to herself. She smiled mischievously, as she remembered stories of Palestinian Arabs—citizens of Israel like herself—who had posed as Jews in order to get a better job.

Her favorite corner, the very center of Jerusalem, was at Jaffa and Strauss Road. To her left, a few doors down King George Street, was where Richie's Pizza used to be. She had loved to stop there on her excursions as a young girl; however, the last time she had been there, it was Passover, and she found herself eating a slice of pizza made without leaven and tasting very much like cardboard.

Passing Davidka Square, Samira finally reached the Mahane Yehuda Market, where the Orthodox bought their fruit and vegetables and fish and nuts and olives. The air was filled with delicious, conflicting aromas. Behind a fruit stand, an Israeli man dumped oranges from a wooden crate onto the counter, while his colleague sampled a dried fig and spat out the pit. The old metal scales had counterweights consisting of ancient bits of steel, their pound and quarter-pound numbers worn with use.

At last, Samira unfolded the wire mesh basket she had brought and began loading it with a fresh harvest of her heart's desire. Now she was humming "Yerushalayim Shel Zahav." Nobody took particular notice of her. Yes. She belonged . . .

Back on the street, Samira saw a female Israeli soldier standing by herself at a bus stop, her little Uzi machine gun slung from a shoulder strap like a purse. Samira's baskets had grown heavy when she reached the bus stop and unloaded them onto a bench and sat down to rest. As she caught her bearings she saw yet another group of young black-coated Orthodox men striding confidently down Jaffa Road. Suddenly she was flooded by an alarming fantasy—that these young men, who had all left the secular world to serve God alone, were like a bevy of nuns, trapped in their black habits on this steaming afternoon, locked into their vows of poverty, chastity and obedience to their religious superiors. Did any of these men, in private moments, ever have secret doubts over the life sentences that they had chosen? She wondered . . .

Her bus screeched to a halt, and Samira climbed aboard and rode back down Jaffa Road to the Old City. She had just gotten off the bus and was heading toward Jaffa Gate with her bag and heavy basket—when she suddenly spotted Rabbi Abram on the street! Her heart lurched within her. But then she remembered how she was dressed, and her mischievous confidence surged within her again.

Chapter 11

Arab and Israeli
Claims to
Western Palestine

PALESTINE

How did Palestinian Arabs like Samira and her father come to lose their land in Palestine? In Munir's case, the house that his wife had inherited, and that they resided in before the war of 1948, was lost when the family fled to the Old City during that war. After that, they had resided in the cramped quarters of their falafel stand in the Old City, which was under Jordanian rule for the next 19 years. When Jordan lost the West Bank in 1967, Munir—now an Israeli citizen living in the reunited capital of Israel—could once again walk outside Jaffa Gate toward his wife's old homestead, but, after all those years, he was unable to reclaim the property.

Israel's victory in the Six Day War sparked religious revival on three levels throughout the world:

> — In Israel, the reunification of the capital city of Jerusalem for the first time in 2,000 years was seen as a sign of God's miraculous championing of the return of Jews into their ancestral homelands during the 20th century. And it accelerated the ingathering of Jews from all over the world and the belief among religious Jews that the time of the Messiah was near.

— In the Muslim world, the sudden, humiliating defeat of four Arab armies by the tiny Jewish state was blamed on the secularization of Muslim society. It demonstrated the urgent need to enforce *shari'a* rule in Islamic countries and to take up arms in the worldwide cause of Islam. The three-year-old Palestine Liberation Organization began to display the image of the Dome of the Rock, and began to claim a pre-eminent Islamic role for Jerusalem and the Haram al-Sharif.

— In the Christian world, and particularly among evangelicals, the Lord's restoration of Jerusalem was interpreted as a sign of the end times. As David Parsons of the International Christian Embassy in Jerusalem once recalled: "I know people who fell on their knees and cried out to God when they heard that Jerusalem was back in Jewish hands. It forced Christians to rethink their views toward Israel, toward Jerusalem, toward prophecy."

But what about the Palestinian Arabs, who once again were treated as mere pawns in history?

In a strange, ironic way, the Palestinian Arabs—especially those scattered refugees outside of eastern and western Palestine—might be called the 'Jews' of the Arab world. Like the Jews who were scattered abroad 2,000 years ago (before there ever were Arabs in Palestine), these refugees refuse to be assimilated into other societies where they reside.

Among all the Arabic peoples who lived in the Middle East under the rule of the Turkish Ottoman Empire until the First World War, only the Palestinians have failed to achieve statehood in the modern world where nations exist as sovereign 'states.' Their immediate neighbors— the Egyptians, the Jordanians, the Syrians and the Lebanese—all became nation states. And then came the State of Israel, in western Palestine, in 1948.

The people now known as "Palestinian Arabs" have lived for several hundred years in western Palestine, on just one-third of the ancient region known as Palestine. As early as the late 1800s, a spirit of nationalism was beginning to awaken among the nomadic Arabs who had been living in Palestine under Turkish Ottoman rule. At the same time, the Zionist movement was beginning to stir among Jews in eastern Europe to reclaim their ancestral homeland in Palestine.

During the First World War, Britain promised to support the establishment of an independent Arab state as a reward for Arabs who were revolting against the Ottoman Empire. But in the Balfour Declaration of 1917, Britain promised to "view with favour the establishment in Palestine of a national home for the Jewish people," adding: "Nothing shall be done which may prejudice the civil and religious rights of existing non-Jewish communities in Palestine." The "existing" communities were Arab and Bedouin. Were those *existing* Arab populations meant to include Arab newcomers from other countries—who would swell the *future* Arab populations in Palestine beyond the natural increase by childbirth?

"Had only actual 'natural' increase taken place among the *existing* Arabs," Jane Peters writes in her book, *From Time Immemorial,* "the European and Arab-born Jews might have had their sanctuary in time to save countless Jewish lives." Instead, she said, there was a "carefully disguised Arab population increase by in-migration and illegal immigration—that matched or possibly even exceeded the Jews' immigration into their 'Jewish National Home.'"

After the First World War, the victorious nations granted Britain a mandate to govern Palestine until the former Ottoman Empire's various peoples were ready for statehood. The British Mandate of Palestine originally covered the entire 48,000-plus square miles on both sides of the Jordan River. But in 1922 the British broke off from "Palestine" all the land east of the Jordan River—two-thirds of ancient Palestine—and this became the state of Jordan in 1947. Jordan was inhabited mostly by Bedouin Muslims under their Bedouin king, and they began to be called *Jordanians*—but today 70 percent of Jordan's residents are Palestinian Arabs whose families fled from western Palestine in 1948 and 1967.

Also In 1947 the United Nations proposed a plan to partition western Palestine into two parts—one part that was already inhabited mostly by Palestinian Jews, the other part mostly by Palestinian Arabs. Although some of the Jewish families and many of the Arabic families had lived in the region for centuries, many Jews and Arabs were fairly recent arrivals. During the British occupation over Palestine, while Jewish immigrants from Europe were "illegally" entering the land to escape the Holocaust, Arab immigrants from Arab countries were "illegally" entering the land as well—not only to take advantage of how the Jews were making the desert bloom, but also to counter the Jews' rising numbers. A demographic race was going on for the future control of the western Palestine. (For more details of Arab migration to Palestine, see Chapter 17.)

After examining the UN partition plan, the Palestinian Jews agreed, reluctantly, to accept their half of western Palestine for a future Jewish state. Unfortunately, the Palestinian Arabs never had a voice in the partition plan. Their self-appointed spokesman, the Grand Mufti of Jerusalem (who had collaborated with the Nazis during the war) rejected the UN plan, as did the neighboring Arab nations, all of them unwilling to share any part of western Palestine with a Jewish state.

The following year, in 1948, when the British pulled out of western Palestine, the Jews declared an independent State of Israel, mostly in the part designated for them under the UN partition plan. In reaction, the armies of seven Arab nations immediately invaded and attempted to crush the Jewish state. Jordanian troops occupied the West Bank, inhabited mostly by Palestinian Arabs, and Egyptian troops took over Gaza, also inhabited mostly by Palestinian Arabs.

Gaza and the West Bank, in fact, constituted most of the territory that the United Nations partition plan of 1947 had assigned to the Palestinian Arabs. But over the next two decades, the Arab nations did nothing to promote the establishment of a sovereign Palestinian state. Both Jordan and Egypt remained technically at war with Israel, intent on destroying it, rather than establishing a sovereign Palestinian state on the land already under their control. In fact Jordan at one point annexed the West Bank (later relinquishing any claim over it) and granted Jordanian citizenship to all of its Palestinian inhabitants.

Israel was admitted as a member of the United Nations in 1949.

*

In 1964 the Palestine Liberation Organization was established by the first Arab Summit as an umbrella organization over numerous factions, including Fatah, headed by Yasser Arafat. Exactly what territory did it intend to *liberate*? Certainly not Egyptian-occupied Gaza or the Jordanian-occupied West Bank, where there were as yet no Jewish settlements.

If the PLO had suddenly decided to recognize the UN partition plan of 1947, it might have rightfully claimed parts of Israel that originally had been designated for Arabs on the partition map. These included central Galilee (including Nazareth), a ring around the south and west edges of the West Bank (including a corridor to Jerusalem), a northern piece of the Gaza strip and a stretch of land south of Gaza, along the border of the Sinai. But the Palestine National Covenant called for eliminating Israel and setting up an Arab state in all of western Palestine.

Then, in June 1967, Egypt, Jordan and Syria (aided by Iraq) amassed their armies, composed of 250,000 troops and 2,000 tanks, on Israel's borders. Their intent was to treat Israel's portion of western Palestine as if it had no sovereignty as a state—despite the UN recognition of Israel. The Arab plan was to seize all of Israel's land—or as much of it as possible—for resettlement by the approximately 700,000 Palestinian Arabs who had fled from that land during the war of 1948-49. The bulk of these refugees were living either in Jordan or on the West Bank, with Jordanian citizenship; the other Arab nations had refused to absorb these refugees, preferring to take them into temporary refugee camps.

Conversely, as many as 800,000 Jews who had been living for centuries in Arab Muslim countries fled to the new Jewish state under pressure from their host countries, which were furious over the establishment of the State of Israel and were stepping up their persecution of their Jewish minorities. (One might ask today: If multitudes of Jews lived as minorities in "Arab countries" for all those years, why should 1.5 million Arab citizens, living in the Israel proper, object to its recognition as a "Jewish state"? And why should 250,000 Jewish settlers living on the West Bank be forced to leave so that the future State of Palestine can be an entirely "Arab state"? If Zionism was 'racism,' what is this?)

The 1967 invasion plan of the Arab nations backfired. Facing an imminent threat to its very existence, Israel struck first, repelling the invaders from its borders and moving on to capture Gaza from Egyptian occupation and the West Bank (including Israel's ancient capital, Jerusalem) from Jordanian occupation. The lightning speed of the Six Day War (bringing to mind the six days of Creation) pointed to the hand of God—and surely He hadn't performed this marvelous feat unless He intended for Israelis to conquer *and settle* the land that He had given them ages and ages ago.

The victorious Israelis then proceeded to do with these conquered, "occupied territories" exactly what the Arab nations had planned to do with a conquered and occupied Israel: The Israelis treated the Arab-dominated portion of western Palestine as land without any recognized sovereignty. In fact, the United Nations never acted on any application to grant sovereignty to the West Bank (and Gaza) until September 2011, when it was asked to recognize a State of Palestine.

"We do not see it as an occupied territory because there was no recognized sovereignty there before 1948," declared Elyakim Rubenstein of the Israeli Supreme Court.

"We'll stay put," said Israeli Prime Minister Levi Eshkol. "We can strangle terror in the occupied territories." His defense would be the Three No's that came out of the Arab summit in Khartoum, Sudan, in August 1967. "No peace with Israel, no negotiations with Israel, no recognition of Israel, and maintenance of the rights of Palestinian people in their nation."

"If Khartoum is the declared position," Eshkol told reporters, "then our answer is, 'We stay here.'"

By the summer of 2005, when Israel evacuated Gaza, 250,000 Jews were living in 125 officially recognized settlements in the West Bank and 180,000 were living in the area of East Jerusalem that Israel annexed in 1980.

In July 1968, a year after the loss of Gaza and the West Bank, the Palestine National Covenant was redrafted to reject the partition of Palestine which, "with the boundaries it had during the British mandate, is an indivisible territorial unit." (It is not clear whether this was meant to include eastern Palestine, now called Jordan.) The document did recognize the existence of Palestinian Jews, defined as those who "resided in Palestine until the beginning of the Zionist invasion," without specifying when that began. Those Jews could continue to live in a future Palestinian state (as they had in Arab countries). However: *"Judaism, being a religion, is not an independent nationality. Nor do Jews constitute a single nation with an identity of its own; they are citizens of the states to which they belong."*

Ironically, these words were written by Arabs who claim today that Israel has attempted to deny that Palestinian Arabs are *an independent nationality* that would *constitute a single nation with an identity of its own.*

*

Why had the Arab nations not pushed for a sovereign State of Palestine from 1948 to 1967, when they controlled Gaza and the West Bank? Wouldn't this have advanced the rights of Palestinian people in *their nation*? That is a question that Palestinian Arabs are asking today, with a deep sense of resentment at having been kept as helpless pawns to be used against Israel. A common saying is that the Arabs are for the Palestinian cause but not for the Palestinians. The Arab nations have encouraged the Palestinians to teach anti-Semitism in their schools (I witnessed this in a Palestinian school in Jordan—see Chapter 18), thus perpetuating their resentment in successive generations, and branding as traitors those wishing to share the land and make peace with Israel. All the while, they have cleverly used the Palestinians as terrorist proxies against Israel. The evidence that the Arab nations hated Israel more than they loved their fellow Arabs was never so clear as when they failed to come to their rescue on the battlefield. They did nothing when Israel invaded Lebanon in 1982 to drive out Palestinian militias that were harassing Israelis across the border. Even when the battle was inside Palestine, when Israel invaded Gaza in 2008 to stop Hamas from firing rockets into Israel, the Arab nations did nothing.

While Arabs and other Muslims across the world have sympathized with the Palestinian Arabs, their leaders preferred that the Palestinians remain stateless and continue to resort to terrorism against the hated Jewish state. Meanwhile, Iran had been smuggling weapons to Hamas in Gaza—and Syria had been arming Hezbollah in Lebanon—to maintain terrorist activities against Israel. What Iran and Syria did not do was commit their own armies against Israel during its showdown against the terrorists.

At the same time, Palestinian Arabs living as refugees have given their Arab host countries reason to fear them as a people. During "Black September" (1970,) the Bedouin king of Jordan expelled the PLO in a bloody crackdown, fearing a Palestinian takeover. Long intent on taking over eastern Palestine, the PLO had set up political and military bases in refugee camps, from which it launched terrorist attacks against Israel. Many PLO fighters fled Jordan to Lebanon, where a new group called Black September emerged (two years later it murdered eleven Israeli athletes in Munich). A generation later Hezbollah has won political control of Lebanon and has amassed thousands of rockets aimed at Israel.

The decades-old Palestinian incremental strategy for winning all of western Palestine—by negotiating land-for-peace agreements with Israel and continuing armed struggle from there—should also raise future alarms for Jordan—as well as Lebanon and Egypt—where Palestinians might someday claim they are historically entitled to certain provinces bordering on their future State of Palestine.

Just as the wandering Jews refused to become assimilated and lose their ancient heritage, the Palestinians have maintained their identity in Arab countries and elsewhere. The difference is that "Palestinian Arabs" scarcely existed as a people with a nationalistic identity until the idea was born out of their rejection by their fellow Arabs.

The Arab nations, then, have been playing with fire. Islamic dictators have long feared that Palestinian fever for secular democracy could be a deadly poison to their own populations. Even Egypt and Syria, long ruled by secular tyrants, feared an infestation of rebellious Palestinian Arabs among their population and excluded them.

But since 2011, during the "Arab Spring" revolts that began toppling Arab dictators, fear was growing in Israel that this fever would spread to the Arabs living in the West Bank and Gaza—and even to the 1.5 million Arabs enjoying citizenship in Israel proper. After decades of anti-Semitic indoctrination in their schools, virtually all Palestinian Arabs have resented Israel's treaties with Egypt and Jordan, which were negotiated by their Arab dictators without the public's support. In effect, the people clung to the myths long after their leaders had brushed aside those myths in order to make peace with the Jewish state. Those dictators are gone, but their poison continues to fester in their people.

The Arab people also resent America's role in bringing about those treaties. In the wake of the Arab Spring, the populace in each liberated country will never forgive America for having supported their tyrant leaders for all those decades. But how would they have felt if, years earlier, the United States had invaded their sovereign Muslim soil and removed their despots, as the U.S. did in Iraq? The very thought of infidel troops on Islamic soil—for *any* purpose!—is anathema to the Muslim mind, which longs for the Muslim world to be united as one.

The question now is: Will the Arab *people* deal more sympathetically with their Palestinian brothers and sisters now that they have toppled the dictators who allegedly betrayed Palestine by making peace with Israel?

Ironically, the pan-Arab movement of the 20th Century did succeed in bringing together scores of rival Arabic tribes—but *only* under the iron fists of dictators who took over the emerging post-Ottoman states of the new Middle East. The sudden fall of any one of these dictators would produce immediate chaos, as in the case of Iraq, where the United States dethroned Saddam Hussein, only to ignite a civil war between his fellow Sunnis and the majority Shi'ites who could now take control and revenge on the Sunnis.

If anything, the long-awaited emergence of one united Arab nation from the ashes of the Turkish Ottoman Empire was held back by the very dictators of Egypt and Syria and Jordan who were hypocritically clamoring for such a unity. Government-imposed national unity proved to be an artificial blanket that concealed age-old tribal rivalries smoldering beneath, waiting to be released at this late date in history to bring chaos to the Arab streets. Libya is the most graphic example, with the fallen regime's weapons now in the hands of many competing militias unwilling to share power. In Syria, in fact, the ruling family actually perpetuated those divisions among its people by a strategy of 'divide and conquer,' keeping rival tribes at odds with each other while they all lay prostrate under iron rule. Then those tribes found it impossible to work together in the civil war that flared up during the revolt against their stubborn dictator.

As for Egypt, the ruling military wanted to preserve the peace treaty with Israel, not eager for war—but their people disagreed. As civilian infiltrators cross from Egypt into the Sinai desert to attack Jews, Israel has urged the Egyptian military to increase its troop strength in the Sinai, above the limit spelled out in the peace treaty signed in 1979 by the late Anwar Sadat. But a mass civilian infiltration of the Sinai could pose such a threat that Israel might declare the peace treaty dead and take back the Sinai by force.

The real nightmare for Israel is the prospect of thousands of civilians pressing on its borders simultaneously—from Lebanon and the Golan Heights in the north, from Jordan in the east, from Egypt in the south, and from Gaza in the west—in retaliation for any Israeli attack on the nuclear facilities in Iran. This could be more threatening than the firing of thousands of rockets by Hezbollah from Lebanon, and by Hamas from Gaza.

Thus, the Arab Spring was either the harbinger of a new order emerging in the Arab world—or, far more likely, the omen of an extended period of chaos.

Curiously, most Arabs in the Middle East—and Palestinian Arabs in particular—have proven unready for the democracy that they so fervently crave. The concept of democracy did not spring naturally from the Old Testament, the New Testament or the Qu'ran. All three religions still look forward to a world theocracy, not democracy, in the end times. In fact, democracy was the slogan but never the goal of the "peace" talks toward a two-state solution. Rather, those talks now seem to have been a cloak for a one-state solution, with all of western Palestine eventually becoming the planet's twenty-third Muslim state.

The Arab "land for peace" proposals, now seen in retrospect, were calculated to fail. Consider just two of the arguments long considered inescapable:

— No Arab leader with knowledge of Middle Eastern history could possibly expect the Israelis to give up all of the occupied West Bank, the heartland of previous Jewish commonwealths under David, Solomon and the Maccabees. Without it, Israel is indefensible, with a depth as narrow as ten miles separating the West Bank from the Mediterranean. The Prime Minister's residence is barely a mile from the "green line" that once marked Israel's border with the West Bank.

— A geographically divided Palestinian State of Gaza and the West Bank would be too weak a country to thrive. Israel voluntarily drove all of its settlers out of Gaza in 2005. But since 1967 it has settled the West Bank with so many Jews—and invested so many resources in building residential and business communities and the roads and infrastructure to serve them—that a Palestinian state on the remaining Arab lands would be hopelessly decimated. As for evacuating Jewish settlers from the West Bank, it most likely cannot be done without driving the settlers to civil war. Many of them are so attached to their biblical land that they would rather live there under the Palestinian flag than return to Israel proper!

That is why so many Arab leaders, and the Palestinians themselves, have been moving away from the two-state solution and concentrating on creating one, bi-national State of Palestine (with or without the Jewish settlements remaining in place). The only role of democracy would be for the Arab population, with its higher reproduction rate, to democratically take over the country in the voting booth. It is hard to imagine Arabs governing themselves democratically in an Islamic state, or even in a secular state like the Kingdom of Jordan. This is because most Arabs in the Mideast don't have the experience of having lived in a democracy that Jews from Europe had.

Israelis have tried desperately to avoid the one-state solution. Three times they offered a Palestinian state in the West Bank and Gaza and part of the Old City of Jerusalem: At Camp David in 2000, at Taba in 2001, and in Jerusalem in 2008. The Palestinian negotiators walked away all three times. Why? Because—while signing cease-fires and interim agreements was easy—signing a final peace agreement ending the conflict for all time would require them to recognize a Jewish state in western Palestine.

A single, Arab-Israeli state is a tempting but deceptive dream. Bi-national states have produced disappointing records, with the notable exception of Canada and possibly Belgium. Failures include Bosnia, Cyprus, Kosovo, Lebanon, Pakistan, Rwanda and Sri Lanka.

Failing to capture all of western Palestine militarily, and stalled by their own recalcitrance at the negotiating table, the Palestinian Arabs then sought statehood unilaterally through the United Nations—without having to sign a peace agreement with Israel in return. How could the UN's declaration of a State of Palestine on paper change anything on the ground? At the very least, it would make Israel guilty of attacking a sovereign foreign country the next time it sent troops into Gaza to stop the firing of rockets into Israeli neighborhoods.

Ever since the IDF forcibly removed 8,000 Jewish settlers and gave up Gaza to Palestinian rule in 2005, Israel has been rewarded with rocket fire aimed at innocent civilians. Hamas took over Gaza through democratic voting and is intent on creating an *Islamic* Palestine, even if it has to wage civil war against the Palestinian Authority. Should Israel make the same mistake and unilaterally withdraw from the West Bank, where Hamas enjoys popularity among voters and could replace the Palestinian Authority's goal of a *secular* Palestine? And so, with no trustworthy Arab partner to negotiate with, Israel continued to settle the West Bank—ancient Judea and Samaria—with Jewish families.

Ultimately, a peaceful resolution would have to materialize, somehow, in the distant future . . .

*

As the years have gone by, the nightmare of being labeled as "occupiers" over another people has cast a different light on the Israelis' lightning victory in the Six Day War, which religious Jews and evangelical Christians have always seen as evidence of the hand of God. It's almost as if a different, sinister force instead was at work, baiting a trap from which Israel could never extricate itself.

Surely this wasn't the first time in history that a militarily stronger people has won over a weaker people and tried to become a *benign* ruler. The Peace Now movement, increasingly popular among Israelis, struggled for years to bring justice to the Palestinians. And in a gesture toward self-autonomy for Arabs, the Israeli government brought about the creation of the Palestinian Authority, so that Palestinians could at least have their own security force and municipal home rule. No, this could never have been enough for a people dispossessed of their land.

But wasn't much of that land *purchased* from individual Arab landowners both before and even after the 1948 war?

"The truth is that from the beginning of World War I, part of Palestine's land was owned by absentee landlords who lived in Cairo, Damascus and Beirut," writes Mitchell Bard, an American foreign policy analyst and executive director of the nonprofit American Israeli Cooperative Enterprise. "About 80 percent of the Palestinian Arabs were debt-ridden peasants, semi-nomads and Bedouins. Jews actually went out of their way to avoid purchasing land in areas where Arabs might be displaced. They sought land that was largely uncultivated, swampy, cheap and, most important, without tenants." In fact, Bard wrote, 37 percent of total immigration to pre-state Israel was by Arabs from neighboring countries "who wanted to take advantage of the higher standard of living the Jews had made possible." In the two decades leading up to the mid-1940s, he said, Arab infant mortality fell from 201 to 94 babies per thousand, and Arabs' life expectancy rose from 37 to 49 years.

In 1920 David Ben-Gurion, who would become the first prime minister of Israel, said: "Under no circumstances must we touch land belonging to *fellahs* [peasants] or worked by them. Only if a *fellah* leaves his place of settlement should we offer to buy his land, at an appropriate price."

Arriving in Palestine in May 1930, British diplomat John Hope Simpson observed that the Jews "paid high prices for the land, and in addition they paid to certain of the occupants of those lands a considerable amount of money which they were not legally bound to pay." The British High Commissioner to Palestine later reported: "In 1944, Jews paid between $1,000 and $1,100 per acre in Palestine, mostly for arid or semi-arid land; in the same year, rich black soil in Iowa was selling for about $110 per acre."

Britain's Peel Commission, rejecting Arab claims that Jews had taken their cultivated land, pointed out that "much of the land now carrying orange groves was sand dunes or swamp and uncultivated when it was purchased. There was at the time of the earlier sales little evidence that the owners possessed either the resources or training needed to develop the land."

King Abdullah of Jordan remarked ironically in his memoirs: "It is made quite clear to all, both by the map drawn by the Simpson

110

Commission and by another compiled by the Peel Commission, that the Arabs are as prodigal in selling their land as they are in useless wailing and weeping."

By 1947, about 463,000 acres of land in Palestine were in Jewish hands—387,500 acres purchased from Arabs, 30,000 acres from various churches, and 45,000 acres acquired from the British Mandatory Government. Nearly three-quarters of the land was purchased from large landowners, not peasants working the land, from 1880 to 1948.

If the birth of the State of Israel in 1948 was a *nakba* (catastrophe) for Arabs living in western Palestine, it was inflicted by the neighboring Arab states, says Efraim Karsh, head of Mediterranean Studies at King's College, University of London. "Had the Arab states pressured the AHC [Arab High Command] to accept [the UN] partition resolution rather than abort it by force of arms," Karsh says, "the Palestinian tragedy would have been averted altogether."

This was admitted in October 2011 by Mahmoud Abbas, president of the Palestinian Authority (and chairman of the PLO), in the wake of his request that the UN accept a State of Palestine into membership. In a rare interview with Israeli television, Abbas said this of Arab rejection of the 1947 partition plan: "It was our mistake. It was an Arab mistake as a whole." If the UN partition plan of 1947 had been peacefully accepted by both sides, Israel wouldn't have had to fight the invading Arab armies in May 1948, in a war that resulted in hundreds of thousands of Arabs fleeing, mostly from land that had been assigned to them under the UN plan. *unaccepted*

Abbas also admitted that Israeli Prime Minister Ehud Olmert had created "a very good opportunity" for peace during negotiations in May 2008 by offering to give up about 94 percent of the West Bank for a Palestinian state and to share sovereignty over Jerusalem. Just before leaving office, President George W. Bush met one-on-one with Abbas in the Oval Office and appealed with him to accept the offer.

"The Palestinian stood firm, and the idea died," Condoleeza Rice, then secretary of state, wrote in her book, *No Higher Honor*, in 2011. The Prime Minister's offer was so generous that it probably would not have been approved by his parliament, the Knesset. Foreseeing this, the Palestinians could well have called the Prime Minister's bluff and, once the deal fell through, could have had a plausible reason for sparking the Second Intifada of 2008.

In a *New York Times* op-ed piece earlier, on May 17, Abbas had already confessed his true motives for going to the United Nations: "Palestine's

111

admission to the UN would pave the way for the internationalization of the conflict as a legal matter. It would pave the way for us to pursue claims against Israel at the UN, human rights treaty bodies and the International Court of Justice."

Abbas, whose Palestinian Authority controls only the West Bank, included Gaza in his UN application for statehood. But Gaza is controlled by Hamas, which forced Abbas' Fatah party loyalists out of Gaza in a bloody takeover that virtually constituted a civil war among Palestinians. A cease-fire was quickly patched together for the sake of unity before the United Nations. Except for the case of the Palestinians, it is difficult to imagine the UN seriously considering statehood for any people engaged in civil war and unable to govern together.

Nor can Israel believe that Abbas and his Fatah party can get Hamas to recognize Israel. "Fatah hasn't thrown the rifle aside," Tawfik Tirawi, a senior Fatah Central Committee member, told thousands of demonstrators during a rally in Hebron in October 2011, as the world awaited a UN decision on Palestinian statehood.

*

As for the morality of taking land by force and keeping it, this has always been the rule of the jungle throughout human history. Nobody gives away land (except Israel, which unilaterally evacuated Gaza and voluntarily returned the Sinai to Egypt after dismantling Jewish settlements there).

Nor is this the first time in history that Samaria has been the scene of conquest and resettlement of populations. From 724 to 721 BC, Assyria deported 27,290 residents, most of them Jewish, from Samaria and replaced them with captives from other regions. (Among the newcomers were the Sepharvim—who burned their children in the fire as sacrifices to their pagan gods. Such an abomination would doom them—as it had doomed the Canaanites before them—to be dispossessed of their land by God.) Samaritans at the time of Christ were descendants of Assyrian colonists who intermarried with Jews who had returned to Samaria.

The 12th Century biblical scholar Rashi made a statement about the ancient Canaanite inhabitants of Samaria and Judea that could also apply today to the Arab Palestinians:

"If the nations accuse Israel of banditry, of illegitimately seizing the lands of the seven nations of Canaan, Israel will say: 'The entire universe belongs to God. He created it and granted its territory to whomever He deemed fit. It was His desire to give it to them [the Canaanites], and it was later His desire to take it from them and grant it to us.'"

And then God allowed it to be taken away from the Jews . . . who wandered the earth for 2,000 years and finally won it back in 1948 and in 1967.

While the Arabs had no intention of sharing the land they hoped to take from Israel in the Six Day War, Israel not only has withdrawn from Gaza but has allowed the Palestinian Arabs to remain and share the West Bank with Jewish settlers since 1967. At last count, there were 2.5 million people living in the West Bank—83 percent of them Palestinian Arabs and just 17 percent of them Jewish settlers, according to United Nations sources.

Why won't the Palestinians recognize Israel as a *Jewish* state? Because Israel proper already has 1.5 million Arab citizens whose families never fled the land. (Isn't it odd, though, that Israel's Arab citizens are seldom referred to as *Palestinians*? When did *victimhood* become a decisive factor in defining a nation's bloodline?) And because the door must be left open to the Palestinian refugees' Right of Return.

Creation of a State of *Palestine*—the first ever in history—has perhaps always been inevitable. But for the record, the region that was renamed *Palestine* nearly 2,000 years ago by the Romans was been carved up in modern times as follows: Jordan, 37,737 square miles; Israel, 7,992; West Bank, 2,165; Gaza, 140.

What is the territorial breakdown between Arabs and Jews on the West Bank (and in East Jerusalem?).

Palestine Monitor: Exposing Life Under Occupation says there are 271,400 Jews living in 121 settlements spread throughout the West Bank, plus 191,000 living in settlements around Jerusalem, for a total of 462,400 Jews.

The separation barrier (which in *some places* is a solid wall) that Israel constructed to keep suicide bombers out of Israel was placed mostly east of the so-called "green line," which was the 1949 armistice boundary between Israel and the West Bank. If that barrier were accepted as a final boundary, it would bring 80 of the settlements—containing 385,000 Jews—into Israel proper. That would leave just 77,400 Jews to evacuate from just 41 settlements to make a State of Palestine *Judenrein.*

The Jewish settlements actually are built on less than 3 percent of the West Bank. But the extensive network of "by-pass" roads linking the settlements (each with 50- to 75-yard buffer zones free of construction) take up 40 percent of the land, according to *Palestine Monitor.* For security reasons, Arabs aren't allowed on 500 miles of "by-pass" roads. Israel has built approximately 50 miles of "fabric of life" roads connecting Arab settlements, including about 60 tunnels and underpasses.

How the descendants of Abraham are to live in peace on this land is proving to be the impossible riddle of our time. Only the God of Abraham can solve it peacefully—and only His Messiah can bring these brothers and sisters back together, at last.

. . . Meantime, Samira and her father continued to live behind their falafel stand just inside Jaffa Gate. And Munir continued to long for a peaceful (or violent, if necessary) restoration of the family home that he and his wife had lost in 1948, in Israel proper, just *outside* Jaffa Gate.

The Rabbi's Apology

Rabbi Abram finally found Samira, getting off a bus and walking through Jaffa Gate toward her father's falafel stand. She was carrying a basket—but he also noticed that she was dressed as a Jewish Israeli woman.

"I must talk with you," he said, and she stopped.

"What for?" she asked. "I have nothing to discuss with a knife-wielding Pharisee." She began walking on toward the falafel stand.

"Please, my daughter—" the Rabbi said.

"I'm not your daughter," she snapped back at him. But she stopped walking and listened to him.

"My, my!" the Rabbi said. "The way you're dressed today, you could *pass* for my daughter! Why are you dressed as a Jew?"

"Because an *Arab* woman isn't treated with respect when she shops in *your* part of town!" she said.

". . . I see," Rabbi Abram said. "But I must tell you that my heart is aching over what I almost did to you."

"It's over now," Samira said.

"I sincerely hope so!" the Rabbi exclaimed. "But for me, it will not be over until I do *t'shuvah*."

"Till you do *what?*"

"*T'shuvah*—repentance!" he said. "You see, we Pharisees have remained very Orthodox in our ancient teachings about God's forgiveness."

"Yes, Rabbi Abram. But you and your little cult—Messiah Now—all of you are looked down upon as fanatics—even by your fellow Orthodox Jews!"

"True," he said, stroking his beard. "Well, every great movement in history has met resistance even from good people. But I will admit that I did become 'fanatical.' And God says that 'a violent man leads his neighbor astray.'"

"Especially violence against a defenseless woman," Samira said.

"I am guilty," he said. "In fact, our teachers say that the worst sin of all is *rage*. Because when we give ourselves over to unrestrained anger, we throw away the one thing that lifts us higher than the animals—our intelligence."

"Really?"

"Yes, my daughter."

"I'm not your daughter," Samira said again.

"The world is reserved solely for the sake of him who knows how to restrain himself at the moment of strife," the Rabbi added. "That maxim is in Chulin 89a of the Talmud."

Samira couldn't help but smile. "But I accept your apology, Rabbi."

"Thank you! Thank you!" he exclaimed. ". . . But I must do more than that. There are four things that I am required to do in order to fully repent. May I tell you what they are?"

"Go ahead, Rabbi."

"First, do I have your forgiveness?"

"You do."

"Thank you. Now, I want to change my ways. I promise never to act that way again."

"Not with me or any other person."

"Absolutely," he said.

"Done!" she said, and smiled.

"Third," the Rabbi said, "I wish that it had never happened."

"So do I," Samira said.

"You see, daughter," he told her, "there are some sins that we commit against another person that we are tempted to hold onto. For example, a man steals another man's car—or his wife!—and then he returns it and concludes the first three elements of t'shuvah to everyone's satisfaction. But . . ."

"But?"

"But," the Rabbi said, "one night he is lying awake in bed, and suddenly he remembers, with pleasure, how much he enjoyed that other man's car—"

"—Or his wife!" Samira said, smiling broadly.

"Or his wife," the Rabbi said. "And his repentance is no longer sincere. Because deep inside, he does not truly wish that it had never happened."

"Rabbi," Samira told him, "I am sure you will never take pleasure remembering this incident."

"Never!"

"Now you have completed your . . ."

"T'shuvah. It means 'return'—return to God."

"Repentance."

"Exactly," the Rabbi said. "Finally, there is the *fourth* element of *t'shuvah* that I must perform, according to the *letter* of the Law."

"Go ahead, Rabbi," Samira said. "I know you're a Pharisee and can't help yourself."

"Right you are! I am Orthodox, I am a Pharisee. But let me tell you who the Pharisees were before they come up in your New Testament. You have heard of the miracle of Hanukkah?"

"Yes," Samira said. "After getting the Temple back from the evil foreign king, the Jews found they had only enough oil to light the lamps for one day in the Temple."

"Yes!" the Rabbi said. "And the oil burned for eight days, until they could consecrate new oil—a miracle."

"A miracle."

"Well," he said, "the Jewish fighters who drove the evil king away from their Temple were known as the Maccabees. They saved Judaism from destruction—and their descendants, the Pharisees, later preserved Judaism after the Temple was destroyed by the Romans and we had nowhere to offer sacrifices."

"And now," Samira said, "a small band of Pharisees—under Rabbi Abram and his Messiah Now movement—are going to save Judaism again!"

"Precisely!" he exclaimed. "Save Judaism from secularism—bring Jews back to Judaism—*and* bring the Messiah and peace to the world!"

"Wonderful!" Samira said, and thought for a moment. "You know, Rabbi," she said, "just hearing you talk about your religion makes me kind of wish I could have lived at the time of the Early Church, when it was still Jewish."

"There was never anything Jewish about your church," the Rabbi said.

"There certainly was."

"Prove it!"

"At the time of Yeshua—Jesus—there was a Jewish leader named Nicodemus, who was a member of the Jewish Council, the Sanhedrin," Samira said.

"Yes," the Rabbi said. "His Hebrew name was *Nakdimon*."

"Okay," she said. "One night, Nicodemus—Nakdimon—came in secret to Yeshua, asking about his teachings."

"A total waste of his time," the Rabbi said.

"And Yeshua told him that you must be 'born again from above' in order to have full repentance and to enter the Kingdom of God. But when Nicodemus asked how it was possible to be born again, Yeshua gave him a Jewish answer. He said to Nicodemus—'You hold the office of teacher in Israel, and you don't know this?'"

"Now, why would a teacher of Israel bother trying to understand some new religion?"

"That's just my point, Rabbi. He *wasn't* trying to convert Nicodemus to a new religion. He was telling him that being 'born again' was Jewish teaching."

"Show me in the Torah where we ever have used such an expression!"

"The idea behind the expression 'born again' can be found in your Book of Ezekiel—'I will give you a new *heart* and put a *new spirit* inside you. I will take the stony heart out of your flesh and give you a heart of flesh.' And you can find it in Jeremiah—'I will make a new covenant with the house of Israel—I will put my Torah within them and write it on their *hearts*'" (See CJB).

"New covenant. New heart. New religion!" the Rabbi said with scorn.

"But it was all predicted by the Hebrew Prophets," Samira said. "And when it finally came true, and Yeshua came as Messiah, his first followers naturally were all Jews—who continued to be Jewish."

"But a Jew who embraces a false messiah is no longer a faithful Jew!"

"Oh?" Samira replied. "What about Rabbi Akiva? He declared Simon Bar Kokhba to be the Messiah, and he turned out to be wrong—but Akiva remains one of the most revered Jewish teachers of all time!"

Rabbi Abram's eyes narrowed as he stared at this Arab Christian woman dressed as a Jew. "Where did you learn all these things about Judaism?" he inquired.

"Every Christian should return to the roots of the only religion that Yeshua of Nazareth ever practiced. Judaism!"

"Well," the Rabbi replied, "for your information, Rabbi Akiva did not worship the man he believed to be the Messiah. And neither will we, when the true Messiah comes!"

"Rabbi, I hate to challenge you on Jewish history, but I must remind you that when the Pharisees confronted Yeshua, they said these words: 'Tell us whether you are the Messiah, *the Son of God*.' And those are the same words of Simon Peter, the first follower of Yeshua to declare him "the Messiah, *the Son of the Living God*.'"

The Rabbi looked baffled.

"The latter is from Matthew 16:16," she explained, "proving that at the time of Yeshua, it was expected that the Messiah would be the Son of God."

Reaching up and twisting the kipa on his head, his face scrunched up in frustration, Rabbi Abram objected: "But Moshiach is supposed to bring peace!"

"But He did," Samira replied. "He brought inner peace for those accepting Him."

"Well," Rabbi Abram replied in a voice of weary resignation, "when Moshiach does come, we will see!"

"And how we long for that day when Messiah comes!" Samira said.

"And so do we!" Rabbi Abram cried. "Rabbi Chanina said that only when God's Shekinah returns to Zion will God's greatness be recognized by the world."

"The Messiah will bring peace to the Holy Land between Jews and Arabs," Samira said. "And He will bring an end to the turbulence of human history."

The Rabbi laughed and said, "In fact, when Moshiach comes to rule the world from Jerusalem, everybody will suddenly want to become Jewish already!"

Samira smiled at him and said, "Maybe someday, Rabbi, *you'll* convert me!" She laughed. "Then I could marry a Jew!"

"Not if you still believe in a false messiah!" the Rabbi said.

"If Rabbi Akiva can do it, any Jew can do it!" Samira replied.

Now the Rabbi turned to go. "Be well, my daughter," he said. But suddenly he stopped. "*Oy vey!* I almost forgot the fourth thing I must do to make sure I have made up for my actions toward you! I must make full restitution for any harm I caused you."

"There was no harm."

"Was your garment torn? A sandal lost in the scuffle?"

"No."

"Did I cause you a sleepless night?" the Rabbi asked.

"No."

"Then what can I give you?" the Rabbi asked. "Please tell me."

Samira thought for a moment. "Well," she said, smiling weakly, "I wouldn't mind having my little heifer back. I miss her so!"

Rabbi Abram was taken aback. "Do you have 5,000 shekels to buy it back from us?" he asked.

"Heavens, no," she said.

"I am sorry," the Rabbi said, ". . . so sorry. . . ."

Samira extended her hand. "That's all right, Rabbi," she said. "Shalom!"

After a long pause, Rabbi Abram told her: "I, ah—I think you should know that it is not customary for the Orthodox to touch an adult member of the opposite sex unless they are related by blood or through marriage."

"I've heard that," Samira said, her hand still extended toward him. "But—"

"—In fact," the Rabbi quickly added, "when a young Orthodox man and woman are courting, they are not to touch hands—much less kiss!—until their wedding night."

"A marvelous idea," Samira said. "But in the case of you and me, I have to ask you, Rabbi—where is it commanded in Scripture that you may not shake my hand as a sign of peace?"

"Well," the Rabbi replied, "you won't exactly find it in the Scriptures . . ."

"So it isn't part of the divine laws of God?" she asked. "The Word of God?"

"Actually," he said, "it's in the Oral Law. Later written down in the Talmud."

"A law of man?" she asked, smiling.

". . . I suppose a Christian would say that . . ."

"I must return to my father, Rabbi," Samira said, extending her hand again. "From the depths of my heart, from the wellspring of my own tradition, I wish you peace. Shalom!"

After the longest pause, Rabbi Abram extended his hand and shook hers. "Shalom," he said.

Chapter 12

Is Rabbinic Judaism a Supernatural Religion?

Judaism is not primarily about personal salvation, the relationship between the individual and God in the inner recesses of the soul. It is about collective redemption, about what it is to create a society that is the opposite of [ancient] Egypt, where the strong enslave[d] the weak.

— Rabbi Jonathan Sacks, chief rabbi of Great Britain

[The Jew] must selflessly join the ranks of the total Jewish community, and must seek his own salvation only in that Divine favor which must be regained by the nation as a whole.

— Rabbi Samson Raphael Hirsch

JERUSALEM

It is a steep walk up the winding road from the Wailing Wall to reach Zion Gate inside the Old City. Just past Zion Gate, a Bedouin nomad named Ahmad sits on his camel with a cell phone to his ear, waiting for tourists who may want to be photographed with his camel. He offers to buy my sunglasses, but I have to decline, several times. Nearby is the entrance to the Diaspora Yeshiva, where Rabbi Simcha Abramson has been teaching for three decades. He grew up in a liberal, Reform family in New York City before becoming Orthodox and moving to Israel.

The father of ten, Simcha was inside his little house down the hill from the yeshiva on the day I came by. In the kitchen his wife, Chaya Malka, was cutting slices of green melon for an afternoon refreshment for us.

"The Red Heifer is impossible to understand," Simcha told me after welcoming me as an old friend. "King Solomon, the wisest man in the world, asked God what it meant, but He said 'No.' The Red Heifer is one of the strengths of the Jewish people—because it's a law that we not only don't understand, but it's contradictory. There are *halachas,* legal factors, about purity and impurity that seem to contradict each other. It doesn't make sense. But we do it. And that's the strength of the Jewish people."

When Simcha heard the story about Isaac Cohen—that the yeshiva boy had deliberately fallen on the Red Heifer in order to exonerate Samira of having desecrated it—he immediately recalled a story about Rabbi Israel Kahan (1835-1933). This Lithuanian rabbinical scholar is known as the Chafetz Chaim, after the title of his main work—on the laws of slander.

"Someone made off with something from his house," Simcha said, "and he chased the man down the street, yelling, 'It's *hefker*!'—meaning, 'I give you the right to it'—just so the man wouldn't be guilty of sin." Similarly, Isaac Cohen thought that Samira had transgressed the law of the Red Heifer, so he risked his good name to protect her from judgment at the hands of his rabbi.

Rabbi Simcha Abramson does not support the movement to find a red heifer. "They shouldn't try to push it, to hasten the coming of the Messiah," he said. "Those who do so are only fringe groups. We are definitely in favor of non-confrontation, non-violence. We just want to teach Torah. In fact, most 'ultra-Orthodox' feel the same way."

As for the red heifer, he said, "I imagine when we need it, it will come. God—if we need it—He will bring it."

And the Temple?

"The Temple is supposed to come down from heaven," Simcha replied. "We don't build it. We built the first one, and we built the second one. The Second Temple was greater because it lasted ten years more than the First Temple. The First Temple was greater because it had the Divine Presence in it."

The widening division between religious and secular Jews in Israel—and the astonishing rate of assimilation of Jews all over the world—seems to be part of a "winnowing" process, he said. "We are winnowing ourselves out."

Could this be the hand of God, sifting the people of Israel to gather together only those who are willing to be obedient to Him?

"There could be a spiritual reason why it happened," Simcha said. "It's unfortunate. But there's a great rise in Torah study and Torah observance among the Jewish people. Because of this, the percentage of Jews who are observant is actually increasing."

Young Jews like Simcha Abramson were searching for answers in the 1970s, he said, sometimes in the wrong places.

"They have a lot of Jews for Jesus in Israel, which I have a big problem with," he said. "Often they take advantage. Depression is a great sickness of this time in history. A lot of people are depressed, for whatever reasons."

*

As a youth, Simcha Abramson visited Israel after high school, and it changed his life. He first told me his story back in 1985, when he and his wife had only four children. The yeshiva boy and I sat on an open porch on the roof of a new branch that the yeshiva had opened on Jabotinsky Street. (Ze'ev Jabotinsky started the Revisionist Movement in 1925, demanding all of western and eastern Palestine for a future Jewish state, as promised by the British in the Balfour Declaration of 1917.) Traffic passed on the street below us, threatening to drown our conversation as I took notes and tape-recorded it.

"I had no religious connection at all," Simcha said at the time. "But I knew I wanted to come back to Israel. I didn't know what I wanted to do. I was interested in philosophy."

Upon his return in 1972, he happened to attend a wedding on Mount Zion, in the Old City—which had been recovered by Israel only five years earlier.

"There wasn't any food served at the wedding," he recalled. "It was in an old building. I didn't know what I was supposed to be doing. But it was beautiful! And there was no pretension or anything. That's when it happened to me."

Before he knew it, he was attending this yeshiva and playing clarinet and saxophone in the Diaspora Yeshiva Band both here and abroad, working to bring Jews back to Judaism.

Simcha talked about how he became a yeshiva boy and then a rabbi after being swept up in the *baal t'shuvah* revival that started in the mid-1960s, after Jerusalem was recovered by Israel. Religious Jews sought out secular Jews and tried to draw them back to the faith. This was a historical first in Judaism—never before had Orthodox rabbis invited secular Jews to study the Torah without first securing a commitment to become Orthodox.

"There had been a falling away," Simcha said. "The Holocaust. Secularism in society. So you try and make up for it now." Some of his friends back home in New York asked him why he would risk his life by moving to Israel. "What are you doing this for? You're going to die," they would say. And Simcha would reply, "We're going to die *anyway*."

As a *baal t'shuvah*—a master of return to the faith—Simcha and other rabbis had to learn *kiruv*, how to share their life-changing experience with other Jews.

"After not having been involved," he said, "I think we have a great love for the Torah—and an understanding of what it means to try to bring someone closer who's not that involved. One of the problems is always: How do you get a person involved without pushing a 'trip' on him? Sometimes we tend to do that."

I told Simcha that I, too, had seen people on fire for the Lord who sometimes tried to force their own experience onto others. In my case, it was the charismatic movement, which began in the same decade—the 1960s—in the church. Fallen-away or lukewarm Catholics and Protestants began attending prayer meetings run by laymen, not clergy. We studied the Bible, sang hymns and danced for the Lord, prayed for each other's needs, laid hands on the sick to heal them, and received other gifts of the Holy Spirit, who is known to Jews as the Ruach ha-Kodesh. Charismatics also listened for God to speak during silent moments in their prayer meetings.

Simcha replied that this sounded a bit emotional to him. "What we do is based on learning," he explained. "It's not based on a revelation or on anything like that. It's not an emotional thing. Judaism is not something that you *go into*. You don't belong to the Jewish religion—you are Jewish. We *do*. We are *doing* now. The more you get involved in the Torah, the more you *do*."

I asked Simcha whether he considers Judaism a supernatural religion, capable of bringing about a spiritual transformation in a totally observant Jew.

"It has its great emotional features," he replied, searching for the words. "But the Torah doesn't really—God created the Torah as the blueprint of the world. The Torah is God's love letters to us! It governs everything: How we wake up in the morning. How we wash our hands. How we pray. How we eat. How we make breakfast, before and after.

124

How we mourn. How we marry people. We want our children to marry Jews. We must continue on as the Jewish people."

And now, a dozen years after our interview on the roof, we walked together out of the Abramson family home on Mount Zion, and Simcha walked me down the hill, on my way back to my room at Mishkenot Sha'ananim.

The Animal Is Returned

Leaving Rabbi Abram and arriving home at the falafel stand, Samira stepped behind the counter and laid her basket on a chair. Her father was making *taboola* salad and waiting for her.

"My most beautiful daughter of Palestine," Munir said, as he tried to conceal a smile of amusement. "Would you please explain to your old father why you are dressed as a Jewish woman?"

"I was shopping," she replied.

"Shopping?" he said. "Where?"

"In Me'a She'arim," she said.

Munir looked at his daughter for a long moment.

"Me'a She'arim?" he said. "The Orthodox neighborhood?"

"Yes," Samira said as she removed her Jewish headdress and fluffed her hair.

"May I ask why?" He wasn't smiling anymore.

"There were some things I needed," Samira said, "and it was the best place to shop for such things." She opened her basket for him to see, but he didn't look into it.

"Well," Munir said, forcing a little smile. "How did it feel to be dressed as a Jewish woman—and in a place like that?"

"I guess I kind of liked it," she said.

"My daughter," Munir said, raising his hands helplessly in the falafel stand. "First you convert from Islam to Christianity after the death of your dear mother—"

"She was a Christian when you married her," Samira interjected.

"—And you started wearing a cross," he added.

"I needed to believe in life after death," Samira said. "Something holy—as I've tried to explain to you for the past two years."

"Now, you're trying out the *Jewish* thing for size!" he shouted.

"I *still* want to understand my faith by tracing its roots, back to the Old Testament," she replied. "As I've told you before."

Munir thought for a moment. "This Christian religion of yours, and your 'born-again' friends," he said. "Doesn't it bother you that they all favor the Israelis over us?"

"We're Israelis too, Father," she reminded him. "Israeli Arabs."

"These Christians favor Israeli Jews over Arab citizens," he said. "And you know it. Can't you see what they are doing to us? They use their Bible to try to justify the Israeli occupation and settlements on the West Bank. They're using all of us Palestinian Arabs as pawns—even Christian Arabs!—like paltry little pawns on their chessboard. For their game of 'final days.'"

After some silence, Samira changed the subject. "By the way," she told her father, "Rabbi Abram apologized to me today."

Munir reached out and touched his daughter's necklace. "Did the Rabbi give you *that?*" he demanded. "A Jewish star?!"

Samira angrily cut him off. "We've been over this before!" she shouted. "I *still* don't know **where** I'm going with this!"

Munir pounded his fist on the counter of the falafel stand, then looked around to see if any customers were near. Stepping closer to his daughter, he hissed: "Next time you go to a Jewish market disguised as a Jew, I'll give you a **bomb** to deliver in your basket!"

"And you call yourself an authentic Muslim!" Samira hissed back. "For shame!" With that, she disappeared into the back of the falafel stand.

*

A few minutes later, Rabbi Abram came lumbering toward Munir's falafel stand. He had the Red Heifer beside him—and for the first time, she was on a leash. Munir's eyes widened when he saw the animal, but he quickly composed himself and pretended not to see it.

"Munir," the Rabbi said, stepping up to the counter. "My kosher special, please!"

Munir poured two cups of tea and placed them on the counter. For a long time, they just drank in silence, ignoring the heifer standing beside the Rabbi.

Finally, Munir could no longer remain silent. "I see your heifer has grown a few inches," he said.

"Yes," the Rabbi replied. "Your heifer is growing."

More silence, as they sipped their tea.

"So," Munir said, "you're happy with your red heifer."

"Oh, your heifer is a fine specimen," Rabbi Abram replied. "No doubt about it." He paused. "*But . . .*"

Munir stretched his neck to get another look at the heifer. "But . . . ?" he inquired.

"Well," the Rabbi said, "at this point in time, this animal is no longer kosher. For purposes of being a red heifer."

Curious, Munir stepped around the counter and, bending down to the ground, examined the Red Heifer. "You found a couple of white hairs?" he asked.

". . . Not exactly."

"I don't see any deformities," Munir said.

"No."

"No blemishes?" Munir asked, rising to his feet.

"No blemish . . . is visible."

"None?"

"No," the Rabbi said and paused. "However . . . There *is* such a thing as what we might call an invisible blemish."

"An—invisible blemish?" Munir said, fascinated.

"Well, for want of a better term . . ."

Munir looked at the Rabbi. "And so . . . ?"

"And so," the Rabbi said, "we'd like to sell it back to you."

Silence, as both returned to their tea. Now and then Munir murmured to himself, "An invisible blemish . . . Hmmm . . ."

Suddenly the Rabbi spoke boldly: "Now, Munir, we paid a handsome price for this, this heifer."

"Of course—but that was before this invisible blemish came to light. No?"

". . . Not exactly."

"Well," Munir said, turning his palms up, "did I sell you an animal with an invisible blemish?"

Rabbi Abram turned silent, a beaten man. Then he blurted out: "All right, Munir, how much for the animal?"

The haggling began.

At this point two passing musicians stopped, and they faced off against each other outside Munir's falafel stand. One of them, an Israeli Jew, began playing his violin, and the other, an Arab, began blowing on his reed flute. They glared at each as they furiously played their music, creating a cacophony reflecting the discord of the Middle East.

A crowd was now gathering.

Now Noor appeared and, mimicking a cattle auctioneer, began to amuse the crowed, while Munir and the Rabbi shouted at each other over how much the animal was now worth.

"Step right up, gentlemen!" Noor said, lifting the head of the Red Heifer for all to see. "What do I hear for this prized specimen cow?

Anybody, anybody, anybody-body-body-body!" She stroked the heifer, then turned its head in her hands to display the merchandise.

"I will let this animal go for no less than 5,000 shekels," the Rabbi vowed.

"Five thousand, from the gentleman in the black hat!" Noor said. "An excellent opening price. And did we hear a response from the other gentleman for this red heifer?"

"Five thousand?" Munir exclaimed. "Preposterous!"

"How so?" the Rabbi asked. "That's what we paid for it!"

"That was then," Munir replied.

"What?"

"And this is now."

The Rabbi thought for a moment. "Very well, Munir," he said. "I'll credit you—oh, 500 shekels—for your trouble. 4,500 shekels!"

"My trouble?" Munir told him. "My friend, it seems *you* are the one who is having the trouble."

"Give us your bid, sir!" Noor said.

"2,500," Munir said.

"2,500 shekels!" Noor echoed. "From the gentleman wearing the checkered scarf."

The Rabbi was incredulous. "2,500?!" he said. "This heifer has lost half its value? How?"

Munir shook his head and squinted. "I can't say exactly how," he replied, "but it has."

"Oy vey, gevalt!" said the Rabbi.

Turning a palm, Munir said, "You know how it is with the red heifer market. One day it's up . . . another day it's—"

"Do not toy with me, sir!" the Rabbi shouted.

"My friend!" Munir said, "I would never toy with you!"

Just then Isaac arrived and ran up to the Rabbi. "Rabbi Abram," he said, "what are you doing here with the Red Heifer?"

The Rabbi was surprised to see Isaac. After staring at him for a moment, he said, "Itzak. Please describe to this gentleman the qualities of this animal."

"Pardon us, folks," Noor told the crowd, "but the auction has been suspended as one of our bidders seeks clarification about the merchandise."

Rabbi Abram began to hum the tune for Isaac, and the yeshiva boy began to chant:

"... *t'meemah*..."

". . . perfect . . ." the Rabbi said.

". . . *asher ayn-bah moom . . .*"

". . . on which there is no blemish . . ."

". . . *asher lo-alah aleyha ol.*"

". . . which was never under a yoke—well—except once," the Rabbi said with resignation.

Now Noor blew a few notes on her flute, looking intently at Munir as if to hypnotize him. Then she said: "Well, I believe we're ready to resume. Our last bid was, ah, 2,500 shekels."

"Well," Rabbi Abram told Munir, "how about 3,500?"

"3,500!" Noor exclaimed. "From the man with the sacred—"

"2,000," Munir said.

"—cow!"

The Rabbi wasn't sure he had heard right. "2,000?" he said. "I thought I just heard you say 2,500."

Glancing at his wristwatch, Munir said: "Rabbi, this business is starting to be troublesome for me as well. And so . . . that particular offer has been withdrawn."

"Withdrawn?!" the Rabbi exclaimed. "I went down on my price!"

"And so I am doing the same," the Arab replied.

Disgusted, Rabbi Abram turned and began to walk away with the heifer.

"Gentlemen!" Noor cried. "Gentlemen! Surely we can—"

"Please don't go away mad, Rabbi," Munir said.

"Does the gentleman have a counter bid?" Noor asked.

"3,000," the Rabbi said, pausing. "Now what's your counter offer? *1,500?*"

"Rabbi! Rabbi! We're friends!" Munir said, smiling helplessly and approaching the Rabbi with open arms. "Now, so that there are no hard feelings—I will renew my offer of 2,500 shekels for this red heifer."

"2,500 from the Palestinian!" Noor cried. "Going once . . . Going twice . . . Last chance . . ."

Rabbi Abram nodded his head.

"Sold! For 2,500 shekels!" Noor announced. "To the gentleman in the checkered scarf. Please note that all sales are final and are payable in cash . . ."

Munir tugged at his empty pockets and said, "Payable tomorrow, in cash!"

"Agreed," said the Rabbi.

"But Rabbi!" Isaac said. "We paid—"

"Silence, Itzak . . ." the Rabbi said, and the two walked off.

Just then Samira emerged from the falafel stand and shrieked for joy to see the Red Heifer. She ran out and embraced the animal.

"Papa!" she cried. "What have we here?"

Taking out a large butcher knife behind the counter, her father said, "Veal cutlets, my princess."

"Oh no you don't!" she told him.

"Hey," Munir said, smiling broadly, "from sacred cows come gourmet burgers!"

As Samira continued to pet the Red Heifer, she noticed that Isaac and the Rabbi had walked only a few steps from the falafel stand and had sat down outside David's Citadel to talk. Samira listened to them . . .

*

"We had to cut our losses," the Rabbi was explaining to Isaac. "At least we got some of our money back—money to buy another red heifer . . . some day."

Isaac was looking so downcast that Rabbi Abram decided to amuse him.

"Yitzak," he said, "I have a riddle for you."

"A riddle?"

"Yes," he said. "On the day the Roman soldiers destroyed the Temple—it was on a Saturday night, at the conclusion of the Sabbath. And even as the flames spread through the Temple, the priests continued to serve—up on the altar—and the Levites continued to sing."

"How brave they were!" Isaac said.

"But history records that the Levites were no longer singing the song for Saturday. They were singing the song for Wednesday! They were chanting: *O Lord God, to whom vengeance belongs . . . shine forth!* Now, why do you suppose they did this?"

Isaac thought for a moment, then replied: "They were reminding Hashem of His promise to 'shine forth' with divine vengeance against the enemies of Israel?"

"Yes," the Rabbi said. "But I tend to think that their immediate purpose was to console the people—who were dying all around them—that God would avenge their blood. To promise God's people that He would make it right for them—someday — maybe on a Wednesday, no?"

131

Isaac closed his eyes and calculated: "Wednesday . . . Let me think . . . June 5, June 6, June 7—Monday, Tuesday, Wednesday. Yes! That's it!"

"What is it, Yitzak?" the Rabbi asked. "Have you come up with another explanation?"

"Yes!" Isaac cried out. "During the Six Day War! June seventh, 1967—the day the Israelis broke through and recaptured the Wailing Wall—that was a Wednesday, Rabbi!"

"Yitzy!" Rabbi Abram exclaimed, and he gave the yeshiva boy a long hug. "In fact, the 94th Psalm, which we call the Mighty One of Retribution, was sung on Wednesdays, because God created the sun and moon on the fourth day, and He will some day punish those who worship the sun and moon."

But Isaac was looking at the ground again, so sad. "Rabbi," he said at last, "do you think it was a mistake for us to obtain a red heifer from a Gentile?"

The Rabbi's eyes widened, and he thought for a moment.

"Actually," he said at last, "the Sages pondered this. Let me tell you a story or two. As you know, there have been nine red heifers since the time of Moses."

"Yes," Isaac said. "And Maimonides has written, 'The tenth red heifer will be accomplished by the king, the Messiah—May he be revealed speedily, Amen—May it be God's will.'"

"One time," the Rabbi began, "the rabbis were looking for a precious gem to replace one that had fallen off the breastplate of the High Priest. Without that stone, he could not serve in the Temple. They heard of a Gentile in Ashkelon who had one. They went to his house, and he agreed to sell it to them for 100 gold coins. The man excused himself to go into another room for the key to his strongbox. But when he returned, he said he could not sell it at this time. They asked why. He said his father was sleeping with the key under his pillow, and he was afraid to wake him. The rabbis thought the man simply wanted more money, so they offered 300, then 400 gold pieces—until they finally offered 1,000. Still, the man said no, insisting: 'For all the money in the world, I will not disturb my father's sleep.' So the rabbis started back to Jerusalem. But they had not gone far before they turned and saw a man running toward them. It was this same Gentile. He explained that after they had left his home, his father had awakened on his own. The man had the gem in his hand. Delighted, the rabbis were about to pay him the 1,000 gold pieces. But this Gentile said, 'No, I made up my mind to sell you the stone before discovering my father asleep.'

And he would accept only 100 gold pieces. The rabbis were greatly moved by this act of honor and respect for one's father. And not long after that, heaven rewarded this Gentile—a red heifer was born on his farm, and he sold it at great profit for the Holy Temple."

"Wow!" Isaac exclaimed. "What a blessing! That reminds me of the story of Rav Safra. He was reciting the *Shema* when a man suddenly offered to buy something from him. The Rav couldn't say 'Yes' because he was praying, but the man misunderstood his silence and increased his offer. So when he finished saying the *Shema*, he sold the item at the original price the man had offered."

"Exactly!" Rabbi Abram said. "Rav Safra is an example of one who spoke truth in his heart—because his heart had already accepted the man's first offer. But another time," the Rabbi continued, "when the Jews ran out of ashes and needed a red heifer, none could be found. Then the rabbis heard of a certain Gentile who owned one. So they went to this man, told him how important it was for the people of Israel, and asked him if he would sell it. He replied, 'If you pay for her, she is yours.' Well, they examined her and then asked, 'How much does she cost?' The man replied, 'Three or four gold pieces.' It was agreed. So the rabbis went to get the money. But while they were gone, this Gentile started thinking about how badly they wanted this animal. So when they returned, he refused to sell it. Well, the rabbis thought he wanted more money, so they offered him 10, 20, 100 gold pieces, but he still refused. Finally, he agreed to sell the red heifer for 1,000 gold pieces. Off they went, to get the gold. Now, while they were gone, this wicked man said to himself, 'I'll make a fool of these Jews. They want this heifer because it is red, it is without blemish, and it has never had a yoke on it.' So he put a yoke on his heifer and went to bed for the night. In the morning, when the rabbis returned with all that gold, the man removed the yoke before bringing his cow out to them. But they examined the heifer carefully and noticed that two hairs on the back of her neck were no longer standing straight up. And they told him, 'We will not be needing her after all. Perhaps you shall find someone else to laugh at.' And they left. Well, the man thought about his lost opportunity, and he also felt guilty. And he said to himself, 'Let this same mouth that mocked the people of God now begin to say, *Blessed be the One that chose this nation.*' Sick with remorse, he went home . . . and took his own life."

Isaac thought about this for a moment. "Sometimes," he told the Rabbi, "I feel like that Red Heifer was, like a, a curse."

"Interesting that you should say that, Itzak," the Rabbi said. "Actually, the Lord sent the first Red Heifer to make up for our ancestors' worship of the golden calf. But the Book of Numbers warns that *'the man who gathers up the ashes of the red heifer must also wash his clothes, and he too will be unclean till evening.'* And our teachers have marveled at this irony, that the very thing that causes purity also causes impurity."

"Can anyone purify the Temple with the ashes without becoming impure himself?" Isaac asked.

"No," the Rabbi said. "No. He must go through purification again. The only way you can purify is to impurify! Nobody truly understands this—it is a *chukah*—a law we are not supposed to understand. As the Holy One said, 'I have engraved an ordinance with no explanation—and you cannot transgress it.'"

"Then only God knows the secret why—why no man can purify the people without becoming impure himself . . . to bring about the Redemption," Isaac said.

Dusk was falling when the two stood up to go home for dinner.

Samira was still sitting on the ground, with her back to the falafel stand and her arms around her Red Heifer, listening to them until they departed David's Citadel.

"Father," she said in prayer, "Yeshua was a lamb without blemish or defect. And Messiah Yeshua brought about the Redemption by taking on Himself the curse of our sins . . . Just like the Red Heifer . . ."

Chapter 13

How Rabbi Yaacov Haber Explains the Red Heifer

Q. As a rabbi, would you say that rabbinic Judaism is a supernatural religion?

A. How do you mean?

Q. Well, suppose the Temple were rebuilt and Jews could observe all of the 613 commandments. By becoming totally observant of the Law, would Jews receive supernatural assistance from the Ruach haKodesh to truly love the Lord? Or would it still be possible to do all those things and not love God?

A. That's always a problem. . . . I believe it is not our actions that stand before God but rather it is we ourselves. God judges not what we do but rather what we are.

JERUSALEM

A few houses down the street from the Frankels, No. 36 was once the home of Rabbi Yaacov Haber. Both Americans were living and working together in Romema in the 1970s, when they were setting out as young rabbis and starting their families. Frankel was from Toledo, Ohio; Haber, from Buffalo, New York. Now they are permanent residents and citizens of Israel.

Their calling is to *kiruv*, that is, bringing lost Jews back to Judaism.

Unlike other rabbis in this book, Yaacov Haber is not a *baal t'shuvah*. Born in an Orthodox family in Buffalo, he moved to Israel at age 14 to study Torah. He eventually became one of the most brilliant disciples of Rabbi Chaim Pinchus Scheinberg at Torah Ohr Yeshiva, serving as his personal secretary and working with him on his halachic responses. Young Haber studied ten hours a day, six days a week at school. In his tiny apartment, he had no television set but scores of books on Jewish law that he read for relaxation. Asked whether his schedule was tiring, he replied: "Of course it is. But I love it. Using your mind fully for ten hours a day is one of the most tiring things you can do (but) I can't remember the last time I was bored."

Young Yaacov had been sent to Jerusalem by his father, Samuel Haber, who had played his own historical role in trying to bring Jews back to their homeland. As a U.S. Merchant Marine officer in 1947, the elder Haber had helped fit and prepare a Chesapeake Bay ferry—the 600-passenger President Warfield—for a mission to post-war Palestine. The ferryboat had been purchased by the Haganah, the underground paramilitary organization that was still struggling against the British Mandate.

The vessel's new name was the SS Exodus. She carried 4,500 Jewish survivors of the Nazi Holocaust. Sam Haber was an eyewitness to the heart-breaking fate of the Exodus—to arrive from Marseilles, France to the port of Haifa, only to be turned back by the British . . .

Toward the end of his decade of study in yeshiva in Jerusalem, Yaacov Haber learned an important lesson about the spirit of the Law, as opposed to the letter of the Law. One night, at the start of Hanukkah, he and his wife, Bayle (who was expecting their first child), were about to light their menorah when they heard a knock on their door. Opening it, they saw a disheveled, unshaven man in filthy clothes. One of his eyes was frozen in a permanent squint.

"Do you think you might have a meal for me?" he asked meekly. His name was Beinish.

Thus began a relationship that found the Habers hosting this man, every Sabbath and several times during the week, serving him meals and even washing his smelly clothes. His presence had become burdensome by the time they finally found a more affordable apartment in the Romema neighborhood. What to do about the man who had worn out his welcome? Turning to the rabbis, they received a religious ruling that they were not required to tell Beinish that they were moving.

After their first child was born, the Habers began to notice scorpions scampering across the floor in their new home at 36 Ma'ane Simcha. It was terrifying. An exterminator came twice but eventually said, "There is nothing more I can do here."

The odd thing was that none of their neighbors had scorpions. Not even the Frankels, just a few doors down the street.

Going to his mentor, Rabbi Scheinberg, he asked: "Have we done anything wrong? How should we view this spiritually? Why is this happening?"

Turning to *Perek Shira*, an ancient book about how everything in creation has a purpose, the rabbi found an entry concerning 'psalms' of creeping creatures. It said, "The scorpion says: God is good to all, and His mercy is upon all His handiwork," elaborating on Psalm 145:9.

"We don't know the purpose of scorpions in this world," the rabbi told his student. "Even though some of them are lethal, God has compassion on scorpions and supplies them with food and what they need to survive. Perhaps you failed to show compassion to someone. The scorpion's song is one of mercy and that's what we must adopt in our lives."

Stunned, Haber realized that he had abandoned Beinish, who had been so heavily relying on the family. Over the next several days, whenever he could, he walked through the neighborhood where Beinish had said he lived. It was most frustrating. Then one day, while riding a bus, he spotted the destitute man, walking aimlessly. He quickly got off the bus and ran after him.

That night Beinish came to supper. Before long he was again their frequent guest. The scorpions disappeared; not one returned. Now, that's the kind of modern-day miracle that might qualify rabbinic Judaism as a supernatural religion. But how many Jews, especially secular Jews, have a clue to the power and faithfulness of the Holy One of Israel?

*

After coming back to Buffalo in 1980 as a 24-year-old rabbi, with his wife and first child, Haber began teaching adults in their home. Soon he was launching the Torah Center, a part-time yeshiva for adults wishing to learn more about Judaism by studying at convenient hours. His inspiration was Amos 8:11: "Behold, the days are coming, says the Lord God, when I shall send a famine on the land, not a famine of bread, nor a thirst for water, but of hearing the words of the Lord." He also interpreted the final verse of Malachi as a prophecy that, in the latter days, the children will not only be reconciled with their parents but will also teach them Torah. This is actually happening today, as *baal t'shuvah* Jews strive to share Judaism with their secularized parents.

Because of his fervent calling and magnetic personality, scores of suburban Jews moved back to the city—not only to study at the Torah Center, but to buy houses within walking distance of the Saranac Synagogue, where he was spiritual leader.

Later, Rabbi Haber moved to Australia to bring Jews back to the fold, and then to New York City, where he became national director of outreach for the Orthodox Union. He and his wife and eleven children later made *aliyah,* and today he lives in the Jerusalem suburb of Beit Shemesh, running his own outreach program. By now, in his fifties, Yaacov Haber has brought thousands of secular Jews back to the synagogue.

*

"You're always the same," Rabbi Haber tells me, recalling the days when I was his *shabbos goy*, living upstairs from the Torah Center (later, I purchased the Habers' home when their family outgrew it). "No matter what changes over the years," he adds, "something in you is a constant that's always there."

No doubt this is the presence of Yeshua's love inside me, but he doesn't realize it.

I tell him about my latest writing project, *The Red Heifer*—in which a yeshiva boy named Isaac Cohen saves the life of a Palestinian woman by making the red heifer impure, thus sacrificing his reputation, rendering it impure for the rest of his life.

Then I ask him: Why must one man become impure in order to purify others with the ashes of the red heifer? My rabbi friend is 14 years my junior, but I respect him for his learning, for his successes in the battle against Jewish assimilation, and most of all for his fervor and warmhearted manner that make him seem so much like a brother in the Lord to me.

"The intrinsic paradox is that it's to purify things but he becomes impure by touching it," Rabbi Haber begins. "The Talmud describes this as the unanswerable paradox—How could it be that the thing that causes purity can create impurity?"

And now—like Samira in *The Red Heifer*—I marvel to myself about how, as the Corinthian believers were once told, *God made Him who had no sin to be sin for us, so that in Him we might become the righteousness of God.*

I ask Rabbi Haber, How can anyone distribute the red heifer's ashes without becoming impure?

"You can't," he says, helplessly. "The only way you can purify is to 'impurify.' Not only is this yeshiva boy ruining his own reputation to save another one—who is pure—but really *that* pure becomes impure. You've got to work out the mathematics!"

And he laughs, ironically. Joy and laughter are seldom absent when the Rabbi is discussing what he learned by studying ten hours a day, six days a week, for a decade.

I ask him: Is this like how the Messiah can't come until the world has become either all pure or all impure—or until the world is polarized between those who are absolutely pure and absolutely impure?

"Well," Rabbi Haber says, "I think psychologists call it 'bottoming out.' You can reach such a *low* where you can derive *purity.* There are two ways to become pure: either from the high, and esoteric, and the spiritual—or you can derive some purity from the street."

Or you can bottom out and have your second wind and be refreshed?

"That's right. So that's the message here. Those are the three that I always felt worked together. It works well."

What about the heifer that's turned loose in the wilderness, carrying the sins of the nation?

"I don't know if it fits in or not," Rabbi Haber says. "The counterparts that we're looking for are this idea of bad, bad, bad equals good somehow."

The red heifer is actually a source of impurity, and yet that's the purifying factor?

"I'll tell you the ultimate example of this," Rabbi Haber says. "The Galus, the Diaspora. Here the Jewish nation was in Jerusalem, and then we're put out into the Babylonian exile, then the Roman exile, and here we are today, waiting for the Moshiach. The real understanding of this is that it's not negative. It's really a positive process. But the positive process is a lowering process, a humbling process—it's a process of purification. The dipping down—like a basketball player—is what allows you to jump high. That's the ultimate metaphor here. The Para Aduma. This is a concept—you see Jacob bow down to his brother Esau seven times."

I suggest to Rabbi Haber my hope that both liberal Jews and the Orthodox will be able to identify with my story about the Red Heifer—one that can somehow bring Jacob and Esau together again, here in Israel.

"I can't wait to see it!" he says.

"Frankly," I confess, "neither can I."

We both laugh.

*

Years earlier, Rabbi Haber and I were discussing a Jewish woman who had 'come back' to Orthodox Judaism—and married an Orthodox man—after reading my article in the Sunday magazine of *The Buffalo News* about his Torah Center. So grateful was the woman for how my article had changed her life that, every year, on or near the anniversary of its publication, she hosted an *oneg Shabbat* meal for everybody after services in Haber's synagogue.

The Rabbi told me what anguish she had gone through, leaving the church for the synagogue. "Many find it a relief to be done with the long troublesome problem of who Jesus is," he said.

It pained me to hear this, but I welcomed the discussion, and before I knew it we were debating the benefits of the Jewish religion versus Christianity. I asked him about the "circumcision of your hearts" that is found in the Books of Deuteronomy and Jeremiah.

Rabbi Haber said circumcision can be of the heart, because the Torah (first five books of the Bible) doesn't spell out in detail what that word really means; circumcision is fully explored in the oral law, which became the written Talmud.

"The point is," he said, "you need the Talmud to understand the Torah. A study of the Talmud (as well as the Torah) would show the way Christianity lifted so many things from Judaism, out of context, and made them sound foolish . . . they magnified small parts."

But rabbinic Judaism, I replied, both magnified and shrank various aspects of Second Temple Judaism so that today it is hardly the same religion practiced in Yeshua's day.

"Not so," Rabbi Haber said. "The Rashi's and the Rambam's (in later centuries) were faithful to what was codified and written into the oral tradition, the Talmud, at the time of Christ. Their writings (commentaries) aren't the Talmud; the Talmud was completed in the First Century AD."

I pointed out to him that rabbinic Judaism was born after the Temple was destroyed in 70 AD, which was 40 years after the birth of the early church. And that Rabbi Akiva and his cohorts had been so opposed to the Jewish believers in Yeshua that they continued to reject the Messiah.

"My belief in Yeshua as Moshiach isn't an intellectual position that I could drop if it was proven false," I explained. "And it isn't an emotional response that you'd dismiss as psychological. It's an indescribable excitement of my spirit, such as I get when I read the Bible. It's the action of the Ruach haKodesh who wrote those books of the Old and New Testaments and who recreates that excitement in my spirit when I read them."

"That's because the New Testament took from the valid Old Testament," the Rabbi replied. "I'd bet that the very lines that excite you spiritually in the New Testament were those taken from the Old Testament, especially spoken by Jesus. You can also find smatters of the Talmud in the New Testament."

I asked my friend how trustworthy the rabbis have been in preserving the critical distinction between the Hebrew Scriptures and the oral law, on which the Talmud is based.

"The Book is holy from God," he said, "but the Talmud, while from man, explains and makes sense of it for us. Let me give you an example. If I give you written instructions, like an outline, but then go on to explain it all to you, you need both. So do Jews, because Moses got the entire oral law at Sinai, along with the tablets containing the Ten Commandments."

I seriously doubted that Moses, on the mountain those 40 days, also received the oral law—which fills a large bookshelf in its written form—but I let it go.

"The oral law is the basis for the Torah," he went on. "So you can't separate the two; only Christians try to grasp the Old Testament without the Talmud; it's foolish. Even in the original Hebrew you can't grasp it."

I told him that it's the Holy Spirit, not the Talmud, that one needs to understand the Bible, and that all of his focus on the Talmud was trapping him in the letter of the Law.

"So I'm a lawyer," he said, and laughed. "The Law is everything."

"And the Prophets?" I persisted. "Some of them, like Ezekiel, talk about how to capture and practice the *spirit* of the Law."

"They're valid too," he said, "but not one single law is in the Prophets."

"Why should there be?" I asked. "Their function is prophecy."

"I'm not interested in the future," he replied and laughed again.

I reminded him of the story Yeshua told about the Jew who was beaten by robbers and left half dead by the road. Two Jews (a priest and a Levite) saw him but walked on, taking no compassion on their fellow

Jew. But the Samaritan man stopped to help him. "This," I concluded, "shows the danger of getting so wrapped up in religion that you don't have a heart for God and your fellow man."

"The Law tells us how to live," Rabbi Haber replied, "as opposed to the Prophets, who are into homiletics. In fact, the Prophets inspire us to keep the Law." (Only later did it occur to me to mention that both Jeremiah and Ezekiel inspired Jews to keep the Law by being born again—as Yeshua had advised Nicodemus, who should have known about these Prophets, being himself a teacher of Israel.)

Finally, I asked whether keeping all 613 laws in the Talmud could in itself cause a spiritual transformation in a Jew, guaranteeing that he or she would love God. He said no.

"*The Torah needs heart* is a phrase we use," he acknowledged. "Torah and Talmud demand that the heart be given to God. So it's incorporated in the Law. Developing a relationship with God . . . "

*

The last time Shirah and I visited the Habers in Jerusalem, Rabbi Haber escorted us from his house to our waiting cab. He and I hugged, and I saw that he had grown serious.

"May the Shekinah be over your house," he said with a solemn wave of his hand. And I saw tears in his eyes . . . for we go back a long way . . . and now I know that his spirit, as a devout Jew, has made a connection with my spirit as a born-again Christian. We can disagree for years about the nature and identity of Messiah, but that is mere theology. What binds us like spiritual brothers is the precious touch of God's hand on each of us, for His kind purposes, for these final days.

God Has a Human Face

"You're so right," Noor was telling Samira as they sat on the ground outside the falafel stand, petting the Red Heifer. "There's so much about Yeshua that's reflected in the Red Heifer."

"Yeshua is also the Lamb of God," Samira said.

"Yes," Noor said, "because He was foreshadowed by the lambs that the Hebrews sacrificed for the Passover before escaping from Egypt. God chose the lamb—not the goat or the cow or the lion—to foreshadow the coming Messiah as the gentle Lamb of God. So they smeared the blood on their doorposts and warded off the Angel of Death, as it passed over and slayed the Egyptians' firstborn."

They were silent for a few minutes. Samira was petting the Red Heifer, whose head was in her lap; it was fast asleep.

"Noor," Samira asked, "what does Yeshua look like? I mean His face."

"He is the image of the unseen God, the firstborn over all creation," Noor replied. "And since His death and resurrection, we can say that He is the beginning and the firstborn from among the dead. For God was pleased to have all His fullness dwell in Yeshua."

"But—what does Yeshua's face look like?"

"Why," Noor said, "Yeshua has the face of the Father!"

"You mean God has a human face?" Samira exclaimed.

"Of course," Noor said. "We are created in God's image and likeness, which means that we have faces that look like the face of God. And that means to me that, before the creation of the world, God had a certain human face in mind for the Messiah. As well as human arms and human legs."

"Really?"

"How do you suppose the Lord walked with Adam in the garden in the cool of the day? He had legs—a face, arms and legs—just like those of Adam. This was the Messiah, in his pre-incarnate body—the body that was the blueprint for the entire human race."

"Now, Moses saw the face of God on Mount Sinai," Samira said.

"Yes," Noor said. "Moses looked into the face of God and saw Yeshua. And God said to Moses: 'I will raise up for them a Prophet like you from among their brethren, and will put My words in His mouth.' In due time, the Messiah was finally born in Bethlehem, and God walked among us in the flesh. They called this man Yeshua—salvation."

Samira sat up straight, causing the Red Heifer to stir in its slumber. "But didn't Yeshua appear in disguise after His resurrection—because the disciples walking on the road to Emmaus at first didn't recognize Him?"

"True." Noor said. "Yeshua can appear in the flesh with a face other than His own. And don't forget, in the Old Testament, how the Lord appeared as a man, with two others, during His visit to Abraham at Mamre. To announce that Sarah would have a son the following year."

"And then," Samira said, "after His resurrection, he appeared to the apostles in his glorified body."

"The same glorified body that He had once displayed on the Mount of Transfiguration, talking to Moses and Elijah," Noor said.

"Just tell me one thing," she said, turning to Noor and staring into her eyes. *"Who are you?"*

Noor looked at Samira for a long moment. Then she told her, "No, I'm not Yeshua in disguise . . . But you should know that the Ruach ha-Kodesh can appear in many different manifestations. And He has made Himself known, once again, for such a time as this."

Chapter 14

This World Will Become God's Condominium

Whenever the world has appeared to be in a state of violent agitation, and whenever the greatest and strongest physical powers shook to their very foundation, the cause of this commotion has always been God's will and His displeasure at the conduct of men.

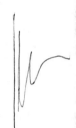

— Rabbi Samson Raphael Hirsch (1808-1888), commentary on Psalm 18:8

BUFFALO, NEW YORK

C hristians claim that God has a human face, the face of Yeshua. And some ultra-Orthodox Jews are preaching that when the Messiah comes, it will be God Himself who comes down to this earth and dwells among men.

Take Rabbi Noson Gurary, a leader in Chabad, the worldwide teaching wing of the Lubavitcher Chasidic movement. His ministering on college campuses for the past generation has rescued scores of Jewish students from loneliness, breakdown, even suicide, and has led thousands back to the faith. The Lubavitchers' brownstone headquarters building in Crown Heights, New York, has been replicated near Tel Aviv.

One day the little gray-bearded rabbi with the Yiddish accent was talking to a group of his students about the floods, hurricanes, earthquakes and other devastations that are a sign of the end times.

"We're living now in a very *moshuganah* time," he said, using the Yiddish word for *crazy*. "But all this is predicted—that it's going to happen right before the coming of Moshiach. No one ever understood what it meant. The waters would rise. Everything with water! We are now very, very close to the coming of Moshiach."

Rabbi Gurary urged his Jewish listeners to look at their lives and ask why they are here.

"We have to look at the big picture," he said. "There's more to life than my needs and my family's needs. We are here for the Boss—God. We are part of God's plan. Everyone is needed for this big plan. If God could manage without any one of us, then He's not a perfect God—*He doesn't create unnecessary beings!* The only way we could explain our existence is that God is perfect and every one of us here are in His plan. We must be here for something that each individual has to contribute that—without him—it's not going to happen."

Many Jews think that the coming of the Messiah is a fairy tale, Gurary said, but nothing could be farther from the truth.

"If a person doesn't understand the need for the coming of Moshiach, he's missing a fundamental principle in the Jewish religion. The fact that we exist, that God created us, is the proof that we are needed in the big puzzle. If it's missing only one piece, it's not a complete puzzle. If you don't hope for the coming of Moshiach, it's like thinking only about yourself. *We* are here for *Him.*"

Suddenly Rabbi Gurary paused and pointed to one of his listeners.

"You—what's your name?"

"Marvin."

"No, your Hebrew name."

"Moshe."

"Good," he said. "There are no Marvins in heaven, only Moshes. If there were already a Moshe like you, then God wouldn't have created you. If you're not needed in the puzzle, you're an extra piece. There's something about your contribution—that *mitzvah* as Moshe does it—that was never done before. And there'll never be another Moshe."

Which brings us, he said, to the reason the world was created.

"God created this world eventually, ultimately, to dwell in this world," Rabbi Gurary said. "This physical world is one day, very soon, going to be the holiest place, higher than the most lofty spiritual worlds that we learn about. This is the world that God chose to be His condominium. His dwelling place. This world will one day be so permeated with God's presence that we will feel and see how God is dwelling in this world."

*

> I saw the holy city, New Yerushalayim, coming down out of heaven from God, prepared like a bride beautifully dressed for her husband. I heard a loud voice from the throne say, "See! God's *Sh'khinah* is with mankind, and he will live with them. They will be his people, and he himself, God-with-them, will be their God." . . . I saw no Temple in the city, for *ADONAI*, God of heaven's armies, is its Temple, as is the Lamb. — Revelation 21:2–3, 22 (CJB)

*

Rabbi Gurary and his rabbi sons are the latest (and hopefully not the last) generation of Lubavitcher Chasidim. The Chasidic (pious) movement goes back three centuries, to an itinerant teacher known as the Baal Shem Tov. He was born in Ukraine in 1698, just three decades after a mystic named Shabbetai Tzevi declared himself to be the Messiah in Smyrna, in modern-day Turkey. After raising the hopes of Jews all over the world, Shabbetai Tzevi traveled to Constantinople to claim his kingdom from the sultan. Arrested and imprisoned, and threatened with his life, he converted to Islam and died in obscurity. His apostasy broke the hearts of world Jewry and was still a source of pain when Israel ben Eliezer arose in Ukraine and earned the name Baal Shem Tov (Master of the Good Name) for his healing of the sick.

This humble teacher stressed prayer and obedience to the Law—more than the study of the Law for its own sake—thus appealing to less educated Jews wishing to soar spiritually. Yet, according to his modern-day followers, he "focused less on the intensely messianic idea of cataclysmic redemption and more on the concept of personal redemption."

The Baal Shem Tov soon gained a mass following throughout Eastern Europe.

"The ultimate of Divine worship is the attachment to the Almighty, a service of the heart rather than the mind," his followers say in his name. "The Baal Shem Tov emphasized [that] merely feeling the holiness

147

of the words was enough for even the most illiterate to express their desire to come closer to the Almighty . . . Above all, the Baal Shem Tov endeavored to instill joy into Divine service."

One day, in meditation, he asked the Messiah a question: "When will you come, Master, to redeem the world?"

"When your well springs shall spread out from one end of the earth to the other," the Messiah replied, "and when all people shall be able to know the Divine as you do."

The Baal Shem Tov's successor, Dov Ber (the Maggid) of Mezhirich, sent out more teachers to spread the word, and he developed the concept of the importance of the movement's righteous leader (the Rebbe) as an intermediary between Jews and God.

Next came his protégé, Shneour Zalman of Lyady, who founded the Chabad school of Chasidism. From the mid-1800s, the movement was centered in Lubavitch (City of Brotherly Love), Russia, and was perpetuated by a dynasty of Rebbes from one generation to the next.

The seventh and last Rebbe was Menachem Mendel Schneerson, who was born in Russia in 1902 and became the leader in 1951. At the Chabad Lubavitch headquarters in Crown Heights, the Rebbe gained such worldwide respect and admiration—among Jews and even those of other religions—that his followers urged him to declare himself the Messiah.

Rabbinic Judaism teaches that in every generation there are 36 righteous men worthy of being the Messiah, if only the Jews have been faithful to God. The Rebbe declined to claim that role, despite all of his qualities and actions that pointed to him as the man chosen by God.

Rabbi Noson Gurary's belief that God will come down to earth and dwell with us during the Messianic Era was no doubt shared by the Rebbe, who respected Gurary as one of the most successful Chabad teachers of their generation. I thought about this one day while reading *Toward a Meaningful Life: The Wisdom of the Rebbe*, published a year after the Rebbe's death and adapted by Rabbi Simon Jacobson. "G-d desired to have an abode in the lower worlds," he wrote, quoting from *Midrash Tanchuma, Nasso 7*. (Outside of prayer books and the Bible, Orthodox Jews avoid spelling out God's name, lest it be dishonored someday when that document is defaced or thrown away.)

But the Rebbe's book contains a parable explaining why God, thus far, has usually not shared His presence with humankind.

"G-d is like a father who hides himself from his child," the story begins. "The father is encouraging the child to demonstrate his ingenuity in finding him, which will ultimately intensify the love and closeness between them. The father . . . hides himself very well—so well, in fact, that the child finally gives up the search, forgets his father, and goes off to something else. Meanwhile, his father remains in his hiding place, sadly waiting for his child to return. Similarly, G-d concealed Himself from us to bring out our deepest abilities and resources in our search for Him. It is G-d's concealment in the material world—which is intended to create a truly profound search for goodness—that allows for the potential of evil."

Christianity teaches that Messiah Yeshua defeated the power of evil spirits (fallen angels now called demons) by his Blood Atonement for sin on the cross. The New Testament draws from eight books of the Old Testament—Leviticus, Deuteronomy, First and Second Chronicles, Job, the Psalms, Isaiah and Zechariah—which refer to evil as being personified—either as 'Satan,' or as 'Lucifer,' or as 'devils.' But the Rebbe did not believe in the existence of evil as a spiritual force.

"Evil is simply the absence of good, it has no real existence of its own, and is dispelled in the light of goodness," the Rebbe wrote. "To believe that evil has its own, positive existence is to incorrectly believe that there are two divine powers rather than one." Therefore, "Rather than battling evil, we should concentrate on cultivating the goodness within ourselves and others."

Thus, in conflicts between nations (or between Jews and Arabs), the Rebbe taught, "War breaks out in the heart of man when the human soul becomes disconnected from G-d, the source of goodness."

As for the coming Messiah, who will end evil by bringing justice and peace to the world, the Rebbe wrote: "The final redemption is no longer a dream of a distant future, but an imminent reality."

The Rebbe believed this so firmly that he opposed the land for peace proposals and encouraged the spread of Jewish settlements in Samaria and Judea. And because of him, Lubavitchers were the only major Chasidic group whose members served in the IDF. That is why his followers were so mystified that the Rebbe never set foot in the Land of Israel, even after the completion of an exact replica of his Crown Heights brownstone headquarters building in Tel Aviv.

Because of the strong messianic expectations that the Rebbe nurtured all those years, his death in 1994 hurled Chabad into an epochal quandary. Not only had the Rebbe not declared himself (or anyone else)

Messiah, but he also had no children, leaving no son to continue the dynasty as the eighth Rebbe. What could this possibly mean? Surely, the end of the dynasty meant the end of days. Now, how could the Messiah come out of Chabad? . . . Unless the Rebbe arose from the dead and ruled as Messiah during the Millennium.

And so, many 'Chabadniks' quietly believed that Reb Schneerson would rise from the dead. All that God required was—as always—that enough Jews throughout the world came back to Judaism and became a light to the nations, preparing the way for Moshiach.

As Rabbi Gurary once put it—without actually committing himself to the Rebbe's return—"When the Rebbe's soul was contained in his body it was limited and we could only experience a ray of spirituality—whereas now, the soul has been raised and knows no limits. We can now benefit from his essence."

Until now, the Jewish narrative of Messiah ben Joseph preparing the way (and possibly dying) for a triumphant Messiah ben David had all but fallen by the wayside. But now, the notion of the Messiah rising from the dead was no longer a Christian invention; it was an authentic Jewish concept embraced by the strictest descendants of the Pharisees, the ultra-Orthodox Chasidim of our time.

The God-Fearers

At the dinner table that evening, Rabbi Abram's thoughts went back to his conversation with Samira outside Jaffa Gate earlier today. While the others carried on their own conversations, the Rabbi told Isaac what the Arab woman had talked about—and how she had been dressed as a Jew.

"Samira was always hanging around with the Jewish boys and girls," Isaac said, recalling the days when he and Simon and Samira were attending the same public school. "She hardly ever hung out with the Arab kids."

"She was a Muslim, wasn't she?" the Rabbi asked.

"Yes," Isaac said.

"When did she become a Christian?"

"After her mother's death—don't you remember that day?"

Rabbi Abram put down his steak knife and thought. "Yes," he said at last. "During that Palestinian riot . . ."

"She's a very devout Christian," Isaac said. "And she's very interested in how her religion evolved out of our religion."

Rabbi Abram, who had been sipping from his cup, slammed it down on the table, causing a brief pause in the other conversations around them. "Oy vey!" he exclaimed. "Not only that—but she even hinted that she might want to convert to Judaism someday! I laughed at her."

Isaac stared at the Rabbi in amazement. "What did you tell her?"

"I told her the first thing she'd have to do would be to give up this *Yeshu* business!"

"Yeshua," Isaac corrected him.

"<u>Yeshu</u>!" the Rabbi insisted.

"That <u>means</u> *fool*," Isaac said. "They don't like it when we mispronounce his name."

"The sages have always called him that," Rabbi Abram said. "So I told her she couldn't believe in a false messiah and become a Jew. There is no precedent for such a thing."

Isaac swallowed and put down his fork. "What about Rabbi Akiva?" he asked. "He believed in a false messiah, but he is still revered today as one of the greatest rabbis who ever lived."

"Hmph!" the Rabbi retorted. "Akiva never bowed down and worshiped Simon Bar Kokhba as a divine messiah! Bar Kokhba was an ordinary man, and so will be the Messiah—a descendant of King David with all the wisdom of his son, Solomon. A divine messiah is a Christian invention."

They ate in silence for a long time. Finally, Rabbi Abram pulled back his chair and folded his napkin.

"What I can't figure out," he said, "is whatever possessed this Arab woman to dress up like an Israeli Jew and walk around Jerusalem as if she was something that she isn't?"

Isaac laughed.

"What's so funny?" the Rabbi said.

"Nothing, Rabbi," the yeshiva boy replied.

"When I asked her about it," the Rabbi said, "she explained that she wanted to shop in the Jewish markets. But I am convinced that there is a great deal more than *that* going on in that woman's head."

"She loves the Jews, Rabbi," Isaac said. "She even came to synagogue with me one day, when we were kids."

"That's *it*!" Rabbi Abram exclaimed, causing the others to pause again in their own conversations. "She is a God-fearer! A God-fearing Gentile!"

"What's *that*?" Isaac asked.

"The God-fearers go back to the time of the Roman Empire," the Rabbi said. "Even before. And they were not only in Jerusalem and Antioch, but in the dispersion across the sea, where Jews were living in their own communities. These Gentiles would come to the synagogue and attend services, but they never converted."

Isaac looked at him. "They never converted?"

"No," he said. "Some of them followed the Sabbath regulations, and some of them kept kosher to one degree or another—but apparently they were afraid of circumcision."

"So, how were they treated by the Jews?"

"Very openly, most of the time. You see, the evil nature of the Roman Empire, and way that it corrupted daily life, caused the good inclination in some of the pagans to look around for something holy. And Judaism attracted them—like an oasis in a desert."

"Didn't the Romans mistake them for Jews, and persecute them along with us?" Isaac asked.

"Not usually," the Rabbi said. "You see, many of the Roman emperors looked up to Judaism as an ancient religion. And they were especially impressed that Jews minded their own busir..... didn't cause trouble or pose a threat to the emperor. And so, only the Gentiles were required to worship the emperor once a year. But if any Gentiles attended a synagogue, they usually were exempt from that idolatry."

"Did these God-fearers come to believe in the Holy One of Israel?"

"They certainly did," the Rabbi said. "They liked the idea of one god—in place of all the false gods that the Romans believed in."

Isaac frowned at the Rabbi. "Why did you call *Samira* a God-fearer? She is a Christian."

"She's a God-fearer, in spite of following a false messiah," the Rabbi said. "She apparently loves the Holy One of Israel and identifies herself personally with our people." Here the Rabbi paused. He stared intently at his yeshiva boy. "And that's the *problem*," he went on.

"Problem?" Isaac asked.

"Yes!" the Rabbi said. "The problem, Yitzak, is that those God-fearers back in the time of the Temple ended up contributing to a movement that would someday cause enormous misery to our people."

Isaac took a sip from his cup and then gave all his attention to the Rabbi.

"You know who Sha'ul of Tarsus was, do you not?" the Rabbi asked.

"No, Rabbi."

"He is better known to Christians by his Roman name, Paulus— Paul the Apostle. Sha'ul of Tarsus was an observant Jew whose teacher was Gamaliel the Elder."

"Wow!" Isaac said. "Gamaliel was the grandson of Hillel and he became head of the Sanhedrin!"

"Yes . . ." The Rabbi pursed his lips to gather his thoughts. "So great a defender of the faith was Sha'ul that he was appointed by the Sanhedrin to track down Jews who strayed from the faith to follow this Yeshu. But one day, according to the early Christians, Sha'ul had a vision from heaven and was told to travel far and wide and convert the gentiles to Christianity."

"Was his vision truly from God?" Isaac asked.

"Of course not!" the Rabbi replied. "But here is what happened. Sha'ul crossed the Mediterranean Sea and traveled to various cities where Jews were living. And the first place he went in each town was to the local synagogue—to preach about his messiah. Well, the Jews threw him out! But guess what happened then?"

"What?"

"Those God-fearing Gentiles—who loved the Jewish religion but weren't willing to convert—would join him outside the synagogue and listen to him preach. And he told them they could have all the blessings the Jews had—without having to convert—because all they had to do was believe in the Messiah,—this Yeshu!"

Isaac smiled. "No circumcision. No mikvah. No kosher food. No Sabbath observance."

"That's right," the Rabbi said. "So they followed Saul and became the backbone of the church that he organized, in every town in the Diaspora. In ancient Corinth. In Philippi. In Thessalonika. And finally, in Rome! And three hundred years later, the Emperor Constantine converted to Christianity—and declared it the official religion of the Roman Empire! And then came the Crusades, the pogroms and—and the Holocaust."

Isaac shook his head. "But Rabbi, can you blame all that evil on the God-fearing Gentiles? Weren't they good people in the eyes of God?"

"Many of them were," he replied.

"And so is Samira," Isaac said.

Rabbi Abram went silent. Something in his mind prevented him from giving his yeshiva boy a simple answer to that question.

"Rabbi Abram?"

"Yitzak," the Rabbi said at last, "I have a sneaking suspicion about that woman."

"Oh, no," Isaac said. "Not Samira!"

"Wait a minute," the Rabbi told him. "Yes, she is a God-fearing Gentile. And she claims to worship the Holy One of Israel. But she prays to God through the spirit of this messiah of theirs. And that sounds to me like a false god."

"No, no, Rabbi," Isaac protested. "It isn't always forbidden to speak in a prayerful fashion to a spirit that is holy. Remember when Yaacov wrestled with the angel? Didn't he ask, prayerfully, for his blessing?"

The Rabbi just looked at his yeshiva boy.

"And what about the *Mamre*?" Isaac went on. "When Abraham was living in Mamre, he was visited by three men—and one of them turned out to be the Lord, in the flesh! And the Lord said that Abraham and Sara's prayers for a son would be answered in the coming year."

"Yitzak," the Rabbi said, rising from his chair, "we are getting into a theological thicket here, and it's almost my bed time."

Isaac also arose from his chair and pushed it under the table.

"Let me just say this—and you think about it," the Rabbi said. "Every Christian wants to spread their religion to others, including Jews—*especially* Jews! And somewhere deep down inside of me, I don't trust that Arab woman. She may mean well now—just as those ancient God-fearers did when they hung around our synagogues as our friends. But in the end, their community turned against us."

As they walked from the dining room, Isaac asked one final question.

"Rabbi," he said, "we should judge people by their fruits. And so far, Samira has borne good fruit. She would never harm another person. Especially having gone through what she went through—with the killing of her dear mother! And yet, she seems to bear no animosity whatsoever against those who caused it to happen. She has a forgiving heart."

"And so?" the Rabbi asked.

"And so," Isaac said, "I have to ask myself why God is so good to this woman if indeed she is an idolater by worshiping a false god, as forbidden by the First Commandment?"

"A good question," the Rabbi replied. "In due time, we may very well find the answer. Good night, Yitzy."

"Good night, Rabbi."

As he stood in the stairway of the yeshiva, gazing out the window at the dimly lit Mount of Olives in the distance, Isaac Cohen asked himself a question that had occurred to him numerous times in his life. Never had he confided in anyone about this unthinkable question.

What, he wondered, would be the consequences for the Jewish people if their Messiah actually had come . . . and they had failed to recognize him?

Chapter 15

Christ Church, and the Salvation of the Jews

For the Jew, faith is not the beginning but the reward for Torah living. One does not begin with faith; faith follows.

— *A Woman of Valour*, published by the Lubavitch Foundation, 1976

JERUSALEM

Christ Church is across from David's Citadel, just down the street from Munir MaTouk's falafel stand. I used to pray here while in Jerusalem, and I imagined that whenever Samira came here, she too liked to sit in the front row, where she could gaze at the wooden altar, carved in Hebrew with the name "Emmanuel" and Yeshua's instruction at the Last Supper, "Do This in My Memory."

I would also say that Samira, too, loved the simplicity of the arched, white-stone church. Built by the English in 1843, it was originally named Hebrew Christ Church and had no cross or other Christian symbols, so that Jews would feel more at home. In fact, the Star of David could be seen in the stained-glass windows. But Samira wasn't in favor of converting Jews to Christianity. All she longed to see was the Jewish people accepting Yeshua of Nazareth as Messiah and fitting Him into their own religion, just as the first Jewish believers did 2,000 years ago.

"And so all Israel will be saved," the Apostle Paul (Rabbi Sha'ul) had told the Romans, leaving us with a promise so mysterious yet so tantalizing that theologians have wrestled with its meaning for two

157

millennia. The salvation of the Jews is about more than each Jew getting his or her ticket punched for entry into heaven (as supremely important as that is). God also has in mind what the rabbis refer to as corporate or collective salvation—the restoration of the royal nation of priests who are to be the final teachers of humankind during the last days before Messiah's coming . . .

Samira won't be here at church tonight.

As the prayer meeting begins, we are all singing the hymn, "Holy, Holy, Holy," from the Christian Book of Revelation (NIV), based on Isaiah 6:3, in which four heavenly creatures were chanting before the throne of God:

> *Holy, holy, holy is the Lord God Almighty,*
> *Who was, and is, and is to come!*

Our hymn continues with the words of the twenty-four elders, who then fell down before God and laid their crowns before the throne:

> *You are worthy, our Lord and God,*
> *to receive glory and honor and power,*
> *for You created all things,*
> *and by Your will they were created*
> *and have their being.*

A woman named Christine takes the pulpit and begins talking about being in the garden of the Lord. Quoting loosely from the *Song of Solomon*, she says: "Take me away with You! Like an apple tree is my Beloved . . . I delight to sit in His shadow, in the shadow of the Cross." Once she had found her Savior, she recalls, "I held Him and would not let Him go."

Then Christine looks up from her Bible and speaks directly to us.

"He wants to have an intimate relationship with you. Give Him time to tell you what's on His mind. Be totally quiet in the Word of God. We *don't* go to Him to develop *our own* resources."

She pauses.

"You are a garden fountain, a well of flowing water streaming down from Lebanon. Then let it flow off you to other people. It delights Him when we put ourselves under the flow. I have come into my garden . . . eat and drink your fill. He's waiting! Don't go in a rush—go for a morning or for a day with Him. My Beloved has gone down to His garden . . . to browse . . . He's not in a hurry."

Some of the people are praying in the Spirit, softly, as Christine continues: "Your eyes are the pools of Heshbon, reflecting His light. Only *quiet* waters can *reflect* . . ."

Another pause.

"Who is this coming up from the desert, leaning on her Beloved? What great gain there is in losing all earthly support and leaning only on the Lord!"

Now we all stand and sing the song, "Shout to the Lord!"— popularized worldwide by the Australian music group Hillsong.

After the people take turns voicing their prayer requests, I have an inner urge to go up and share my "testimony" about how my life has been changed through belief in Yeshua of Nazareth, Messiah of Israel. But as usual, I remain seated. Instead, in my mind's eye, a man looking just like me arises from his pew and walks up to the altar.

The man begins by saying that he was once tempted to go outside his home for the love that he craved. He says he used to pray earnestly to God, asking why he had been created as a healthy young man with the normal desires of a husband, only to be spurned. He also mentions that it was his practice each night, after coming home from work, to make himself a whiskey drink before dinner.

But one night, he says, he came home from work and decided to go immediately to a charismatic prayer meeting that he had heard about. Toward the end of that meeting, all fifty Christians stood and raised their hands and prayed as one for the Holy Spirit to come down upon them. Men and women were praying in the Spirit, or simply singing their praises to the Holy One of Israel.

"You know," the man tells his listeners tonight in Christ Church, "God dwells in the praises of Israel!"

As the man continues his story, he gazes up at the white arched ceiling of the church, spreads his hands, and speaks slowly, his words penetrating the congregation to the last pew. He recalls that the loud sounds of all the men and women praying that night—at first a cacophony of individual cries—gradually melded into a symphony that lifted them higher and higher into heavenly places, until at last he felt that he had pierced the clouds and was praying with his brothers and sisters, as one, before the very throne of God! It was then that he realized that yes, he had been created as a man suited for love making, but now he was virtually making love with the Creator! And it was a love that he had been born for, a love that far surpassed anything he had ever experienced in his life!

Now the people in Christ Church are on their feet, clapping their hands and giving all the glory to God for what He had done for this man.

"As it says in the Letter to the Hebrews," the man adds, *". . . You have tasted the heavenly gift, and have become partaker of the Holy Spirit. And you have tasted the good Word of God, and the powers of the age to come"* (See NKJV).

Just as the man is about to step away from the pulpit, amid the cheers and the tongues, something stops him, and he signals for silence.

"I have to tell you one more thing," he says quietly. "When I got home that night, filled with the Holy Spirit, I found myself alone in the dark house. Suddenly I remembered that I hadn't had my drink tonight. So I poured a whiskey and took a sip. It tasted like bitter medicine! I added ginger ale and stirred it into the drink and took a sip. It still tasted horrible. I poured it down the sink and went to bed."

. . . It was the kind of testimony that Samira would have loved to hear, if only she had come tonight. Lately, however, her concern had centered on the salvation of the Jews, especially Israelis like Simon who didn't even believe in God, much less His Son, the Messiah. In addition to wanting the man she loved to spend eternity with God and His people, she also wanted Simon to become a believer so that she might someday become his wife—his dark-skinned Shulamite from the *Song of Solomon.*

But the New Testament forbade Christians to marry non-believers, warning against expecting them to eventually come to accept Yeshua, after years of being married to a believer. Noor, too, had warned her about this problem, even while encouraging Samira in her love for the soldier who guarded the Western Wall. "Do not yoke yourselves together in a team with unbelievers," Paul/Sha'ul had told the believers at Corinth. "What does a believer have in common with an unbeliever?" And what of her friend Simon's fate as an unbeliever? What would happen to him at the moment of his death? Yeshua had said most plainly, "I am the way, the truth and the life. No one comes to the Father, except through Me."

The question of whether God would accept a penitent and righteous person into heaven without a specific acceptance of Jesus as Savior of the world has rattled Christian theologians for centuries. Especially in the case of Israel, God's chosen people.

"Did God reject His people? By no means!" the Apostle Paul declares in his Letter to the Romans:

Most of the Jews have not found the favor of God they are looking for. A few have—the ones God has picked out—but the eyes of the others have been blinded.

God gave them a spirit of stupor, eyes so that they could not see and ears so that they could not hear, to this very day. — Isaiah 29:10

This is what our Scriptures refer to when they say that God has put them to sleep, shutting their eyes and ears so that they do not understand what we are talking about when we tell them of Christ.

I will provoke them to jealousy by those who are not a nation — Deuteronomy. 32:21

Does this mean that God has rejected his Jewish people forever? Of course not! His purpose was to make his salvation available to the Gentiles, and then the Jews would be jealous and begin to want God's salvation for themselves. Now if the whole world became rich as a result of God's offer of salvation, when the Jews stumbled over it and turned it down, think how much greater a blessing the world will share in later on when the Jews, too, come to Christ. — Romans 11:7–12 (Living Bible)

Samira found comfort in this. Yes, the church had taken up Israel's burden as a light to the nations, but only temporarily, until the time of the Gentiles be over and Israel be restored to her homeland and come to recognize her Messiah. Tragically, the church had presumed itself to have inherited Israel's role in history for all time. (So had the early Muslims, who built the Dome of the Rock on the foundation of the Jewish Temple that Israel's God had not saved from destruction.)

In the meantime, Samira knew that, outside of Christ Church, some teachers had suggested that the Father would be merciful to those who had sought Him with all their heart but had not known about Yeshua. Anyone who would have accepted Yeshua, *had he or she only known*, would be recognized by the all-knowing God as one of His own. In fact

Samira even wondered to herself whether the Father—who had allowed scales to blind the eyes of most of the Jews to His Son—would remove them today for Jews, somewhere on their journey between death and the hereafter, to see whether they would accept their Messiah at last.

But Samira wasn't entirely comfortable with such lenient theology, for she wanted to take the Scriptures literally wherever possible. Yeshua's warning kept coming back, again and again: "I am the way, the truth and the life. No one comes to the Father except through Me." At times she found this a terrifying truth, because her own father hadn't yet accepted it, even though he and other Muslims revered Yeshua as a great prophet. As for those who didn't know enough to follow this command, Samira's own teachers simply suggested that God would offer them an opportunity to repent of their sins and choose Yeshua as their Savior before their death. The Father would accept Jews even if they acknowledged Yeshua with their final breath (after reciting the *Shema* for the last time).

Once, when Samira was discussing the Holocaust with Isaac Cohen, he told her that the six million Jews who perished—more than a million of them children—were all accepted by God as martyrs, who had sanctified God's name by dying as His people. That's what Judaism taught . . .

*

Rabbi Abram and other *baal t'shuvah* teachers blame the Holocaust for the great falling away of the Jewish people from their God. But the process of assimilation was well on its way long before the rise of Nazi Germany. During the 1920s the International Hebrew Christian Alliance—active in 18 countries on four continents—was keeping its hand on the pulse of European Jewry. In 1928, a Dr. Deszo Foldes delivered a paper during an Alliance conference in Hamburg, Germany, titled "The Religious Position of the Jews in Hungary." The 'Emancipation'—the loosening of restrictions on Jews in the emerging European nations—had brought Jews out of their ghettoes and allowed them to live in Gentile society and attend public schools and universities. Now, in 1928, a few decades later . . .

> This sudden change and unforeseen contact with Christian knowledge and culture has altered to a great degree the Jew's ideas of the world, his consciousness of life in general, and his perception of Judaism, and in this way an undoubted religious indifference was brought

about. . . . The Jewish belief and the traditions of the Talmud which had taken root through the centuries—of which they gave practical proof by the minutest observance of all rabbinical and statutory orders—lost their power . . .

We must confirm the sad fact that Hungarian Judaism as well as Judaism in general all over Europe shows, in the last ten years, with regard to religion, a distinct weakening.

The author then points out that "polarization," as we would call it today, was already taking place between religious and secularized Jews in pre-Holocaust Europe:

We find amongst these groups on the one side an Orthodox conservative intolerance against the flood of modern culture . . . and convulsively clinging to their old established views; on the other side there exists an enlightened body of intelligent Jews who—after they have thrown off the fetters of Talmudism . . . and when they have progressed intellectually, economically, and socially—[it turns out that] unbelief and atheism more and more pursue their course, and they still further lose their association with Jewish religion and the Jewish nation . . .

This is what is occurring universally today in united Judaism.

Many Jews, through their free contact with Christianity in Germany and Poland and a host of other European countries, were joining Christian communities. The Hebrew Christian Alliance was determined to avert the tragedies of past centuries in which Jews accepting Jesus joined a denominational church and forgot their Jewish heritage. The Alliance was considering the formation of a 'Hebrew Christian Church,' which would replicate the First Century Church that sprang up in Jerusalem, where Jews accepting Yeshua as the Messiah continued to follow virtually all the rules and ceremonies of Judaism. The Holocaust crushed any chance of such a church being formed in Europe. Much later, starting in the 1970s, the Messianic Jewish Alliance of America (MJAA) became a kind of godmother over scores of 'messianic synagogues' throughout America and around the world, including Israel, gathering Jews (and Zionist-minded Gentiles) in worship communities that retained Judaic trappings, in varying degrees; retaining, for example, the Torah reading and Haftorah reading each Sabbath, while adding a *B'rith Chadoshah* reading from the New Testament. In this way, secular Jews recognizing Yeshua of Nazareth as the Messiah retained (and often strengthened) their bond to their Jewish heritage—although often enduring excommunication from their religiously observant families (Messianic Judaism hasn't been recognized as a Jewish denomination by traditional Jewry). And so, in 1928, this Dr. Foldes was struggling with how to minister to emancipated Jews open to the Messiah now that they had left the old Jewish ghettoes and were becoming forgetful of their Jewishness.

> It will be our mission to advance and hasten those approaching the healing process of the spirit of the Gospel. I am not thinking here of conversion or baptism, for we must be extremely careful about these subjects, and recognize the many elementary [freedoms] of the Jews to the independent formation of their religious life.

> We must attempt nothing that appears like strong influence, but we must encourage the independent strength of Judaism to remain in its comprehending spiritual truth, declaring the same to the world.

> Not human work, not human art, but the constantly operating Holy Spirit of God will accomplish the work of the spiritual development of Judaism, the knowledge of the truths of Christianity, and the Messiahship of Jesus Christ.

In 1932 the Hebrew Christian Alliance, based in Britain, had Continental chapters in Germany, Austria, Hungary, Poland, Latvia, Russia, Switzerland, Sweden, Denmark, Rumania, and Yugoslavia. It had acquired property in Jerusalem, within view of the Mount of Olives, for a Hebrew Christian colony to be called Abraham's Vineyard. All of the plans and dreams of the Alliance were shattered by the onset of World War II, and most of their members throughout Europe are believed to have perished in the Holocaust.

*

As Samira wrestled with the challenges of bringing Simon to Yeshua without compromising the soldier's Jewish heritage, she remembered how the New Testament told of two thieves who were crucified with Yeshua. The Bad Thief mocked the Lord, saying: "Aren't you the Messiah? Save yourself and us!" But the Good Thief defended the Messiah, acknowledging that He was innocent and begging: "Yeshua, remember me when You come into Your kingdom."

"Today," Yeshua replied, "you will be with Me in paradise."

Samira found this remarkable: The only person in the entire Bible who was told by the Savior of the world that he would enter heaven had never been baptized, never said the Lord's Prayer or the Sinner's Prayer, never received the Holy Spirit, never taken the Lord's Supper, never gone up for an altar call, and probably never read a single word of Scripture. Salvation, indeed, was in the hands of the Lord, not human theologians. As it said in Deuteronomy 29:29:

> *Things which are hidden belong to Adonai our God. But the things that have been revealed belong to us and our children forever, so that we can observe all the words of this Torah. (CJB)*

At the end of tonight's service, the people file out, into the night. Whenever Samira left this church, she always felt like she was floating her way down the street, all the way home to the falafel stand.

The Betrayal

The next day, late in the afternoon, Simon and Samira paid a visit to Isaac in the prayer and study room near the Wailing Wall. Isaac was still subdued from what had happened with the Red Heifer, and he only reluctantly let them in. He didn't invite them to sit at the study table, so they all stood.

"Itzak," Samira began, "when you hid me behind the curtain, you saved me from your angry Rabbi. But now I've learned what you did *after* that, and why I was able to walk away without harm."

Isaac looked down at the book-strewn table and said, "I did what I had to do."

Samira looked at Simon and then turned back to Isaac. "I believe you fell deliberately on the Red Heifer—so that your Rabbi would never go after me in the future," she told Isaac. "Isn't this how it happened?"

Isaac looked very uncomfortable. ". . . I don't feel at liberty to discuss the matter," he said quietly. "It's over now."

Simon spoke up: "Not exactly . . . Itzak."

Isaac looked at the soldier: "What do you mean?"

"Itzak," Simon told him, "it took a lot of courage for you to fall on top of the Red Heifer and smear your own reputation." There was an awkward pause. Finally, Simon spoke again: "Itzak, I'm not a religious man like you—"

"—It's never too late to repent and make *t'shuvah*," Isaac retorted.

"Itzak," the soldier said, and he sighed in exasperation. "I think back to the days we shared together during Peace Now . . ." Here he glanced at Samira. "And I realize that we now live in two different worlds. But I want you to know that I am still a Jew."

"Of course!" the yeshiva boy said. "A Jew never stops being a Jew."

"Yes!" Simon continued. "And, as far as your being a 'black hat'— being so religious—there are some things that I really *want* to believe the way you do—but can't." Here Simon paused, and he seemed to be going through some turmoil as he tried to choose his next words. "I have the conscience of a Jew," he said. "And that's why I'm here. I . . . I must tell you the truth."

"About what?" Isaac said.

"Itzak!" the soldier said, and paused. But then he summoned the courage to say it. "I know you may never forgive me for this. But I must confess the truth to you. *Samira never touched the Red Heifer!*"

Isaac whispered to himself, "What?!"

"I lied to you, Itzak," Simon said. "Never mind why . . ."

The yeshiva boy stared at the soldier, stunned. ". . . Is this the truth?" he finally asked.

Samira raised her hands toward Isaac and said, "Yes, Itzak." Pain was on her face.

". . . Do you swear it?" Isaac said, looking at both of them.

Taking a small prayer book from a pocket of his uniform, Simon held it in his hands and said, "I solemnly swear, Itzak, I am telling you the truth."

"I'm sorry, Itzak," Samira said. Then she and Simon turned and left the prayer room.

Alone, Isaac began to walk slowly in a circle around the table piled with prayer books, whispering to himself, "**I** was the one . . . **I** was the one after all!"

Then the yeshiva boy cried out in a loud voice of anguish. Feeling suffocated, he ran out of the prayer room and escaped to the outdoors for fresh air. Within a few moments he was standing at the Wailing Wall, and the sun was going down. At the Wall, he tore his garments and rubbed his face with dirt from the ground. Then he pressed his face against the ancient Wall and sobbed.

*

After nearly an hour, when darkness had fallen, Isaac was alone. He stepped away from the Wall and looked up to see a full moon shining above the Temple Mount.

"O Jerusalem, holy city," he said out loud. "The Lord once said to His disobedient people, whom He had scattered—'I will gather you from all the countries, and return you to your own soil. Then I will sprinkle clean water on you'—the water of purification!—'I will cleanse you from all your uncleanness and from all your idols. I will give you a new heart and put a new spirit inside you.' Then the Holy Spirit—the Shekinah Cloud of God's Glory—will return and dwell in the *hearts* of His people!"

Suddenly Isaac rushed to the staircase and began to climb up the steps leading to the Temple Mount.

"O God," he cried out, "You are My God; I will seek you eagerly. My soul thirsts for You, my body longs for You in a land parched and exhausted." Looking up toward where the Temple once stood, he said, "I long to contemplate You in the sanctuary, seeing Your power and glory . . . In Your name will I lift up my hands—to You who dwell *forever* in the praises of Israel!"

Isaac continued his climb, almost to the top step.

"When will You send Your Messiah?" he asked. "I will offer sacrifices of joy in His Temple; I will sing, yes, I will sing praises to the Lord!"

At the very top step, Isaac stretched out his hands toward the Temple Mount.

"In the future, peoples and inhabitants of many cities will come," he said. "When that time comes, ten men will grab hold of the cloak of a Jew and say, *We want to go with you, because we have heard that God is with you.*"

Sadly, Isaac resisted the temptation to enter the forbidden Temple Mount. As he stood there, shivering in the night, he remembered what the Kabbalah said about the Shekinah—how she returned at night to the Holy of Holies and—seeing how the spot had been defiled and made desolate—raised her voice and cried bitterly. She would even repeat the words from the *Song of Solomon*, where the Bride calls out to her Divine Bridegroom for unity.

Then Isaac turned and began climbing back down the steps.

"My heart is broken," the yeshiva boy cried as he recalled the words of the Prophet Daniel, while in exile in Babylon. "We have no sacrifice to offer the Lord, and no altar on which to offer it, in order to find favor with God. But with contrite heart and humble spirit, let us be received, as though we were offering a thousand lambs and heifers in the Temple. Let us follow the Lord with our whole heart.'"

Isaac was back on the ground now and was walking along the Wailing Wall.

Suddenly he stopped as he saw a figure approaching him in the night.

It was Samira.

She stopped several steps before him, and they looked at each other in silence for a long time. Then she said, "Yitzak, if I could only undo what has happened. It was never my idea to lie to you. Simon did it, without telling me."

"I know," he said softly, through his tears. "It's just—" and he stopped to wipe his face with his fingers. "It's just that I wanted Moshiach to come in my time."

"So do I, Yitzak," she said, calling him again by his Hebrew name.

"And—and—we were coming so close to making it happen. Because Rabbi Abram says we can't just sit by and wait for him to come. We've got to be working and working for him to come!"

"Yes," she said.

"You know . . . the Talmud says that a great sage was asked what he would do if he was out in the field, hoeing his crop, and suddenly received word that Moshiach had come."

"And what did he say?"

"He said—he said he would keep right on with his hoeing—because we're all supposed to be working to repair the world *already*—and we can't suddenly start doing it when it's too late and he's already here!"

Samira choked back a sob. She wanted so much to reach out and hug her old childhood friend. But Orthodox men forbade themselves to touch a grown woman unless she was family.

"The Lord knows full well your devotion to Moshiach," Samira told him. "You *can* work for the coming of His kingdom."

"But what can I do *now*?" Isaac said. "Now that the Red Heifer is no longer kosher, and we don't know how or where to find another one."

Taking in a deep breath, Samira told her friend what she would tell anyone seeking to become born again.

"Religion is more than ethics," she began. "Even atheists have ethics of their own, including some of the Ten Commandments. But religion is really about worship, Yitzak. You want to become as close to God as you possibly can."

"It's called *kavanah*," Isaac said. "Rabbi talks about it now and then."

"But what does he do about it?" she asked. "How close can he be to God if he was willing to go crazy and chase me with a knife?"

"He made *t'shuvah*," Isaac said.

"Yes," Samira said, "and that's fine. Now, what about you? What are you doing to come closer to God? Do you see Him not only as your Creator but also as your Redeemer?"

"Of course," Isaac replied. "We refer to Him as our Redeemer every day after saying the *Shema*—and in the seventh benediction of the *Amidah*."

"Can you pray to the Lord, addressing Him as your Redeemer, and ask Him to lift you up on high?"

Isaac thought a moment. "We lift our prayers on high," he added, "because God dwells in the praises of Israel."

"Yes!" Samira exclaimed. "When we do that, Yitzak, we are presenting ourselves as a living sacrifice—which is much better than offering an animal to be slaughtered on an altar."

"Well," he replied, "Rabbi Yerucham Levovitz said that our soul is also called our glory, because our only function in the universe is to glorify God."

"That's what I mean by a perfect sacrifice," Samira said.

"In fact," Isaac continued, "the Talmud says that when Moshiach comes and is present in his Temple, the only sacrifices offered will be for praise and for thanksgiving."

"I believe that," she said. "We should praise God all day long, without ceasing. The Temple once contained the Glory of God, hidden inside the Holy of Holies. But now it's gone. And we believe that when Messiah comes, the Temple will again be filled with the very Presence of God, our Redeemer!"

"Yes," Isaac said. And now he had another idea. "In the Talmud," he said, "in *Sanhedrin 22a*, Rabbi Hana Ben Bizra says—in the name of Rabbi Shimon the Pious—that when we pray we should regard ourselves as if the Shekinah, the Divine Presence, were standing before us—as it is written, 'I have set the Lord before me always.'"

But then the yeshiva boy turned sad again.

"The only thing is . . ." he began, "what if we lose it again?"

Before Samira's very eyes, Isaac went into a trance and, his eyes gleaming, and he began paraphrasing from Ezekiel 8:5-18:

"King Solomon built the Temple," Isaac said slowly, as if in a daze, "but there came a day when Solomon began to worship false gods. And some of the people followed him. This offended the Lord. Until now, God's Cloud of Glory had dwelled deep inside the Temple. But one day, there were twenty-five Jewish men standing with their backs toward the Temple and their faces toward the east, and they were worshiping the sun. And so, the Lord's Cloud of Glory departed from the Temple. It floated up from the city and stood on the Mount of Olives. And it waited. But still the people worshiped the sun. Then the Shekinah Glory of God departed, taking away the Lord's protection of the Temple and Jerusalem. Never to return, to this very day."

Isaac broke down and began sobbing uncontrollably. Samira took out her handkerchief and carefully reached out to wipe her friend's tears. "Tears of sorrow in the evening," she said, "followed by tears of joy in the morning."

Giving back her handkerchief, Isaac said, "My tears are my food, day and night—while all the people ask me, *'Where is your God?'*"

"Psalm 42," she whispered to herself.

"I recall, as my feelings well up within me," Isaac said, "how I'd go with the crowd to the house of God, with *sounds of joy and praise* from the throngs observing the festival!" (CJB).

Isaac walked away from her, his eyes half shut, and began wandering in the plaza below the Wailing Wall, reciting the rest of the psalm. "My soul, why are you so downcast?" he said. "Why are you groaning inside me? Hope in God, since I will praise Him again for the salvation that comes from his presence!'"

Samira began walking back home.

But Isaac continued to pray, still in his trace, wandering in little circles across the plaza.

"No, the destruction of the Temple by the Romans was *not* the greatest tragedy for our ancestors," Isaac was saying to himself in the night. "The greatest catastrophe for all of us—and for the whole world!—happened much earlier—when God's Cloud of Glory departed from *this spot* . . . never to return."

Walking away from the Wall, Isaac opened his eyes and made his way to the path that would lead him through the Old City and to his room. But he turned back once more to behold the Wailing Wall, and the Temple Mount above it, with the full moon shining brightly in the night sky. And he remembered a prophecy made in 572 BC, nineteen years after Ezekiel had seen the Shekinah departing from the Temple.

"Then the man—whose appearance was like bronze—brought me to the gate that faces the east. And behold, <u>the glory of the God of Israel came from the east.</u> His voice was like the sound of many waters. Then <u>the glory of the Lord came into the Temple by the Eastern Gate.</u> The Spirit lifted me up and brought me into the inner court; and behold, the Shekinah of the Lord filled the Temple! And he said, 'Son of man, this is the place of My throne—where I will dwell in the midst of the children of Israel forever!'" (Ezekiel 43:1–9)

In the distance, the yeshiva boy thought he could hear the triumphant sound of the shofar horn.

Chapter 16

Alan Dershowitz and Shabbat At Mishkenot Sha'ananim

JERUSALEM

All across the Land of Israel in 1998, people young and old, secular and religious, Jew and Gentile, were talking about what might happen if a genuine, kosher red heifer were found in our time. Only a few of them had heard parts of my story of how Rabbi Abram was raising a red heifer and watching carefully for blemishes or white hairs before her third birthday, when she might be slaughtered if found to be still kosher.

[Alan Dershowitz] and his wife were having breakfast one Sunday morning at Mishkenot Sha'ananim (Serene Dwellings), the city of Jerusalem's guesthouse for writers, musicians and artists. Its windmill can be seen from blocks around. In the sunny breakfast patio this morning, guests helped themselves to eggs and toasted bagels, fresh tomatoes and cucumbers, cottage cheese and yogurt, watermelon, oranges, grapes, bitter olives, pickled herring and other fish choices.

At his table, Dershowitz was being interviewed about a new book he had just completed. I listened from the next table, where I was having breakfast during my stay here. The reporter was suggesting that Dershowitz was now **the** Jewish lawyer in the world today. I smiled to myself, because the supremely self-assured Dershowitz was having a hard time finding the words to deny it . . .

Dershowitz is a lawyer's lawyer and has no interest in the law of the red heifer. Born in Brooklyn and raised an Orthodox Jew, he boasted in his autobiography, *Chutzpah*, about "my gradual transition from passive observance of (Jewish) ritual to active participation in causes."

He has defended disgraced football legend O.J. Simpson, felonious fighter Mike Tyson, Israeli spy Jonathan Pollard, and race-baiting Rabbi Meir Kahane. And if Hitler were to turn up alive and face trial without a lawyer, Dershowitz told a reporter, he would take his case, although "holding my nose and feeling horrible about it."

A champion of free speech, Dershowitz mentioned the Batsheva controversy, which had exploded in the cultural wars between secular and religious Israelis during his stay in Israel. The famous Batsheva Dance Troupe had been invited to perform during a gala celebration of the 50th anniversary of the State of Israel. At the last minute, the government of Benjamin Netanyahu—which relied heavily on the Orthodox—discovered that the dance troupe intended to conclude its performance in its usual way—by disrobing. Officials tried to persuade the dancers to wear tights underneath their costumes, but Batsheva angrily pulled out of the event.

"We Protest the Attack on Creativity," said a banner carried in the protest rally in Tel Aviv by the arts community, whose ranks were swollen by activists on the Left who resented the religious.

"Modern dance," the *Jerusalem Post* editorialized, "to all but its adherents, is a strange language that to the uninitiated is likely to provoke a variety of reactions, ranging from amusement to outrage. When the dance is set to a song from the *Haggada* (Passover narrative), which invokes the name of God, and the dancers disrobe, albeit not completely, one does not need the vision of Theodor Herzl to realize that this has the potential to offend not just the *haredi* [ultra-Orthodox] world—for whom performances in which women sing in front of men are anathema—but also a sizable portion of the modern Orthodox community."

During the many days of public outrage by the secular community, Mayor Ronni Milo of Tel Aviv vowed to run for prime minister without seeking the support of the Orthodox—a political feat that has never been pulled off by anyone to this very day.

"Take the Batsheva Dance group," Dershowitz was telling his interviewer in the breakfast patio, as he searched for a possible legal defense for the Netanyahu government's ultimatum to the dancers to wear tights. "You can take the argument that the government would have fallen, and that would have been a national security issue. You can turn anything into national security."

He continued: "I have no question that if the dance group—instead of having done something offensive to the *haredim*—had done something

174

that was offensive to the Left in Israel, the Left would have demanded censorship . . . They're both pro free speech when their speech is being involved."

The following Saturday I was having breakfast in the patio with a beautiful poetess who edits poetry and her companion, a handsome poet from Tel Aviv. They liked to join others at Mishkenot Sha'ananim every Saturday to share the creative process of poetry. The man, who was smoking a cigarette, was in no rush for the Temple to be rebuilt or for the Messiah to come.

"To a secular Israeli, the red heifer would spell the end of democracy in Israel," he said. "If you have the red heifer, you don't need democracy anymore. You will have a theocracy."

*

Here at Mishkenot Sha'ananim, Saul Bellow conceived and wrote *To Jerusalem and Back* in 1976. Others who have stayed in these Serene Dwellings include writers Elie Wiesel and Graham Greene, musicians Pablo Casals, Arthur Rubenstein and Isaac Stern, artists Alexander Calder and Marc Chagall. Its garden-like location in the middle of the city's 'Cultural Mile' puts it within walking distance of the Cinematheque, the Khan Theatre, the Jerusalem Centre for the Performing Arts, the Jerusalem Music Centre, and a host of other cultural resources.

The windmill and main building was commissioned by the British philanthropist Sir Moses Montefiore and was completed in 1861. As the first residential settlement outside the Old City's walls in modern times, it marked the beginning of modern Western Jerusalem.

Mishkenot Sha'ananim was abandoned during the 19 years of Jordanian rule over the West Bank, which placed it right on the 'Jordanian border' and attracted fire from enemy snipers. After the Six Day War it was renovated with the help of the Jerusalem Foundation. Since then it has become not only a peaceful place for quiet study, but a discreet meeting place for Israeli and Palestinian leaders, fostering cordial, informal working relationships.

*

That Sabbath at Mishkenot Sha'ananim, I returned from breakfast to my room and soon found myself lounging on the long veranda facing the Old City, which is just a short walk across the valley from here. After thumbing through the entry on Redemption, in Volume 14 of the *Encyclopedia Judaica* in the hallway, I wandered down to the far end of the veranda to eavesdrop on a family that was celebrating a leisurely Shabbat on the upper porch of the house across from the hedges. The sounds coming from their porch so intrigued me that I crept up the stone steps leading to my roof so I could be closer. I said my prayers as the Sabbath keepers picked on their food and, now and then, at the suggestion of one member, they spontaneously broke out in yet another Hebrew song, clapping their hands and making a joyful noise to the Holy One of Israel. I longed to be up there with them—or just to catch a glimpse of them—but they were in a world I could not enter—for they were God's people, rejoicing in their return to the Land on this Sabbath.

In mid-afternoon I went inside to put on a long-sleeved shirt so I could continue to enjoy the wonderful breeze on the veranda. The day was overcast but the sunlight was still pretty bright. I thought I heard a cardinal chirping loudly in the tall arbor vidi evergreen tree that was entwined with painted leaves, but I never saw the bird that the Cardinale family reveres back in America.

At 5 o'clock I found myself deep in the olive garden above Mishkenot Sha'ananim, asking myself yet again: With whom may I share this beauty? *Won't You send me a woman to love, a woman I can marry?* Perhaps this is a godly loneliness, I told myself. Maybe He created the universe first, then asked: With whom may I share all this? And then was born Love . . . which I would finally experience seven years later, when I married Shirah.

I heard crickets in the dense underbrush. Birds. Children's cries. Church bells. Then I climbed to my favorite overlook spot, with its slim olive tree. My little bricked nook juts out far enough to give a view of Mishkenot Sha'ananim to the left and the Old City in the distance. Now a Shabbat group was walking past my perch, conversing in Hebrew . . . that language that almost died after being confined for two thousand years to the pages of Bibles, Talmud tractates and prayer books.

Growing restless in the late afternoon (was all of this really 'inactivity'?), I took a walk around the curved bridge leading to the Cinematique. Looking down into the grassy canyon, I saw a horse and rider, followed by a barebacked horse, galloping along the bottom of the Hinnom Valley. In this valley, even up to the time of Christ, fires smoldered day and night with the refuse dumped here by Jerusalemites, inspiring the Greek name *Gehenna*, transliterated from the Hebrew *Hinnom*. Also in this valley, human sacrifices had been offered to Molech by pagan tribes . . . suggesting to me a demonic mockery of the blood sacrifices that God would someday require in the Jewish Temple . . . and a mockery of the ultimate sacrifice of atonement by the Messiah, here in Zion.

Back in the olive grove, I sat on Johnny's Bench, with the carving in its wood honoring John Rubens, "a dear friend of Jerusalem," on his 80th birthday. As I leaned back on the bench and crossed one leg over the other, as my Dad used to do, I pictured him and tried to remember what he was doing when *he* was my age . . . certainly not sojourning comfortably in Israel.

I remembered how I'd struggled before taking this second journey to Jerusalem. One day, while walking down a hall in the city library, I'd been drawn into a dark room where a film was just ending. Elie Wiesel was wrapping up his narration with words to the following effect: Once you have been to Jerusalem, you will never be the same. And once you have been to Jerusalem, she too will never be complete without you. Tears came to my eyes, and I knew that I would return again and again.

The Lovers Quarrel

The next day, Samira and Simon were walking through the streets of the Old City, locked arm in arm, now and then pausing to embrace. Outside the Dung Gate, they stopped on a grassy spot overlooking the Kidron Valley (or Valley of Jehoshaphat) and opened Simon's backpack. They shared a lunch of *shwarma,* slices of mutton roasted by Munir on a vertical spit and then stuffed into *pita* bread with salad. They washed it down with red wine, which Simon had already started sipping on their way here.

Simon kissed Samira on the cheek, and she returned his kiss. Now they were in a deep embrace, kissing on the lips.

"Does your father know that you have been kissing a Jew?" said Simon, before taking another sip from the bottle of wine.

"Simon, you've had too much wine!" Samira exclaimed, smiling. "Still, the Arabs and the Jews are *cousins*, aren't we?"

"Kissing cousins!" Simon said, and they both laughed.

As he lifted the bottle to take another drink, she said, "Simon, you still haven't told me where you were the past two years."

"I told you," he said, "in the Golan Heights."

"But why were you there?" she asked. "You're not in the Golan Brigade."

"You might call it a special assignment," he said.

Touching his face, Samira asked, "Is that where you got this scar?"

"Yes—No!" he blurted.

"How did you get it, Simon?" she asked. "You can tell me."

Simon took a swig from nearly empty wine bottle and thought for a few moments. "All right," he began. "I was sent away after an incident here in Jerusalem. We were called out to put down a riot of young Palestinians."

"We want our land back," she said softly, as if to herself.

"You have your Israeli citizenship," he replied. "Since 1967."

"What about my relatives outside Jerusalem—on the West Bank?" she said. "They're not citizens of Israel. And the Israelis keep spreading new settlements on this Palestinian land."

"It's the Land of Israel," he insisted.

"You even have personal friends living in settlements—like in Tekoa, smack dab in the middle of Palestinian land!" she exclaimed.

"My friend Abraham HaCohen," he replied. Then he added, "Tekoa goes back to King Jehoshaphat, twenty-eight hundred years ago. It's always been our land."

"Oh?" Samira said sharply. "Who *gave* it to you?"

"Don't, Samira," he said. "We weren't going to let this come between us, remember?"

"Your rabbis say that *God* gave this land to you."

Simon turned the bottle over in his hands and said nothing.

"But—who do *you* say gave the land to you?" she asked. ". . . Simon?"

"Samira, please . . . The Jews have *always* needed a safe place to live, free from the hate of the world."

"You know, Simon," she said, "in all my reading on your religion, the most remarkable thing that I keep coming across is a certain teaching. It goes like this: You shall act justly toward the stranger who is living in your midst. For *you* were once strangers . . ."

"—in Egypt! Yes. We were slaves. But no more! And I have this scar to prove it!"

". . . Where did it happen?"

"Not far from here, just below the Temple Mount," he said. Simon had a very pained expression on his face, and he began speaking as if he were in a dream. "There were only a couple of us soldiers, and scores of young Palestinian men were beginning to surround us. They were burning tires and throwing stones, and some of them waving knives. Suddenly, I thought I saw an opportunity to divert them. I saw a ditch not far from us, and it was deep and nobody was near it. So I threw a grenade—but as it rolled toward the ditch, a little Arab child began running after it. The grenade looked like a toy! That's the kind of toys their parents give them to play with nowadays . . ."

Samira suddenly was trembling.

"That—that was my little cousin . . ." she said.

Still in his reverie, Simon took a final swig from the wine bottle, as if he hadn't heard her.

". . . and before anybody could do anything, an Arab woman ran after the boy, shouting—shouting the child's name . . . but he wouldn't stop. And then the woman threw herself on top of the boy—just before the grenade exploded."

"That . . . was my . . . mother . . ."

Slowly Samira rose to her feet, her eyes open wide, and, looking one last time at Simon, she hurried away. "I can't marry the soldier who killed my mother!" she screamed as she ran. "What a fool I was— to think I could marry an unbeliever!"

In a daze, Simon let the bottle drop to the grass with a dull thud.

"The Arabs beat me mercilessly," he said. "More soldiers arrived and drove them off, before they could kill me. I spent two months in the hospital in Tel Aviv. And the government promised me a settlement for my injuries. I still have the money coming. Then the army sent me to the Golan, where no Arab would recognize me."

In the distance, Munir was at the falafel stand when he heard his daughter crying out for him.

"Father! Father!"

"What is it, my daughter . . . ?"

*

That night, a masked figure dressed as a warrior, in an Arabic battle gown, stood on top of the Wailing Wall, his hands folded over his chest. After glaring down at the darkened plaza below, where Jews pray, he whipped out a huge Oriental sword, curved like the Crescent. In rhythm with the war drums and Jihad music in his mind, he slashed the air as he danced acrobatically along the top of the Wall.

When it was over, Munir recited this from the Qu'ran, Sura V:32:

"We decreed upon the Children of Israel that whoever kills a person—unless he kill because of a murder or because of corruption in the land—it is as if he had slain the whole people," he boomed. Then, quoting from Sura IX:5, he cried out: "Fight and slay the pagans wherever you find them. Capture them! Besiege them! Sit in wait for them at every place of ambush!"

His voice echoed in the night throughout the Jewish Quarter of the Old City.

*

Hearing this, Isaac came out of the study room and looked around. There was Simon, kneeling in the dark at the Wailing Wall, embracing the stones and weeping. Hesitating at first, Isaac bent down and laid a hand on Simon's shoulder.

180

Simon turned and, seeing his boyhood friend, pulled Isaac down in an embrace. Too distraught to speak, he whispered in Isaac's ear what had happened.

Isaac was not surprised.

"There is only one course of action, Simon," he said. "You must make *t'shuvah*."

"Repentance...."

"You probably don't remember the four points," Isaac told him. "You must feel regret—which I know you do. You must apologize—to both Samira and her father. You must change your ways. And you must offer restitution.

"Restitution?" Simon said, his voice hoarse. "How can I replace her mother? And his wife?"

"...Simon...I don't know."

"Oh, Itzak..."

"Remember," Isaac told him. "He who has gathered us back to the Land of Israel will surely *keep* us, as a shepherd his flock. God will give you an answer...Shalom..."

Isaac sadly walked away, and Simon resumed his mourning at the Wall.

Chapter 17

A Settler in Tekoa, on the 'West Bank'

TEKOA

Simon's friend Abraham HaCohen is most enthralled by the land, which he loves to roam day and night in Judea (on the West Bank), a few miles from Jerusalem.

HaCohen had a silver .45 pistol tucked in his belt, behind his back, when he climbed into his Jeep one night in May 1998 and drove out of Jerusalem. He was driving home to Tekoa, a desert settlement southeast of Bethlehem, in the Israeli-occupied West Bank. Bouncing over rutted roads in the night, he passed through four Arab villages before arriving home.

Located just about as far east as Israeli settlements go, Tekoa is on the edge of a desert, within sight of Mount Moab. The village of 300 families has no fence surrounding it. Arabs pelt the settlement with stones, but to HaCohen and his neighbors, not having a fence makes an important statement.

Tekoa has a mushroom packing plant, and a Russian immigrant has opened a computer software business here. The Tekoa Agro-Technology Farm was cited as Enterprise of the Year in 1989 by the Israeli *Journal of Agricultural Settlements*.

Among the crops grown here are grapes.

Amos the Prophet was a shepherd in Tekoa in ancient times. Now, inside Abraham and Shoshanna HaCohen's house in Tekoa is a poster quoting Amos: "They will plant vineyards and drink their wine; they will plant gardens and eat their fruit. I will plant Israel in their own land, never again to be uprooted."

"We make wine here," HaCohen says. "I have crushed it with my feet. The Temple, too, will be rebuilt by prophecy. I can't tell you how it's going to happen . . ." As a religious Jew—of the priestly line, no less—HaCohen takes the Scriptures literally and believes that the prophecy of Amos is coming true in our time.

Another prophet, Jeremiah, mentioned Tekoa when warning the inhabitants of Jerusalem to flee from the advancing Babylonian armies: "Sound the trumpet in Tekoa!" Jeremiah cried. "For disaster looms out of the north." Tekoa was one of the towns that had been fortified as a defense for Jerusalem.

Three centuries earlier, the armies of Moab, Ammon and Edom were attacking from present-day Jordan. It was in the wilderness of Tekoa that King Jehoshaphat exhorted the army of Judah to have faith in God and His prophets. Shortly after that, singers went out ahead of the army, praising the God of Israel, and the invaders were defeated. The rabbis teach that angels of the Lord so confused the enemy armies that they began attacking each other.

Today, Abraham HaCohen follows the teachings of Rabbi Zvi Yehuda Kook, the mentor of the Gush Emunim movement. It was founded in 1974, seven years after Judea, Samaria and Gaza were regained by Israel. This group has created settlement blocks of Jewish families on these "occupied territories," often in defiance of the Israeli government. More than 250,000 Jews now live there. Unlike Meir Kahane and his Kach Party, which wanted to remove the Arab residents, Gush Emunim envisioned Jews and Arabs living side by side on those lands—for the Messianic Age was about to unfold.

"We are in the middle of the Redemption," Kook wrote. "The Kingdom of Israel is being built anew. This is the revelation of the Kingdom of Heaven. The Israel Defense Force is total sanctity. It represents the rule of the people of the Lord on His land." He added: "The borders, these kilometers, are sacred and cannot be relinquished by those who consider themselves guardians of the entire Jewish people." He was referring to the leaders of modern-day Israel.

Rabbi Kook's father, Avraham Yitzak HaCohen Kook, had moved from Russia in 1904 and was elected the Ashkenazi chief rabbi of Palestine in 1921. He was the leader of Mizrachi, a group of religious Zionists who saw the return to the Land as "the beginning of the messianic process" and predicted that Jerusalem would become the center of the world. And he wrote: "All the civilizations of the world will be renewed by the renaissance of our spirit. All quarrels will be resolved and our revival will cause all life to be luminous with the joy of fresh birth."

The Talmud quotes the Book of Exodus—"And let them make Me a sanctuary, and I will dwell among *them*"—and asks why that sentence ends with the word *them* instead of *it*. The answer given is that the Shekinah left *it* (the Temple) but continued to dwell with *them* (the Jews) who kept the faith while scattered across the globe. The return of the Jews would bring the Divine Presence back to the Holy Land and bring Redemption to the whole world.

Sharing his vision of a rebuilt Temple, Kook went on:

"Here stands the Temple upon its foundation, to the honor and glory of all peoples and kingdoms, and here we joyfully bear the sheaves brought forth by the land of our delight, coming, our wine presses filled with grain and wine, our hearts glad over the goodness of this land of delight, and here before us appear the priests, holy men, servants of the Temple of the Lord God of Israel."

The elder Kook—who died in 1935—stressed the centrality of the land, and he passed this on to his son, Zvi. The mentor of Gush Emunim, Zvi once wrote that if the Israeli government were to attempt to remove all the Jewish settlers from their land on the West Bank, "a war of brothers may be required."

Walking outdoors tonight, under the stars in Tekoa—his silver pistol still tucked in his belt—HaCohen looks off into the distance. "You can't be frenetic out here, because the land itself is calming," he says quietly. "We're only twenty minutes from Jerusalem, but they don't have the lifestyle and quality of life that we have here."

If it weren't for the Muslim shrine on the Temple Mount, HaCohen adds, there would probably be more interest in rebuilding the Temple now. HaCohen is interested in the red heifer but is wary of the attempt by an American Pentecostal minister, Clyde Lott, to breed cattle on his ranch for this purpose. Rabbi Richman of the Temple Institute had long shown a keen interest in Lott's plan—even visiting him and finding Lott's Red Angus cattle most promising for breeding—but broke with him in late 1998, following Lott's legal and financial problems in Israel. The rabbi later referred to Evangelicals' end times interest in Israel as "doormat theology."

"We're all interested in the red heifer, to have the Third Temple," HaCohen says. "But I wouldn't give ten shekels to feed oats to the red heifer. It's not a fruit of Israel. The cow has to be born here."

*

Abraham HaCohen well remembers the events that led to the establishment of Jewish settlements in the "occupied territories" following the Six Day War. Cited for decades now as the main obstacle to peace, the settlements were inspired by a messianic vision going back two thousand years. But the settlements that sprang up after 1967 were also a political strategy to avoid a repeat of what had happened after the 1956 war in the Sinai desert. Egypt had nationalized the Suez Canal and closed the Straits of Tiran, isolating the port of Eilat at the southernmost point of Israel—and cutting off the Jewish state from its shipping lifeline to Asia through the Suez Canal. With the approval of Britain and France, Israel sent an invasion force under Chief of Staff Moshe Dayan, and the IDF captured the entire Sinai Peninsula in three days. But under pressure from the United States, Israel soon withdrew, having achieved its purpose of reopening the Suez Canal.

On the eve of the Six Day War, Dayan—ever the bold *sabra*—was determined to retain the bulk of any land that Israel might conquer as it prepared its pre-emptive attack against Egypt, which had amassed 120,000 troops in the very desert that Israel had returned to Egypt a decade earlier.

"Our basic aim will be the destruction of Israel," declared Egyptian President Gamal Abdul Nasser.

From the loudspeakers of the muezzin on the Dome of the Rock came the cry, "Take up your weapons and take back your country stolen by the Jews!"

Egypt had kicked out the United Nations peacekeeping force, which had been in the Sinai since the end of the 1956 war. Israel's return of the Sinai to Egypt in exchange for peace had been in vain.

On the morning of the third day of the Six Day War—Wednesday, June 7, 1967—the United Nations Security Council was about to call for a cease-fire. The Egyptian air force had been decimated on the ground, the Sinai was being recaptured by Israel, and the Jordanians were being driven out of the West Bank.

The Old City of Jerusalem lay at the feet of the Israelis, ready to be conquered. And soldiers of Dayan's generation wanted to atone for their failure to capture Jerusalem in the 1948 war.

That morning, Israeli paratroopers landed on the Mount of Olives and advanced down towards the Garden of Gethsemane. Tanks blew open the Lions' Gate (also known as St. Stephen's Gate) and paratroopers entered the Via Dolorosa and soon found themselves in the open plaza surrounding the Dome of the Rock, where the Temple had stood.

Meanwhile, members of the Jerusalem Brigade crashed through Zion Gate and stormed down the hill to the Jewish Quarter and were joined by their cohorts entering the Dung Gate—and now they all proceeded to the Western Wall.

While soldiers wept and danced for joy at the liberated Wailing Wall, Rabbi Shlomo Goren, chief rabbi of the IDF, blew the ram's horn and read from a Torah scroll, declaring that today's victory was "heralding redemption." This happened on a Wednesday—fulfilling the prophecy that the Levites had made on the day the Romans destroyed the Temple—a Saturday—by singing instead the song for Wednesday: *"O Lord God, to whom vengeance belongs . . . shine forth!"*

Moshe Dayan slipped into a crack in the Wall a piece of paper on which he had written: "May peace descend on the whole house of Israel."

But then, Dayan unilaterally prevented Rabbi Goren from establishing a Jewish presence on the Temple Mount, informing the Muslims that Israel was claiming sovereignty over the 35-acre plot but was returning control to the Muslim Waqf. Jews would be permitted on the Temple Mount as tourists but not as worshipers, lest a religious war break out. Israel's Chief Rabbinate ordered that Jews observing the Law should not even walk on the mount for fear that "we shall be faulted, God forbid, in breaking a most severe prohibition regarding the desecration of this holy place" (without first being sprinkled with the water of purification containing the ashes of a red heifer).

A committee immediately began plans for enlarging Jewish west Jerusalem to include the Old City. The municipal line would also stretch north, past Neve Ya'akov, whose Jewish land owners had been forced to flee in the 1948 war; this is the town where Eric Mahr would settle his family three decades later.

Israel had conquered 26,000 square miles of territory—three times the size of the Jewish state—containing more than a million Arabs. Prime Minister Levi Eshkol instructed his cabinet to tackle "the question of how we'll live in this land without giving up what we've conquered, and how we'll live with that number of non-Jews."

*

Abraham HaCohen still carries a gun wherever he goes, and no one can doubt that he would use it—but only in self-defense. However, some Jewish settlers have become increasingly violent in recent years, attacking Palestinian people and Muslim institutions without provocation. The image now emerging of Jewish settlers as violent interlopers—apparently intent on terrorizing Palestinian Arab residents—makes a mockery of their idealistic desire to resettle Samaria and Judea in preparation for the coming of Messiah.

The most infamous Jewish extremist, Baruch Goldstein, opened fire outside the Tomb of the Patriarchs (the Ibrahimiyya Mosque) in Hebron on the West Bank, slaughtering 29 Muslim worshipers in February 1994. It was on the Jewish Feast of Purim, when Jews commemorate their deliverance by Queen Esther from destruction in ancient Persia. Goldstein's apparent motive was to torpedo the peace process by inciting anger against Israel on the Arab street. A devotee to the late Rabbi Meir Kahane and his banned Kach party, Goldstein was an army man, not a settler, but he was eulogized by many Jewish settlers for what he had done.

A key follower of Kahane, Baruch Marzel—who saw himself as the martyred leader's successor—endorsed the "price tag" vandals in 2008 but insisted that he was against violence. He told members of his Jewish National Front that any Israeli official who orders the evacuation of a Jewish settlement "commits a crime against your people" and must "pay a price" to make him "think twice about committing the crime" again.

Marzel had been active in Hebron, the West Bank city that was King David's first capital, before moving to Jerusalem to the north. Overwhelmingly populated by Palestinian Arabs, Hebron has a small Jewish community that seeks to protect the tombs of Abraham, Isaac and Jacob—which the Muslims claim as their site.

Also active in Hebron is Rabbi Shalom Dov Wolpe, a Lubavitcher who believes that the Rebbe will come back from the dead to reign as Messiah. Wolpe, too, claims to shun violence but says this of violent "price tag" activists: "I understand them, and you can blame only our government that brought them to this point." Wolpe once declared on Israeli television that Prime Minister Ehud Olmert should be "hanged from the gallows" for making his generous offer to Palestinian peace negotiators in 2008. His outburst provoked a rare public rebuke from his Chabad superiors, who remembered how an ultra-Orthodox talmudic scholar, Yigal Amir, had assassinated Prime Minister Yitzhak Rabin in 1995 after hearing violent rabbinic statements against Rabin and his peace plan. Such rabbis had been citing the Talmudic 'law of the pursuer,' which requires a Jew to kill or maim a Jew who is perceived as intending to kill another Jew.

After the Palestinian leadership applied to the United Nations for unilateral recognition of a State of Palestine in September 2011, Jewish extremists vandalized mosques, cemeteries and farmlands, not only on the West Bank but inside Israel. "Death to the Arabs" was spray-painted in Arab Muslim and Arab Christian cemeteries in Arab Jaffa, outside Tel Aviv. In Galilee, a mosque was burned in a Bedouin village, even though its Muslim residents were known for their loyal service in the IDF. Vandals spray-painted the words "revenge" and "price tag" on the mosque walls, as they took vengeance not only on the latest Arab attack, but also on the latest actions by the Israeli government and IDF to make things better for the Palestinians. Radical settlers even attacked Israeli soldiers and vehicles sent to restore peace, as well as vandalizing an army base and the home of an Israeli anti-settlement activist in Jerusalem.

Many of the "price tag" attacks were in retaliation for decisions by the Israeli Supreme Court, which has habitually ruled against the government in lawsuits bought by Arab citizens of Israel. For example, the court has upheld the right of Israeli Arabs to buy homes in Jewish neighborhoods where the land belonged to the Jewish National Fund and had been developed by the Jewish Agency for Israel.

The Supreme Court has also ordered the government to shut down and demolish illegal Jewish settlements created on the West Bank on land owned by Palestinian Arabs.

As the "price tag" vandalism and violence spread to Israel proper—affecting *Arab citizens* of the Jewish state—many began asking whether this was the early dawning of a civil war within Zionism itself. Israeli officials and rabbis denounced the actions as betrayals of Jewish values, which are shared by the vast majority of settlers, like Abraham HaCohen.

*

But the settlers' case against certain Palestinian Arabs goes back many decades, long before the Arabs deserted Israel at the bargaining table and went straight to the United Nations for statehood. What most galls Jewish settlers like HaCohen is that thousands and thousands of Arabs from outside Palestine entered and claimed to be *Palestinian* Arabs during the years of British control. The British usually looked the other way, mainly to placate Arab concerns over Jewish immigration, especially during the wartime effort to win the Arab powers to their side against Germany. British Prime Minister Neville Chamberlain told his cabinet on April 20, 1939: "If we must offend one side, let us offend the Jews rather than the Arabs."

The Grand Mufti of Jerusalem, Haj Amin al Husseini, wrote extensively in his diary about his meeting with the Fuehrer in Berlin in November 1941. "The objectives of my fight are clear," the Mufti was told. "Primarily, I am fighting the Jews without respite, and this fight includes the fight against the so-called Jewish National Home in Palestine."

The following April, Joachim von Ribbentrop, the Nazi foreign minister, wrote to the Mufti and assured him: "Germany is consequently ready to give all her support to the oppressed Arab countries in their fight against British domination, for the fulfillment of their national aim to independence and sovereignty and for the destruction of the Jewish National Home in Palestine." Ironically, Arab support of the Nazi Holocaust only made it more urgent for Jews to escape Europe and flee to Palestine!

"Only through funds made available by Germany to the Grand Mufti of Jerusalem was it possible to carry out the revolt in Palestine," according to captured files of the German High Command in Flensburg, Germany. The Mufti saw to it that Arabs took part in "espionage, propaganda, establishment of pro-Axis Muslim military units [and] training of Arabs as Nazi agents," wrote Joan Peters in *From Time Immemorial*. In June 1942, Marshal Erwin Rommel's Afrika Korps battled the British 8th Army in northern Africa; eventually Rommel, the Desert Fox, was defeated by combined Allied forces. But if the Germans had succeeded in taking over those Arab countries, they could have extended the Holocaust by annihilating hundreds of thousands of Sephardic Jews living under Arab rule.

Thus the question can be asked again: If untold numbers of Arabs who migrated to western Palestine in the years before and during the war can be classified as *Palestinian Arabs*, why could not the Jewish refugees flocking from Arab countries after 1948 be classified as *Palestinian Jews*? And today, can't Israelis of Sephardic descent claim a right to live on the West Bank alongside Palestinian Arabs, many of whom came originally from the same Arab countries that those Jews fled?

Even before the war, the British in Palestine were doing all they could to keep the Arabs content. In 1926, the Controller of Permits for Jerusalem instructed: "It is agreed that refugees who would appear to be Syrian, Lebanese or Palestinian by nationality may be admitted into Palestine without passport or visa."

In 1935 Winston Churchill candidly admitted: "So far from being persecuted, the Arabs have crowded into the country and multiplied till their population has increased more than even all world Jewry could lift up the Jewish population."

For example, between 30,000 and 36,000 Syrians "entered Palestine and settled there" in 1934, according to the minutes of the Permanent Mandate Commission of the League of Nations.

During the war, thousands of laborers from Syria, Lebanon and Egypt were illegally brought into Palestine by "trucks" and by "train" to fill the "demand for labour exceeding the local supply," according to the Anglo-American Committee's 1945-46 *Survey of Palestine*. It added that they were believed to have "remained in Palestine illegally." Other illegal immigrants came from Jordan, Persia, India, Somaliland, Abyssinia and the Hejaz. In that particular report, 9,687 Arabs were counted, of whom an estimated 6,500 settled in the Haifa district, more than 1,000 around Jaffa, 990 in Galilee, 472 in Samaria and 140 in Gaza.

In fact, Yasser Arafat himself was born in Egypt!

Prof. Moshe Braver of Tel Aviv University published a study in 1975 titled, "Immigration as a Factor in the Growth of the Arab Village in Eretz-Israel." He wrote: "The major increase in the population of the Arab villages in the coastal plain, during the British period, had come largely from immigrants from neighboring countries." In one village, he found that "the great majority . . . had been born in Egypt, some of them came here toward the end of World War I with the British army, and some of them infiltrated into Palestine later on to join members of their families or friends."

In other villages studied, he went on, "there were Arabs from Egypt, from Jordan, from Syria, and even further away—from Yemen."

Braver found 200 to 300 cases of Jordanians whose relatives had crossed the Jordan River into western Palestine as refugees. "Some of them of course are still refugees," he added. "You see, the benefits of being refugees are so considerable that they didn't go back to their villages, or even if they did go back to their original Jordanian village after 1948, they went and registered as refugees when the refugee camps were established, in order to get the refugee benefits."

Braver said Egyptians continued to settle "in villages and towns along the coastal strip between Jaffa and Gaza" well after World War II. Other researchers have identified 'Palestinian' Arabs whose families actually came from Algeria, Iraq and Turkey.

"If the Jews had not come to Palestine," British Colonial Secretary Malcolm McDonald wrote, "the Arab population of Palestine would undoubtedly have remained fixed . . . where it had been for ages before."

*

What also bothers Abraham HaCohen and other Jewish settlers is that so many *legitimate* Palestinian Arabs moved from Arab areas to Jewish areas of western Palestine in the years leading up to 1948. The world has heard little about the record of Arab "in-migration" within western Palestine before the rebirth of the State of Israel. Palestinian Arabs, attracted by the economic and infrastructure improvements made by Jewish immigrants from Europe, moved their families to those areas. The towns they left behind continued to be Arab (and in fact were off-limits for Jews to purchase land after 1939).

Philip Hauser, director of the Population Research Center at the University of Chicago, described a study of census reports from the Turkish authorities, and later from the British authorities over Palestine. Between 1893 and 1947, an estimated 168,000 Arabs moved from Arab settlements to predominantly Jewish settlements within western Palestine. All of this is rather startling, in light of the repeated Arab claim that Jews arriving from Europe before, during and after the Holocaust had pushed Arabs out of their native soil.

And now Abraham HaCohen has made his home back in ancient Tekoa, fulfilling Amos' prophecy, "never again to be uprooted."

Last Chance for Peace?

Noor, too, heard Munir's voice booming from above the Wailing Wall. Hastening up to the Temple Mount, she approached his dark figure in the night. He was still wearing his Arab battle gown, and his sword was at his side.

"Pardon me, Munir," she said to her temporary landlord. "Did I just hear you shouting something about ambushing non-Muslims and slaying them?"

"Only if they murder a member of your family," Munir assured her.

"What brought this on?" she asked, shivering in the night.

"I just found out that the soldier who guards the Wall was the one responsible for the death of my beloved wife."

"I know," Noor told him. "Samira just told me. I am so sorry that the wound from this terrible loss has suddenly been torn open again."

Munir just looked at her and shook his head.

"Thank God that Samira is asleep," Noor said. "If she had heard your voice—and seen you up here, risking your life in such an emotional outburst—"

"—I would gladly give my life to avenge this injustice!" Munir shouted.

"Please calm yourself, Munir," Noor said, motioning for him to walk with her. "Don't forget—this all happened two years ago. Nothing has changed. Her suffering is long over—and she is in heaven with God. Nothing has changed."

"Everything has changed," Munir roared. "The man who murdered her has been courting my daughter, and now he has broken Samira's heart!"

Noor was walking Munir over the lawn to the steps leading to the Dome of the Rock. He walked with her, oblivious to his surroundings, and listened.

"Munir," Noor told him, "the person responsible for that terrible tragedy has been carrying a burden of his own, these two years."

"The only burden I will add," Munir said, as if to himself, "is the weight of my blade in his Zionist heart."

193

As they climbed the steps, they could see the star-studded sky coming down to meet them, and the Dome of the Rock looming ahead.

"Let me ask you something, Munir," she said. They stopped at the top of the steps. "Did it ever occur to you that your wife was a martyr? She died to save her little nephew."

"Oh, she's a martyr, all right," he replied, suddenly upbeat. "She died at the hands of the Zionists, and she went straight to paradise!" Then he raised his hand toward the Dome: "Look—here on the Haram Al-Sharif! Where Muhammed, blessed be he, mounted his steed, al-Buraq, for his night ride to paradise!"

"But didn't she roll over on that grenade so her little nephew wouldn't be killed?" Noor persisted.

"Of course!" he roared. "She will forever be our heroine!"

"Yes, Munir, a heroine. But also something of a deliverer—giving up her own life to save another. Now, imagine that God had come down to the earth in the form of a man—and gave his earthly life to save the human race!"

Munir looked away from the Dome and almost smiled at Noor. "My friend," he said, "you sound just like my daughter, preaching to me about her Christian savior." He shook his head.

Noor just smiled back at him. "Do you ever listen to her? It could save your life."

"Nobody dies for another man's soul," Munir said at last.

"No, but your wife died for a little boy's life," she said. "Don't you see? The Jews used to sacrifice an unblemished animal on God's altar." She turned and pointed toward where the Temple once stood. "Not only does the Jew give up this animal, which could have fed his family. He also hopes that by shedding its blood, on God's altar, he himself won't have to shed his blood before his time. For all of us have sinned and fallen short of the glory of God."

"My beloved wife died indeed before her time," Munir replied. "And the man responsible for it must die now—for his time has come." Munir drew his sword and held it by both hands, above his head. "*Whoever kills a person,*" he declared, "*it is as if he had slain the whole people.*"

"Sura five, thirty-two," Noor said, citing the Qu'ran. "But then again, whoever saves a life, it is as if he had saved the whole world. Your wife saved not only your nephew, but all the children who will follow in his name."

"I will kill this Zionist," Munir shouted, his voice trembling, "and cut him off from marrying and giving birth to more of his kind in our land!" He swung the sword around, above his head, flipping it with one hand high into the air and catching it with the other.

"Put your sword away!" Noor commanded. "Those who live by the sword will die by the sword!"

"Then let me die for the honor of my family," he said.

"Munir," she said, "do you want to rise to your rightful place in heaven—which no man can rob you of—and be with your wife? Or will you kill this soldier out of pure spite, and spend eternity in hell? Listen to your daughter—she can teach you about the peace that comes from forgiveness."

"There is no peace in our land," he sighed.

"On the contrary," she replied, "the time for peace is at hand. And if you let it pass, it won't come again for another generation. You, Munir, were born for such a time as this. Haven't you all had enough bloodshed? Or will it take more for you to say, *Enough!*"

Munir sheathed his sword and began to walk around the Dome of the Rock. Noor followed. They were across from the Golden Gate— the one that has been closed up, its stairwell covered with barbed wire—when Munir stopped and pointed east.

"We should have fled across the Jordan when this all happened in 1967," he said. "Then none of this would have happened to us. We would all be living in Jordan, and she would still be alive." He turned to Noor. "Instead we stayed. We had lost our home years before, but we still had our falafel stand and all of its rooms to live in."

"Munir," she said quietly, "what would you have accomplished in a refugee camp in Jordan?"

"We could be with our brothers—citizens of Jordan—the country that has since signed a peace treaty with the Zionists. And we'd all be looking forward to the day when the peace process will grant us our Right of Return, not only to our falafel stand but to our house—my wife's family home—just a few blocks away!"

Noor looked at Munir for a long time. Then she said, "Munir, the peace process has never guaranteed Palestinian Arabs a Right of Return to their families' former homes in Israel proper. How many Palestinians living in Jordan originally came from the West Bank? Or from Gaza? Only one in ten—*they* are the only ones who could return to their families' original homes. All the others would have to take their chances and move to some strange town on the West

Bank, or in Gaza. I think most of them would stay where they are in Jordan."

"I have relatives in Jordan," Munir said quietly.

"Then ask them," Noor said. "Ask them where they would rather live—in Jordan, where they make up 70 percent of the population, or in some strange town in a new state called Palestine—under the strict Islamic rule of Hamas."

Then they slowly walked back to the falafel stand.

Chapter 18

In Jordan with Zerach

JORDAN

On our first morning in Amman, we woke up to a mist in the air following an overnight rain. On the balcony of our hotel, across the street from the sandbagged U.S. Embassy, I kept glancing in the direction of Jerusalem—some 50 miles to the west—while praying in the Spirit and reading Psalm 90.

> *Oh, satisfy us early with Your mercy,*
> *That we may rejoice and be glad all*
> *our days!*

Inside our room, Zerach was also facing toward Jerusalem. He had wound the leather tefillin around his arm and attached it to his head while reciting Psalm 145, the prayer that Orthodox Jews say three times a day, to become worthy of a share in the world to come. A tall, spidery figure with spectacles and a perpetually boyish demeanor, Zerach's head bobbed and his back bent reverentially at the waist as he rattled off the Hebrew from memory.

> *I will extol Thee, my God, the King,*
> *and evermore will bless Thy name . . .*
> *One generation to another shall*
> *praise Thy works*
> *and recount Thy mighty acts . . .*

My devout friend Zerach had taken a crash course and learned just enough Arabic—and I knew just enough Hebrew—to get us both into a lot of trouble here in Jordan. We had boarded a bus at the American Colony, the favorite hotel for journalists in Jerusalem, and crossed from the West Bank to Jordan at a time when the two countries were still technically at war, with no direct air, postal or telephone service. We'd even had to procure clean passports, because a Hebrew notation stamped by Israeli Customs would disqualify anyone from entering Jordan from "the Zionist entity."

"You've got to stop saying *Shalom* in this country," Zerach kept admonishing me. "It's *Salaam aleikum!*"

Our mission here in March 1985: To scoop the world media by interviewing Palestinian Arab refugees in Jordan about the recently announced peace proposal by King Hussein and the Palestine Liberation Organization. Both Jordan and the PLO were offering to make peace with Israel in exchange for withdrawing troops and Jewish settlers from the West Bank and Gaza, making way for a Palestinian state.

Arabs and many Israelis alike were touting the proposal as "the last chance for peace." We had come to hear from Palestinian refugees themselves whether this was true. And if so, we were about to witness a historic opening—not only for peace in the Holy Land, but for the Zionist dream to *fully* come true by Israel's obedience to Leviticus 19:34—"But the stranger *[exile?]* who dwells among you shall be to you as one born among you, and you shall love him as yourself; for you were strangers *[exiles?]* in the land of Egypt." The Bible doesn't use the word *exile*, or *refugee*—but these strangers today surely see themselves as exiles from their homeland. To what extent does God require Israel to give up part of her inherited land permanently to another people? The Jewish Study Bible commands that the stranger be treated as a citizen. Does God require Israel to make Palestinian Arabs citizens, capable of someday outnumbering Jews and turning Israel into an Islamic republic?

Zerach was on assignment from his Jewish newspaper in New York, which has sent him to more than a dozen countries as a correspondent. I had secured a freelance assignment to write a full-page article in the *Jerusalem Post*, which had been unable to get a reporter into Jordan for three dozen years, because the two countries were still technically in a state of war. All communications had to be routed via a neutral country, such as Cyprus. Even a year later journalist Wolf Blitzer, our fellow Western New York native, was denied entry by the Jordanian government to cover Vice President George Bush's visit, despite strenuous efforts by the U.S. Embassy in Amman. Jordan's leaders were afraid Blitzer would announce at a public news conference that he represented the Zionist *Jerusalem Post*. Of course, I flew under their radar by showing them only my credentials from *The Buffalo News*.

Later I wrote a five-part series for my newspaper, and it was Best News Story of the year by the Society of Professional Journalists in Buffalo. So, what was the startling disclosure that came out of my series? Simply this: *Only one out of ten Palestinian refugees living in Jordan is from a family originally from Gaza or the West Bank—the other nine are from families that fled Israel proper.* The United Nations knew this, and surely American, Israeli and Arab diplomats were aware of it—but still they went forward with a "peace" process that was doomed from the start: How could anyone believe that Yasser Arafat had the power to persuade 90 percent of his Palestinian constituents to lay down their arms for such a deal?

"Real estate won't buy you peace—peace is a state of mind," we were bluntly told by Nayef Mawla, public relations director for the Jordanian Ministry of Information.

While visiting a Palestinian school overseen by the United Nations, I saw an ominous warning of the attitude of the next generation(s) of Palestinian Arabs in Jordan toward Israel. A drawing on the door of the school director's office portrayed an Arab terrorist pointing a rifle at a map of western Palestine, where a flame of freedom is chained by Stars of David. I can never forget these innocent little Palestinian children I watched dutifully reading out loud in unison during class . . .

Bordering on the West Bank, Jordan was the key place to find Palestinian refugees, because the bulk of them lived here and in fact had been given Jordanian citizenship. Thousands of others were scattered in other Arab countries, most notably Lebanon, but they were far from welcome. By 1985 Palestinian Arabs made up 60 percent of Jordan's population; today it is over 70 percent.

It was Zerach's idea to go to Jordan, and he generously invited me to come along and made arrangements for visas and a tour of a United Nations refugee camp. We had first met four years earlier while covering the historic World Gathering of Jewish Holocaust Survivors in Jerusalem for our newspapers.

Our choice of Jordan for our search for Palestinian Arab refugees was confirmed during our meeting at the English-language *Jordan Times* with Rami Khouri, then senior editor: He saw Jordan as a buffer zone and a shock-absorber between Israel and the Arab world. As the only Arab country to extend full rights to its Palestinian population, Jordan had gained much experience in dealing with both sides. At the same time, Khouri told us, Jordanians know a great deal about Western culture and politics. Palestinians are avid news hounds, tuning daily in to Western broadcasts and open to Western culture.

Our weeklong visit to Jordan almost turned into a disaster. (In fact, we arrived the day after the American journalist Terry Anderson was kidnapped in Lebanon.) We had just crossed the Allenby Bridge over the Jordan River when armed Jordanian soldiers burst onto our bus and informed us that nobody could return the way we had come. They suggested that we make plans to fly from Jordan to a neutral country, such as Cyprus, from which we could then fly back to Israel. (I supposed that they wanted us to enrich the Jordanian economy by purchasing tickets from Royal Jordanian Airlines.) Zerach and I spent the next two days at the Interior Ministry in Ammon, begging bureaucrats for a special exit visa that would get us back across the River Jordan a week hence.

A *baal t'shuvah*, Zerach had shed his kippa for a floppy hat that didn't look Jewish but was at least a size too big for his head. For all that subterfuge—and for all his pathetic knowledge of Arabic—he kept giving in to the temptation to tell people on the street that he was Jewish to see their reaction. He even asked, in Arabic, if they had any kosher food! They were surprisingly friendly, having never met a Jew in their life. They explained that as long as we were Americans—and not Israelis living on 'Arab land'—we could enjoy all the benefits of tourists (along with the customary rip-offs reserved for American tourists, as we shall see shortly).

The United Nations Relief and Works Agency welcomed us at a refugee camp outside Irbid, a city in northern Jordan that's a few short miles from the Syrian border and the Golan Heights. Beginning with 4,000 refugees in tents in 1951, the Irbid camp had switched to mud huts and now had graduated to concrete shelters for more than 17,000 residents, along with schools, clinics and food distribution centers. By the time of our arrival, the camp had become a suburb of Irbid, the third largest city in Jordan. City streets run into the camp, which isn't marked by any fences or signs. The camp's architecture is barely distinguishable from the rest of the city, where some of the refugees also live and work.

In addition to the five camps serving refugees from the 1948 war, Jordan also had six "emergency camps" for those who fled the West Bank after the Six Day War of 1967.

Before embarking on a tour of the camp—and interviews with Palestinians themselves—the United Nations area officer, Ahmed Abu Faddah led us into the office of the camp services officer, Abdul Muti Salman, whose family was from Haifa. Faddah played with his string of red beads as Salman spoke in his tiny office, with its bare concrete floor, kerosene stove, and a single light bulb against the stark concrete walls.

"If the Palestinians (move to the West Bank), I'll throw away my house in Irbid and go," Salman said. "I want to return to Haifa and live under the Israeli government. My father was a chef in Haifa; he has a letter from Ben-Gurion. We'd live together as a family, Jews and Palestinians. Just to have my land—not to live as a foreigner here" in Jordan.

"Most of the people have crossed over from the northern half of Israel," Faddah told Zerach. Faddah's family had fled Hebron, in the southern part of the West Bank. "The PLO is banned here and has no offices," he said, "but no doubt the people are looking to the PLO and to their return to their homeland." Still, the Palestine Liberation Organization operated small sewing and typing workshops for the women.

The PLO was banned after the country's civil war in 1970, when PLO fighters based here had fought Jordanian soldiers on the outer fringes of the camp. In fact, Israel has always considered Irbid a strategic location, because whoever controls Irbid will control Syria's military access to Israel, and Israel's military access to Syria (and the Golan Heights), through Jordan.

"Today," Zerach later observed, "the only hazards are donkeys braying under heavy loads, soccer balls misfired from school boys in a street corner game, and low-slung laundry hung across the narrow side streets."

The most striking thing that I remember after meeting dozens of Palestinian Arabs in this refugee camp is that very few of them were able-bodied men. Asked where the young men were, the women said they were working in the oil fields of the Arabian peninsula, earning money to send home. But I wondered how many of those men had virtually abandoned their families to train and fight with militant factions of the Palestine Liberation Organization.

Salman led me and Zerach to one of the poorest families in the camp. Living in two rooms, 12 people were seated around a small kerosene stove on which hot tea was brewing. Tapestries hung on the chipped blue walls, and a woman with a checkered kaffiyeh on her head was smoking a cigarette. The family offered us hot, sweetened tea and crushed salted olives. Speaking in Arabic, Salman asked the mother what her children were being taught in the UN school. She answered in Arabic.

"They taught their children," Salman told us, "that Israel conquered us and put us here, and if there is a peace and we have land there, we can go back to our land there."

But this family was from Tiberias, in northern Israel—not the West Bank.

In another home, a family from Nazareth, in northern Israel, pointed proudly to a picture on a wall of a young man who had died in the 1967 war. Salman pressed them for their realistic expectations of the proposed land-for-peace deal.

"They feel it's a very good chance," he reported to us. "Yes, they're optimistic. They want to go to Nazareth, not the West Bank. If they (still) have a house there, they surely want to go back."

Out the open market place, looking at oranges and lemons, was Shafik Abu Libdeh, known as "something like a mayor" of the community. Would he like to move to the West Bank if peace came?

"If he could not return to Haifa," Salman told us, "he would prefer to stay here." Speaking for many others in the camp, Salman added: "If there is any chance for them to have a good life here in Jordan, they will stay."

In fact, Zerach and I learned, only about 10 percent of the Palestinian Arabs living in Jordan had originally come from Gaza or the West Bank. The others were in families that once lived in what is now Israel. And the land-for-peace proposal held out little or no hope that Israel would grant a "right of return" to former Arab inhabitants as it had granted to Jews since 1948.

*

Even within the Palestine Liberation Organization, some expressed doubt that the proposal sponsored by King Hussein of Jordan and Yasser Arafat of the PLO could deliver peace to Israel in exchange for Gaza and the West Bank.

Take Samir Al-Khatib, a former PLO fighter who lived down in Karak, 50 miles south of Amman and near the Dead Sea. His cousin back in Buffalo had recommended that we interview him. On our way to Karak, as the bus jostled us down the aging King's Highway, Zerach and I struck up a conversation with some Jordanian soldiers and two Arabs wearing red-and-white checkered kaffiyeh headdresses (the PLO's black-and-white checkered scarves are banned). Zerach insisted on revealing to them that he was Jewish, just to watch their reactions. One of the Arabs persuaded Zerach to remove his floppy cap and put on his kaffiyeh. A cheer went up on the bus, and I snapped a picture to show Zerach's mother back in Buffalo.

Karak had once been the main city of ancient Moab and dominated the caravan route from Syria to Egypt and Arabia. Crusaders controlled it until 1188, and the golden stone ruins of their fortifications still stand in Karak.

Here we interviewed Samir Al-Khatib, who owned a bookstore. His passport had been revoked by the Jordanian government for his activities in Lebanon with the PLO.

Asked about the peace proposal, Al-Khatib told us: "This latest agreement that was signed between King Hussein and Yasser Arafat . . . didn't really satisfy the people of Palestine or their rights to go back to *their own* land and form their own state." Al-Khatib—who was born in 1949 near Beersheba, in southern Israel—was then asked whether he would move to the West Bank if he could. His answer seemed to betray the PLO's continuing ambition to take over Jordan as well as the West Bank for a Palestinian state.

"It doesn't really matter if I stay in Jordan to be a Jordanian," he said, "or go back to Palestine to be a Palestinian—because Palestinian and Jordan people are one body that shares the same course and the same goal, now and for days to come."

When we were leaving, Al-Khatib called a Palestinian cab driver he knew, so we wouldn't have to take the bus back to Amman. The fellow also knew a faster way back to our hotel than the King's Highway. So we agreed to pay him 20 dinars ($50). The cabbie in the red-and-white checkered kaffiyeh and baby-blue suit seemed a friendly enough sort. He even tuned his radio to an Israeli music station for our enjoyment. But we were in for the ride of our lives. Soon Zerach would be reading his Hebrew prayer for safe travel, and I would be praying in the Spirit for our lives.

After we left Karak the Jordanian countryside disappeared and became a wilderness. First I looked out my window at the goats, sheep and donkeys and wondered how they could live on this barren soil. This wasn't even a flat desert, with maybe an occasional cactus, but rolling hills of gravel and stone. Then we found ourselves overwhelmed by barren mountains of rock. Our cabbie had a heavy foot on the accelerator, and he was climbing a winding road and wandering close to the edge of the abyss. At times all we could see through our vertigo was the sky, then suddenly the badlands below as our car plunged toward the wadi floor.

On the map, the place where Zerach and I were emotionally dry-gulched is called the Wadi al-Mawjib.

Later, after the terrain had grown more to our liking, we asked him to stop at Mount Nebo, where Moses had been permitted to look to the west and behold the Promised Land before dying.

We walked around the Christian church that stood at the top of this craggy hillside overlooking a canyon. Tough little plants with tiny white flowers blossomed here and there among the rocks and stones and infertile earth, and Zerach later reported seeing some olive sprigs.

From the top of Mount Nebo we looked to the west and beheld, in the late-afternoon mist, the Promised Land as Moses saw it before he died here! There was the Dead Sea and, just north of it, the shallow Jordan River. Jerusalem was too far away in the distant mist for us to see. We took our time, even wandering away from each other, each trying to breath it all in. I picked up two little golden stones and put them in my pocket, for my collection of stones from the Mideast (starting in 1981 with the heart-shaped stone I'd scooped up from the bottom of the Sea of Galilee).

Zerach and I spent 45 minutes there, but apparently that was too long for our driver. The sun was beginning to set, and I saw our driver relieving himself at the edge of the hill. When we got back into his cab the Palestinian had turned sullen at the wheel, a quiet anger rising within him. He was especially enraged when he had to stop for directions. It was nightfall when he pulled up to our hotel in Amman and demanded 40 dinars ($100) instead of the 20 dinars we had agreed to. When we balked, the cab lurched forward and didn't stop for another block. I wanted to drop the agreed-upon $50 into his lap and leap out of the cab, but Zerach didn't feel like spending the next several days wrangling with those bureaucrats downtown. We might have faced a criminal offense. So we paid up.

What had gotten into Samir Al-Khatib's cabbie friend with the checkered kaffiyeh? Was it a mysterious change of heart? Or had he planned this hijack all along? Wasn't this the dilemma that Israelis had faced every time they sat down at a negotiating table with a Palestinian Arab?

(Ten years later, Zerach returned to Jordan, after it had finally signed a peace treaty with Israel. He found the people lukewarm, at best. "Peace for us is really a final admission of defeat, " a Jordanian Christian told him. *"Israel is a reality."*)

Back at the Intercontinental Hotel, Zerach was still subsisting on kosher Israeli food out of his suitcase, because there were no Jews in

Jordan, no kosher shops, no lox and bagels, no matzo, not anything for an Orthodox Jew. Back in Jerusalem, he had furtively packed his suitcase with nonperishable kosher food. His worst fear had been that Jordanian officers would search us at the border (*did they really fear terrorists coming from Israel?*), open his suitcase and confiscate his kosher crackers and jelly in their Hebrew-marked packages, leaving him stranded for a week in this Moslem country that was virtually *Judenrein*.

Jews once dominated this land. The Arab world has long forgotten that 800 years before Christ, more than half of "Israel" was east of the Jordan River. In fact, all of what is now northern Jordan was Jewish as late as 64 BC, when Roman rule began. A century later, when the Jewish rebellion against Rome began, the Church at Jerusalem—which was still entirely Jewish—fled across the Jordan to a town called Jerash and its friendly Judeo-Christian environment. (On our way to Irbid we had driven past Jerash, or Pella, with its row of ancient columns, but not a messianic Jew was to be seen.)

Anyway, with Zerach eating out of his suitcase, I'd been subsisting on cheese, bread and olives that I would pick up on the run in the marketplace. I'd grabbed a hamburger and fries one day but felt guilty about what Zerach was going through. One night I decided that I needed a real meal. And so I announced that I was going upstairs to the fancy restaurant in our hotel for some fine dining. Zerach said he'd come along to keep me company. I was well into my steak when Zerach closed his menu and absently-mindedly asked the waiter that fateful question: "Do you by any chance have any melon?"

The waiter said sweet melon wasn't in season in Jordan, but a few minutes later he returned from the kitchen with half a melon mounted on a silver pedestal. Zerach put on his napkin and lit into the melon with his spoon. Before long he was down to the rind.

"Ask him for the other half of the melon," I told him. "The treat is on me."

When the check came, my steak dinner was $15. Zerach's two half-melons had been priced separately and came to $17.50.

I asked the waiter if he was serious, and he said the melon wasn't on the menu so he had asked the chef what to charge. I asked to see the chef, but he had gone home. So I paid. But the next day I returned and asked for the chef. Out came a chubby-cheeked Frenchman in chef's whites and tall cap. He was big, pink, well-fed and completely at ease.

"You see, monsieur," he began, "sweet melons are not in season. We have to order them from France when they are in season. But we have to pay a high price for them because of the shipping costs, plus the 75 percent import tax."

I opened a menu and pointed to the crabmeat appetizer, priced at a mere $15. How could one sweet melon go for $17.50?

He looked around in the quiet restaurant and gestured as if to take me aside. "Confidentially," he said in a half-whisper, "I don't think melons are in season in France, either. I suspect that *this* melon was actually grown in *Israel*—and had to be shipped (and taxed) to Europe and then to Jordan."

I went back to the room and told Zerach that he had just eaten an Israeli melon that had been exported to Europe and reshipped 1,600 miles to the Intercontinental Hotel in Amman, a mere 50 miles from the Zionist melon patch from which it had been weaned.

"Sure!" he exploded. "Always a way to blame it on Israel!"

Noor Seeks Out Simon

None of the soldiers seemed to notice the tall Bedouin woman walking across the square on her way to the IDF barracks where Simon was stationed outside the Old City. As she strode up to the front doors, a slight breeze stirred her lavender gown, trimmed in gold, but her footsteps made not a sound. Inside, she walked past the officer at the duty station and made her way directly to the room that Simon shared with seven other soldiers. He was alone, sitting on the floor, with his back to the wall near his bunk, listening to music, when Noor suddenly materialized before his eyes. Startled, he jumped up and almost raised his right hand, as if to salute, but checked himself.

They stared at each other in silence for a long moment.

"You don't look well, my friend," she said.

"You call me *friend?*" Simon retorted. He turned off the music player.

"I've come to comfort you," she said.

"No one can comfort me—least of all *you!*" Simon blurted.

"Shimon, I know you are upset and I understand—"

"Upset?" he shouted, suddenly shaking a fist at her. "Does that puny word describe a man—a soldier—who has been wounded again, two years after that catastrophe that changed my life forever? A man who now has lost the only woman he could ever have loved—because now she knows that *I killed her mother?*"

"Please try to calm yourself," Noor said gently, stepping closer to Simon. "Let me be your Comforter."

"Get away from me!" he shouted, his voice echoing in the barracks. *"You're* the one who made all these things happen!" His face had turned red.

"Yes," she said, "I suppose you could say that. But—"

"First you bring this animal into the city and give it to who?— an Arab. Then you go and tell this lunatic Rabbi and his yeshiva boy where to find the animal they've been waiting for. Then—*and then!*— you had the audacity to come up to *me* and tell *me* about your little game of mischief."

Simon was visibly shaking.

Noor looked into his eyes. "Shimon, if I hadn't done that, you never would have renewed your friendship with Samira."

"But now, because of *you*, our whole world has been turned inside out! She hates me now!" he roared, his voice nearly deafening her ears in the barracks. "Because of you and your meddling religion!"

With that, the soldier lunged at the woman, grabbed her by the golden lapels of her gown, and shook her several times. When he let go of her, she almost fell backwards.

An officer popped his head through the open door. "Hey—everything okay, Shimon?"

"Yeah, yeah," Simon replied, his voice hoarse. *"B'seder!* Even *Sababa!* Whatever."

"Hey, Shimon—are you sure you took your medication today?"

"Yeah, yeah, everything's cool," Simon replied.

The officer left.

Noor was looking at him with profound pity in her eyes.

Simon stepped away and paced back and forth in front of his bed, then turned his music back on. He was playing "Sabra Girl," from the music album *Purple Heart*, by the American singer Shirah.

"Sabra girl," he sang along with Shirah, *"oh, ohhh, Sabra giiirlll . . . I'm standing at a stop sign, and it's flashing red . . ."* Just as abruptly, he turned off the music, threw his back against the wall and let himself slide to the floor, where he had been sitting when Noor came in. "Forgive me," he said quietly. His eyes were closed.

"Of course," she said softly, as she sat on the edge of his bed. "That's a good album you're playing. You need the Ruach ha-Kodesh to help you control your temper."

They were silent for a whole minute or more. When Noor spoke again, it was like the still, small voice that Elijah had heard on the mountain—after the mighty wind, after the earthquake, and after the fire.

". . . You still don't know who I am, do you?" she breathed. "The Pharisees didn't know who Yeshua was, either. Do you want to know why, Shimon?"

Simon was sitting on the floor with his eyes shut.

"The same problem exists today," she went on. "Experts in Hebrew, Aramaic and Greek have not the slightest idea of the meaning behind much of the Bible. With all the knowledge they have when they approach the Scriptures, it is as if they had dissected a baby heifer and discovered nothing but a dead animal. The only way to approach the Scriptures, Shimon, is with an attitude of *submission. It must be a heart response!* Only then will God reveal to you His deepest secrets."

Simon opened his eyes and asked: "What has that to do with knowing who this Yeshua was?"

"I'll tell you," she said. "The Pharisees were experts in the Law, and in all the prophecies about Messiah. But when He finally came, they didn't recognize Him because—for all their intellectual knowledge of the Scriptures—their hearts were not right. They dissected their Messiah and ended up with a dead body on a cross. Even when He arose from the dead, they refused to look at Him with their hearts. Two thousand years later, Shimon, they *still* don't get it!"

Then Noor spoke in Hebrew, quoting the *Shema*: "You shall *love* the Lord your God with all your heart, with all your soul, and with all your might!"

Simon had opened his eyes. Finally, he whispered, "I *love* her so . . ."

"And she loves you," Noor replied.

"Not anymore," he said.

Another minute of silence. Then he opened his eyes and looked past her at the opposite wall.

"I remember the first time I laid eyes on Samira. It was at the first Peace Now rally that I went to with Itzak—we were best friends then. And there was Samira! We sang peace songs together. We chanted slogans together. We held hands—*oh!* Her hand . . . it was so soft but alive! And those *eyes* . . . !"

"You don't hear much about Peace Now these days," Noor remarked.

"No—the whole political left has lost its way. So much has happened since that day. But I'm still a believer."

"A believer?" she said. "In what?"

Simon pulled his knees back, wrapped his arms around them, and thought. "I believe in the basics of the Zionist dream. That we Jews have returned to our land and rebuilt our country again. That we can survive and conquer our enemies by our blood, sweat and tears . . . and finally make peace with them." He looked straight into Noor's eyes. "We don't need religion. Not anymore, anyway."

"That's how the Israelites felt when they were about to cross the Jordan into the Promised Land, after forty years of wandering in the desert, totally dependent on God for all their needs," Noor said. "They thought they could just walk away from God and start doing things their own way."

Simon said nothing.

"Why do you so hate Itzak?" Noor asked.

"I don't hate him. I just disagree with his approach to life. I don't even really mind the black hat and the whole get-up—that's his choice and I respect it. In fact, I think all religions are a civilizing force on people, making them better."

"So why were you and he on the outs for so long?"

"It's his infatuation with Rabbi Abram," he said, "and their demented plot to take back the Temple Mount, ignite World War III, and bring this Messiah of theirs."

"He's your Messiah, too," Noor said.

"Messiahs are for the religious," he said. "The religious are too enthralled with their books and their studies—too lazy to work for a living!—not willing to work to make the Zionist dream really come true—for all of us. They expect this Messiah to come and do it all for them."

"The Millennium," she said.

"The Millennium."

"So you're trying to bring about a millennium of peace and justice by human means."

"How else can we do it? "

"Only God can bring it about," Noor said. "Remember the Tower of Babel? How they all tried to unite themselves and climb up to heaven without God's permission?"

"I don't believe in those Bible stories," Simon said. "They're just too fantastic."

"All right," she said. "Name me one nation that has ever succeeded in creating a peaceful society—with total tolerance for one another—by its philosophy or by sheer force."

"I think socialism should be given a chance," Simon said. "That's how each kibbutz operated in our early days of statehood. Then, on a larger scale, just divide up all the world's wealth and distribute it equally to everyone."

Noor just looked at him. "Shimon," she said, "this was supposedly tried in the Soviet Union. For more than 70 years, it was illegal for anyone to practice anti-Semitism (except of course for Soviet officials!). If you picked on a Jew for being a Jew, you could be arrested. Did you know that?"

"No."

Noor was on her feet: "So this Russian family is sitting at its kitchen table in 1917, after the Russian Revolution. A generation later, their children are sitting with them at that table. A generation later, their grandchildren are also gathered with this poor family at that old kitchen table. And suddenly it's 1989 and the Soviet Union is no more—and nobody can go to prison anymore for being anti-Semitic. But they're still in poverty. So what happens now?"

"What happens?

Noor raised her hands above her head and shouted: "The grandchildren run out into the street and yell, 'The Jews, the Jews, the Jews! It's all their fault that we're poor!'" She lowered her hands. "You see, Shimon, an atheistic country can't force people to love one another by sheer force of law—even after three generations of trying!"

Simon shook his head helplessly. "I still think we should try."

"But you've already tried it in Israel!" Noor cried out. Now she looked really frustrated. "Socialism on the kibbutz years ago was one thing, but now that secular Zionism has played itself out, we're seeing just how self-destructive it is! Israel has bought into the whole liberal package! The public schools don't teach the Holocaust anymore, because the Palestinians are seen as greater victims, and their suffering is still going on. And liberal Israelis absolutely *despise* their religious brothers and sisters—"

"—They should all serve in the IDF, and they should get a job when they're out!" Simon shouted. "And they should stop throwing stones at Jews driving on Shabbat."

Turning her palms up, Noor gave him a half smile but went on: "All over the world, liberalism is turning against Israel, the 'occupier'—and now it's quickly turning into flat-out anti-Semitism! Those liberal Jews who thought that all they had to do to serve God was to fight for all the victims of the world—without doing it in God's name—well, in atheistic Russia, you had Bolshevik Jews working their hearts out to help build a communist system that ended up turning *everybody* into a victim."

"They took pity on the underdog," Simon said.

"Yes," Noor said, "and after the Holocaust the whole world took pity on the poor, emaciated Jews. *Oh, those poor Jews—let's let them have their homeland back in Palestine!* A generation later, Israel became a world power, and now what were the liberals saying? *Oh, those poor downtrodden Palestinians! Let's support their struggle against the Zionist state!* And next, Shimon, what do you suppose all these do-gooders will say if Hamas and the Islamist terrorists finally have their way with your land? *Oh, look at all those poor Israelis, thrown into the sea! Tsk-tsk! Let's have a fund-raiser for those poor, pathetic victims!*" Noor glared into Simon's face. "So much for the value of pity, that perverted liberal substitute for *love!*"

The soldier was deep in thought. "Those poor downtrodden Palestinians," he murmured, as if to himself. "But they *are* downtrodden. They call us Nazis for the way we treat them . . ." With his hands clasped over his face, his words came out muffled, as from a bad dream: "I have stood over a bunch of Palestinians as they waited to go through our security checkpoint in the hot sun . . . and I have felt such *power* over them! Some days it made me *feel* like a Nazi!"

Noor told Simon, "Yes, Shimon, the occupation has made you a victim as well. But we must strive for peace again."

Simon lowered his hands, and his reddened face was contorted in a helpless expression: "All we can do is try again."

"Of course, we never give up," Noor said. "But don't even bother trying to make the world better without God. Only God can bring about a transformation in the human spirit. We all need to renew our minds, after the mind of God. All those nice friends of yours in Peace Now have good intentions, Shimon, just like you. But without putting the Lord first, they will only be trying to fashion a false unity of society. Another Tower of Babel. And God won't stand for people trying to unite the world in their own image and likeness instead of His. Because basically we're all prone to evil."

"I disagree," Simon said. "All people are basically good. The only problem is, we can't get everybody to work together for what it is that all of us really want. We thought Peace Now was going to start the ball rolling. We had Arabs and Jews and Bedouins and everybody else under the sun in our tent."

"All these people singing and chanting together—did they really *love* one another?" Noor asked.

"Of course!" he said. "It was a love feast! We danced and sang and ate and drank and hugged—I hugged Samira and she hugged me back! And now she's gone . . ."

Noor began to pace the floor, deep in thought. "I wonder," she said, still pacing, "I wonder how many of the Jews and Arabs in that group were really ready to share the land as brothers and sisters? Had they really learned how to *love* each other, in spite of all that hate that each of them has felt now and then toward the other?"

Simon looked at her. "I think they did. I think they do. What more does it take to love each other if we're already coming together and agreeing about peace—Peace Now?"

"Love isn't just a feeling," Noor said. "Love isn't just a political agreement to no longer act like enemies and fight over the land. Love is a divine impartation from God Himself into the heart and spirit of every person who is ready for love."

"All I know about real love," Simon said, "is that I will *always* be in love with Samira!"

"And Samira was in love with you," Noor said.

"But not anymore," he said again,

Noor came closer to Simon and sat on the floor next to him. "Shimon," she began, "when you fell in love with this Arab woman, you set aside her culture and her religion. You made a decision to love her as herself."

"Yes. That's right!"

"And I presume that Samira did the same in your case—setting aside your blood, your dedication to the Zionist movement, the occupation of the land . . . This was a decision that she made."

"Once," he said.

"Shimon, it's a decision that she can make *again!* That's what *forgiveness* can do to the injured heart. Give her time."

Simon looked at her for a long time and didn't blink.

"What about you?" he said at last. "How do you go about loving others in this land, that was taken from *you*, too?"

"Bedouins don't claim ownership of the land."

"Come on, you know what I mean."

"All right," Noor said. "I get along with everybody in this land not only because I don't need the land, but because—because I have decided to put aside all of their faults and accept them as people whom God loves without measure."

"No," Simon replied. "You didn't make any decision on your own. You just adopted the principles of the Christian religion and follow them religiously—just like Itzak and his Rabbi counting the days till Shabbos and going through all sorts of contortions to buy only food that is absolutely kosher. You're as much a slave of the Law as they are."

"You really think so, huh?"

"Yes," he said. "You've just admitted it yourself—you made a *decision* to love everybody, regardless of their faults and their bad ways. And that decision came out of your religion."

Noor winked an eye at him and said, "Suppose I were to agree with you, for argument's sake? Tell me, then, what you have against religion if it was able to transform *me* like that?"

Now it was Simon's turn to be silent. Finally, he said, "But religion is so *divisive!* If only we all had the same religion, it would be a uniting force."

"Right," she said. "And that's what Yitzak and the other Orthodox wish to happen in Israel, at least among all Jews—that they all follow the laws set down by God, from Mount Sinai down through the ages."

"But these radical fanatics want to force every Jew to follow their way!" Simon shouted. "How can I as a Jew make a decision to follow things that I can't believe in? These religious people are divisive—and they're tearing apart our society!"

"Is divisiveness always a bad thing?" Noor asked.

"Of course! It's the enemy of unity. How can we have peace with Arabs if we can't have some sort of unity among ourselves?"

"I hesitate to tell you this, Shimon," Noor said, "but I have a sneaking suspicion that the Holy One of Israel is in favor of *divisiveness* at this time in history. At least while the danger exists that the people of the world will come together in a *false* unity, based on lies and misconceptions about the truth."

"Well, now you've admitted it!" Simon exclaimed. "Your religion is divisive."

"Shimon," Noor said with a smile, "allow me to quote what Yeshua of Nazareth once said to His disciples—'Do you think I came to bring peace on earth? No, I tell you, but division . . . father against son . . . mother against daughter.'"

"There you are again!" Simon replied. "Even the founder of your religion admitted that his plan was divisive. I rest my case."

Noor looked at him and smiled again. "Your Prophet Isaiah said this about God: 'He comes to sift the nations with the sieve of destruction.' And listen what the Prophet Amos says of the Lord—'I will sift the house of Israel among all nations, as grain is sifted in a sieve, yet not the smallest grain shall fall to the ground.'"

"And what does all that mean?" Simon asked.

"It means," Noor replied, "that at this time in history, the God of Israel is about to force the nations to take sides—either for Israel or against Israel. And He is also forcing His people to take sides—for their God or against their God. He is being divisive in order to bring about a final unity of people devoted to their divine Creator. All the others will perish."

Simon's face was starting to turn red again. And there was a twitch in his neck as he gathered his thoughts and let them pour out of him like a blazing torch.

"You Christians are divisive, all right," he said. "All those evangelical churches that send missionaries to Israel, to convert us to their religion. They claim to love Israel, but they don't give a damn about us! I've read some of their literature about the final days. And if you ask me, all they care about is hastening the day when their Messiah will return—and when all the bloody predictions in their Book of Revelations come true!"

"Revelation," Noor corrected him. "It's called the Book of Revelation."

Simon was on his feet. "Oh, you can't wait for Jacob's Trouble to begin, can you?" he shouted. *"Here, Israel, let us hold your coats while you go and fight the Antichrist—who will slaughter one-third of you from the face of the earth! Then we will have our Messiah!* So much for Christian love!"

Now Noor was on her feet, and Simon was lurching toward her again. Quickly she escaped his grasp and stood in the doorway.

"Pray to the God of Israel—Pray to *God your Redeemer!*—for the power to control your temper," she commanded. Then she turned and left the barracks.

Chapter 19

Terror in a Downtown Restaurant

Israel is still in the service of God and bears within its
bosom the future of all nations, so that all of Israel's
troubles are simply the birthpangs of the dawn of the
morning that is to come to all mankind. Israel's enemies
are the foes of the kingdom of God, and their very
abuses are the footsteps of the coming Messiah.

— Rabbi Samson Raphael Hirsch's commentary on
Psalm 89

JERUSALEM

Eric and Jody Mahr were out on a long-overdue night on the town,
thoroughly enjoying each other's company, when they suddenly
got into an argument: Jody said she was hungry. It was already 10:30,
so Eric suggested they go home, where he would make her an omelet.

"No way!" his wife shot back. "We're spending the night out,
including eating in a restaurant, even if it kills us."

With that, they hopped a cab and went to the pedestrian mall to eat
at Off the Square, the restaurant where Eric was then working as a chef.
Jody ordered a chef's salad. Eric ordered an omelet special.

As they ate, all the waitresses passing by said hello, and Robert
Vasl, one of the owners, joined the Mahrs for a cup of coffee. While they
chatted, Robert kept a wary eye on a bunch of rowdy teenagers sitting in
the front room. Then Robert brought out a lemon pie that Eric had baked
that morning, pointing out how hard the filling was. Had Eric used too
much starch? It was just like Robert: all business!

217

Alone again, Jody laughed about it, and Eric jokingly suggested that he might go back into the kitchen and bake another pie. "That will make Robert feel guilty," he said.

Suddenly they heard a bloodcurdling sound, like dozens of firecrackers going off at once. The youths in the front room all jumped up and the girls started screaming.

Terrorists were racing up the street, automatic guns blazing. The teens could actually see the fire spouting from the barrels of the guns.

"Into the back of the restaurant, *quick!*" Eric yelled to everyone, and he and Robert directed customers to the rear. "Everyone on the floor!" Eric shouted. "Hug the ground and stay down!"

Seeing that the terrorists would have a direct line of sight to where they were lying, Eric overturned a table to give them protection from flying bullets.

"Rimonim!" a voice was shouting in the distance. "Hand grenades!"

Eric kept pushing heads onto the floor, repeatedly reminding the teenagers to stay down.

Lying at the bottom of the pile of huddled bodies, Jody urged everyone to say the *Shema.*

Meanwhile, Robert had herded the four waitresses to the back of the restaurant.

"We're going to die!" one of the waitresses yelled. "They're going to kill us!" another cried. But another waitress grabbed them and said, "No. *'Hashem Ro'ee lo echsar '"*—meaning "The Lord is my Shepherd; I shall not want." The other women repeated this verse from *Tehillim* together and calmed down a bit. Some of the teenagers joined in.

Now the shooting grew louder.

"I think this is for real, kiddies!" Robert warned as he and Eric stood up and peered out the long aisle leading to the front gate. Then the shooting grew louder—and in the doorway was one of the terrorists, his back to them as he held his Kalashnikov in two hands, spitting death into the street.

Ducking down and making his way back to the rear, Eric told the others that they would have to take a chance and try to escape through the back door into the alley behind the restaurant. The girls crawled over, stood up and ran down the steps. One man on his hands and knees seemed petrified. Eric grabbed him by the collar and belt and dragged him, while Robert went to gather up the kitchen help to escape with them.

"I remember not being afraid for myself so much as for my wife and all the students," Eric recalled later. "I also remember feeling very, very angry—angry at this disruption in our lives, angry at the insanity that grips people, even angry that they weren't letting me finish my dinner!"

In the dark, Eric knew the way out and pushed the group, then cautiously opened the door leading to a corridor, which in turn led to the outside door and, hopefully, safety. As they stumbled on piles of garbage and boxes in the darkness, he met Robert coming through the kitchen with the girls. Eric opened the rear door and slowly stuck his head out.

"Be careful," he heard his wife say. "Please!"

Ping! Ping! Ping! Ping! went the bullets, and Eric quickly closed the back door. After a minute or so, Robert stepped forward and opened the door and said, "It's clear now," and they ran into the alley, struggling to climb over fences to get away as quickly as possible.

But Eric looked back at the kitchen and saw the restaurant's Arab workers—Shoeb, Umzed, Samir and Bassam. He and Robert shouted for them to follow, but they didn't.

"Which way?" Eric asked Robert.

"Straight up to Ben Yehuda," he said. "Go!"

Another *Ping!* and Eric yelled, "Help the girls over the fence!" Jody snagged her skirt on some barbed wire, and, breathless, they all started across a vacant lot toward the street ahead.

"He has a gun!" Jody suddenly cried, and one of the girls started screaming.

Eric stared at the figure standing before him. He was short, and his rifle looked bigger than him. But he was an officer responding to the emergency.

Looking back, Eric realized that two of the waitresses and some of the teens, as well as the Arab workers, hadn't caught up with them. But Jody insisted that they had to go home to their children right away. They took a taxi, and some time after arriving home, Eric was able to reach the restaurant by phone. The waitress who had initiated the *Tehillim* prayer answered the phone and said the border patrol had the situation in hand.

"Her story was incredible," Eric recalled later. "She and the others had waited for the Arabs, but the Arab workers had told them to leave first. The girls wouldn't hear of it. The shooting started coming very close, and they all feared they would be shot in their backs, so they stayed down. The Arab workers kept the girls down and protected them as best they could. The Arabs hadn't joined us when we called them because they feared they would be injured or shot by the Israelis if they ventured into the street for any reason. In fact, later, as the police prepared to put them in a van and bring them in for questioning, a crowd of angry people mercilessly beat these innocent men."

The police held their ground and took Shoeb, Umzed, Samir and Bassam in for questioning, later releasing them.

The final toll: one young Israeli woman, one Arab-Israeli citizen, and both terrorists died.

"The miracles that night were quite tangible," Eric reflected. "Had the terrorists come the night before, *motzaei Shabbos*, the area would have been packed with people. Had they come a half hour earlier, before the rain drove people away or indoors, more would have been shot. None of the terrorists' hand grenades explored! One terrorist actually pulled a grenade and tried to blow himself up and take the border patrol with him—but it didn't work!"

Eric Mahr also asked himself how he and Robert had managed to keep their cool, at least outwardly.

"A partial answer occurred to me a couple days later," he said, "as I spoke with our *Tehillim*-saying waitress as well as with one of the other, less religious girls—who had served in the army. The army had counseled her to remain cool and in control of each situation. Yet here, when the chips were down and she was not in control, she panicked. But her religious friend hadn't. The nonobservant girl couldn't understand it. The religious waitress explained: Her whole life she had been taught that *hakol bidei Shamayim*—Everything is in God's hands. If that is the case, we are never in control of circumstances . . . This is a lesson in faith we could all benefit from."

Munir and His Nephew
Discuss Murder

The next morning, as he arose from his bed, Munir was still thinking about his conversation with Noor on the Haram al-Sharif the night before. Samira was probably in her room, mourning the loss of her mother all over again. As he brooded darkly behind the counter, Munir also thought about his little nephew, whose life was saved when his wife jumped on the grenade thrown by Simon two years ago.

And then he thought of the boy's older brother, Ahmad. Yes, Ahmad should be told about this. Locking up the falafel stand, Munir hurried to the Petra Hotel, just down the street. Climbing the stairs of the crumbling building, he made his way up to the fourth floor. Pausing to catch his breath, he walked over to a window and looked down at the huge garbage-strewn courtyard, landlocked by the hotel and surrounding buildings. Munir grimaced as he wondered why nobody was cleaning up this wasteland, invisible to passers-by going to the Chain. It would be an ideal plaza for an open-air bazaar.

Turning from the window, Munir walked down the hall and knocked on a door. Opening it without waiting for a reply, he found Ahmad sitting up on his bed, fully clothed and shod, reading a book. Ahmad jumped to the floor and embraced his uncle.

"Uncle," Ahmad asked, "have you heard the latest news regarding our Arab Spring?"

"I have some very startling news for you," Munir told him. "News of a more personal nature."

The 17-year-old youth lit a cigarette and waited.

"Your cousin Samira has been seeing this Israeli soldier," Munir said.

"I could have told you this would happen," Ahmad replied, blowing cigarette smoke. "Leaving the faith—and then pretending to be a Jew. Now just watch this Zionist pig break her precious heart!"

"Well, he already has," Munir said.

"Good!" Ahmad said. "Now she can start getting over him and—"

"No," Munir said, scowling. "Not good. He has just confessed to her that he was the one who threw that grenade that your little brother almost grabbed that day—"

"What!"

"—and that your dear aunt smothered with her poor body!"

"No!" shouted Ahmad, and he dropped his cigarette to the floor and ground it out with his boot.

They stared at each other for a long moment.

"Where is he?" Amhad asked at last.

"Hold off," Munir said, and he sank into a chair facing the bed. Ahmad sat on his bed, his short legs barely reaching the floor.

"This soldier had been kept under wraps in the Golan Heights all this time," Munir said, "so none of us would recognize him. They never did tell anybody his name."

"And now he's back," Ahmad said. "Where is he stationed?"

"Hold off," his uncle said again. He had his beads in his hand, and he was working them silently.

Ahmad reached under his pillow and pulled out a pistol. Checking the safety, he handed it to Munir, handle first. With his beads hanging from a finger, Munir turned up his palms and held the gun on both hands, much as one would hold a dinner tray.

"Is it loaded?"

"Of course!" Ahmad retorted. "What good is an empty gun under one's pillow?"

Munir smiled at his nephew, the gun still balanced on his hands. "Ahmad, you must have many enemies."

"Don't you, Uncle?" he replied. "A faithful Palestinian has many enemies."

Munir handed the gun back to him.

"Can you count even *one* enemy, Uncle?"

Munir made a face.

"Not counting this Zionist soldier, of course," Ahmad added. "Surely you want him dead—no?"

"I see him dead, every time I think of him," Munir said, his voice rising. "Bloody, and broken, and quite dead. Yes."

More silence, as Amhad lit another cigarette.

"Tell me honestly, Uncle," he said. "Why did you come and tell me all this?"

Shrugging, Munir replied, "Who else can I tell? Everybody else has moved to Jordan. Even *you* were there for a while."

"They took my passport, and I had to *sneak* back here," Ahmad said. "I'm a fugitive in my own country. Now, all I do is wait for the day."

"The day!" Munir blurted, and almost laughed. "The day that never comes."

"It will."

"Did you every consider the possibility that it came and passed?" Munir said.

"There'll be another."

Munir sighed and stood up to look out the window. "What a waste of valuable real estate," he said to himself. "Just a parched, abandoned field."

"The parched earth was once covered with water and was called Hezekiah's Pool," Ahmad told him. "Some say this was where that man was crucified."

His uncle just shrugged.

"One time," Ahmed went on, "a group of archeologists began to clear the rubbish after being given access through one of the buildings. But that didn't last long. The building's tenant—a Palestinian, of course—was quickly threatened with cancellation of his lease. And why? Because allowing the archeologists into the courtyard might disturb the perceived status quo." Now Ahmad raised his hands in judgment and spoke in a mocking voice: "'Whoever had the power to grant such permission must have more authority than other contenders for ownership of this abandoned parcel! This cannot be allowed!'"

Munir returned to his chair. "Isn't it funny how it all comes down to the land?" he said.

"What else is there on this earth but the land?"

"People!" his uncle roared.

"I can see where this is going," Ahmad said. "Look—even when they conduct ethnic cleansing, it's still all about the land. See? The Zionist enterprise has been about ethnic cleansing from Day One."

"We had a chance to share the land," Munir said. "The Jews thought that once they settled here and 'made the desert bloom,' the flourishing farming economy would mollify us and bring us into business relationships."

"You mean employer-and-lackey relationships, don't you?"

"Even so . . ."

"Even so?"

"Ahmad," Munir said, "your grandfather believed that by cooperating with the Zionists, with all their wealth and ingenuity, we would all prosper again in Palestine."

"He was wrong," Amhad replied. "With all due respect to my grandfather."

Munir switched his beads to his other hand and said, "They called him a traitor. But in his heart, he was more loyal to the Arab cause than our national leaders were."

"More loyal than the Grand Mufti of Jerusalem?" Amhad said. "With all due respect."

"May Amin al-Husseini's soul rot in hell for what he did to us!" Munir shouted. "We had a chance to divide the land in 1947 and he opposed it."

"Rightfully."

"Stupidly!" Munir retorted. "Because look where we are now!"

"You just can't forgive him for siding with the Nazis," Amhad said.

"It wasn't that at all," Munir said. "Because of al-Husseini, the Higher Arab Command opposed the UN partition—and any Palestinian who supported partition was assassinated! He liquidated the opposition! So much for brotherly love."

"I guess my grandfather was lucky to escape," Ahmad said.

"Yes. And you can thank him that you were ever born. But if you look at how few of our people actually fought in the war against the Jews—Grand Mufti or no Grand Mufti behind them!—you'll realize how many of us really wanted to divide the land—or at least live in peace under one roof."

"So the Zionists took their portion of Palestine—according to the United Nations map—and then they went on to take 25 percent more—from the portion the UN had offered *us!*"

Munir smiled bitterly. "We would have done the same thing, no?"

"Of course," his nephew said. "But don't forget—the role played by my grandfather and so many other collaborators never got credit in Zion's history books. And do you know why? Because after the Jews drove the collaborators out, they didn't want to admit any reason for letting them back *in*."

Munir arose from his chair and picked up the pistol from the bed, feeling its weight in his hands. Then he began pacing the room, the pistol hanging in his left hand.

"Ahmad," he said, "I keep asking myself what kind of a life we will have, once we have our Palestinian state." He stopped and looked at him. "Do you ever ask yourself why Arabs like me who are citizens in Israel have no desire to become citizens of the 'State of Palestine'? With such corruption and savagery among our leaders?"

"The Jews are just as corrupt"

"But not as savage," Munir said.

"Oh, no?" his nephew retorted. "All of the Zionist fathers of the state of Israel started out as terrorists—murdering the British occupiers until they finally retreated from Palestine in 1948!"

"But there's one difference," Munir said. "The Irgun and the other terrorist groups were able to create a functioning democracy after they drove out the British. Sure, Hamas drove the Zionists out of Gaza—but they still show no ability, not even the inclination, to form a working government for all the people."

"That's Hamas," his nephew said. "But the Palestinian Authority is making progress in stabilizing the West Bank—if only the Jews would leave."

"Ahmad!" Munir cried out. "Don't you get it? Hamas and the PA are in a civil war! Throwing brothers off buildings in Gaza! They'd keep on killing each other if they could! What does that say about our *people*?"

Ahmad stared at Munir for a long moment, then said slowly, "That sounds like a racist statement, to me, Uncle."

"I'm not saying our people are *inferior*," Munir reassured him. "Although you do have to admit that the Zionists look pretty good to the world when they're willing to free a thousand of our most ferocious fighters from prison in exchange for just one measly IDF soldier we've captured."

"They're sooo stupid," Ahmad marveled in a loud whisper.

"Come on and admit it, Ahmad," Munir said. "Our Arab brothers can't get along with each other unless we're all under the heel of Hamas or some other dictatorship." Munir paused. "No. We're not inferior. It's just that the Zionists had plenty of experience living and working in democracies in Europe before they came here. And so I ask you again: Can a million Arab citizens of Israel all be wrong when they prefer *that*, to living under Hamas or the PA?"

"They prefer to stay in Israel," Ahmad replied, "because most of them never left—they're still living in their family homesteads. Why would they leave?"

"They're happy enough living as second-class citizens, surrounded by Zionists," Munir said ironically. "Just like the Palestinian refugees living in *Jordan*, who'd rather stay there than move to the West Bank once it's under Arab control. Every wonder why?"

Ahmad reached under his pillow and took out the extra ammunition magazine for his pistol. "I'd like to see the shoe on the other foot," he said. "I'd like to see a million Jews on the West Bank try to live under Palestinian rule!" he said, shaking the magazine at his uncle. "Now, are you going to tell me where I can find that sonofabitch who murdered my aunt, or am I going to have to track him down myself?"

"Just hold off," Munir told him again.

"My baby brother deserves revenge, too, you know!"

"Ahmad, you ask an interesting question: How could the Jewish settlers remain on our land if we succeed in raising the Palestinian flag over all of the West Bank?"

"They have to go!"

"Yes, of course," his uncle said. "But now and then we hear some of those settlers say that living on the land is more important to them than living under their Zionist flag. I think those religious fanatics are serious. Not only that, but everybody knows there's going to be a civil war breaking out between them and the IDF if the Israeli government ever agrees to evacuate those settlements and give it all back to us."

Ahmad popped a bullet out of the magazine and played with it in his hand. "That's why I favor the one-state solution. That's what most of our rich Palestinians are leaning toward now."

"But not the PLO," Munir said, "not the old guard. Because they know they'd be out of the picture. And rightfully so."

"And rightfully so."

Munir extended his left arm and aimed the pistol at the window overlooking Hezekiah's Pool. "You know," he said, "I used to see the West Bank as a great big chunk of Swiss cheese. We were the cheese, and those Jewish settlements were all the holes in the cheese. And I used to ponder this—is it possible that with all these Arab and Jewish towns scattered all over the place, neither side would dare use advanced weapons, or chemical warfare, because they'd only end up killing their own as well?"

"You're an idealist, Uncle," Ahmad said and laughed.

"But then," Munir said, drawing back the pistol and cocking his arm, so that it was aimed at the ceiling. "But then it dawned on me that this Swiss cheese arrangement would never work. Know why? Because one of these two sides doesn't give a damn how many of their own people they kill along the way! And guess which side I'm talking about."

Ahmad screwed up his face and said nothing.

"It's us, Ahmad! We're the ones who have become capable of such savagery." And with that, Munir tossed the pistol on Ahmed's bed and headed for the door.

"Wait, Uncle!"

Munir stopped.

Ahmad walked over to him. "Don't you see how the Jews have trapped themselves in this piece of Swiss cheese? Don't you see? *We* surround *them*. And until they decide to leave, they will continue to be harassed and vilified and boycotted and ostracized by the rest of the world. That's going to be *our* 'price tag'!"

Munir smiled broadly. Putting a hand on his nephew's shoulder, he chuckled to himself, then said, "Ahmad, you are so right. I must take you one of these days for another of our outings at the zoo. Do you remember the day we were standing with hundreds of spectators, gaping at the animals in their cages, and wondering to ourselves— *Wouldn't it be funny if the animals actually thought that we were the ones behind the bars, and they were the ones on the safe side, gaping at us?*"

Ahmad gave him a hug. "You've always been a real philosopher, Uncle. That's the only reason why I still speak to you these days. Here I am, risking everything to live back home in El Quds, and there you are, armed with nothing but a butcher knife, selling falafel to Jews and American tourists at Jaffa Gate."

Munir playfully kissed his nephew's forehead. "That's why *I* still like *you*, Ahmad. Because you don't give a damn what anybody thinks."

Munir reached for the doorknob, but his nephew stopped him.

"Let's get one thing straight, Uncle, before you return to your tourists. *We* are the ones who are the holes in the Swiss cheese. We've got less than 60 percent of the land. And I swear to you, whatever is left of the West Bank today is no longer sufficient to sustain itself as a sovereign state. The grid of Israeli settlements, towns and cities and highways has a stranglehold over us. So you can just forget about negotiating for a two-state solution."

"I disagree."

"Palestine must become a part of Israel—one sovereign, bi-national state—before Israel can be assimilated into Palestine!" Ahmad said.

"I'm the philosopher," Munir replied, "and you're the hopeless dreamer. In my humble opinion, Ahmad, the only way your dream will come true is if enough Jews are forced to leave Palestine and go back to the United States, or wherever they came from, for a better life and a safer life. The Israelis call it *reverse aliyah*, their worst nightmare."

"But *we're* the ones who are suffering this reverse aliyah!" Ahmad cried. "Our people are shriveling up, just like their brothers in Gaza! Do you know which Palestinians are leaving the West Bank? Our very elite! They can't take it anymore, and they're the ones with the resources to get out! We're being drained of our business leaders and our potential political leaders."

"Well," Munir replied, "I hope they're not moving to any Arab countries—because educated Palestinian Arabs who think for themselves are the last people those Arab nations want living in their midst!"

"That's for sure," Ahmad said.

"We've become the Jews of the Arab world," Munir said, swinging open the door and stepping into the hall. "'Shalom!'" he said sarcastically.

"'Shalom!'" Amhad called after them, and they heard each other laugh sardonically as Munir walked down the hall and to the stairs.

Chapter 20

What the Khatib Family Lost

Samir Al-Khatib of Kerak, Jordan, the book seller whose passport was revoked by the Jordanian government because of his activities with the Palestine Liberation Organization, comes from a family of Palestinian activists. Nor is their activism out of the ordinary for Palestinian Arabs.

I met Samir through two of his cousins living in the United States—Marwan Khatib and his sister, Samira Khatib. They told me stories of how their mother, Yusra, threw hand grenades at Israeli fighters during the battle for Jerusalem in 1948. Samira later spent several years writing for Arab publications in Jerusalem (where she was jailed in 1973), London and the Persian Gulf, interviewing the likes of Moammar Gadhafi of Libya and Saddam Hussein of Iraq.

Born in 1948 during Israel's War of Independence, Marwan was hidden between piles of mattresses during the bombing of Jerusalem. He says he is doing well in America but would leave everything and return if a Palestinian state were formed—or even if war broke out and he had a chance to fight for statehood.

Dressed in a three-piece suit, the chain-smoking Marwan is the image of success in the Palestinian Arab community and is one of its articulate spokesmen. But his emotional attachment to Palestine transcends intellectualism and politics: I saw tears in his eyes, behind his thick glasses, the night they raised $2,000 for the Palestinian victims in Lebanon after the Israeli invasion of 1982.

"We owe the PLO to the Israelis," he told me with his typical bitter irony. "From 1948 to 1967 we got things shoved down our throat by the Israelis. The PLO was born in 1965 as a tiny, minute, ineffectual resistance movement. It took us 17 years to fire a shot."

That shot was fired when Palestinian fighters in Lebanon faced the invading Israeli army. At the same time, he and other Palestinians

229

remain bitter that the Arab world stood by while the IDF routed the PLO and drove it out of Lebanon.

Marwan remembers picking and eating figs in Jerusalem outside his grandfather's house. He was 19 years old and again hiding from bombs during the Six Day War, when Jordan joined other Arab countries that were amassing their forces on the Israeli borders, intent on destroying the Jewish state. In the end, Jordan lost the West Bank, Egypt lost Gaza, and Syria lost the Golan Heights.

Marwan told me that the Jordanian defeat left his grandfather's house under Israeli occupation. He says he saw the Israelis bulldoze the house, in the Old City, not far from Jaffa Gate, in their cleanup operation after the war. And he still savors the figs that he will never again pick from that tree.

"After the Israelis came in," he says, "I was in a demonstration against the occupation. That must have got me a police record. I worked for a bank, but it closed. I lost the tourist guide job too. We went to Jordan. . . ."

In 1972, he says, his father suffered sunstroke while waiting in line to visit the West Bank from Jordan. He died. That year, Marwan moved to the United States. He purchased a country property in upstate New York with a house for himself and a house for his sister and their mother.

"So America is the only country that got us back together as human beings," he says, the irony returning to his voice. "Every time I'm asked where I was born, I have to say I'm Palestinian. That was the curse the moment I was born, but I'm proud of it. They say, 'Oh, terrorists!' I say, 'Ask what made them terrorists. We didn't create you a problem, you created us one. My ancestors had been there for centuries.'"

Marwan Khatib says Jews who had lived for generations in Palestine before 1948 have as much right as Palestinian Arabs to live there now. But since then, Zionism brought in hordes of Jews from around the world on grounds that God had given the land to Abraham's *Jewish* descendants for all time.

"If they go by the Biblical right," he says, "all the Protestants may move to Canterbury, all the Catholics to Rome, all the Moslems to Mecca. We know Israel started there—way back—but not the Poles or Russians who adopted their religion. Don't tell me just because you converted to the Jewish religion that makes you a Palestinian Jew."

Moshe Dayan was born in Palestine and was a legitimate Palestinian Jew, Marwan says, but Menachem Begin was born in Poland and was "an illegal alien." As for Israeli Jews who came from Arab countries after 1948, he argues, they have no rights in Palestine.

Marwan was the first Palestinian Arab who predicted to me that the Israelis will have a civil war, sooner or later, and that is when they will lose Palestine. (I think of this often . . .)

"In Jerusalem," he smiles behind his metal-rimmed glasses, "you'd think God was running out of real estate. You've got Moslems in the mosque praying, you've got Jews outside the Wall praying, and you've got Christians in their holy shrines praying. I say Palestine is for the Palestinians of all religions; it was Jesus' birthplace, and there are Palestinian Christians too."

Marwan doesn't take much comfort in still having a Jordan passport. The Jordanian massacre of PLO fighters during a crackdown in 1970 was proof, to him, that the Palestinian refugees have not become Jordanians in the eyes of the government.

Can Palestinians and Israelis ever live in peace in the Holy Land?

"Yes," he says, "I can see recognition of Israel if a Palestinian state is formed in the West Bank and Gaza. And we'd be a good buffer for Israel against the other Arabs—because we can deal with them. But I don't want to be a part of Israel. I just want to feel that sovereignty."

*

Marwan's sister, Samira Khatib, is an angry woman. A dissident writer and political activist, she was jailed several weeks during the 1973 Yom Kippur War while working for a Palestinian Arab newspaper in Jerusalem. A few months later, she says, after a late-night rendezvous with his staff, the editor disappeared and was never heard from again.

"I think they kidnapped him," she told me. "We covered all the issues—nothing scary—but we printed what we thought of the occupation and how it corrupts the occupier and destroys the occupied."

Since then, she has been all over the Mideast and Europe, starting newspapers and trying to tell the story of the Palestinian "diaspora." Palestinian Arabs are scattered all over the world, she noted, and they build successful businesses and careers. "They're not really brighter than other Arab people," she said. "But they had a 70 percent education level in 1948 (when Israel was born) and now 100 percent of them are educated."

Born in Jerusalem in 1954, Samira Khatib speaks both Arabic and Hebrew and studied creative writing at the University of Iowa in 1974. She left her native Jerusalem again in 1977 to cover Mideast politics.

In London, she wrote for the *Al Manar* and the *July 23 Magazine*. The latter's name commemorates the day in 1952 when Gamel Abdel Nasser came to power in Egypt; later it opposed Egyptian President Anwar Sadat's peace talks with Israel.

Then she wrote for *Al Khateej*, a daily newspaper in the United Arab Emirates, but left when it sided with Iran in the war with Iraq. She remembers meeting Saddam in Iraq in 1978, 1979 and 1980 when the Iraqi president was courting the Arab media.

"What he liked was the pan-Arabic mentality that we had," she recalls. "I was coming from Palestine, and he felt the same way that I felt about what's happening to us in Palestine. He's the best listener I have ever seen."

She and other female journalists also found Saddam attractive as a man.

"He's as handsome as hell," she told me. "I remember a girl from Lebanon who was with me in '78, and she was just looking at him. And he said. 'Do you have a question?' She said, 'Damn, you are so nice looking.' And this guy blushed! He turned red."

In 1991 Samara Khatib opposed the U.S.-led invasion that drove Iraqi forces out of Kuwait. "They want Saddam to withdraw from Kuwait," she told me at the time. "If they'd just go to any history book—the man can't withdraw from his own land."

Iraq had always considered Kuwait a part of Basra, Iraq's only port on the Persian Gulf, she said. Iraq never recognized Kuwait as a British protectorate in 1897, nor as an independent nation when the British withdrew in 1961 and left it to the Sabah family.

Samira Khatib dreams of a "secular democracy" in Palestine, ruling Jews and Arabs with an even hand. "I can live with Jews and they can live with me—worship is their right," she says. "To me, the biggest thing about Palestine is the Arab culture—the beauty of the area—the colorful Arab world."

If that secular state were born on the West Bank, she says, within 10 to 15 years it would establish "some kind of unity, not only with the rest of Palestine (Israel) but with Jordan. I want one Arab world; I am tired of passports."

Samira Khatib's temperamental moods swing from the sublime to the horrifying. The poetess can speak of her love of God—"Sometimes in a field I feel so close to Him, that's how beautiful He is"—but suddenly she can paint a picture of catastrophic nihilism—"A lot of Palestinians can reach despair and decide we are not going to die in vain; then every oil well in the Arab countries is going to be exploded . . . we'll explode the whole world if you don't listen."

And, as a mother, she could rock her son in her arms and wonder about the future of her people. In her poem, "Song of the Diaspora," she writes:

Far away from home,
in your diaspora, my baby,
I'm sure you will excel even in wandering.
You're going to starve, I know.

So fight the greedy ones
and don't accept any kind of chains.
Yet I know you're going to ask me:
"Mother,
why was I born wearing a soldier's uniform?
Why do they split the earth
into countries, states and closed borders,
when my love for humanity
and life
has no borders?"

Who Is Noor?

Up on the Temple Mount the next day, Samira was deep in prayer, seated in her favorite spot. Concealing her head in the *hijab* that she used to wear as a Muslim, she sat on the steps of the 500-year-old Fountain of Qaytbay, where Muslims wash their hands before entering the Dome of the Rock. But since becoming a Christian, she no longer sat facing the mosque. Instead, she sat facing east, toward the Mount of Olives. Within her line of sight was the Golden Gate, which Jews believe the Messiah will use when he arrives in the Old City. The gate had been sealed shut with building blocks and adorned with barbed wire by Muslims, who had also created a burial ground outside the gate—all to prevent the Jewish Messiah from ever entering Jerusalem without defiling himself by contact with the dead.

Samira was sitting under a cyprus tree, bringing to her mind the vision of trees growing in the old Temple precincts, and her favorite verse from Psalm 82, "planted in the house of the Lord, they shall flourish in the courts of our God." But today she did not feel like a flourishing cyprus, palm tree, or cedar of Lebanon.

Looking at her hands, which were wet with her tears, Samira felt moved to pray from Psalm 26, a purification prayer associated with pilgrims about to enter the Temple.

"I will wash my hands in innocence," she prayed, "and walk around your altar, Adonai, lifting my voice in thanks and proclaiming all your wonders. Adonai, I love the house where you live, the place where your glory abides. Don't include me with sinners or my life with the bloodthirsty . . . My feet are planted on level ground; in the assemblies I will bless Adonai!" (CJB)

Suddenly she shook off the *hijab* covering her head, letting her long hair fly freely.

"Israel knows You as God the Father," she prayed. "Please let them come to know you also as God the Redeemer! And may your Divine Presence soon return to this holy Mount Moriah!"

She paused to wipe her eyes with her cloak. These were tears of joy, not tears of mourning. "Yeshua," she cried out loud, "You are the visible image of the invisible God. You are supreme over all creation!

For me, You are the very presence of God in this place. The Divine Presence that the prophets longed for." Turning her head to glance at the golden Dome, where the Temple once stood, she murmured to herself, "If indeed the blood of goats and bulls, and the ashes of a red heifer sprinkled on those who are ceremonially unclean, can purify us, how much more will the blood of Yeshua . . . which was offered, unblemished, to God! You have made me a temple of God! Fill me, O Lord, with Your Divine Presence!"

Someone was approaching her. She turned.

"Go away, Noor!" she cried. "Can't you see what I'm going through?"

"Of course I do," Noor told her. "I saw it coming . . ."

Samira stared at her. "You knew what Simon had done? And you told me nothing?!"

"How could I?" said Noor, reaching out to comfort her.

"Get away from me!" Samira screamed, shrinking away from Noor. "You're just a—meddling troublemaker!"

"Samira—"

"Who sent you here, anyway? I mean—"

"Everything in its time, Samira," Noor said.

"Why—you were the one who brought the Red Heifer to us! You sold it to us!"

"But don't forget, you were the one who picked the Red Heifer out of my flock."

"And then you went and told *Itzak* we had it! Simon heard the whole thing! Why have you come here? And why did you bring this animal to Jerusalem? It's a curse! Isn't it?"

". . . Yes, and no."

"Why . . . ?"

"Samira," Noor told her, "the Red Heifer will someday bring us the New Jerusalem. And I believe the time is near, because of the rising hatred in the world—hatred for Jews and other people of God. But first, the New Jerusalem must begin to take form in the heart of just one person. Like you. Then another person. And another . . ."

Samira was frantically shaking her head.

". . . I trusted you. 'Noor'—'Light.' Huh! But now I'm all confused."

"Noor is my Bedouin name. I have another name—a Hebrew name."

"So you even travel with an alias!"

"It is . . . Moreh."

"*Moreh*? That means *Teacher*. So . . . who are you, then? *Tell me!*"

"Did not Abram become Abraham? Did not Saul of Tarsus become Paul? Even Moses had an Egyptian name before he led his people out of bondage," Noor said. "And then there was Simon—who became Peter."

Softening, Samira begged her, "Won't you tell me who you really are?"

"First, let's remember who *you* are: 'Samira'—the watcher in the night," Noor told her. "Be watchful! And remember: If the mountain won't come to Mohamed—"

Samira was suddenly enraged to hear this again.

"Just go!" she screamed. "**Gooo!**" And her voice echoed across the Temple Mount, as Noor quietly departed.

Moments later, Samira felt a calm come over her, and she sensed the presence of the Lord here on the Temple Mount, where He was presented as an infant by His parents, where He taught for three years, and where He drove out the money changers. *Abide in Me, My beloved*, the voice said, and she sobbed for joy. *You Mother is with Me, and I am with you all the days of your life . . .*

*

Hearing Samira's voice from above, Simon stepped away from the Wall and looked up. Rushing to the steps, he climbed to the top of the stairs leading to the Temple Mount. At the Maghrubi Gate, the Muslim guard, seeing his IDF uniform, was about to block his entry—but then he recognized Simon as the soldier who guards the Wall. Although they served two bitterly divided peoples, the two guards had a nodding acquaintance and in fact had discussed, briefly, how tragic it was that the descendants of the patriarch Abraham—Isaac and Ishmael—were still at each other's throats over the land.

Simon began walking through the grassy park leading to the beautiful blue-tiled Dome of the Rock, resplendent in the afternoon sun. A gentle breeze barely stirred the fir trees. In the distance, he could see the Old City to his left and the Mount of Olives to his right.

Muslim women were seated on a brick bench, smothered head to foot in their *burqas*, talking quietly or not at all. One of them turned and looked at him for a long time, following him with her eyes. Nearby, a cluster of Muslim men sat on the grass beneath a spreading olive tree whose trunk was several feet in diameter, surely making it at least fifteen hundred years old.

Then he spotted Samira, seated by herself under a cyprus tree, not far from an ancient fountain. Her eyes were closed and she seemed to be deep in prayer. Simon looked at her for a long time, until she sensed his presence and turned her head away.

"Samira," he said, "I can't tell you how it fills me with sorrow, what I did. When I learned in the Army hospital the name of the woman—and realized it was your mother—I requested the transfer to the Golan Heights and stayed away as long as I could . . . Can you ever forgive me, Samira?"

She only shook her head and sobbed . . .

"Samira, I love you with all my heart," Simon pleaded. "Everything I thought I could have *after* all—a woman like you!—I can't bear to think that I've lost you too! Will you forgive me?"

"Simon," she said. "This came on so fast. I haven't sorted out my feelings about you yet . . . Now I must go."

"Samira . . . ?"

Standing up to go, Samira told Simon, "I am wondering why God would have put us on the same land. Are you Jews here in Palestine to somehow turn us into better Arabs?"

"I'm afraid we have brought out the worst in you," he replied.

"Or," Samira said, "is it possible that God sent us to this land in order to test and prove you Jews—to see if you would obey His command to act justly toward the strangers living in your midst?"

"Wait, Samira—don't leave!" he called after her.

Hurrying toward the steps, she turned her head back and said, "This is the mountain where Abraham was about to sacrifice his son. It's also where Yeshua of Nazareth taught and prayed, and where he drove away the money changers. And, yes, Isaac was right—Yeshua *did* refer to it as his Father's house."

"So—what about—Christian forgiveness?" he asked.

"Christian forgiveness!?" she exclaimed, stopping at the top step and turning toward him. Suddenly she turned silent, staring at him for a long moment. Then she said: "Simon, if you truly want Christian forgiveness—then you must confess with your mouth that Yeshua is the Messiah, and you must believe in your heart that God raised Him from the dead. Then you will saved."

Simon was startled for a moment. "I want to believe as you do, Samira," he pleaded. "I want to have what you have! But I can't believe in something I can't see. If only he would show himself to me!"

"Just step out in faith," she said. "When anyone acknowledges that Yeshua is the Son of God, God dwells in him, and he in God."

Simon shook his head, confused and frustrated. "It's always about religion, isn't it?" he shouted.

"It isn't at all about religion!" she shouted back at him. "It's about a *person*—the Messiah!"

"Samira," he said, "why have you let the Red Heifer come between us? You and I could be having an intelligent conversation about our future together, if it weren't for Isaac and his Rabbi and their mad mission to rebuild the Temple!"

"You know something, Simon?" she retorted. "I have been reading the New Testament again, and I now believe that the Jews *should* rebuild the Temple—so it will be here for Yeshua, when He returns as Messiah!" And sneering spitefully at him, she turned and hurried down the steps from the Temple Mount.

"So you have become a religious fanatic, like the others!" Simon shouted after her. "Like the ones who are always on a religious Crusade!"

"If only the Crusades had been successful," Samira shouted from the ground below, "there would be a *cathedral* up on that spot, instead of a phony Muslim mosque!"

Shaking his head as he looked down from the Temple Mount, Simon replied: "You really *are* a flaming fundamentalist!"

"And you are an anti-religious bigot!" she shouted back. "Like Cain—jealous of his brother's love for the Lord! Cain called Abel a 'fundamentalist' for being so religious—and killed him!"

"*You* are the fundamentalist!" he shouted. "You Christians can't wait to start World War III—so soldiers like me can die in a bloody massacre that will bring this Yeshua of yours back as your Messiah!"

"—Please don't say that!" she cried.

"I am a Jew!" Simon cried out, his voice echoing through the plaza beside the Wailing Wall. "And I do not want to fight and kill one more Arab over the Temple Mount!"

*

Samira hurried back to the falafel stand and disappeared inside. "Betrayed," she whispered as she sat down in her room and began flipping through her Bible. "Betrayed. Betrayed!" When she stopped flipping pages, the Bible stood open at a chapter about the Last Supper. Yeshua was telling His disciples that He would be arrested late tonight, and that tomorrow He would die. Peter boldly told Him, "Lord, I am prepared to go with you both to prison and to death!" Yeshua replied, "I tell you, Kefa, the rooster will not crow today until you have denied three times that you know me."

Then, after His arrest, Yeshua was taken to the home of the high priest. A crowd gathered around the bound prisoner in the courtyard, awaiting Yeshua's trial. Peter had hidden himself in the crowd. In the course of that long night, Peter was asked three times whether he was one of Yeshua's followers. Three times Peter denied it. Then the rooster crowed, and Yeshua, looking across the courtyard, made eye contact with Peter.

Peter went out and wept bitterly.

Samira had always found this the saddest, most heart-wrenching moment in the entire New Testament. For Peter had been the first Apostle to identify Yeshua as the Messiah.

*

Meanwhile, Simon had come down from the Temple Mount and was on patrol at the Wall. But soon he took a little prayer book out of the pocket of his uniform.

"It has been said," he reminded himself, "that the destruction of the Temple was a blessing for the Jewish religion. Without an altar for animal sacrifice, the Jews had to learn how to pray on their own, as they wandered the world with their portable religion."

Simon stood still and opened the prayer book.

"Sometimes I actually open this little prayer book. It comes with the Army uniform, and it's to be kept in the pocket. Maybe it can give me the comfort I need . . . Not that I'm going to become a black hat religious Jew like Itzak . . . but there happens to be one Psalm that has always fascinated me."

Simon flipped through the pages and stopped.

"Ah, here it is—these foreign kings got together and approached Jerusalem for the attack. But suddenly they saw something that stopped them dead in their tracks. It says here, 'Terrified, they took to flight.'" Keeping a finger in the book, he recalled a story he had once heard from some soldiers who had fought in the Six Day War back in 1967.

"It seems that this tiny Israeli unit, with only a couple tanks, was out on patrol in the desert when they came over a sandy hilltop and suddenly saw scores of Arab tanks grouped below them. The

Israelis stopped and prepared to retreat. But then a very strange thing happened. All the Arab tanks turned and headed in the other direction—as if *they* were in retreat."

Simon began walking slowly along the Wailing Wall.

"The Israelis followed the retreating Arabs and were able to capture one tank. When the Israelis asked why all the Arab tanks had retreated, the Arab soldiers said they had looked up and suddenly saw a hundred Israeli tanks up on the hilltop! It was a desert mirage—or something."

He stopped and opened the little book again.

"If ever I found a prophecy that seemed to have come true, it was in this Psalm, where it says: *'Terrified, they took to flight,'* And it continues, *'We heard it, and now we see for ourselves . . . in the city of our God'"* (Psalm 48, CJB).

Closing the book, Simon resumed his patrol of the Wall.

"I have wondered for years about the little Psalm . . . and that incident in the desert. Mirage? Or a *new* miracle in the desert? I have read on, the next verse or two, for an explanation of why these kings—who had advanced upon Jerusalem to attack her—abruptly fled. But it is unsatisfactory."

Stopping, he opened the book again and read: *"'. . . in the city of our God. May God establish it forever. God, within your—'"*

Suddenly he stopped reading and stared at the page in disbelief.

"'God, within your—temple'—the Temple!—*'within your temple we meditate on your grace.'"*

Closing the book again and returning it to his pocket, Simon stepped forward and marched along the Wailing Wall.

Isaac had been eavesdropping on him from outside the prayer room at the end of the Wall.

"March on," Isaac whispered, "Watchman on the Wall!"

Now a bomb went off somewhere, and Simon headed toward the source of the **Boom!**

"O Shepherd of Israel," Isaac prayed as he watched Simon leave, "save us from the plague that wreaks havoc at noon. You make our enemies fight over us, and our enemies mock us. God of armies restore us!"

Isaac stepped out in front of the Wall and spread his arms toward the sky. "You brought a vine out of Egypt, you expelled the nations and planted it . . . Why did you break down the vineyard's wall, so that all passing by can pluck its fruit? God of armies, please come back! Make your face shine, and we will be saved."

The air was shattered by another **Boom!**

Isaac refused to run for cover but continued his prayer to the sky: "And they say, 'Come, let us cut them off from being a nation—that the name of Israel may be no more.'" He paused. "O God, we wait for peace, to no avail. For a time of healing, but terror comes instead."

His words were drowned out by yet another loud **Boom!**

Chapter 21

Young Sabras at Lev Smdar Bar

JERUSALEM

Today is the 50th anniversary of the founding of the State of Israel, and that "**Boom!**" was the sound of Arab Palestinians holding protests across the land. Eight people were killed today, and eighty injured. In Gaza and the West Bank, they staged marches to commemorate what they call the *Nakba*, the catastrophe of 1948.

After seething for 19 years over the existence of the Jewish state, its Arab neighbors in 1967 sought to force a permanent change in the geography of the Mideast. Mobilizing their armies on Israel's borders, they prepared to invade and take over all—or least some—of the land occupied by Jews. They planned to settle the land with Arabs whose families had fled western Palestine in 1948 (most of them living today in eastern Palestine, or Jordan).

Faced with a threat to its very existence, Israel struck first, repelled the Arab armies on its borders, and went on to take Gaza from Egypt, the Golan Heights from Syria, and Judea and Samaria (the West Bank) from Jordan. Since then, Israeli families had been allowed to create settlements on the West Bank, from which they had been driven by the Romans 2,000 years earlier. Like the Arab nations that had tried to alter the borders of Israel forever, the Israelis had no serious intention of ever evacuating the "occupied territory" of the Judea and Samaria, once the euphoria over their unexpected victory faded and political reality set in.

CNN television says today that 770,000 Arabs fled western Palestine during Israel's War of Independence in 1948 (Israel says it was 550,000). Their families now number between three million and four million, about half of them living in the occupied territories. In addition, another 1.5 million Arabs are Israeli citizens whose families never left western Palestine.

Today, in the Lev Smdar restaurant and bar, attached to the Little House in the Colony, these matters are being discussed by several young *sabras* (Israelis born in Israel). A young bartender named Joel pours Leffe, a dark Belgian beer, into a goblet. Smoking a cigarette, Joel looks Germanic with his blond hair. He wears earrings and a white shirt, with the sleeves rolled up and the buttons open to reveal an orange T-shirt.

Joel has been studying a small Torah, issued by the Israel Defense Forces to its reservists. The book is open on the bar. Looking up from his study, Joel asks: *"Why were they commanded to kill everyone in Canaan?"*

"Because of their idols," I reply. "It's the First Commandment."

"You're going to kill your brother or sister if they worship idols?" Joel asks.

"Yes," comes my reply. "The Canaanites were sacrificing their babies to demons. And the Israelites would be tempted to follow their example."

There is talk of more Palestinian riots. Also tomorrow, students plan a rally on King George Street to protest the Orthodox-leaning government's pressure on the Batsheva Dance Troupe to wear tights so as not to offend the religious when disrobing during the coming celebration of Israel's independence.

"The difficulty is photographing the riots," Joel says. He has a Nikon camera with a 70- to 200-millimeter zoom lens.

"We must act justly toward the stranger living in our midst," Joel says, returning to his Torah. Now he is making a boiling *kalva* tea in a glass cup.

"There is a cultural war going on," Joel says, referring to developments that have occurred since the Batsheva Dance Troupe abruptly pulled out of the national celebration. "Now the president of Israel has canceled the IDF singers because some of them are women, and the Orthodox do not approve of women singing to men. *But Miriam sang as they crossed the Red Sea!*" he says, pointing to his Torah. "Sometimes living in Israel is like living under the old Shah of Iran. I mean, if women can't sing in the Knesset . . ."

A young man sitting at the bar is saying that the Mideast is awry because, "People are running away from God." He says this includes the ultra-Orthodox who are intent on rebuilding the Temple. Although he isn't wearing a kipa, he says he has returned to God in the past year.

His friend Michael opens a lukewarm bottle of Merlot and offers everyone a toast, *"L'chaim!"* Michael has spent some time in Britain, and his English is excellent. A philosophy student and an agnostic, he feels we must stop looking outside ourselves to blame others (including God) for our failures. The answer, he feels, must lie somewhere within us; but he hasn't yet found it.

A bar maid, Efat, has been sitting between them but says nothing. She is reading a leaflet for the Diva International party that is to be held at Benyanei Haooma, the city's convention hall, this Saturday.

Michael says that today he made some African drums, which is his hobby. Despite being an agnostic, he says he admires Joel's Torah study, which he understands to be "for his project" of photographing the street protests.

Soon Michael and Joel are drinking tall Carlsbad beers at the bar.

A thin girl with black bangs, wearing a mint-green top with a sash, comes into the bar from the cinema next door and takes a cigarette from Michael's pack.

A young man named Elan comes in and stands at the bar. All he asks for is a glass of water. Elan works at Sergio's, an Italian restaurant north of Machane Yehuda, on Agrippa Street, and he hopes someday to have his own restaurant. His mother is from Naples, his father from Livorno, so he speaks Italian as well as Hebrew and English. Elan sips his water, spinning somebody's cell phone on the bar, now and then popping into his mouth a green olive from the little bowl that Joel has put out for customers.

Now I see a young woman named Michel taking a break at the bar. She works at the adjacent cinema while studying film at the Sam Spiegel Film and Television School here in Jerusalem.

"What if there were an Arab who possessed a genuine red heifer?" I ask.

Shrugging off the question, Michel says that her film project is to make a twelve-minute video titled "Genetics." It's about her grandmother—who was widowed by suicide—and whose granddaughter was born out of wedlock. Michel says she wants to shoot some of the video in a nearby cemetery.

"The cemetery gate is locked," she says. But she knows a cemetery employee who happens to be in love with her mother.

His Torah still open on the bar, Joel mixes two whiskey-and-Cokes. Then he makes a pressure-fizzling drink from the coffee maker. As it foams, Joel deftly pours cream into it from a pewter pitcher and serves it to a patron.

What the Imam Said

Not until he was in the presence of the Imam did Munir happen to put a hand into a pocket and feel the single bullet in his fingers. Instantly, he realized that his nephew Ahmad, in their parting embrace, had slipped him the bullet he had been playing with in his room that day at the Petra Hotel. Withdrawing his empty hand from the pocket, Munir looked into the eyes of the Imam and wondered if he had sensed anything.

The Imam was talking about the chaos that had engulfed the Arab world after the people rose up in Tunisia, in Egypt, in Libya and other Muslim countries and deposed the dictators who had ruled them since the creation of modern Arab 'states' by the Western colonial powers following World War II.

"We were told that our Muslim brothers were rising up against their rulers because they wanted democracy," the Imam was saying. "But what did they mean by 'democracy'? They must have known very well that Western-style democracy is the creation of infidels with no respect for Islam."

"Well," Munir ventured, "at least our brave brothers have toppled their secular political leaders. Now the way is clear for Islamic republics to emerge from the dust."

"Exactly!" the Imam replied. "Islam is stirring from its slumber once again, and _Sharri'a_ law can take its proper place again. But look at all this chaos—as the tribes of Libya turn against each other and struggle for power—and for revenge against each other. At least those secular dictators knew how to keep all these tribal rivalries under lock and key."

"Imam," Munir asked, "do you think the Arab Spring has been more of a curse than a blessing for Islam?"

"Munir," the Imam replied, gesturing for him to pour more tea for both of them, "this chaos and dividedness in Islam was prophesied centuries ago—and you and I are privileged to live in the day when it all will come true. For when the Mahdi comes, he will bring together all the fractured pieces of Islam before he leads us in battle to win the whole world for Allah!"

The Imam sipped his tea, and Munir sipped his. Then Munir told the Imam why he had asked for an audience today. After hearing Munir's

246

story, the Imam began talking about how the Jews will be driven out of Palestine during the present generation. The Europeans who had adopted the Jewish religion had no right to colonize Palestine after the Nazi Holocaust. However, those Jews already living in Palestine might have been permitted to stay.

Munir asked the Imam about the 800,000 Jews who moved to the Zionist state from the Arab countries where they had lived for centuries. The Imam replied that those Jews had already been living in peace in the Islamic world when they betrayed their hosts' generosity by colonizing parts of Palestine along with the European Zionists.

The Imam then gave Munir a brief Islamic teaching on the coming of the Muslim savior, who is not mentioned in the Qu'ran but has always been part of Islamic tradition, since the seventh century. To Shi'ite Muslims, he is the Promised One—descended from the Prophet Muhammed as the 12th Imam, who disappeared as a youth in a cave in the year 878 in what is now Iraq. The Promised One will reappear at the end of the age, when the world is in chaos, and he will lead his warriors to conquer the world for Islam.

To Sunni Muslims, he went on, it is al-Mahdi, the Guided One, who will complete this Islamic conquest. Then, after seven years, he will die.

The Imam said that, according to one authentic *hadith*, the Prophet Muhammed said: "Our Mahdi will have a broad forehead and a prominent nose. He will fill the earth with justice as it is filled with injustice and tyranny. He will rule for seven years."

Another authentic *hadith* says that the Prophet declared: "He will be among us. Allah will conclude his religion through him just as he began it with us."

The Imam then went on to quote from other sources—saying that the Mahdi will be 40 years old when he appears, that he will be fair complexioned but will have a black spot on his left cheek, and that he will speak with a slight stutter.

Finally, he quoted a source claiming that the Prophet Muhammed once declared: ". . . the members of my household shall suffer a great affliction and they shall be forcefully expelled from their homes after my death—"

—And here Munir blurted a sound that caused the Imam to stop and look at him.

"Yes, Munir," the Imam said, "we all were driven from our homes by the Zionists. But I say to you that the Mahdi will come in our time! And he will cause the Zionists to sign a seven-year treaty with Islam! The

Zionists will be permitted to rebuild their temple somewhere on the Haram al-Sharif and resume their ritual sacrifices—"

"No!" Munir cried.

The Imam smiled. "Do not worry, Munir. For after the first three and a half years, the Mahdi will come upon the Zionists with all his troops and force them to worship Allah!"

"What?!" Munir cried out.

"Yes," the Imam said. "This is why the Islamic world will agree to sign the seven-year treat with the Zionists. To entrap them—and convert them for Allah!"

Munir marveled at this. "But how will the Jews ever embrace Islam?" he asked.

"Munir," the Imam replied, "have you ever heard of the Jew named Shabbetai Tzevi? The 17th Century mystic from Smyrna?"

"No."

"Well, a Jew named Nathan of Gaza had a vision, and he persuaded this mystic, Shabbetai Tzevi, to declare himself the Messiah. Which he did in 1665. And he was well received in his native Turkey. This caused great excitement and expectation throughout the Jewish world. But then, in 1666, he went to Istanbul to receive his kingdom from the Sultan. Instead, he was immediately arrested and imprisoned!"

"Hah!" Munir said.

"Yes—and not only that, Munir. When threatened with death, Shabbetai Tzevi converted to Islam!"

"No!" Munir shouted, and the Imam joined him in laughter.

"But then," the Imam went on, "some of his followers adopted Islam too—while continuing in secret to observe many of their Jewish customs, along with Shabbetai's prayers and rituals. And for more than a century, long after his death, the followers of this cult worked out a rationale that, somehow, at some time in the distant future, all of Jewry will do as they have done and convert to Islam."

As Munir rose to leave his presence, the Imam handed him a slip of paper on which he had written a verse from the Qu'ran.

"Munir," the Imam said as he embraced him, "the Mahdi will wear a crown and ride a white horse as he leads all of us to world conquest! So, you can forget about this Israeli soldier for now. The Mahdi will take care of him. In fact, maybe we shouldn't discourage them from building their temple somewhere up on the Haram al-Sharif—so long as it doesn't disturb the Dome of the Rock."

Munir departed, with visions of the crowned Mahdi on a white horse galloping through his mind.

Chapter 22

From Daniel to the Book of Revelation

And the final phase of the history of nations preceding the advent of the kingdom of God, to which Psalm 93 looks, will end with the rise of one single world-conquering power which will swallow up all the other nations. Ezekiel calls this power Gog. Then there will be only one world power on earth which will unite all other nations beneath its rule. But there is still One Who will be mightier than even this conqueror nation—the Lord, "Who alone is mighty on high."

— Rabbi Samson Raphael Hirsch, *The Psalms*, 1882

PATMOS, GREECE

But the Imam visited by Munir was mistaken. In the Book of Revelation, the conquering rider on the white horse is identified not as the Muslim Mahdi, but as the Antichrist.

John, who outlived all the other apostles of Messiah Yeshua, is credited with writing this final book of the New Testament. The youngest of the apostles, John was also the most mystical and wrote the Gospel introducing Yeshua as the "Word" that had existed from the very beginning with God, and that in fact was God. Before his death Yeshua made this prophecy: "Jerusalem will be trampled on by Gentiles until the times of the Gentiles are fulfilled" (Luke 21:24) (NKJV).

That time is now imminent. The elderly apostle saw it coming.

Composed as late as 96 AD, the Book of Revelation is based on a vision the elderly apostle had while living on the rocky island of Patmos in the Aegean Sea, where he had been banished by the Roman Emperor Domitian. The Greek island, with an area of only 13 square miles, is off the coast of modern-day Turkey, and not far from the sites of ancient Smyrna and Ephesus.

Much of John's book reflects the end times prophecies found in the Old Testament, particularly in the Book of Daniel. Christians believe that Daniel, the last major Hebrew prophet, foresaw the Book of Revelation more than six centuries before John wrote it. Another six centuries later, Muhammed wrote the Qu'ran in the 7th Century AD, drawing from both testaments of the Bible. Today, Islam's end times prophecies borrow extensively from John's last book, adding twists and turns to fabricate an entirely different outcome of human history.

Perhaps the most remarkable similarity is Islam's expectation that the Mahdi will reign for seven years, echoing the seven-year treaty that John (and Daniel) said Israel would make with her enemies.

Some Islamic commentators claim to identify the Mahdi in Revelation 6:2, where John says: "I looked, and behold, a white horse. Who sat on it had a bow; and a crown was given to him, and he went out conquering . . ." One of the so-called Four Horsemen of the Apocalypse, this one is the Antichrist, according to John. Later, John mentions *another* rider on a white horse—this one is the triumphant Messiah Yeshua who will conquer and cause the Antichrist to die at Armageddon:

> Now I saw heaven opened, and behold, a white horse. And He who sat on him was called Faithful and True, and in righteousness He judges and makes war. His eyes were like a flame of fire, and on His head were many crowns.
>
> — Revelation 19:11–12 (NKJV)

Muslims acknowledge that the Mahdi will die after his seven-year reign, but they don't know who will slay him. As for the seven-year period, it is based on Daniel:

> He (the Antichrist) will confirm a covenant with many for one (seven-year period). In the middle of the seven (after three and a half years) he will put an end to sacrifice and offering. And on a wing (of the Temple) he will set up an abomination.
>
> — Daniel 9:27 (NIV)

The Jewish Temple, then, will be rebuilt and the altar sacrifices will resume before the coming of the Messiah. And the Muslim nations will permit the Temple to be rebuilt (as the Rambam predicted) and to stand *somewhere* on the Temple Mount (just as Rabbi Fogelman said). And who but the most religious Jews will be pushing for the reconstruction of the Temple? Certainly not secular Israelis (although they are the ones most likely to sign a treaty with the Arabs, even if they are all brought together by a messianic figure who isn't Jewish). The Pharisees remain the most intent on reinstituting the long dormant animal sacrifices on the sacred altar, because they still sense very strongly that a blood sacrifice is required to atone for sin. And only a relatively few of them have had the scales fall off their eyes to see that God Himself has made the Blood Atonement for sin, once and for all.

Meanwhile, Islamist extremists will continue to play out their own need for blood sacrifice by training suicide bombers, whose attacks on civilians were checked only after Israel built a security fence, which in critical spots actually consisted of a high concrete wall.

Facing continued terrorism, Israel will sign a peace treaty with her enemies, in good faith, under the sponsorship of a great world leader, headquartered in Europe, promising world peace. Rabbi Hirsch warned more than a century ago that "whenever Israel has attempted to play politics on its own in the manner of the other nations, and has placed its trust in the help offered by other states, it thereby brought about its own ruin and incurred the loss of its independence."

According to John, it is the Antichrist who will broker a seven-year treaty between Israel and her enemies, who today are the Arab Muslim nations. But after three and a half years, the treaty is broken by some of those nations—such as Iran, Syria, and Egypt—by attacking Israel. Then the Antichrist seeks to "enforce" the treaty by launching a massive invasion of his own. Once he invades the land, he takes the opportunity to capture Jerusalem and force the Jews to cease their sacrifices in the rebuilt Temple—sacrifices that all the Muslim nations had originally permitted under the treaty. In place of the traditional Jewish sacrifices, the Antichrist will erect an abominable image of himself and demand to be worshiped as a god. John borrows from Daniel:

> And armed forces of his shall appear [in the holy land] and they shall pollute the sanctuary, the [spiritual] stronghold, and shall take away the continued [daily

burnt offering]; and they shall set up [in the sanctuary] the abomination that astonishes and makes desolate.

— Daniel 11:31 (AMP)

The first time Daniel's prophecy came true was during the time of the Maccabees, in 168 BC. Antiochus Epiphanes IV of Syria forced the Jews to cease their sacrifices in the Temple and placed a pig on the altar for a mock sacrifice. This "abomination of desolation" will be repeated on a utterly blasphemous scale at the end of the age, according to John. Daniel also recounts the mandatory worship of the abomination of desolation by describing how King Nebuchadnezzar of Babylon raised a 90-foot statue of gold for universal worship. His command to the people was: "At the time you hear the sound of the horn, flute, harp, lyre, and psaltery, in symphony with all kinds of music, you shall fall down and worship the gold image" (Daniel 3:5). (NKJV hereafter.)

At the time he was writing the Book of Revelation, John was well familiar with New Testament scriptures already written: In Paul's second letter to the congregation at Thessalonika, he had warned about what must happen before Yeshua Messiah's return:

> For that day will not come unless the falling away (from the faith) comes first, and the man of sin is revealed, the son of perdition, who opposes and exalts himself above all that is called God or that is worshiped, so that he sits as God in the temple of God, showing himself that he is God.
>
> — 2 Thessalonians 2:3–4

"Therefore," Yeshua prophesied, "when you see the abomination of desolation, spoken of by Daniel the prophet, standing in the holy place, then let those who are in Judea flee to the mountains." He added: "Then if anyone says to you, 'Look, here is the Christ!' or 'There!' do not believe it. For false christs and false prophets will rise and show great signs and wonders to deceive, if possible, even the elect" (Matthew 24:15–16, 23–24).

John then prophesies that Israel (portrayed as a woman clothed with the sun) will flee to the wilderness before the Antichrist can kill her children—the 144,000 Jews who will herald the coming of Messiah (Revelation 12:14).

The Hebrew scriptures have numerous prophecies—never fulfilled—about how Israel will flee to Ammon, Edom and Moab for protection. These were kingdoms that opposed the Israelites' passage to the Promised Land, and that harassed the Jews in ensuing centuries. Now, their land—modern-day Jordan, in eastern Palestine—will become a place for faithful Jews to hide from the Antichrist when he invades Israel.

"He shall also enter the Glorious Land," says Daniel (11:41) "and many countries shall be overthrown; but these shall escape from his hand: Edom, Moab, and the prominent people of Ammon."

Isaiah 16:4–5 says: "Let My outcasts dwell with you, O Moab; be a shelter to them from the face of the spoiler . . . In mercy the throne will be established; and One (the Messiah) will sit on it in truth, in the tabernacle of David, judging and seeking justice and hastening righteousness." (It is interesting that David went to the king of Moab and asked him to protect his parents, Jesse and Nahash, when David was fleeing from Saul—1 Samuel 22:3–4.)

And here, in the wilderness of Jordan, God will plead with His people to accept His ways—and His Messiah. "I will bring you into the wilderness of the peoples, and there I will plead My case with you face to face. Just as I pleaded My case with your fathers in the wilderness of the land of Egypt. . . ." (Ezekiel 20:35–36).

Hosea likewise has God say: "Therefore, behold, I will allure her, will bring her into the wilderness, and speak comfort to her . . . She shall sing there, as in the days of her youth, as in the day when she came up from the land of Egypt . . . I will betroth you to Me forever . . ." (Hosea 2:14–15 and 19).

The Bridegroom, Yeshua, will take to Himself the Bride, comprising all of His believers alive on the earth. "Then I looked," John wrote, "and behold, a Lamb standing on Mount Zion, and with Him 144,000, having His Father's name written on their foreheads" (Revelation 14:1).

The Book of Revelation predicts that all of these things will happen after the Antichrist and the enemies of Israel allow the Jews to resume the ancient sacrifices in the rebuilt Temple—the Temple that cannot be rebuilt without the ashes of a red heifer.

In light of all these things, should Christians encourage the Jews to rebuild the Temple?

Can *any* Christian today claim to know God's answer to that question?

Repentance

During the Arab demonstrations on the anniversary of the founding of the modern State of Israel, Simon was suddenly called from his patrol at the Wall by a shattering "**Boom!**" and then another, and another. Rushing toward the echoes, he saw a swarm of young Palestinian Arab men coming toward him through the Dung Gate. They were carrying metal pipes and knives, and a few of them were waving pistols in the air. But the "**Boom!**" was coming from an Israeli artillery piece that they had commandeered outside the gate.

Simon and several other IDF soldiers aimed their weapons and fired them over the heads of the advancing mob. The Arabs paused briefly, but then they advanced toward the soldiers, only to be stopped by armored vehicles crawling toward them, forcing them to retreat through the Dung Gate. Soon IDF reinforcements arrived and recovered the IDF's howitzer, scattering the mob in all directions.

It was over in a matter of minutes. But for Simon, it was a terrifying experience, and he asked another soldier to drive him back to the barracks. There, he took his medication, undressed, and lay on his cot, his body soaking wet. The hammering in his head would not go away. After a while, as his medication took hold, he lay semiconscious on the cot, his eyes blinking at the ceiling.

Simon was having a waking nightmare. He saw hordes of armed Arabs, many of them in uniform, tramping over him and running toward the Wailing Wall. After driving off the IDF soldiers who had been summoned to protect the Wall, the Arab mob parted like the Red Sea to make way for a truck, which then drove around the concrete barriers and made its way down the pedestrian path to the Wall. There, it stopped by the Wall—and suddenly exploded, balls of fire rolling and roiling in the midst of smoke and choking fumes. When the smoke cleared, the ancient Western Wall was a pile of rubble—yet the Temple Mount looked secure up above, and in the distance the golden Dome of the Rock glistened in the sun.

Simon started to wake up but rolled over on his cot and blacked out. The nightmare wasn't over. His ears would not stop ringing . . .

The next day, Simon was excused from military duty but showed up at the Wall anyway. The bombing incident of yesterday was already forgotten, but he had been given the day off to rest. Simon watched the door of the prayer room until Rabbi Abram left. Then he followed him. The Rabbi crossed the plaza and began walking up the steps of the busy Jewish Quarter, passing restaurants and souvenir shops. Then he turned left and was soon walking west on Chabad Road. Eventually the Rabbi stopped outside David's Citadel—and here the soldier caught up with him.

"Rabbi—I have a question!" Simon said.

From his falafel stand, Munir eavesdropped on their conversation, while toying with his butcher knife—now and then glaring angrily at Simon.

"I have nothing to discuss with a Jew who dares walk on the Temple Mount," Rabbi Abram replied to the soldier. "As Jeremiah lamented, *My people have forgotten Me—days without end.*"

"But Rabbi," said Simon, "according to your own theory, I've walked only within 60 feet of where the Temple once stood."

"Why do you go up there at all?" the Rabbi demanded.

"To patrol the Wall from up above, and watch for any danger to our nation. An Arab attack . . ."

"They wouldn't be attacking us if we all followed our Jewish faith," the Rabbi retorted. "*Then* the Holy One of Israel would protect us by standing in their way."

"Is that what he did during the Holocaust?" Simon shot back.

The Rabbi became angry. "If *every* Jew had been faithful back then, the *Shoah* could not have happened," he said. "God would have stopped it."

"But Rabbi," Simon said, "if it weren't for the Holocaust, the nations of the world wouldn't have let us Jews return to the land and create the State of Israel!"

"True," the Rabbi replied. "But listen to what those nations are saying now, a generation later: 'We Gentiles are not responsible *after all* for what happened to the Jews during the Holocaust—because, look at what tyrants the Israelis have become—like Nazis!—persecuting the poor, downtrodden Palestinian Arabs!'" And with that, the Rabbi spat on the ground.

"That's why I must patrol the Wall," Simon said, "watching for any Arab that might try to attack us."

Glancing toward the falafel stand, the Rabbi said, "There's one of them now. He's looking for his chance."

"*I'm* the one *he's* after," the soldier said.

"He's after *me*, too—for wanting to rebuild the Temple," said Rabbi Abram. "Oh, he's a sly one."

"Be careful, Rabbi," Simon told him. "Even the other Orthodox are afraid that your 'Messiah Now' movement will go too far—and provoke the Arabs and start World War III."

Rabbi Abram looked at the soldier for a long moment. "So, you think you are the Watchman on the Wall?"

"That I am."

"A modern-day Maccabee warrior, are you?"

"I'd be pleased to follow in the footsteps of the Maccabee warriors, who were granted the miracle of Hanukkah!" Simon answered.

"Well, for your information, the Maccabees were the ancestors of us Pharisees."

"Yes, I know," Simon replied. Then he pointed at the Rabbi and said, "But today, not every Pharisee is a true Maccabee. When did **you** ever serve in the IDF?"

Offended, the Rabbi said, "Young man, if you were faithful to your own religion, you might truly *be* a modern Maccabee! For your information, it is only the prayers of us religious Jews that can keep Israel from destruction." He paused. "Now, what do you want with me?"

Simon stepped closer to the Rabbi and told him: "Well, Rabbi— believe it or not, I want to make *t'shuvah*."

"You want to *repent*?" the Rabbi exclaimed. "For what offense?"

From his falafel stand, Munir strained his ears to hear the reply.

"Two years ago I caused the death of an Arab woman," Simon said.

"I know all about that. Yitzak Cohen told me," the Rabbi said. "But it was an accident. You were not responsible. Besides, you were defending the Land."

"I still feel guilty, Rabbi," Simon said. "I also feel somewhat responsible for what happened to your red heifer."

"Oh?"

"If I hadn't plotted with the Arab woman about the heifer, she wouldn't have raised your suspicions—you wouldn't have run after her like that—Yitzak wouldn't have had to save her life—and you wouldn't be looking for another red heifer now."

At his falafel stand, Munir was stunned to hear all this. He was no longer clutching his knife.

After a long silence, Rabbi Abram said, "There are four ingredients of repentance."

"I know, Rabbi," Simon said, counting on his fingers: "I apologize to you. I will change my ways. And I wish to make restitution."

"Restitution?"

"See, I am expecting a large settlement from the Army for my injuries," Simon said, touching the scar on his face.

"No. Keep your money. I forgive any debt," the Rabbi said and started to walk away. "Give it to that Muslim, for all I care."

"Now, what about—?"

"What about what?" the Rabbi asked, pausing.

"I mean, what are you going to do now?"

"We'll look for another red heifer, of course."

"Does it matter what gender?" Simon asked.

"It's referred to as she in the Book of Numbers, Chapter 19," the Rabbi said.

"But where will you find one?"

"God will provide," Rabbi Abram said, and was about to walk off again.

"Rabbi, what if—?"

"What if what?"

"What if this heifer, when she was old enough, what if she were bred?" Simon asked. "She might have a fine baby red heifer."

Rabbi Abram thought about this. "Not a bad idea," he said at last. "But I just sold her back to that hot-headed Arab. I'll never see her again. Shalom!"

"Shalom . . ."

Now Munir unfolded the slip of paper that the Imam had given him and read out loud this verse from the Qu'ran: "Fight and slay the pagans wherever you find them . . . But if they repent—and establish regular prayer—and practice charity—then let them go on their way. For Allah is forgiving and merciful."

Munir then disappeared inside his falafel stand.

*

Now Noor went to the Wailing Wall, where Simon had gone again to attempt to make t'shuvah, as advised by Isaac and by Rabbi Abram.

"Excuse me, Soldier," Noor said to him.

"Go away," Simon said. "I have a problem and I need to be alone."

"What is your problem, friend?" she asked.

"I need to do *t'shuvah*. Big time!"

Noor thought a moment and said, "I understand that one needs four ingredients of repentance."

"Go away!" Simon shouted at her. "Do I really need *you* to tell me about my religion?"

"Well . . . yes!" she replied.

Now Noor walked around Simon at the Wall, playing her flute like the Pied Piper. He looked at her inquiringly. She blew some more notes and turned toward the steps to the Temple Mount.

Simon couldn't stop himself from following her up the steps to the top. There, Noor led him to her surveyor's transit and motioned for him to bend down and look through its telescope. Pointing into the distance, she asked him, "Do you see where that street ends at the corner?"

"Come on, now," the soldier said. "Why would *you,* a Bedouin nomad, have any interest in our city streets?"

"Nomads know a great deal about land," Noor told Simon. "We even see things that are overlooked by people who have their own land to live on."

"All right," Simon said, bending down to look through the telescope. "What do you want to show me?"

"Around that corner, to your left, what do you see?"

"It's a—"

Noor stepped closer and whispered in his ear.

"Are you sure?" Simon said. "How do you know this?"

"Never mind," she replied. Stepping close she whispered a suggestion.

"Yes! That's it!" Simon exclaimed. "Yes!"

Simon quickly ran down the steps from the Temple Mount.

Alone, Noor resumed playing on her flute.

Chapter 23

Benji Levine's
'Four Faces of Israel'

JERUSALEM

When Rabbi Benji Levin heard the story about what Isaac Cohen had done to the Red Heifer, he told me, "That's a beautiful, beautiful story. A person who's willing to take upon himself the losing of the Red Heifer in order to save another person's life—which is really, ultimately more important than the heifer itself. Which is the whole *raison d'etre* of the heifer."

Chimes constantly ring in Benji's office at the Gesher ("bridge") Foundation in downtown Jerusalem. His organization's goal is to build bridges among factions of Jews in order to avoid civil strife (and even *civil war* someday if the government tries to evacuate all of the Jewish settlers from the West Bank for a Palestinian state and the settlers fight back).

An actor, Benji tours the country, visiting schools and playing four characters: An ultra-Orthodox rabbi, an Eged bus driver who is a secular Jew, a French artist living in Safed who is married to a non-Jewish woman, and a tourist from Los Angeles, California, who is a generous donor to the State of Israel.

Called "The Four Faces of Israel," his show is presented in English and Hebrew and explores serious questions about Jewish identity.

"It goes very well with the kids," he said. "What happens is that when you try to break down stereotypes, each person gets upset about the way your portrayed him. But when you say to them that the other side is also upset about how they were portrayed, they reply: 'No, that was very good, that's exactly the way they are!' And I talk about that at the end. If we don't know how to respect one another, there's never going to be peace in the country. And I say to them at the end that Jewish history has taught us that the worst wars we've had to fight were the wars from within, not the wars from without."

Benji is the grandson of Rabbi Aryeh Levin, who was known as the Tzaddik of Jerusalem. Born and educated in yeshiva in Lithuania, the rabbi arrived in Jerusalem as a teenager around 1900 and began teaching Torah. But soon he began visiting patients in a leper hospital, and inmates in prison.

During the Jewish struggle against British rule in the years leading up to Israel's independence in 1948, Reb Aryeh visited Jewish prisoners who had fought the British. He became their only link to the outside world. Gifted with an extraordinary memory, he carried hundreds of messages each week between the prisoners and their families, at great risk to himself. For those Jewish men condemned to die for using violence against the British, Reb Aryeh was the only one who stayed with them, giving them courage and consolation to the very end.

Benji used to come from America to spend summers in Jerusalem with his grandfather. On prominent display in his office is Reb Aryeh's old brass teapot, still in use.

"He lived in a little room about the size of this room," Benji said in his office at the Gesher Center in downtown Jerusalem. "In his room I met Martin Buber, S.Y. Agnon, Sulzberger from *The New York Times*, many of the greats of the past generation who came to see him. He was like Mother Teresa. He became a very close friend of the Chief Rabbi of Israel, Rabbi Avraham Yitzak Kook."

Benji has dedicated his own life to solving what he calls "the religious/secular problem" in Israel. He would have appreciated Rabbi Abram's wry reply when Isaac Cohen asked whether the Messiah will bring peace between Arabs and Jews—"The real question is: Can the Messiah find a way for all the Jews to live together in peace?"

"We can't have peace with the Arabs if we can't have peace with ourselves," said Benji. "Everyone wants peace. Even the settlers, on the extreme right—their kids go into the Army—they have eight or nine kids, so they have the most to lose if there's a war. Not so, families of liberals in Tel Aviv, with two kids and a dog."

As for Muslim fundamentalists, he said, "they have nothing to lose. So let's raise their lifestyle, give them a garden and a home. Then they'd have something to lose."

High Above Jerusalem

On the winding highway from Jerusalem to Tel Aviv, the mountains become hills, lined with broken stone walls keeping the goats from the groves, and finally settle into a rolling pattern. The kibbutzim are covered with a variety of hardy grasses and grain fields and bales of straw cut from those grain fields; burnt stubble fills the air with incense where the land has been cleared. The Israelis have planted orange groves and sunflower fields and acres of corn, melons and grapes.

Up the Mediterranean coast, from Tel Aviv to Netanya and on to Haifa, the terrain goes through every conceivable variation in less than two hours. Dairy cattle graze on flatlands, next to fields of roses. Around Hadera comes the lush fruit section, and on the highway are open tractor-trailers loaded with potatoes.

Soldiers of the IDF, in clusters of two or three, can be seen hitchhiking rides with civilian motorists.

Abruptly, the Mediterranean comes into view on the left, and desert dunes on the right. Then wide, flat farmlands under cultivation, with picturesque mountains in the background. The smell of fertilizer prickles the nostrils, and a creek cuts across the landscape, then fields of palm trees.

East of Haifa lies the Galilee—and the town of Nazareth, where Yeshua grew up—and the richest soil in Israel, which attracted the country's kibbutz settlers. The Synagogue Church in Nazareth, where Yeshua read from the scroll of Isaiah and first claimed to be the Messiah, is now surrounded on all sides by bazaars, and its door is almost impossible to find without a guide. Not far off is the cliff from which they tried to throw Yeshua to His death.

To the east is Tiberias, on Lake Kinneret. From the hill where the Sermon on the Mount was first heard, the city can be seen on the shore of the lute-shaped lake of cobalt blue, surrounded by purple-shaded foothills. Along that shoreline promenade, visitors at an outdoor café dine on charcoal-broiled Peter's fish, of the perch family, while schools of fish dance in the water, and stray cats prowl for handouts.

Driving up the steep road north of Tiberias, past the Mount of Beatitudes, the visitor finds himself stymied behind a slow watermelon truck. Behind both vehicles, a Sabra bobs and weaves impatiently waiting for the right moment to pass. Just beyond the next hairpin turn, the Sabra's car roars by and disappears up the hill, on the way to Safed, at the top of the world.

The air is noticeably cooler in Safed, where the ancient mystics taught, and where artists paint today. Past that town are the archeological excavations of Hatzor, a city that Joshua captured and that now has several layers of civilization exposed to the naked eye. Beyond are the Golan Heights, where Simon was stationed after the Arab woman was killed during that Palestinian uprising.

Here, Simon returned to his former unit and filled out the final paperwork in order to receive his settlement for the injuries he suffered during that uprising two years ago. After receiving permission from the commanding officer to take military leave, Simon returned to Jerusalem and spent the next several days moving about the city in his civilian clothes. He had many stops to make, and many people to see.

Now back in Jerusalem, his mission accomplished, he took a casual stroll up to his favorite spot. It was a place where he could hide in plain sight while observing the city from above.

Leaving the walls of the Old City, Simon walked down the Jerusalem Brigade Road, past Zion Gate. He walked past Abie Nathan's rusting peace sculpture of swords beaten into plowshares. At the bottom of the hill, near the dried-up Sultan's Pool, he headed up Hebron Road, passing the windmill and elongated porch of Mishkenot Sha'ananim on his right. At the top of the hill, just before reaching the Oriental arch of the Ariel Hotel, he stopped on Ramiz Square and looked around. Then he climbed the rustic hill above the Railway Station by walking up a winding path whose old steps were nearly buried in the tall grass and bushes bursting with yellow flowers in the golden sunlight. At the top, he wandered along the rough terrain, then sat on one of the large rocks. Years ago, he used to see a flock of goats up here in this miraculously preserved hideaway, from which he now looked down on the Railway Station, and on the Jerusalem Khan Theater. Turning around and gazing into the distance, he looked past the Cinematique movie house toward the Hinnom Valley, where pagans offered human sacrifices to Molech three millennia ago.

Below Simon's little hill, a Bedouin man was leading a donkey laden with bags of cement, as automobile traffic droned up the hill.

Nobody noticed him up here.

Simon breathed in the sweet aroma of wildflowers in the breeze and felt the sun beating down on his forehead. Now he took from his pocket a little book, a gift that Samira had presented to him only a few days ago, before the world they were trying to build for themselves suddenly crumbled. Thumbing through the *Song of Solomon*, he stopped at one of the passages where he recalled encountering an image that now seemed utterly remarkable.

"My beloved is mine!" the Shulamite woman declared. "And I am his! I will hold him and not let him go, until I have brought him to the house of my mother, into the chamber of her who conceived me."

Skipping down a few stanzas in the *Song of Solomon*, Simon stopped again and read: "I am my beloved's, and his desire is toward me. If I should find you outside, I would kiss you; I would not be despised. I would lead you and bring you into the house of my mother, she who used to instruct me."

Closing the little book, Simon squeezed it in his hands and felt a thrill pass through his body. This was almost too good to be true! Surely, what was happening today was more than just a stroke of good luck—more than just a brilliant idea. Surely, this was proof that there is a God and that He watches lovingly over the affairs of men.

Simon chuckled to himself. Then he laughed out loud. Standing on top of his rock, above the City of Jerusalem, he stretched out his arms, clutching the little book in one hand, and laughed and laughed and laughed until he began to cry. Then he sat down again on his rock, his head bent low, and wept for joy.

Chapter 24

Eric Mahr Puts on His Tefillin for the Last Time

> God, as we have seen, has already transfigured our sufferings by making them [an] instrument that cuts, carves and polishes within us the stone which is destined to occupy a specific place in the heavenly Jerusalem.
>
> —Fr. Pierre Teilhard de Chardin, *The Divine Milieu*

BUFFALO, NEW YORK

My earliest recollection of Eric Mahr was some thirty years ago, when he was turning to traditional Judaism and was about to make his first trip to Israel. I had gotten to know him when I was a reporter covering Rabbi Meir Kahane's first speech in Buffalo, where Eric was president of the Jewish Defense League.

It was Saturday afternoon, the Sabbath, when observant Jews are not permitted to do any business, such as driving a car. Eric's passport hadn't arrived in the mail, and he was scheduled to leave for Israel tomorrow, Sunday—when the post office would be closed.

However, the postal facility at the airport was always open on Saturdays; but it would be closed before sundown, when Shabbat ends and business resumes for Jews. *Could Eric's passport possibly be sitting there right now, ready to be delivered Monday?*

I happened to be at Eric and Jody's house that day, and I immediately volunteered to drive to the airport and find out. Eric made it clear that he wasn't asking this 'Shabbos Goy' to do what he himself couldn't do on the Sabbath. (This is an important stipulation, if one is to receive such a favor from a 'Sabbath Gentile.') I insisted that it was my idea, and

265

off I went. Nearly an hour later I pulled into the Mahrs' driveway and knocked on their door. When it opened, I stepped inside and gave the Mahr family a sad look. Eric just looked back at me. Then I pulled out the envelope and tossed it at him!

What marvelous rejoicing erupted in the house! I felt like a hero of heroes. It reminded me of the night they blew a fuse in the Amherst Synagogue, where the Sabbath meal was still cooking on automatic pilot and a party was starting. I had to beg Arnold Weiss, president of the shul and publisher of *Buffalo Jewish Review*, for permission to grab the flashlight and change the fuse, so the party could go on. And that it did . . .

Many years passed, and I still can't believe that the incident with Eric's passport had slipped out of my mind—until Eric reminded me of it at his dinner table in Neve Yaakov in 2007. I had my bride with me, Shirah, and we all were recalling our past encounters for the sake of her and the Mahr children, who were grown but still living at home. A wonderful chill went down my spine when Eric recounted the story.

Then Shirah had a story for the Mahrs, as we sat around their table eating steak that Eric had barbecued out on their upstairs patio, in sight of two distant Arab villages on the West Bank. Some years ago, Shirah said, she had stopped dating and told the Lord that she was going to wait for Him to send her the right husband. During those solitary years, she spent most of her free time reading the Bible and writing her impressions of this lengthy "journey in the desert of singleness," as she called it. Years went by, as all her friends married and began having children. Nobody seemed to believe that she was doing the right thing by remaining out of circulation. Then, one night, as she was taking the chicken out of her oven, the Lord told her that she would meet her future husband the next day. Shirah had been sick, but the next day she went to services. Afterwards, as everybody was filing out of the sanctuary, Shirah found herself alone, in her pew, on her side of the aisle. Across the aisle, a man was the last person to leave. He had a heavy heart that day, and as he arose from his seat, something prompted him to ask the lone woman across the aisle—who had a reputation as a prayer warrior—to pray with him.

And this I did.

Shirah told the Mahrs that the moment she saw me standing over her, asking for prayer, she joined her hands with mine and we prayed together, and she knew her years of prayers had been answered. Ten days later, I knew she was the wife for me, and we married eight months later.

Chavi, the Mahrs' only daughter, was so moved by Shirah's story that she asked her to pray that Hashem (God) would find the husband for her, too. We agreed to pray for her—and added that if possible we would come to the wedding.

Three years later, we learned that Chavi was having her engagement party at the end of January. A young Orthodox man named Moshe had proposed marriage, and her father was delighted with this man. The wedding date was set for May 2. But then Eric and Jody were called back to Buffalo, where Jody's father was dying. Eric gave the eulogy at the funeral.

This man had stepped in after Eric's father was murdered during a robbery when Eric was still in his teens; his broken-hearted mother died later. Now an orphan, Eric became part of Jody's family when the two devoted *baalei t'shuvah* couple married. Eric and Jody had studied at Rabbi Yaacov Haber's Torah Center (downstairs from my apartment) and come back to Judaism.

Yet there was another older man who had taken young Eric under his wing. It was his late father's best friend, Hyman Obstein. This was the man who sold Silverstein's kosher butcher shop to Eric. Now, while the Mahrs were still in Buffalo mourning Jody's father, Mr. Obstein suddenly died. This delayed their return to their home and children in Israel so they could attend the funeral . . . where Eric was to deliver the eulogy.

Eric wanted to do more for his mentor. Although he was exhausted after the flight to Buffalo and the stress and strain of the death in the family, and preparing and delivering his father-in-law's eulogy, Eric decided that he must remain at the funeral home with the body to assure that it was treated with respect, according to halakhic law, until the funeral the next morning.

Morning came, and his brother Sanford and sister Marilyn arrived at the funeral home. But Eric said he couldn't join them yet, even as people were arriving for the service—because he hadn't yet put on his tefillin and said his morning prayers. Returning to Jody's parents' house, he rushed over to his tefillin bag, and felt the familiar warmth and holiness rush over him as he wrapped the leather straps around his arm and head. Everything in his life was changing—the two deaths, and the coming marriage of his only daughter—but his sacred tefillin would always be the same. He prayed. He studied. A peace washed over him . . .

To understand why it was so important for Eric Mahr to put on his tefillin that morning, of all mornings, we must go back to his early days as a *baal t'shuvah*. In the days before he operated Silverstein's, he had received training as a kosher inspector and was working grueling hours. One time his shift took him through the night and into the next day. By the time he left the company, he had missed the morning *shacharis* prayer and still hadn't yet put on his tefillin. He decided to put them on during the afternoon prayers, which would begin soon at the Saranac Synagogue.

And so, before going home to bed, Eric arrived at the shul and entered the sanctuary, where he put on a pair of tefillin, picked up a prayer book and began praying. When the men had finished praying, an old man named Shmuel Fixler approached him, his shuffling gait and weak legs belying a strong iron-willed personality. A direct descendant of the Rav, he had been a student of the Nitra Rav back in Europe.

"Young man," Mr. Fixler began.

"Yes," Eric replied.

"Why are you putting on your tefillin in the middle of the afternoon, instead of during *shacharis*?"

Eric explained that he had worked through the night and hadn't had the opportunity to put his tefillin on that day.

"You didn't put your tefillin on yet today because you didn't have time?" the man exclaimed. *"How could such a thing ever occur?"*

Mr. Fixler then took the young man aside. Rolling up his sleeve, he revealed the number that had been tattooed in blue ink. They sat down together at the back of the shul, and the old man told him a story. He had been in a Nazi concentration camp as a young man, he began, and he had somehow been able to bring his tefillin with him, in spite of searches by the guards.

"I guarded my tefillin with my life," Mr. Fixler said. "I kept them on me at all times and nobody ever managed to take them away from me. I had a giant question, though: How on earth would I manage to put them on every day while I did my utmost to walk between the raindrops of death?"

There was no privacy whatsoever in the camp, and he didn't even trust his fellow prisoners with his secret. His assigned job was to pull a wagon loaded with garbage from one side of the camp to the other and dispose of it.

"When I began my route," he told Eric, "I kept a sharp lookout for the perfect opportunity to put on my tefillin—and I found it. There was one spot along the endless path of garbage removal and collection that was perfect for my needs. There was a short window of precious time when I would be pulling the wagon up one final hill to the place where the guards would dump the garbage over the side and down into the abyss."

The young prisoner was able to sneak about ten seconds of time out of sight of the guards to slip on his tefillin, say a quick prayer, and slip them off.

"When I reached the middle of the hill," Mr. Fixler explained, "both the guard standing at the top of the hill and the guard stationed at the bottom weren't able to see me for a short time. And so, every single day of the week, as soon as we reached this particular spot, I would jump under my wagon, don my tefillin in seconds and return to my place without anyone ever realizing what I was doing, or that I had even ducked under the wagon in the first place. There, in the miserable world of Satan, under the probing gaze of a sea of the worst *reshaim* ever to walk this earth, I managed to wrap my tefillin on my arm and head every single day."

Eric looked at Mr. Fixler and knew that he would love this man for the rest of his life.

"Thank you," he said, and knew that he would feel close to the man forever.

Not long after that, Eric Mahr went to the rabbi of his shul, Rabbi Haber, and asked for his assistance.

"I have emptied out my entire bank account," Eric explained, "and I am going to purchase two tickets to New York for me and you, so we can fly down there together."

"And what are we going to do in New York?" Rabbi Haber asked.

"We are going to go to a Judaica store," Eric said, "wherever you think it's best to go, and I will purchase the most expensive pair of tefillin in the store. And you, Rabbi, will check them to ensure that I am really and truly receiving what I am paying for. Can you do this for me?"

The Rabbi was touched. "Yes," he said. "I will be honored to help you in your quest to become the best Jew you can possibly be."

Years later, when each of Eric's three sons reached bar mitzvah age, he purchased the most expensive tefillin from one of the best shops in Jerusalem.

"Guard them with your life," he told his oldest son, Benjamin.

Now, on this freezing February day in Buffalo in 2010, Eric Mahr took off his tefillin and rushed to the funeral home to deliver the eulogy for his beloved mentor, Hyman Obstein. Two people he loved so much were suddenly gone, and he was utterly exhausted after a virtually sleepless night, yet he still felt a peace in the consolation that he at least had been able to put on his tefillin this morning without fail.

At the crowded funeral home, people greeted him and shook his hand. Slowly he made his way to the podium to speak. Every step felt like an eternity. This was it. The final goodbye to this dear man. *Thank you so much for everything . . .*

The world spun around as he climbed the steps to the stand, feeling a great deal older than his 54 years. He took his place at the microphone. And he began his eulogy. After speaking for some time, he paused to look down at his notes.

"The Talmud says that when Rabbi Chanina ben Tradyon was burned alive, the parchment went up in flames, but the holy letters flew away towards the heavens."

He paused again. Turned to the side.

There was a mad rush to the podium—relatives, friends, medics rushing up to see if he was all right.

But Eric Mahr was gone. He had put on his tefillin for the last time.

*

But the souls of the virtuous are in the hands of God . . .
If they experienced punishment as men see it,
their hope was rich with immortality;
slight was their affliction, great will their blessings be.
God has put them to the test
and proved them worthy to be with him;
he has tested them like gold in a furnace,
and accepted them as a holocaust.
When the time comes for his visitation they will shine out;
as sparks run through the stubble, so will they.
They shall judge nations, rule over peoples,
and the Lord will be their king forever.

— *Book of Wisdom, 3:1–8 (Jerusalem Bible)*

*

Jody had to telephone their daughter and sons back in Jerusalem to tell them what had happened to their father. She and her relatives flew to Jerusalem with her husband's remains. During the funeral, Rabbi

Haber—now also living in Israel—recalled one of the many days when he had visited Eric's kosher butcher shop back in Buffalo. Eric happened to remark that day that the Rabbi's tab was getting pretty high. The Rabbi sadly told him that things still hadn't picked up at the Torah Center. On hearing that, Eric suddenly opened his cash register, scooped up all the cash, and handed it to his Rabbi, insisting that he take it home, along with his groceries. Others spoke of how his Marwood Publications had become the leading producer of hardcover graphic novels, beautifully illustrated, designed to tell young people the stories of the great heroes of Jewish history.

In keeping with his wishes, Eric was buried in the cemetery on the Mount of Olives, where the Messiah is to make his appearance, according to Jewish tradition. In fact, he was buried next to Mr. Fixler, the man who had shown him what it means to live and die for a mitzvah.

The Most Embarrassing Question of All

The assassination of Rabbi Meir Kahane by an Arab in 1990 had been the turning point in Rabbi Abram's life. A follower of Kahane and his outlawed Kach Party, Rabbi Abram had been a frequent visitor to its office on Ussishkin Street, named after the Russian Zionist who settled in Palestine in 1919 and later headed the Jewish National Fund, purchasing large tracts of land for lease to Jewish settlers. The Museum of the Potential Holocaust was also at that address.

Rabbi Abram had also gotten to know Eric Mahr, and mourned with him again on the day Kahane's son and heir in the movement, Benjamin, was shot to death with his wife in a highway ambush.

Now, in his study room near the Western Wall, the founder of Messiah Now shook his head and fought back tears as he read the obituary of Eric Mahr. They hadn't seen each other since the Kach Party broke up and they had all gone their separate ways.

"A true Maccabean warrior," he mumbled to himself as he recalled how bravely Eric had acted when terrorists stormed a downtown street while the Mahrs were having a meal in the restaurant.

There was a knock on the door, a knock so soft that Rabbi Abram didn't hear it. But Isaac, seated closer to the door, heard it and got up from their study table. When Noor stepped into the room, her footsteps were so silent that the Rabbi was still wiping his eyes as he sat before the obituary.

"Rabbi Abram . . . ," Isaac said, and the Rabbi looked up. Startled to his feet, the Rabbi blurted out, "What can you possibly want with *me*? Didn't we air all our differences the other day in that alley?"

"I've come to give you my explanation," Noor said. Her voice was soft but sharpened: the whisper of a tiny whip.

"No," the Rabbi replied. "I know exactly why you blocked my way in that alley. And I have since apologized to that Arab woman and made *t'shuvah*."

"I know," came her soft reply. "But that's not what I came to explain today."

Isaac came closer until the three of them were standing by the study table in the center of the room.

"We have nothing further to discuss," the Rabbi told her.

"Rabbi Abram," Noor began, "for several days I have been praying, seeking the proper explanation to the biting question that you and so many others have been confronting me and Samira with."

Both men stared at the Bedouin woman in silence. Folding her hands in front of her, she began to slowly pace the room. "Please be seated," she said. They both took their chairs at the table, and the Bedouin dressed in white robes began to slowly walk around them.

"You want to know why so many Christians like me love Israel and the Jewish people," she began. "You don't trust religious Christians, because you know very well that we expect the Moshiach you've been waiting so long for to be Yeshua of Nazareth."

Suddenly Noor stopped and picked up a book from the table, opened it apparently at random, and began reading the Hebrew out loud.

It was the Book of Isaiah, Chapter 9, Verse 6: "For unto us a child is born, and unto us a Son is given; and the government shall be upon His shoulder: and His Name shall be called Wonderful, Counselor, The Mighty God, The Everlasting Father, the Prince of Peace."

Noor looked down at their startled faces.

"I direct your attention to the next verse," she said. "Of the *increase* of His government and (of) peace there will be no end." Looking up at them again, she asked: "Can you tell me why the word for *of the increase*—*l'marbay*—is spelled that peculiar way? We all know that the letter M—mem—is open on the bottom except when it appears at the end of a word—then it is written as a **mem sofit**—*closed*. So tell me, please, why does a final mem appear here *inside* of a word?"

Isaac had found the verse in his Bible and was staring at the **mem sofit** in disbelief.

Rabbi Abram cleared his throat. "I believe," he said, "that this is the only place in the entire Tenach where the **mem sofit** appears inside a word. Our sages pondered this for centuries, and the Talmud explains that when Moshiach comes in the final days, Jerusalem will no longer be *open* to the Gentiles and their ways—but will be *closed*."

"Closed to us Gentiles," Noor said, placing the book back on the table. "So when *your* Messiah comes, we Christians will become outsiders?"

"Not really," Isaac interjected. "The Gentiles simply won't be allowed anymore to convert to Judaism. They didn't join us when it was so difficult to be a Jew—so why should they be allowed to climb on the bandwagon, now that our day has finally come?"

"I see," Noor told him. "Now, from our perspective, if Messiah comes—and he turns out *not* to be Yeshua—we Christians will be on the outside looking in. As a Christian, shouldn't I feel offended by that expectation on your part?"

They were silent.

"I mean," she went on, "*we* teach that when Messiah Yeshua comes, He will rule the world from Jerusalem for a thousand years. The Jewish people will be at the center of His government—just as you teach. But the Gentiles won't be shut out—we will come and pay homage to the Prince of Peace. Even Egypt will come and pay tribute in Jerusalem—or they will suffer a terrible drought."

They still said nothing.

"And so," Noor told them, pacing again, "it seems to me that the millennium that Christians expect to come will be the most wonderful, triumphant time in history for the Jewish people. Which comes back to why I am here today to answer your repeated objections to Christians like me who love Israel."

"We don't believe that you truly love us," the Rabbi said. "Your purported love is a sham—a cover-up for your missionizing."

"I have never tried to convert a Jew to the Christian religion," Noor said, standing still before them.

"She's right, Rabbi," Isaac said.

"Yitzak, be silent!" the Rabbi said. "Let me put it this way: You want to see the Jews flock to Eretz Israel in order to hasten the fulfillment of the prophecies in your Book of Revelations—"

"—Revelation," she corrected him.

"Whatever," Rabbi Abram said. "You can't wait for the Battle of Armageddon to start, even though your Bible says that one-third of the Jews will perish in that bloodbath. And you Christians can't wait for that calamity to befall us—as long as it brings your Messiah to the earth."

Noor began slowly pacing around the table again as Isaac and the Rabbi looked up at her, waiting for her answer.

"That," Noor finally confessed, "is the most embarrassing question that a Jew could ever ask a Christian."

She paused and let it sink in.

"First of all," she said at last, "Revelation 9 refers to one-third of the *world* perishing—and there are a lot more Gentiles than Jews in the world. And second, that prophecy may not necessarily come true. Remember how Jonah prophesied that all of Nineveh would be destroyed—but the people repented, and God relented. But what sort of Christian would make up his mind to travel to Israel and befriend Jews for the sole purpose of hastening a bloodbath that will affect us all?"

"Rabbi, the Rapture," Isaac said.

"Yes," Rabbi Abram said. "Your so-called Rapture! All you good Christians will suddenly be whisked away by some—some divine helicopter in the sky—and go to heaven!—while the rest of us remain on earth to suffer the Tribulation! How shameful!"

Noor stopped by his chair and looked him in the eye. "I totally agree, Rabbi," she said. "You are right. This goes to the very heart of the most embarrassing question of all."

"Well, what do you say to that?" the Rabbi demanded. "Are you going to say that you're sorry—this time saying it even before you make it come to pass? After the Holocaust, Madam, we have heard enough of '*I am sorry*' already!"

"Rabbi Abram—and Isaac—let me try to explain something to you," Noor pleaded. "A Christian who truly loves Israel is someone who has been called by God to Israel's cause. This person does not make a political decision, or a philosophical decision—or even a *theological* decision! Those are decisions of the mind. But a *spiritual* calling is a gift out of the blue from Almighty God Himself. It is a moving of the Holy Spirit that touches the person's heart with a true, unselfish *longing* for the Jewish people. Many of these Christians would gladly *die* for Israel."

"Huh!" the Rabbi grunted.

"Let me ask you then," Noor said. "Why is it that during the most dangerous times in the Middle East, only born-again Christians venture to fly to Israel—while even Jews are afraid to come here?"

"Fanatics!" the Rabbi said. "Religious fanatics!"

Suddenly Noor was smiling and covering her face with her hand to hide it. "I should be rather flattered to be called a religious fanatic," she said. Lifting her hands toward both of them, she added: "I'd be in some pretty good company, don't you think?"

"Yeshua was a fanatic," Isaac said.

"I think you're right, Yitzak," Noor said. "But so are you."

"Go ahead and call *us* fanatics!" the Rabbi told her. "But at least we're not out to harm millions of innocent people."

"No?" Noor replied. "What about trying to rebuild the Temple and bringing on World War III?"

"We would do no such thing!" the Rabbi shouted at her.

"Well," Noor replied, "your old friend Rabbi Kahane once said that starting World War III would, in his words, 'bring the Messiah'!"

Chapter 25

Chasidic Followers
of Messiah Yeshua?

KFAR CHABAD

Two American pastors were traveling across the Land of Israel when they received a message that a man in Kfar Chabad wanted to meet with them.

Secretly.

The pastors—one from New Hampshire and the other from New York—had just had an unpleasant encounter with Yad L'Achim, an Orthodox anti-missionary organization. Although Israeli law forbids actively attempting to convert a Jew to another religion, many Christian ministers visiting Israel were suspected of violating the law, and Yad L'Achim was on the lookout for them.

Could this message to the two American pastors be a trap? Was the 'Hand of the Brethren' trying to set them up for arrest?

Now, the little village of Kfar Chabad, on the Tel Aviv-Jerusalem highway, is the Israeli headquarters of the Chabad Lubavitcher movement, started by Chasidic Jews in the Russian town of Lubavitch in the 1700s. Today there are 40,000 Lubavitchers living in Israel. Its world headquarters is in Crown Heights, New York, where its dynastic leader, Rebbe Menachem Schneerson, died in 1994, leaving no successor. A brilliant, compassionate teacher and universally recognized holy man in the Orthodox world, the Rebbe had been pressured by his million worldwide followers to declare himself the Messiah, but he never did.

After his death many Lubavitchers actually believed that the Rebbe would arise from the dead and reign as Messiah. Why the delay? Because, they argued, the Jewish people had not yet completed their

277

spiritual transformation that would make the world ready for the final Redemption. Most Jews, including mainline Orthodox, were shocked by the cultish sound of all this, especially since the death and resurrection of the Messiah was no longer taught by the rabbis—because it had become a Christian teaching.

With these thoughts in mind, the two messianic pastors prepared to meet this unnamed Chasidic Jew who had mysteriously sent for them.

"Everything had to be hush-hush," one of the pastors recalled later. "Not even our driver was permitted."

Billboards with the familiar face of the bearded Rebbe were everywhere when they arrived at Kfar Chabad on the appointed day.

"We arranged for our driver to let us off at a certain street corner," the pastor recalled. "One o'clock rolls around, and a large car pulls around the corner. There are two gentlemen in the front seat and one in the back, and he opens up the back door for us. We very timidly got into the car. Then we're wending our way through all these streets. . . . We were absolutely terrified."

Then they got out of the car with the three Chasidic men and entered a dark building. There, Chasidic women served them pastries, fresh fruit, coffee and tea. Then the leader, sitting behind his desk and flanked by the other two men, told the pastors why they had been invited here.

"They wanted to meet us to tell us that they believed in Yeshua!" the pastor exclaimed.

Reaching into his back pocket, the rabbi behind the desk took out a book whose covers had been torn off. It was a Gideon's Bible that he apparently had picked up in a hotel room. Opening it to the first chapter of the Gospel of John, he told them: "I could see the *Mamre* of God coming down and dwelling among us!"

Mamre was where Abraham was living when he looked up from his tent one day and saw three human figures approaching him. One of them was the Lord, according to Genesis 18:1—"And the Lord appeared unto him by the terebinths of Mamre." Before leaving, the Lord informed Abraham that Sara would have a son by this time next year. It was Isaac.

The term *Mamre* was used by many theologians to refer to the ability of God to appear as a man. The ultimate manifestation of the Mamre was God becoming incarnate as Yeshua.

Here are the opening words of the Gospel of John (Yochanan), where the Chasidic man said he recognized the Mamre:

In the beginning was the Word, and the Word was with God, and the Word was God. He was with God in the beginning. All things came to be through him, and without him nothing made had being. In him was life, and the life was the light of mankind. The light shines in the darkness, and the darkness has not suppressed it.

. . .This was the true light, which gives light to everyone entering the world. He was in the world—the world came to be through him—yet the world did not know him. He came to his own homeland, yet his own people did not receive him. But to as many as did receive him, to those who put their trust in his person and his power, he gave the right to become children of God. . . .

The writer, of course, was referring to Yeshua of Nazareth. And the key sentence of John, Chapter 1, is verse 14:

The Word became a human being and lived with us, and we saw his *Sh'khinah*, the *Sh'khinah* of the Father's only Son, full of grace and truth. (Yochanan 1:1–14, CJB)

"You see," the pastor later explained, "the Mamre is the Word coming down and dwelling among us. It's an Aramaic term well familiar to First Century Judaism. And he had made that connection—from John 1:1 all the way back to Genesis 1:1, the whole Creation story."

Later the two pastors traveled to Mea Shearim, the ultra-Orthodox sector of Jerusalem, and met other Chasidics who believed Yeshua of Nazareth to be the Messiah.

The author of this Gospel was Yochanan (John), the youngest of Yeshua's followers—the one closest to him—and the one who lived the longest. Unlike the earlier Gospel of Matthew, John's account begins not with the human genealogy of Yeshua, going back to David and beyond, but with His existence before time began. Only after living sixty years after Yeshua's death and meditating on the meaning of all that he saw was the elderly John able to write a cosmic account of Messiah in the Book of Revelation.

Many theologians claim that John's concept of the Word was of strictly Greek origin, with no authentic Jewish foundation.

But, the pastor continued, "from a Jewish perspective, a word was more than just a sound. A word had an independent existence. A word had power, that when it went forward, you could not bring it back."

When the Hebrew Scriptures were translated into Aramaic, the language of the people, the Targum used the expression "the Word of God" to avoid anthropomorphism, which would liken God to a man or a thing and sound blasphemous to the common people. For example, "the Word of God is a consuming fire " was substituted for "God is a consuming fire." Also, the cosmos was created by "the Word of the Lord," not by His hands—for God spoke the Word and breathed everything into existence.

The Chasidic men told the two American pastors that there are hundreds of ultra-Orthodox Jews in Israel who are secret believers in Yeshua. They meet privately under their leader, who calls himself Reb Tzlav (Cross), but they continue to practice rabbinic Judaism, and on Shabbat and religious holidays they attend their old synagogues . . . while waiting for Yeshua ha-Moshiach to make His Second Coming, which will settle the matter among the Jews once and for all.

". . . And they will look on Me, Whom they pierced."

They will mourn for Him as one mourns for an only Son . . .
        — Zechariah 12:10 (CJB)

Restitution

Munir was in prayer, up on the Temple Mount, outside the Dome of the Rock. He didn't notice his daughter climbing up to join him, as she sometimes did.

"The most learned men of the Children of Israel knew it was true that Mohamed's message was from God," Munir said, reading from the Qu'ran. "In fact, one of them, Muk-hair-riq, was a Jewish man of property, which he left to follow Islam." Closing the book, Munir added bitterly: "But see how they now have robbed us of our property!"

Then he noticed Samira joining him. She sat on the ground next to him, and they both faced the Dome of the Rock.

"The Jews want to take over the world," Munir said. "They pray that when their messiah comes, all the nations will bow down and bring gifts to Jerusalem." He paused and smiled: "But then, *everybody* wants to take over the world! The Christians say that when their Jesus returns, he will rule the world from Jerusalem. And we Muslims believe that someday the Mahdi will come and the whole world will become Muslim."

"Father," Samira murmured, for she had heard him say all this before.

"If you ask me," her father continued, "one religion is as good or bad as another. Let the Jews build their temples in the sand . . . let the Christians make their mud pies by the sea . . . let the Muslims pitch their tents in the wind . . . He thought about this for a moment, then added, "You know, Samira, if all these beautiful, religious people would just leave each other alone, everything would be fine! After all, how can all of these religions be wrong?"

"But I ask—'How can they all be *right?*'" Samira replied. "God's first commandment to Moses was to avoid false gods. And if there are false gods, there are false religions."

"Yes?"

"So, Father, how can *all* religions lead us to God?" Samira asked. "That's why I'm searching for the true one."

"Well," he told her, "I hope you finally find the religion that's right for *you.*"

"The religion that's right for *me*?" she exclaimed. "We're not choosing ice cream flavors here! There is only *one* true God that can be right for *all of us*!"

"Here we go again," Munir moaned.

Samira got up from the ground, sat on her haunches, and looked down at her father. "Listen," she said. "An Islamic suicide bomber kills himself and an Israeli Jew—and expects to go straight to heaven, as a Muslim martyr, while the Jew, who stole his land, goes to hell."

"Yeah," he said, gazing up at his Christian daughter.

"But the Israeli Jew expects to go straight to heaven, as a Jewish martyr—and expects the bomber to go to hell, for murdering him."

"Hmmmm . . ."

"So, Father," Samira told him, "they can't both be right—can they?"

"No," Munir agreed. Suddenly he smiled: "But they might both be wrong!" and he laughed.

Samira couldn't help laughing, and she hugged her father and sat back on the ground next to him, facing the Dome of the Rock.

"Are you through for today?" he asked.

"Listen," she said. "Suppose three people enter a cave by its only entrance. And after they are deep inside the cave, they get lost."

"Yes?"

"And they find themselves standing at a spot where the cave goes in three different directions. So, one of them says they must take the north tunnel to escape. Another says let's take the south tunnel. And the third says no, the tunnel going east is the only way out, to our freedom."

"What now?" her father asked.

"We know that only one of them can be right," Samira said. "But they have three points of view to consider."

"You're talking about the world's three great religions," he noted.

"Now, tell me, Father," she said. "Are all three points of view equally valid?"

"No . . ."

"Even in a democracy?"

"No. You've got me there."

"Because only one tunnel leads out—"

"*If* only one tunnel leads out—as *you* say," he retorted. "What if you're wrong about that?"

"But if I am right," Samira said, "then there is only one path to God. Every other way leads to darkness and death."

Suddenly Munir began laughing uncontrollably. He was laughing so hard that even his daughter joined in, though not knowing why. When he had regained his composure, he said: "And—and what if the *right* path—which has given the Western world *Christian* culture—is so *wrong* that we see their society falling apart morally, before our very eyes? Christian couples committing adultery, Christian stockbrokers swindling the poor, Christian ministers marrying homosexuals, Christian movies filled with vulgarity and blasphemy—what then, dear Daughter?"

His daughter just looked at him, speechless.

Glancing down from the Temple Mount now, Samira noticed Simon walking up the steps toward them. Noor was right behind him. The odd thing was that Simon wasn't wearing his Israeli uniform—he was dressed in casual clothes. Quickly, Samira left her father, slipped into the olive grove north of the Dome, and disappeared into the busy Muslim Quarter.

*

When Simon reached the Temple Mount he began walking toward Munir. The angry Arab tried to brush past him—but Noor was blocking his way to the Mughrabi Gate.

"Please," Simon cried out to Munir, "I must speak to you."

"No," Munir shouted back at him. "Go away, *Israeli!*"

"I beg your forgiveness for the death of your wife," Simon said.

Munir just looked at him, as if stunned.

"I have already asked Samira for her forgiveness," Simon said.

Standing behind Simon, Noor put a veil over her face. "Munir," she said, "listen to him."

"You broke our hearts two years ago," Munir said to Simon, with sorrow in his voice. "And now you've gone and broken my daughter's heart again. Won't you just go away?"

"Fine," Simon told him. "But first I have something to show you. Munir, look past your falafel stand . . . look down that street. You won't need a telescope."

Munir turned and looked into the distance.

"At the corner, look to your left," Simon said excitedly. "What do you see?"

Munir looked, then turned to face him, enraged. "How dare you mock me!" he roared. "Is this your final insult? I wish I didn't know that *you* were the one that butchered my Beloved! How can I forgive you *that*?"

Stepping closer to Munir, Noor raised her veil and looked straight into his eyes. Munir stared at her in astonishment—then quickly looked away.

"You can forgive him, dear Munir," she said in a voice he recognized, "because **I** have forgiven him."

Munir stared at her again, as if she were a ghost. Then he turned away and headed for the steps. But as he passed, Simon took a folded blue document out of his pocket and shoved it into the Arab's hand.

At the bottom of the steps, Munir stopped, unfolded the blue document and stared at it for a long time.

"Just sign your name!" Simon shouted from the Temple Mount, where he was standing on top of the Wailing Wall.

"Is it really yours?" Munir called out to him.

"Yes—I bought it yesterday," Simon replied.

"The price?" Munir asked, stepping back from the Wall to view him better from below.

"Munir," Simon called down to him, "this is going to cost you more than you ever thought you'd be willing to pay!"

"The price?" Munir repeated.

*

Something made Samira stop in her footsteps on the Via Dolorosa and look around herself. Something was happening—or about to happen. Retracing her steps, she left the Muslim Quarter and returned to the olive grove, looking about her.

Lord, what is it? she asked. *Come, Holy Spirit, guide me, please.* Stepping out of the olive grove, she retraced her steps back to the Dome of the Rock. Her Father was no longer there. *Holy Spirit,* she implored, *guide me—in the name of Yeshua, our Messiah!* She walked past the Dome and made her way to the Maghrubi Gate—walking right past Simon, whose perch on top of the Wall was obscured by the row of fir trees. Stepping through the gate, she looked down, toward the foot of the Wall.

"Father!" she called out.

"Samira!" he shouted, "come quickly, now!"

Scampering down the steps, Samira hit the ground and rushed over to her Father. She was out of breath. Munir handed her the document, and she read it, shaking her head in unbelief.

"My mother's house!" she cried out. "How could you have made such a purchase?"

"With my settlement!" Simon called out to her from the Temple Mount. "From the government!"

Samira looked up at Simon in unbelief.

"The **price?!**" Munir cried out, almost screaming.

Spreading his arms wide, Simon shouted grandly from the Temple Mount: "One . . . red . . . heifer! Without blemish! Never ridden nor sat upon . . . except once!"

From his prayer room next to the Wailing Wall, Rabbi Abram came out to see what all the shouting was about.

Simon climbed down the steps and approached Munir and Samira. Now Noor was standing behind him.

"Father, that's blood money!" Samira said. "He only wants the Red Heifer so he can chop her up and throw her parts into the sea where the Rabbis will never find her!"

"Daughter," Munir replied, almost with a chuckle, "after all we've gone through with that animal, I don't care *what* he does with it!" Then, stepping closer to Simon, he gave him a bear hug. "This is the first deal I've ever closed without haggling!" Munir told him.

"You were too busy hugging for haggling!" Simon said, laughing.

"Oh, I can get used to this!" Munir told him, shaking the document.

Samira just stared at the two of them, not knowing what to think or say. So in her heart she prayed: *Come, Holy Spirit, tell me what's going on!*

"Well," Simon told Munir, "in the absence of the customary haggling, how about throwing in a sweetener to close this deal?"

A frown crossed Munir's face. "What sweetener?" he snapped.

Raising her veil again, Noor looked into Munir's eyes and said: "Give him whatever he asks."

"Father—who *is* she?" Samira whispered to Munir.

"My Daughter," he replied, "you don't *know?*"

"Munir," Simon said, "I told you this may cost you more than you ever thought you'd be willing to part with."

"Name it!"

"Your daughter's hand!" Simon said quietly.

". . . Simon the Zealot . . ." Samira marveled to herself, and smiled. *Thank You, Holy Spirit of God! And now I know my heart!*

Munir turned and took his daughter aside. "Would he become a Muslim to marry you?" he asked her.

"Why should he?" she said. "I'm a Christian."

"Then would he become a Christian?" he asked.

"Why should he?" she replied. "He's a Jew."

Squeezing his eyes shut, Munir confessed, "Daughter, I am confused!"

Now Noor spoke up. "Samira, now is the time to act," she said. "If the mountain won't come to Mohamed, Mohamed must go to the mountain!"

"Yes," Samira told Noor. Then, turning to Munir, she said: "Father, I can marry a Jew and convert to Judaism—all the members of the Early Church were Jewish and remained Jewish! And they believed the Messiah had come."

"And your children?" Munir demanded. "How would you teach them? What god would they serve?"

"Father," she said, "there is only one Creator of us all."

Scowling at her, Munir retorted, "Are you telling me *now* that all religions *are* the same!"

"No, I am not," she said. "There is only *one* way to holiness and everlasting life."

"I thought so!" he said. "Because you refuse to call God 'Allah'! Even before your beloved Mother died, she was teaching you to believe in this 'Yeshua.'"

"If Yeshua is God, then God is a Jew," Samira said. "And I want to become a Jew—and marry the man I love—Simon!"

"A Muslim woman is forbidden to marry a Jew," Munir muttered to himself. "But my daughter is no longer a Muslim. I don't know what she is. I leave her to the mercy of Allah, the compassionate."

Still shaking his head, Munir placed his daughter's hand in Simon's. Then he handed the document to Samira.

Noticing Rabbi Abram approaching, Simon ran over and whispered in his ear. Then Simon turned to Munir—and the Arab quickly left to fetch the Red Heifer. A few minutes later, Munir came strolling down the plaza to the Wall with the animal on a leash.

Simon's eyes suddenly widened—for this was the first time he had ever seen the Red Heifer.

"So *this* is the creature we have been fighting over!" Simon exclaimed.

"She's been here all along, Simon," Samira said. "But your eyes weren't open to her until now."

Rabbi Abram held the Red Heifer by her leash.

Now Isaac came out of the prayer room to see what was going on. "Rabbi!" he exclaimed. "Why are we taking back the Red Heifer?"

The Rabbi just shook his head ruefully, as if to say, *Don't even ask!* Then he led the Red Heifer back to their prayer and study room.

Now Simon took Samira aside.

"Samira, will you marry me?" he said.

"Yes, Simon! But on one condition."

"Anything!"

"I want Rabbi Abram to marry us!" she said.

Simon was stunned. "But—you're not Jewish!" he said.

"I want the Rabbi to be my Jewish teacher, so that I can become a Jew," she told him.

"But—but he wouldn't marry us unless I was a religious Jew, too!" Simon said.

"Maybe we could take classes from him—together!" Samira said. "Are you ready to return to the faith of your fathers, Simon?"

Simon's mouth dropped open. "This will be *t'shuvah*—big time!" he said.

Then he led Samira to the prayer room, where Isaac and the Rabbi were busy grooming the Red Heifer.

"Rabbi," Simon said. "Samira has something to say to you."

"What is it, my daughter?" the Rabbi said without looking up.

"Rabbi, I would like to convert to Judaism. Would you be my teacher?"

"No," came his quick response.

"Ask him a second time," Simon told her.

"Rabbi," Samira said. "would you be my teacher so I can convert?"

"No."

Noor had arrived on the scene again.

"Now ask him the third time!" she told Samira.

"Oh, what's the use, Noor?" she said, walking toward her. "He said no."

"No, Samira," Noor told her. "A rabbi isn't permitted to consider a conversion until he has been asked the third time."

"Oh, Noor—I'm getting cold feet!" Samira said. "I'm not sure I should take this step."

Noor took her aside. "Samira, you'll be making history," she told her. "When Yeshua of Nazareth returns to rule the world from Jerusalem, he'll still be a practicing Jew. Christians must get ready for that surprise."

"But I'm only *one* Christian!"

"Samira," Noor said, "the Church has completed its mission of preparing the nations for the coming of Messiah. Now it's time for the Church to come back to its mother—and to *become one* with its Jewish mother—and *protect* her from her *enemies*—as Israel, too, prepares for the coming of Messiah."

Her eyes wide open, Samira turned back toward the prayer room. "Rabbi, Sir," she pleaded, "would you please be my teacher for my conversion?"

"I will think about it," Rabbi Abram told her. "But I must be satisfied about your reasons. You cannot convert simply to get married. You must sincerely want to become an observant Jewish woman."

"Please don't reject me, Rabbi," she said. "Don't forget—when Ruth the Gentile was leaving her home and going to Bethlehem to live with Naomi—she said to Naomi: 'Your people will be my people and your God will be my God.'"

"We will see . . . Come to our prayer room tomorrow," the Rabbi told her. "And bring your soldier friend!"

"At last!" Noor shouted, overjoyed. "The Church begins to return to its roots in the Temple—through one couple today . . . And what a wedding it's going to be!" She stopped herself, and a look of mischief crossed her face. "Oh, but let me think: What sort of music do you suppose they should play at such a mixed wedding?" She paused. "Why, of course, they will sing—'Oy Vey, Maria'!"

Simon and Samira laughed.

"And *then* they're going to dance the 'Hava Novena'!" she cried out, and they laughed louder.

Chapter 26

Israeli Arabs and Jews, Working in Holy Cahoots

BETHLEHEM

One morning an Israeli Jew named Yossi got out of his cab and walked into the Olive Tree, a hotel on the invisible border between an Orthodox Jewish neighborhood and Arab East Jerusalem. He was looking for an American couple. He didn't know their name, but he was certain that Yeshua of Nazareth would send them to him.

My wife and I came out of the elevator and began walking toward the lobby. Yossi was walking toward us from the opposite direction—down a long corridor. Our eyes met as we all reached the lobby, and now the three of us were standing still, facing each other.

"Here I am," Yossi told us. "Where do you want to go first?"

Startled, we told him we hadn't called anybody—but we *did* need a cab.

Yossi just smiled and led us outside to his cab. After taking us to a bank in Rechavia, Yossi suggested a souvenir shop nearby, on Metudela Street, that was owned by a friend. When we got there the owner, Jonathan, said he too was a believer in Yeshua, the Messiah. Jonathan had recently been forced to move his shop from a busier part of Jerusalem because the Orthodox found out about his faith and organized a boycott. (Three years later, on our return, he had again moved his shop.)

Jonathan then proceeded to show us his rugs, produced by Jewish families that had brought their age-old craft from Iran and needed the money. All of them are Christian believers, he said, and they secretly attend Jewish messianic services in someone's house in Modi'in. This ancient town was the birthplace of the Maccabees, who in the second century before Christ conducted guerrilla warfare against the Syrian soldiers who had set up a pagan altar in Modi'in and pressured Jews to abandon Judaism in favor of Greek pagan customs. The Syrians had even profaned the Temple. The Maccabee victory is celebrated on Hanukkah.

Today Modi'in is one of 15 Israeli cities and villages where more than 25 Jewish messianic synagogues operate, some in public, some in private homes. Today an estimated 15,000 Jews in Israel now believe in Messiah Yeshua, some privately to avoid persecution, some boldly in public. Ultra-Orthodox Jews have sometimes been violent in their opposition, such as fire bombing a building in Kirykat Arba, and sending a package with a bomb, which severely injured a boy when he opened it at his kitchen table.

Seating me and Shirah now on two chairs decked like thrones, Jonathan served us hot tea with mint leaves freshly picked that morning from his mother's garden. After purchasing a large rug, some souvenirs, and a large bottle of holy oil for use by our congregation back home, we returned to the cab, and Yossi drove us to the Mount of Olives. There we had a spectacular view of the Old City as seen by Yeshua from here, in his favorite place of prayer. At an Arab bazaar, Yossi introduced us to Shlomo, another Jewish believer. Shlomo sold my wife a beautiful green-and-cream gown that had been sewn by female soldiers to support the families of Israel Defense Force casualties.

Yossi then drove us to the Garden of Gethsemane, where the Lord spent His last night before His arrest. Some of the olive trees were several feet in diameter, and might have been here as saplings on that night, two thousand years ago.

All over Israel, motorists are in such an impatient hurry that they are constantly honking their horns at each other. Shirah remarked that they were probably leaning on their horns to relieve the tension on these dangerous streets and highways, and that it was comical, in a way, as if they were all honking their nation's real national anthem. Surely, Shabbat—or Shabbos, as the Ashkenazi from Europe pronounce it—is the key to Israeli time. Without a mandatory shutdown once a week, hurly-burly Israeli society would surely have burned itself out by now.

Back at Jonathan's souvenir shop, we all went inside and took a break. Another Jewish cab driver, named Adam, showed up. After being introduced to this Jewish believer in Yeshua, I excused myself and went to find my wife at the other end of the shop.

"You've got to meet this man," I told her. "He looks to me like the young David—I think he's a born leader."

Adam warmly embraced us, then prayed with us—blessing us with "joy, happiness, love and peace." Later Shirah told me that she had felt the anointing coming down on us as this charismatic man prayed.

Several days later, we were standing outside the hotel, looking for a cab, when Adam drove up in his Mercedes and greeted us as an old friend. He offered to drive us to Bethlehem.

"Today," he said grandly as we drove off, "will be your first real day in Israel!"

Outside the walled Old City, our cab stopped for a light at a congested corner—and here a moment of truth forced itself on my wife: Our cabbie was waiting to turn left, and a cab in the oncoming lane—driven by a man wearing an Arab headdress—was at a standstill, facing us. The two cab drivers looked into each other's faces for a long time. Shirah told me later that she found it heartbreaking. She could see in both their faces a kind of tenderness, a helplessness over the circumstances that paralyzed them, like their ancestral brothers Isaac and Ishmael.

On our way to Bethlehem, the IDF halted us at one of several West Bank security checkpoints and asked to see our passports. Once we entered Bethlehem, Adam stopped his cab outside an Arab shop, the King Solomon Bazaar, and—without explanation—went inside. He soon returned with a Palestinian Arab named George. He would be our guide at the Church of the Nativity.

We passed a field—now built up with modern housing—where it is said that Ruth met Boaz, her future husband. George quoted from the Book of Ruth, where the Moabite woman said to Naomi, her Jewish mother-in-law, "Your people will be my people, your God will be my God. Where you die I will die, and there I will be buried." Then George added an Arab touch, "Your land will be my land." At Shepherds Field we got out of the cab and walked down to a cave similar to where Yeshua was born; this one had a manger carved out of stone. On the way, I tasted brown carob seeds hanging from a tree and thought of the *carubi* that my grandmother had eaten as candy in Sicily.

After our tour of the Church of the Nativity, we all slowly ambled back to the cab, singing a hymn that we all happened to know, and Adam drove us back to the King Solomon Bazaar. Inside Adnan, the owner, served us refreshments and ordered a falafel lunch. Adam and Shirah and I dipped our pita bread into the hummus—made of mashed chickpeas, oil, lemon juice and crushed sesame seeds—and scooped up chunks of tomatoes, pepper and onions. Then we looked over jewelry and Christian souvenirs.

George, a lifelong Greek Orthodox Christian, supplies the shop with religious ikons from his relatives, who need money. Adnan, born and raised a Roman Catholic, said he was born again five years ago and stopped drinking. Adam said he had been drug-free for the past six years and ten months.

According to George, 50 percent of Israel's Palestinian Arab Christians are Eastern Orthodox, 35 percent are Catholic, and many of the others are Lutheran Evangelical believers.

Among Jewish believers, Adam attends Congregation HaCarmel in Haifa, one of the larger messianic synagogues. Traditional Jews in Israel and America balk at accepting messianic congregations as "synagogues," looking on them instead as churches with Jewish trappings. Messianic Jews long to be accepted as a legitimate denomination of Judaism. In fact, they see themselves as the latter-day reincarnation of the Early Church in Jerusalem, which was composed entirely of Jews who continued to worship in the Temple in spite of the ongoing persecution of the followers of Yeshua. Never disqualified as legitimate Jews, their congregation at Jerusalem nevertheless fled across the Jordan before the Roman soldiers came to destroy the Temple.

We spent quite a bit of money at Adnan's shop. As we drove out of Bethlehem, Adam remarked that our purchases today had come just in time for Adnan to pay the rent and utilities on his shop.

Back in Jerusalem, after Adam had dropped us off, I said to Shirah: "Isn't it amazing? We just had a Jewish cabbie drive us American tourists to an Arab souvenir shop so he could share his good fortune with the shop owner and his tour guide friend. I mean, who would have thought of such a thing as Jews and Arabs working in cahoots to support each other in the tourist trade? These three citizens of Israel have found the answer—and those poor 'peace negotiators' haven't got a clue!"

"What finally brought them together was their belief in the Messiah of Israel," my wife said. "That's the only way there will ever be peace in the Holy Land."

> For he himself is our peace, who has made the two one and has destroyed the barrier, the dividing wall of hostility . . . His purpose was to create in himself one new man out of the two, thus making peace, and in this one body to reconcile both of them to God through the cross, by which he put to death their hostility.

— Ephesians 2:14–16 (NIV)

The Final Question

Still standing outside the prayer and study room, near the Western Wall, Simon turned to Samira and said, "Return now to your mother's house."

"Come with me!" said Samira, still clutching the deed to the house.

But Isaac shouted after them, "No! Wait!" and the couple stopped.

"Itzak," Samira said, "are you going to wish us well?"

"I'm sorry but I cannot," Isaac said. "Jewish law forbids a Christian to convert to Judaism without renouncing her false messiah."

"Stay out of this, you *black hat*!" Simon told Isaac.

"You're about to become religious like me, and you call me a *black hat*?" Isaac retorted.

"All right," Simon told Isaac. "I've come to believe that the God of Israel still lives." He thought a moment, then said: "And now, since I believe in the miracles in the desert, I also believe God will someday send His Messiah!"

"*Baruch Hashem!*" Isaac said. "You are a Jew after God's own heart! So why would you violate God's law and marry a Christian?"

"She's going to convert to Judaism!"

"It will be a false conversion unless she renounces Yeshua of Nazareth," Isaac said.

Samira spoke up.

"Isaac, the only difference between Simon and his Jewish wife will be that she thinks she knows the name of the Messiah we're all waiting for. And she will be proven right when Messiah Yeshua returns just as he departed—on God's Shekinah Cloud of Glory!"

"But you're wrong!" Isaac insisted.

"Suppose that I *was* wrong," Samira told him. "There have been lots of Jews who were wrong—but they were still Jewish."

"They were *born* Jewish," Isaac said. "They were not converts."

"Oh rubbish, Itzak!" she shouted.

"Nobody will be in violation of Jewish law if we marry," Simon said.

*

293

Back at the falafel stand, Rabbi Abram was having a kosher tea with Munir.

"So, Rabbi," Munir was saying, "you will gain a convert out of all this!"

"Only if your daughter passes all my tests," the Rabbi replied. "And *you* have regained the house you lost in the war!"

"It's a beginning . . ." Munir said.

"But *my* victory is that Simon, a lost son of Israel, is returning to the faith!" the Rabbi said.

"So," Munir said, eyeing the Rabbi, "the Red Heifer has done its work."

". . . Part of its work," the Rabbi replied.

"Rabbi," Munir said. "May I speak frankly?"

"Why not, Munir?" Rabbi Abram said, a bit of sarcasm in his voice. "We are friends—in spite of all the hatred that we still feel for each other. Abraham's two sons—Itzak and Ishmael—began fighting each other inside Sara's womb—and they are still locked in the throes of brotherly war over the Promised Land."

"Never mind that for now," Munir said. "Rabbi Abram—if your God truly wants you to rebuild your Temple up there—where we have our Mosque—surely he will send you another red heifer, some day, one that is perfect and free of any blemish."

"I suppose you're right."

"This particular heifer has done its work. Now it's time to put this little veal cutlet out of its misery. We can put the meat in the freezer—for the coming wedding!"

"This is my Red Heifer!" the Rabbi exclaimed.

"Right you are!" Munir assured him. "And it's yours to give—as a wedding gift! So, let's butcher it now—and put it in the freezer—before my sentimental daughter catches on and tries to stop us."

The Rabbi pondered this . . . After all, the soldier had gotten back the Red Heifer so she could be bred and possibly produce another genuine *Para Aduma*. What should he do?

*

Back at the prayer room, Isaac, Simon and Samira were still having their theological debate.

"Samira, what about Christian law?" Isaac was saying. "Doesn't your bible also forbid intermarriage?"

"Do not harness yourselves in an uneven team with unbelievers," Samira said, quoting from the New Testament.

Simon was getting impatient.

"What are you two fools talking about?" he demanded.

"Nothing, Simon. Forget it," Samira told him.

"Samira," Isaac said, "do you think you can turn Simon into a Christian?"

"What does he mean by that?" Simon asked Samira.

"Nothing, Simon," she said.

"Simon," Isaac said, "haven't you heard what that Bedouin woman keeps telling her? 'If the mountain won't come to Mohamed, Samira, then Mohamed will have to come to the mountain.' So now that Samira has gotten *you* to come to *her*, Simon, she hopes to convert you to Christianity."

Simon stared at Samira: "Is that true?"

"Don't be ridiculous, both of you!" she retorted. "I want to become a Jew—and I'll be one of thousands of Jews in Israel who believe they already have found the true Messiah of Israel."

"All of them are wrong!" Isaac snapped.

"We have all experienced the *presence* of the Messiah," she replied. "You call it *kiruv*, closeness to God."

"In your imagination!" Isaac retorted.

"Isaac," Samira said, "you were wrong the other night when you said the Presence of the Lord disappeared from us when the Shekinah left the Temple, never to return."

"It's all in the Book of Ezekiel, Chapter 9 and 10," the yeshiva boy said.

"So you didn't read on, to Chapter 11?" Samira said. "God then tells Ezekiel that He will return us to the land and give us a new spirit and a heart of flesh in place of our heart of stone. We will be born anew."

"We're still waiting on that promise," Isaac said.

"No, Isaac," she said. "Read Chapter 43—after the Temple was restored, God's Presence returned from the east—'*and the Glory of the Lord came into the Temple*'—but now it appeared in the form of a Man—whom Ezekiel had seen earlier—a Man who shined in all His Father's glory above His throne. Yeshua!"

*

Meanwhile Munir and the Rabbi were discussing if—and how—they should butcher the Red Heifer.

"Maybe you're right, maybe you're wrong," the Rabbi was saying. "But an animal must be butchered the proper way."

Pulling out his butcher knife, Munir said: "I will butcher it! The little beast . . ."

"No!" said the Rabbi. "It must be kosher."

"But of course," Munir said. "We have rules similar to your kosher. We will do it together!"

"No!" said Rabbi Abram, pulling out his dagger. "It must be butchered with the proper knife—one that has never touched unkosher meat or dairy products."

"Agreed!" Munir said. "And the animal must be slaughtered in such a way that it does not feel fear or pain."

"Of course," the Rabbi said.

*

Back in the prayer room, Isaac was continuing to put pressure on Samira.

"And your children will be taught as 'believers,' too, won't they, Samira?" he said. "Let me hear you deny that."

"Itzak," she replied, "all of this is none of your business!"

"That's right, Samira," Simon spoke up. "He should mind his own business. But what do *you* have to say to all this?"

"Don't you see what Itzak is trying to do to us?" she said. "He hasn't forgiven us for what happened to the Red Heifer. He hates us!"

"I don't hate anyone," Isaac said.

Turning to Samira, Simon demanded: "Are you going to marry me or not?"

"Of course I am, Simon!" she said. "I love you!"

"And what if Rabbi Abram refuses to convert you?" Simon persisted. "Where would we get married?"

Samira thought about this. "Well," she said at last, "we could always get married in Christ Church—it's—"

"—Oh, wonderful!" cried Isaac.

"—it's right down the street," she said.

"Your *church*?" Simon said, his anger rising. "*What?!*"

"All she wants is to 'save your soul,' Simon," Isaac said. "That's what this 'love' is all about."

Simon placed his hands on Samira's shoulders and stared her in the eyes.

"So you think that my soul needs saving?" he demanded.

"Simon!" she said. "Everyone needs to make things right with God! Why else would you have agreed to study with me under Rabbi Abram—to do *t'shuvah* and return to the God of Israel? We all need our sins forgiven."

*

Outside the falafel stand, Rabbi Abram and Munir were standing face to face, their knives out.

"Now, Munir," the Rabbi said kindly, "here is how we slaughter an animal for kosher meat." He placed his dagger at Munir's neck. "We must sever the jugular vein."

"Yes," Munir answered cheerfully, "that's how we do it too," and he demonstrated with his butcher knife on the Rabbi's neck.

"But Munir," the Rabbi said, "that isn't the way the knife is held. This is the proper way."

Eyeing the dagger at his throat, Munir said: "No, my friend. This is how the blade must be wielded . . ."

*

Now Simon was filled with rage. "You never forgave me for killing your mother, did you, Samira?" he shouted. "Did you?"

"I swear to God, Simon, I have forgiven you!" Samira said. She was in tears. "Oh, Simon—we serve a God who is *so eager* to forgive! Don't you know by now?"

"Sure she's forgiven you, Simon," Isaac said. "Like the Christians have forgiven us for the death of their messiah!"

Angrily turning on Isaac, she said: "I have news for you, Itzak! Even if all the Jews had accepted Yeshua—and crowned Him *King*—the Romans would have crucified Him—and all the Jews following Him— for challenging the Emperor's authority! Don't you see? The Messiah's mission was to die as a Blood Sacrifice for all the sins of the world."

Then, turning to Simon, she said, "I love you, Simon!" Tears were streaming down her face, and Simon could see the anguish in her eyes, and her love for him.

*

Munir and the Rabbi were now in agreement.

"This beef will make a perfect wedding banquet, my friend," said Munir.

"Ah, this is a perfect animal, for a perfect sacrifice," said the Rabbi. "It is without blemish."

"Except for that invisible blemish, my friend," Munir said, trying to conceal a smile.

"It is still kosher," the Rabbi assured him. "It is kosher . . ."

"Don't forget," Munir told him, "it must be a flawless slaughter. The animal must not cry out."

"None of its bones will be broken," said the Rabbi.

"Amen, 'brother'!" said the Muslim, with a comical wink of his eye. And they laughed together.

*

"But, Samira," Simon said earnestly, "how could you forgive me for what I did? Surely your mother would still be alive today if it weren't for me."

Gathering her thoughts, through her tears, Samira told him: "I forgave you, Simon, because you did the following: You apologized to both me and my father. You wished that it had never happened. You resolved never to do such a thing again. And now, Simon, you have offered restitution—my mother's house!"

Stunned, Simon said, almost to himself: "I—I have made *t'shuvah* . . .

"Yes!" said Samira. "And now you have fully repented. So I forgive you . . ."

*

Munir reminded the Rabbi, one last time: "And the victim must not cry out in pain."

"Like a lamb led to the slaughter," Rabbi Abram agreed. "But wait! What about its coat?"

"It is fine fur," Munir said. "We can divide it."

"No," said the Rabbi. "It's too precious to be cut in two."

"I'll flip you for it."

"That would be gambling, my friend," the Rabbi said. Then, raising his voice, he called: "Itzak! Bring us the Red Heifer!"

"*Wait*, my friend!" Munir said.

The Rabbi waited.

"So," Munir told him, "you're not a gambling man."

"I am not."

"But it *is* a gamble whether Samira can qualify to become a Jew."

"It's not a sure thing at all," the Rabbi replied.

Smiling, Munir said: "And even if she does, my friend—I'm not sure how good a Jew my daughter will make. She might move right on to Buddhism!"

"Just between you and me, Munir," the Rabbi said, "if she fails the course, I will give her an 'F.'"

Munir looked relieved: "Then there might not be a wedding after all!"

"Then you would get to keep Samira!" Rabbi Abram told him.

"And you would get to keep Simon!"

And with that, they both smiled and sheathed their knives.

"But I still say, my friend, that we should have our celebration!" Munir said. Raising his voice, he called: "Bring us the animal!"

"Itzak! Come quick!" the Rabbi cried out. "Bring us the Red Heifer!"

*

Now Isaac turned to Samira one last time. "Samira," he said, "you admitted a while ago that your religion forbids you to marry a man who doesn't believe in your messiah."

Samira was silent.

"Isn't this true?" Isaac persisted.

". . . yes," she whispered.

"So," Isaac said, "you cannot marry this man without stepping outside of your Christian faith."

"That's true," Samira said.

Simon suddenly looked very alarmed.

"So what—what are you going to do, Samira?" he asked.

She looked into his face for a very long time. When she finally spoke, her voice was choked up. "I'm sorry, my love, but I cannot marry you," she said. "You do not believe in the Messiah."

Simon was outraged, his face red and his fists clenched. "What makes you think that I don't believe in the Messiah? Haven't I told you of the miracle that took place in the desert, when a battalion of Arab tanks retreated from a single Israeli tank? Didn't I tell you that it was the God of Israel who did that?"

"Yes, Simon, I remember!" she said.

"Well—what I *haven't* told you yet is the miracle that happened to *me*—just in the past few days!"

299

Isaac called out, "What miracle? What are you talking about, Simon?"

"What miracle?" Samira pleaded.

Simon took in a deep breath. "I have had a tempestuous week, while I was on leave from the Army. Everything fell into place for me to get my settlement from the government—and then to persuade the owner to sell me your mother's house."

"It was the grace of God, Simon!" Samira exclaimed.

"Yes," Simon said. "And then I went to the top of the city—I climbed up on my favorite hill—above the Railway Station. And there I thanked God for what I had accomplished. But then something took hold of me! And I climbed on top of the highest rock and stretched out my hands to the heavens! And as I thanked God—as I thanked God with all my heart that I was going to have you back—I was filled with such joy that I began to laugh! And I laughed so hard that I began to cry! Real tears—like a baby! And that was when I saw Him!"

*

Suddenly the two men at the falafel stand—and the three young friends at the prayer room—were startled by the sound of a shofar blowing. The sound was coming from up on the Temple Mount.

They all ran to the Wailing Wall and looked up to behold Noor, standing up on the Temple Mount. She had a veil over her face.

"Rabbi Abram!" Noor called down to him. "Do you forgive Simon and Samira for sabotaging the Red Heifer?"

The Rabbi stared up at her for a long moment.

"Who **are** you, anyway?" he asked at last.

"Just answer her, Rabbi," Isaac told him.

"But who is she?"

"I could tell you, my friend," Munir said mysteriously, "but you would never believe me."

"Rabbi Abram," Noor called out again, "do you forgive Simon and Samira for what happened to the Red Heifer?"

"Until I see with my own eyes who you are, my answer will be No!" he retorted.

"Samira," Noor called out, "do you forgive Itzak for trying to prevent your marriage?"

"No."

"Munir," Noor called out, "do you forgive Itzak and the Rabbi for still wanting to rebuild the Temple up here?"

"No."

Raising the veil to expose her face, Noor said: "But Munir, you forgave Simon for the death of your wife—for he has returned her family's home to you."

"It is not enough," Munir said. "Don't you understand, my beloved? We must have **all** of Palestine back!"

"Simon," Noor called out, "do you forgive Munir for wanting all of Palestine?"

"No! Never!" Simon shouted. "And stop calling it 'Palestine.'"

Finally, Noor called out to the last one standing below her.

"Itzak Cohen," Noor said, "do you forgive Simon and Samira for sabotaging the Red Heifer?"

"... Well ..." Isaac said. "Yes ..."

Now Noor raised her hands and cried out to them all.

"Only *one* of you knows the meaning of t'shuvah!" she said. "The rest of you know how to *ask* forgiveness—but you don't know how to give it! Very well. Itzak, bring me the Red Heifer!"

Isaac walked through the door to the prayer room and came out, holding the Red Heifer. Slinging the creature over his shoulders, like a shepherd carrying his lost sheep, he climbed up the steps to the Temple Mount and placed the Red Heifer at Noor's feet. Then he descended the steps again.

Noor had the Red Heifer on her shoulders now. She was no longer wearing the veil over her eyes.

"Then I saw a new heaven and a new earth," she proclaimed. "I saw the holy city, New Yerushalayim, coming down out of heaven from God. It shown with the glory of God . . . I saw no Temple in the city, for Adonai, God of heaven's armies, is its Temple, as is the Lamb."

Below, they all stared up at Noor, dumbfounded. What was she going to do with that Red Heifer on her shoulders?

"As we came, so we depart," Noor cried out, "until another generation!"

And with that, she raised her hands in prayer until a white cloud gathered around her and lifted her and the Red Heifer up, out of sight, to the sound of flute music.

On the ground, Rabbi Abram shouted, "The Shekinah!" and ran for the steps.

"Where do you think you are going?" Munir called out after him.

"Bring it back!" Rabbi Abram shouted into the sky as he stood on the top step to the Temple Mount. "Please! It was *our* Red Heifer!"

Looking all around him, Munir cried out: "Stop him! Stop him, brothers!"

"Rabbi!" Isaac cried out. "I saw it too! God's Cloud of Glory!"

"No Jew is allowed on the Haram al-Sharif!" Munir shouted.

"Rabbi!" Isaac shouted. "What can we do?"

"Itzak!" the Rabbi called down to Isaac. "I saw the Shekinah Glory of God! I saw His Divine Cloud!"

"So did I!" Isaac said. "Oh, Rabbi!"

"Brothers!" Munir cried out to any Muslims who might be within earshot. "Ahmad!," he shouted, reaching into his pocket for the bullet from his nephew. "To the Haram al-Sharif! Stop the Jews! Come, let us cut them off from being a nation—that the name of Israel will be no more!"

"Rabbi Abram!" Samira cried out. "Please come down now!"

"Oh, Itzak!" the Rabbi wailed. "That was our last chance! **Our last chance for p e a c e !**"

He began climbing down.

Waving his butcher knife, Munir shouted: "There will never be peace! And I will tell you *this,* Rabbi Abram! My daughter Samira will *never* marry a Jew! I'll see to that!"

On the ground now, the Rabbi unsheathed his dagger: "And our Simon will never marry a Gentile! *We'll* see to that!"

Chapter 27

A Man Called Peter

Immediately, while he was still speaking, a rooster crowed. And the Lord turned and looked at Peter. Then Peter remembered the word of the Lord, how He had said to him, "Before the rooster crows today, you will deny Me three times." So Peter went out and wept bitterly.

— Luke 22:60–62

JERUSALEM

R abbi Fogelman . . . Rabbi Frankel . . . Rabbi Haber . . . Rabbi Abramson . . . Abraham HaCohen—all of them had one thing in common: They were introduced to me by Zerach, who was my very close *baal t'shuvah* friend from America.

Zerach's father had fled Germany during the Holocaust, and his mother came from an Orthodox family in New York. They did not raise their children to be religiously observant. After becoming Orthodox in his twenties, Zerach became editor of the *Buffalo Jewish Review*, located just a few blocks from my *Buffalo News*. Then he moved to New York and became a world correspondent for *Jewish Week*, the largest English-language newspaper in the Jewish world. As the years went by he also traveled every Passover to countries in Eastern Europe to assist the remaining Jews who have no rabbi and have forgotten how to put on a *seder* meal. Sponsored by the Jewish Joint Distribution Committee every year, Zerach goes to a town and leads the *seder*, recounting their deliverance from Egypt. Thus far, he has gone to two dozen countries. Each time, he prepares by studying the language. Fluent in English, German and Hebrew, he quickly learned how to carry on a basic conversation in Russian, Polish, Hungarian, Romanian, Albanian, and a host of other tongues. He even studied Amharic before flying to Africa to visit Ethiopian Jews still living there.

I first encountered Zerach one Friday night in 1980. I had invited myself to Erev Shabbat dinner in the home of a Jewish man who had accepted Yeshua of Nazareth as the Messiah, and who—like the Jews who formed the early church in Jerusalem—continued to live and worship as a Jew. The couple and their children had several other guests that night, including this tall, lanky guy called Zerach. He kept pretty much to himself on the living room couch all evening, not eating and not joining in the Sabbath songs that we were singing in English and Hebrew, celebrating the Sabbath and honoring Yeshua as Messiah. I later learned that Zerach, who had been a school friend of the host, had recently decided to become an Orthodox Jew. This meant that he couldn't eat at his old Jewish friend's table without kosher approval of the food by his own rabbi—who would never extend such a courtesy to a Jew who had accepted Yeshua as Moshiach and become *meshumad* (allegedly dead as a Jew). In fact, Zerach had just attended Orthodox services nearby and was spending the rest of the Sabbath at his old friend's house because he lived too far away to walk home and, being Orthodox, wasn't allowed to drive on the Sabbath.

The next time I saw Zerach was the following year, on the plane to Israel with hundreds of Holocaust survivors from across New York State. Zerach was covering the World Gathering of Jewish Holocaust Survivor for the *Buffalo Jewish Review*. When Zerach learned that I planned to spend the following week touring the country, he said that he, too, was staying to write other stories, and asked when I might be passing through Tel Aviv. I gave him a date. Unfortunately, after I left the Sea of Galilee the following week and was returning south, I stopped for a day and an extra night at the seaside resort town of Netanya.

Only later did I learn that Zerach had been in Tel Aviv on the appointed day and had gone to a dozen hotels, asking for a Mr. Cardinale. He never let me forget that! Over the ensuing days, weeks and months, he would call me on the phone, invite me to his newspaper office, and compare notes on reporting and writing style. We soon became the closest of friends. He even invited me to write a full-page piece, "A Christian Looks at Israel," for his newspaper, which was published by an Orthodox couple.

One of the funniest people I have ever met, Zerach was cons
playing tricks on his friends—but he was also researching a subject
no one had ever touched before: How the Jews had employed
humor and irony to help them get through the Holocaust. The result,
based on interviews with Jews in America and Europe, was a book
entitled *Laughter in Hell.* It made the Jewish Book of the Month
Club (getting better play in the newsletter that month than a new
book by Elie Wiesel).

Zerach and I traveled together to Israel and Jordan in 1985, to talk
to Jews and Palestinian Arabs about the new "land for peace" proposal,
and again in 1998, after I'd become interested in the red heifer. Zerach
had encouraged me to apply for a residency at Mishkenot Sha'ananim,
introduced me to rabbis in Jerusalem, and even accompanied me on
some of my interviews.

In fact, while we were in Jordan, he shared most of his sources with
me, so that we interviewed them together. He knew that I was going
through a very sorrowful time in my life, and he did everything to make
it possible for me to accompany him to Jordan. I was often in a fog that
time in Israel, and when we approached the Wailing Wall he saw me
burst into tears. Well, after my series appeared in *The Buffalo News*,
Zerach's stories began to finally appear in his *Jewish Week.* Not until
many months later, when I studied his articles more carefully, did I
discover that Zerach had not used a single direct quote that I had used.
He had let me take the pick of the quotes that both of us had heard, then
used for himself only the scraps that I'd left behind. It was the kind
of super-caution that an Orthodox journalist might take to avoid being
falsely accused of copying quotes from another newspaper. But much
more significant, it was an act of charity—and self-sacrifice!—that I
cannot recall ever witnessing between two Christian writers. This man
is truly a *tzaddik* and a *mensch.*

Zerach has traveled to Israel more than twenty times. Whenever he
is in Jerusalem, he travels light and stays at the home of the Frankels,
where they keep a closet with his things and have assigned him a bed
in their sons' large bunkroom. For years Zerach has been a favorite
of the Frankel children, romping around the house with them, taking
them on outings, and playing tricks on them. And he loves to jog on
the road below the cliff off their back yard, running along the green
fields of Judea.

On this particular trip, the children's mother, Shalamis, had played
a trick of her own on Zerach by packing Jell-O in the showerhead.

When Zerach turned on the faucet, red water flowed over him. The kids laughed hilariously.

But Zerach could also be his own worst trickster. Late one night he had returned to the Frankel house, sauntered into the kitchen and helped himself to a hamburger and some chicken—only to learn a few minutes later that Salamis had baked his favorite cheese blintzes and left them in the oven to cool. Since the kosher laws don't allow dairy products to be eaten with meat, Zerach had to wait till morning to have his cheese blintzes. The Frankel children laughed and jumped all over him with mischievous delight.

On the day he left Israel, Zerach gave me several dollars that he hadn't gotten around to giving to the poor. That night in Jerusalem, I was getting into bed at my usual hour when I suddenly discovered that I had been short-sheeted! Laughing out loud, I pictured Zerach on his plane, no doubt looking at his watch right about now and smiling at the mischief he had left behind.

But my most singular "trick" on Zerach occurred on March 28, 1991, when he was visiting Buffalo and was about to leave for Israel to lend his hand during the Iraqi rocket bombardment of Tel Aviv. Many civilians were volunteering to fill the gap left by reserve soldiers called up to duty. I was driving Zerach to a kosher pastry shop in Buffalo, and as I parked my car I noticed the license plate of another parked car. It began: NU 326. I asked him to open the Bible in my front seat to Numbers 32:6. He did so. And to his astonishment he read:

> And Moses said . . . *'Shall your brethren go to war while you sit here?'*

"How did you do that?" he demanded, staring again at the license plate.

I could hardly stop smiling from ear to ear. "I didn't do it," I said at last. "It was Yeshua ha-Moshiach!"

"No, really, how'd you do that . . . ?"

*

In Jerusalem, Zerach had also introduced me a *baal t'shuvah* woman named Tova, who made her living as a tour guide. She once gave the elderly actor Kirk Douglas his first tours of Israel, as he made *t'shuvah* and returned to the faith. "I have come full circle," he told her. "I grew up . . ."

A native of Pittsburgh, Pennsylvania, Tova had an apartment in the Old City and had invited Zerach and me for a Erev Shabbat meal. As Zerach was giving the *kiddush* blessing over the wine and bread (which Christians will recall from the Last Supper), I suddenly broke into song, chanting the rest of the Hebrew blessing. Tova and her woman friends—all Americans studying Torah in Israel—said they were most impressed and vowed to learn the Hebrew prayer too.

(The Apostle Paul's Letter to the Romans says that Gentiles who gained salvation by accepting the Jewish Messiah would provoke the Jews to jealousy. He was quoting Deuteronomy 32:21, where God vows to provoke the Jews to jealousy "by those who are not a nation," namely the Gentiles. Most serious Christians today hope that such "jealousy" will bring Jews to Yeshua. Many of our Jewish friends marvel, sometimes enviously, at how good the God of Israel has been to me and my wife, even though we pray to Him in the name of a 'false' Messiah. In addition, however, as supporters of today's historic *baal t'shuvah* movement, it also gives me and Shirah great joy to use our knowledge and love of Judaism to shame fallen-away Jews into coming back to Judaism. For Biblical Judaism was the religion of Yeshua, the same religion practiced and never renounced by the Jews who formed the so-called 'Church' at Jerusalem—and who, a generation later, fled across the Jordan before the Roman destruction of their Temple in 70 AD, never to be heard from again.)

A beautiful, energetic woman, with long, black hair, Tova seemed a perfect match for Zerach the bachelor, at least in my mind. But so far neither of them had shown any romantic interest in the other.

One day Tova gave me and Zerach a tour of Mt. Herzl Cemetery, where Israelis were observing their memorial day. Afterwards, the three of us walked down Jaffa Road to a kosher restaurant, the Center Café. Over a tomato *foccacia* snack, Tova suddenly asked me why, with all my interest in Judaism and my love for Israel, I didn't convert. I explained my devotion to Yeshua of Nazareth as the Messiah, and I pointed out that Orthodox rabbis always required Christians to renounce Christ before converting to Judaism, and this I would never do.

Then Tova boldly asked what I thought would become of Jews who died without accepting Yeshua as their Savior. She demanded an answer: Did they go to hell?

Zerach had an impatient look on his face, wanting no part in the conversation. The Orthodox Jew and his born-again friend from Buffalo had long ago stopped debating religion. Zerach longed for the coming of Messiah and, it seemed to me, was surely walking on the path that God had ordained for him to follow on his way to that salvation that I just knew God had in store for him.

After a long pause, I told Tova that, as far as I was concerned, Jews who faithfully followed not only the letter of the Law but also the *spirit* of the Law given by God to Moses could have such a love for God that they would instantly accept Yeshua as the Messiah, once they encountered Him.

But how to encounter the Messiah, without faith?

In the *B'rith Chadoshah* (New Testament), I said, Yeshua tells Nicodemus that he must be born again. When this member of the Sanhedrin protests, Yeshua says: "Are you the teacher of Israel, and do not know these things?" In other words, becoming born again is originally a Jewish concept.

That was all that I told Tova and Zerach that day.

*

Not long after that day at the Center Café in Jerusalem, I paid Tova a visit alone. Her second-floor window was open to the Jewish Quarter of the Old City on this sunny afternoon. I brought with me two cans of cat food, because Tova was known as the Cat Lady of Jerusalem, taking in stray cats, nursing their kittens to health, and finding homes for them.

Tova put up signs in churches where American tourists were likely to read them: "HOLY LAND KITTENS—Adopt a Jerusalem kitten to the USA. Be the only one on your block with a kitten that walked in the footsteps of Jesus. These kittens have been saved!"

Right now a brood of calico kittens were swarming the apartment, some of them on the table where Tova and I sat over hot tea and apple pie. We were talking about the difficulty of finding (and keeping) the right mate, and I was trying to find a way of working Zerach into the conversation.

Then we talked about the red heifer. Tova had never heard of rabbis like Chaim Richman, and her position on the red heifer was: "No rabbi would say we have to rebuild the Temple now—in order for Messiah to come." Being an animal lover, she added: "I have a real hard time with sacrifices and stuff."

However, she wasn't so kind toward Muslims intent on taking over the ancestral homeland of the Jews. "Jerusalem isn't mentioned once in the Qu'ran," she said. "What's ridiculous about it is that if they wanted to make up a new religion, why didn't they take a different hill? And the exact spot where the Temple was!"

The Temple will be rebuilt after Messiah comes, Tova said. And Messiah won't have to die and atone for the sins of the nation.

"Where do you think Christians got the idea of sin?" she demanded. "Jews are concerned about avoiding sin, or—once having sinned—to make direct atonement to others and directly to God. Christians let Jesus into their heart and that wipes everything clean. And he happened to die for them. Well, millions of people have died for me; not just one."

After a while, over our tea and apple pie, Tova asked that question again. "What do you need Jesus for?" she asked. "Do you really believe that all the Jews are going to burn in hell for not believing in Jesus?"

I tried to frame my answer in a different way from what I'd said at the Center Cafe.

"Tova," I began, "you and Zerach are both *baal t'shuvahs* who have left the secular lifestyle and given your lives to the Lord. You truly believe in the Holy One of Israel—God the Father—who appeared to Moses at Mount Sinai and gave us the Ten Commandments."

"Yes," she said.

"And in your prayer book, in the synagogue, I notice that you sometimes refer to the Lord as the Redeemer of Israel."

"Yes," she said.

"Well, Tova," I said, "we believe that when Moses saw the face of God on that mountain, he was looking into the face of God the Redeemer—that is, Yeshua of Nazareth in His pre-incarnate body. So, when religious Jews, like you, pray to God as *your Redeemer*, you are really praying to the Messiah."

"That's what you actually think?" she said.

"Yes," I said. "And so, as best as I can determine—and this is the opinion of just one born-again Christian—you *are* praying to Jesus, and if you were to realize this, you would *consciously* pray to Him. Because He is the Savior of the world."

"So I'm not going to hell," she said.

I thought about this for a moment, trying to dispel any doubt creeping into my mind. "Tova," I said, "if you really love God—in your heart as well as in your actions in following the Law—now that you have made *t'shuvah* and returned to God—then it seems to me that you have come as close as you can to Yeshua without actually being aware of who He really is."

At that moment, a rooster crowed outside Tova's window!

It was a terrifying moment for me . . .

The rooster crowed again!

"Tova," I asked, my heart thumping in my chest, "why is that rooster crowing at three o'clock in the afternoon?"

"Oh," she said, "it's the neighborhood rooster, and it crows whenever it feels like it."

After leaving Tova's apartment, I walked through the maze of narrow streets of the Jewish Quarter and made my way down to the Wailing Wall. There, I pressed my hands on those golden stones, and laid my head against the Wall, while my heart wept bitterly.

Salvation

Now Isaac left all the others and drifted away from the Wall, as if in a dream, and wandered down to the Dung Gate. Then he began walking down the road, in the direction of the Mount of Olives . . . where the Red Heifer was to have been sacrificed.

"Abba," he prayed, "send us your Messiah *now!* Send Messiah now! Messiah now! *Moshiach achshuv!*"

He paused to catch his breath, his eyes focusing on the Mount of Olives, where the Talmud predicts that the Messiah will someday appear on his way to the Golden Gate, which the Muslims have blocked up and barbed-wired to prevent his entry.

"Messiah, come now!" he prayed. Then he blinked his eyes in disbelief at what he had just said. "I am asking Messiah himself to come?!" he marveled to himself. "Messiah, please—you, who are about to be sent by Abba, the Holy One of Israel! You, whose name was written before the Creation—and who must have *existed* before time began!"

Isaac continued his walk up the road, the Mount of Olives never out of his sight.

"Come, Messiah, and redeem Israel from all our woes," he prayed. "Forgive Israel all our sins. Come, Messiah Redeemer, come and save us now!"

Enraptured in deep prayer, Isaac closed his eyes.

"Oh, *Moshiach!* What love I feel for you, even though I don't know you. Well—even though I *hardly* know you. You must have been there when I was conceived in my mother's womb. So you know me thoroughly, when I sit and when I stand."

Silence.

"Does that mean that I know *you*, to some extent?" he asked. "Can I ever know you as I am known by you?"

Suddenly the sun broke brilliantly through the clouds and shone on Isaac, the yeshiva boy from Jerusalem.

Isaac opened his eyes.

"You call me—'friend'? *Friend! Toda raba, Adonai!* Come now, Messiah Redeemer—come to those who love you, those who long for you—come now and save us! Yes—*Baruch haba b'shem Adonai!* As Moses told the people at the Red Sea, "Remain steady, and you will see how Adonai is going to save you." *Ooh-roo et yeshuat Adonai! Yeshuat Adonai! Yeshua! Y e s h u a . . .*

From somewhere in the distance, now, he heard the wail of the shofar—

Haaa-RIIIII-ooooo!
T'-RUUUUU-ahhhh!
T'KEEEEEEE-yaaaaaahhhh!

Israel and the Occupied Territories

A HISTORICAL CHRONOLOGY

2000 BC, Abraham's calling

1800 Joseph in Egypt

1440 Moses and the Exodus. **Instructions for the Red Heifer (Numbers 19)**

1000 David reigns as King; his son Solomon builds the First Temple

586 Babylonians destroy the First Temple; *Book of Daniel written, giving end-times prophecies*

164 Maccabees' victory over Syria and the miracle of Hanukkah in the Temple

63 Romans take over Palestine

33 AD Yeshua of Nazareth's death

50 The Council of Jerusalem declares that Gentile believers need not convert to Judaism

70 First Jewish Revolt ends; Romans destroy the Second Temple; **ashes of the ninth red heifer are hidden**

90 *Book of Revelation written by elderly Apostle John, extending end-times prophecies*

135 End of Second Jewish Revolt, supported by Rabbi Akiva; Jews banished from Palestine

620 Muhammad's Night Journey from the Rock on the Temple Mount

638 Muslim conquest of Palestine

691 Dome of the Rock completed as a shrine to Muhammed, also called the Mosque of Omar
The huge Al-Aqsa mosque is completed on the southern end of the Temple Mount

1204 Death of Maimonides (the Rambam), who codified Jewish law

315

1897 Theodor Herzl and the World Zionist Organization

1917 Balfour Declaration favoring Jewish homeland in Palestine

1918 World War I ends; League of Nations grants Britain a Mandate over all of Palestine

1945 World War II and Holocaust end

1947 UN Partition Plan (offering Jews 56 percent of western Palestine) Britain assigns eastern Palestine to the new Kingdom of Jordan

1948 Israel's War of Independence, winning 78 percent of western Palestine

1949 Armistice; Israel becomes a member of the United Nations

1956 Egypt launches Suez War; later a UN peacekeeping force is stationed in Sinai desert

1964 Palestine Liberation Organization born

1967 Six Day War: Egypt evicts the UN peacekeepers from Sinai; Israel seizes West Bank, Gaza, Sinai and the Golan Heights
A red heifer is found but disqualified; the *baal t'shuvah* revival among Jews; Christian charismatic movement starts

1973 Yom Kippur War

1979 Egyptian President Anwar Sadat signs peace treaty with Israel and regains the Sinai desert.

1981 Anwar Sadat is assassinated

1982 First Lebanon War to drive PLO out of Lebanon; rise of Hizbollah in Lebanon

1987 First Intifada begins

1993 Oslo agreements signed

1994 Jordan signs peace treaty with Israel

**1996 A newborn heifer named Melody is declared, for a time, to be an authentic red heifer
Organizations are created to advance the rebuilding of the Temple**

2000 Camp David talks fail; Palestinians reject offer of East Jerusalem, all of Gaza and 95 percent of the West Bank
Second Intifada signals the final collapse of the Oslo agreements

2005 Israel evacuates its settlers and troops from Gaza

2006 Hamas defeats Fatah in elections in Gaza; Fatah wins in the West Bank
Second Lebanon War as Israel attacks Hizbollah to stop rocket fire into northern Israel

2007 Hamas takes over Gaza by force, ending the unity government with Fatah, which still rules the West Bank

2008 Peace talks fail; Israel had offered 94 percent of the West Bank and shared sovereignty over the Old City of Jerusalem

2008 Israel attacks Hamas in Gaza to stop rocket fire into southern Israel

2011 Arab Spring revolts begin toppling dictators in the Middle East
United Nations membership is sought for a State of Palestine
"Price tag" attacks by Jewish settlers spread to Israel proper

OTHER RELATED RESOURCES

Available at Messianic Jewish Resources Int'l. • www.messianicjewish.net
1-800-410-7367
(See website for discounts and specials)

Complete Jewish Bible: *A New English Version*
—Dr. David H. Stern

Presenting the Word of God as a unified Jewish book, the *Complete Jewish Bible* is a new version for Jews and non-Jews alike. It connects Jews with the Jewishness of the Messiah, and non-Jews with their Jewish roots. Names and key terms are returned to their original Hebrew and presented in easy-to-understand transliterations, enabling the reader to say them the way Yeshua (Jesus) did! 1697 pages.

Hardback	978-9653590151	**JB12**	$34.99
Paperback	978-9653590182	**JB13**	$29.99
Leather Cover	978-9653590199	**JB15**	$59.99
Large Print (12 Pt font)	978-1880226483	**JB16**	$49.99

Also available in French and Portuguese.

Jewish New Testament
—Dr. David H. Stern

The New Testament is a Jewish book, written by Jews, initially for Jews. Its central figure was a Jew. His followers were all Jews; yet no other version really communicates its original, essential Jewishness. Uses neutral terms and Hebrew names. Highlights Jewish references and corrects mistranslations. Freshly translated into English from Greek, this is a must read to learn about first-century faith. 436 pages

Hardback	978-9653590069	**JB02**	$19.99
Paperback	978-9653590038	**JB01**	$14.99
Spanish	978-1936716272	**JB17**	$24.99

Also available in French, German, Polish, Portuguese and Russian.

Jewish New Testament Commentary
—Dr. David H. Stern

This companion to the *Jewish New Testament* enhances Bible study. Passages and expressions are explained in their original cultural context. 15 years of research. 960 pages.

Hardback	978-9653590083	**JB06**	$34.99
Paperback	978-9653590113	**JB10**	$29.99

Psalms & Proverbs *Tehillim* תְּהִלִּים-*Mishlei* מִשְׁלֵי
—Translated by Dr. David Stern

Contemplate the power in these words anytime, anywhere: Psalms-*Tehillim* offers uplifting words of praise and gratitude, keeping us focused with the right attitude; Proverbs-*Mishlei* gives us the wisdom for daily living, renewing our minds by leading us to examine our actions, to discern good from evil, and to decide freely to do the good. Makes a wonderful and meaningful gift. Softcover, 224 pages.

978-1936716692	LB90	$9.99

Messianic Judaism *A Modern Movement With an Ancient Past*
—David H. Stern

An updated discussion of the history, ideology, theology and program for Messianic Judaism. A challenge to both Jews and non-Jews who honor Yeshua to catch the vision of Messianic Judaism. 312 pages

| | 978-1880226339 | **LB62** | $17.99 |

Restoring the Jewishness of the Gospel
A Message for Christians
—David H. Stern

Introduces Christians to the Jewish roots of their faith, challenges some conventional ideas, and raises some neglected questions: How are both the Jews and "the Church" God's people? Is the Law of Moses in force today? Filled with insight! Endorsed by Dr. Darrell L. Bock. 110 pages

| English | 978-1880226667 | **LB70** | $9.99 |
| Spanish | 978-9653590175 | **JB14** | $9.99 |

Come and Worship *Ways to Worship from the Hebrew Scriptures*
—Compiled by Barbara D. Malda

We were created to worship. God has graciously given us many ways to express our praise to him. Each way fits a different situation or moment in life, yet all are intended to bring honor and glory to him. When we believe that he is who he says he is [see *His Names are Wonderful!*] and that his Word is true, worship flows naturally from our hearts to his. Softcover, 128 pages.

| | 978-1936716678 | **LB88** | $9.99 |

His Names Are Wonderful
Getting to Know God Through His Hebrew Names
—Elizabeth L. Vander Meulen and Barbara D. Malda

In Hebrew thought, names did more than identify people; they revealed their nature. God's identity is expressed not in one name, but in many. This book will help readers know God better as they uncover the truths in his Hebrew names. 160 pages.

| | 978-1880226308 | **LB58** | $9.99 |

The Return of the Kosher Pig *The Divine Messiah in Jewish Thought*
—Rabbi Tzahi Shapira

The subject of Messiah fills many pages of rabbinic writings. Hidden in those pages is a little known concept that the Messiah has the same authority given to God. Based on the Scriptures and traditional rabbinic writings, this book shows the deity of Yeshua from a new perspective. You will see that the rabbis of old expected the Messiah to be divine. Softcover, 352 pages.

"One of the most interesting and learned tomes I have ever read. Contained within its pages is much with which I agree, some with which I disagree, and much about which I never thought. Rabbi Shapria's remarkable book cannot be ignored."

—Dr. Paige Patterson, President, Southwest Baptist Theological Seminary

| | 978-1936716456 | **LB81** | $ 39.99 |

Proverbial Wisdom & Common Sense
A Messianic Commentary
—Derek Leman

A Messianic Jewish Approach to Today's Issues from the Proverbs
A devotional style commentary, divided into chapters suitable for daily reading. An encyclopedia of practical advice on topics relevant to everyone. 248 pages

Paperback	978-1880226780	**LB98**	$19.99

Matthew Presents Yeshua, King Messiah *A Messianic Commentary*
—Rabbi Barney Kasdan

Few commentators are able to truly present Yeshua in his Jewish context. Most don't understand his background, his family, even his religion, and consequently really don't understand who he truly is. This commentator is well versed with first-century Jewish practices and thought, as well as the historical and cultural setting of the day, and the 'traditions of the Elders' that Yeshua so often spoke about. Get to know Yeshua, the King, through the writing of another rabbi, Barney Kasdan. 448 pages

978-1936716265	**LB76**	$29.99

Rabbi Paul Enlightens the Ephesians on Walking with Messiah Yeshua
A Messianic Commentary
—Rabbi Barney Kasdan

The Ephesian were a diverse group of Jews and Gentiles, united together in Messiah. They definitely had an impact on the first century world in which they lived. But the Rabbi was not just writing to that local group. What is Paul saying to us? 160 pages.

Paperback	978-11936716821	**LB99**	$17.99

James the Just Presents Application of Torah
A Messianic Commentary
—Dr. David Friedman

James (Jacob) one of the Epistles written to first century Jewish followers of Yeshua. Dr. David Friedman, a former Professor of the Israel Bible Institute has shed new light for Christians from this very important letter.

978-1936716449	**LB82**	$14.99

Jude On Faith and the Destructive Influence of Heresy
A Messianic Commentary
—Rabbi Joshua Brumbach

Almost no other canonical book has been as neglected and overlooked as the Epistle of Jude. This little book may be small, but it has a big message that is even more relevant today as when it was originally written.

978-1-936716-78-4	**LB97**	$14.99

At the Feet of Rabbi Gamaliel
Rabbinic Influence in Paul's Teachings
—David Friedman, Ph.D.

Paul (Shaul) was on the "fast track" to becoming a sage and Sanhedrin judge describing himself as passionate for the Torah and the traditions of the fathers typical for an aspiring Pharisee: "...trained at the feet of Gamaliel in every detail of the Torah of our forefathers. I was a zealot for God, as all of you are today" (Acts 22.3, CJB). Did Shaul's teachings reflect Rabbi Gamaliel's instructions? Did Paul continue to value the Torah and Pharisaic tradition? Did Paul create a 'New' Theology? The results of the research within these pages and its conclusion may surprise you. Softcover, 100 pages.

978-1936716753　**LB95**　$8.99

Debranding God *Revealing His True Essence*
—Eduardo Stein

The process of 'debranding' God is to remove all the labels and fads that prompt us to understand him as a supplier and ourselves as the most demanding of customers. Changing our perception of God also changes our perception of ourselves. In knowing who we are in relationship to God, we discover his, and our, true essence. Softcover, 252 pages.

978-1936716708　**LB91**　$16.99

Under the Fig Tree *Messianic Thought Through the Hebrew Calendar*
—Patrick Gabriel Lumbroso

Take a daily devotional journey into the Word of God through the Hebrew Calendar and the Biblical Feasts. Learn deeper meaning of the Scriptures through Hebraic thought. Beautifully written and a source for inspiration to draw closer to Adonai every day. Softcover, 407 pages.

978-1936716760　**LB96**　$25.99

Under the Vine *Messianic Thought Through the Hebrew Calendar*
—Patrick Gabriel Lumbroso

Journey daily through the Hebrew Calendar and Biblical Feasts into the B'rit Hadashah (New Testament) Scriptures as they are put in their rightful context, bringing Judaism alive in it's full beauty. Messianic faith was the motor and what gave substance to Abraham's new beliefs, hope to Job, trust to Isaac, vision to Jacob, resilience to Joseph, courage to David, wisdom to Solomon, knowledge to Daniel, and divine Messianic authority to Yeshua Softcover, 412 pages.

978-1936716654　**LB87**　$25.99

The Revolt of Rabbi Morris Cohen
Exploring the Passion & Piety of a Modern-day Pharisee
—Anthony Cardinale

A brilliant school psychologist, Rabbi Morris Cohen went on a one-man strike to protest the systematic mislabeling of slow learning pupils as "Learning Disabled" (to extract special education money from the state). His disciplinary hearing, based on the transcript, is a hilarious read! This effusive, garrulous man with an irresistible sense of humor lost his job, but achieved a major historic victory causing the reform of the billion-dollar special education program. Enter into the mind of an eighth-generation Orthodox rabbi to see how he deals spiritually with the loss of everything, even the love of his children. This modern-day Pharisee discovered a trusted friend in the author (a born again believer in Jesus) with whom he could openly struggle over Rabbinic Judaism as well as the concept of Jesus (Yeshua) as Messiah. Softcover, 320 pages.

978-1936716722 **LB92** $19.99

Stories of Yeshua
—Jim Reimann, Illustrator Julia Filipone-Erez

Children's Bible Storybook with four stories about Yeshua (Jesus).
Yeshua is Born: The Bethlehem Story based on Lk 1:26-35 & 2:1-20; *Yeshua and Nicodemus in Jerusalem* based on Jn 3:1-16; *Yeshua Loves the Little Children of the World* based on Matthew 18:1–6 & 19:13–15; *Yeshua is Alive-The Empty Tomb in Jerusalem* based on Matthew 26:17-56, Jn 19:16-20:18, Lk 24:50-53. Ages 3-7, Softcover, 48 pages.

978-1936716685 **LB89** $14.99

To the Ends of the Earth – How the First Jewish Followers of Yeshua Transformed the Ancient World
— Dr. Jeffrey Seif

Everyone knows that the first followers of Yeshua were Jews, and that Christianity was very Jewish for the first 50 to 100 years. It's a known fact that there were many congregations made up mostly of Jews, although the false perception today is, that in the second century they disappeared. Dr. Seif reveals the truth of what happened to them and how these early Messianic Jews influenced and transformed the behavior of the known world at that time.

978-1936716463 **LB83** $17.99

Passion for Israel: *A Short History of the Evangelical Church's Support of Israel and the Jewish People*
—Dan Juster

History reveals a special commitment of Christians to the Jews as God's still elect people, but the terrible atrocities committed against the Jews by so-called Christians have overshadowed the many good deeds that have been performed. This important history needs to be told to help heal the wounds and to inspire more Christians to stand together in support of Israel.

978-1936716401 **LB78** $9.99

Jewish Roots and Foundations of the Scriptures I & II
—John Fischer, Th.D, Ph.D.

An outstanding evangelical leader once said: "There is something shallow about a Christianity that has lost its Jewish roots." A beautiful painting is a careful interweaving of a number of elements. Among other things, there are the background, the foreground and the subject. Discovering the roots of your faith is a little like appreciating the various parts of a painting. In the background is the panorama of preparation and pictures found in the Old Testament. In the foreground is the landscape and light of the first century Jewish setting. All of this is intricately connected with and highlights the subject—which becomes the flowering of all these aspects—the coming of God to earth and what that means for us. Discovering and appreciating your roots in this way broadens, deepens and enriches your faith and your understanding of Scripture. This audio is 32 hours of live class instruction audio is clear and easy to understand.

9781936716623 **LCD03 / LCD04** $49.99 each

The Gospels in their Jewish Context
—John Fischer, Th.D, Ph.D.

An examination of the Jewish background and nature of the Gospels in their contemporary political, cultural and historical settings, emphasizing each gospel's special literary presentation of Yeshua, and highlighting the cultural and religious contexts necessary for understanding each of the gospels. 32 hours of audio/video instruction on MP3-DVD and pdf of syllabus.

978-1936716241 **LCD01** $49.99

The Epistles from a Jewish Perspective
—John Fischer, Th.D, Ph.D.

An examination of the relationship of Rabbi Shaul (the Apostle Paul) and the Apostles to their Jewish contemporaries and environment; surveys their Jewish practices, teaching, controversy with the religious leaders, and many critical passages, with emphasis on the Jewish nature, content, and background of these letters. 32 hours of audio/video instruction on MP3-DVD and pdf of syllabus.

978-1936716258 **LCD02** $49.99

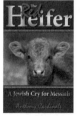

The Red Heifer *A Jewish Cry for Messiah*
—Anthony Cardinale

Award-winning journalist and playwright Anthony Cardinale has traveled extensively in Israel, and recounts here his interviews with Orthodox rabbis, secular Israelis, and Palestinian Arabs about the current search for a red heifer by Jewish radicals wishing to rebuild the Temple and bring the Messiah. These real-life interviews are interwoven within an engaging and dramatic fictional portrayal of the diverse people of Israel and how they would react should that red heifer be found. Readers will find themselves in the Land, where they can hear learned rabbis and ordinary Israelis talking about the red heifer and dealing with all the related issues and the imminent coming and identity of Messiah.

978-1936716470 **LB79** $19.99

The Borough Park Papers
—Multiple Authors

As you read the New Testament, you "overhear" debates first-century Messianic Jews had about critical issues, e.g. Gentiles being "allowed" into the Messianic kingdom (Acts 15). Similarly, you're now invited to "listen in" as leading twenty-first century Messianic Jewish theologians discuss critical issues facing us today. Some ideas may not fit into your previously held pre-suppositions or pre-conceptions. Indeed, you may find some paradigm shifting in your thinking. We want to share the thoughts of these thinkers with you, our family in the Messiah.

Symposium I:
The Gospel and the Jewish People
248 pages

| | 978-1936716593 | LB84 | $39.95 |

Symposium II:
The Deity of Messiah and the Mystery of God
211 pages

| | 978-1936716609 | LB85 | $39.95 |

Symposium III:
How Jewish Should the Messianic Community Be?

| | 978-1936716616 | LB86 | $39.95 |

On The Way to Emmaus: *Searching the Messianic Prophecies*
—Dr. Jacques Doukhan

An outstanding compilation of the most critical Messianic prophecies by a renowned conservative Christian Scholar, drawing on material from the Bible, Rabbinic sources, Dead Sea Scrolls, and more.

| | 978-1936716432 | LB80 | $14.99 |

Yeshua *A Guide to the Real Jesus and the Original Church*
—Dr. Ron Moseley

Opens up the history of the Jewish roots of the Christian faith. Illuminates the Jewish background of Yeshua and the Church and never flinches from showing "Jesus was a Jew, who was born, lived, and died, within first century Judaism." Explains idioms in the New Testament. Endorsed by Dr. Brad Young and Dr. Marvin Wilson. 213 pages.

| | 978-1880226681 | **LB29** | $12.99 |

Gateways to Torah *Joining the Ancient Conversation on the Weekly Portion*
—Rabbi Russell Resnik

From before the days of Messiah until today, Jewish people have read from and discussed a prescribed portion of the Pentateuch each week. Now, a Messianic Jewish Rabbi, Russell Resnik, brings another perspective on the Torah, that of a Messianic Jew. 246 pages.

978-1880226889   **LB42** $15.99

Creation to Completion *A Guide to Life's Journey from the Five Books of Moses*
—Rabbi Russell Resnik

Endorsed by Coach Bill McCartney, Founder of Promise Keepers & Road to Jerusalem: "Paul urged Timothy to study the Scriptures (2 Tim. 3:16) advising him to apply its teachings to all aspects of his life. Since there was no New Testament then, this rabbi/apostle was convinced that his disciple would profit from studying the Torah, the Five Books of Moses, and the Old Testament. Now, Rabbi Resnik has written a warm devotional commentary that will help you understand and apply the Law of Moses to your life in a practical way." 256 pages

978-1880226322   **LB61** $14.99

Walk Genesis! Walk Exodus! Walk Leviticus! Walk Numbers! Walk Deuteronomy!
Messianic Jewish Devotional Commentaries
—Jeffrey Enoch Feinberg, Ph.D.

Using the weekly synagogue readings, Dr. Jeffrey Feinberg has put together some very valuable material in his "Walk" series. Each section includes a short Hebrew lesson (for the non-Hebrew speaker), key concepts, an excellent overview of the portion, and some practical applications. Can be used as a daily devotional as well as a Bible study tool.

Walk Genesis!	238 pages	978-1880226759	**LB34**	$12.99
Walk Exodus!	224 pages	978-1880226872	**LB40**	$12.99
Walk Leviticus!	208 pages	978-1880226926	**LB45**	$12.99
Walk Numbers!	211 pages	978-1880226995	**LB48**	$12.99
Walk Deuteronomy!	231 pages	978-1880226186	**LB51**	$12.99
SPECIAL! Five-book Walk!		5 Book Set **Save $10**	**LK28**	$54.99

Good News According To Matthew
—Dr. Henry Einspruch

English translation with quotations from the Tanakh (Old Testament) capitalized and printed in Hebrew. Helpful notations are included. Lovely black and white illustrations throughout the book. 86 pages.

978-1880226025	**LB03**	$4.99
Also available in Yiddish.	**LB02**	$4.99

They Loved the Torah *What Yeshua's First Followers Really Thought About the Law*
—Dr. David Friedman

Although many Jews believe that Paul taught against the Law, this book disproves that notion. An excellent case for his premise that all the first followers of the Messiah were not only Torah-observant, but also desired to spread their love for God's entire Word to the gentiles to whom they preached. 144 pages. Endorsed by Dr. David Stern, Ariel Berkowitz, Rabbi Dr. Stuart Dauermann & Dr. John Fischer.

978-1880226940   **LB47** $9.99

The Distortion *2000 Years of Misrepresenting the Relationship Between Jesus the Messiah and the Jewish People*
—Dr. John Fischer & Dr. Patrice Fischer

Did the Jews kill Jesus? Did they really reject him? With the rise of global anti–Semitism, it is important to understand what the Gospels teach about the relationship between Jewish people and their Messiah. 2000 years of distortion have made this difficult. Learn how the distortion began and continues to this day and what you can do to change it. 126 pages. Endorsed by Dr. Ruth Fleischer, Rabbi Russell Resnik, Dr. Daniel C. Juster, Dr. Michael Rydelnik.

978-1880226254   **LB54** $11.99

eBooks Now Available!
*All books are available as ebooks
for your favorite reader*

Visit www.messianicjewish.net for direct links to these readers
for each available eBook.

God's Appointed Times *A Practical Guide to Understanding and Celebrating the Biblical Holidays* – **New Edition.**
—Rabbi Barney Kasdan

The Biblical Holy Days teach us about the nature of God and his plan for mankind, and can be a source of God's blessing for all believers–Jews and Gentiles–today. Includes historical background, traditional Jewish observance, New Testament relevance, and prophetic significance, plus music, crafts and holiday recipes. 145 pages.

English	978-1880226353	**LB63**	$12.99
Spanish	978-1880226391	**LB59**	$12.99

God's Appointed Customs *A Messianic Jewish Guide to the Biblical Lifecycle and Lifestyle*
— Rabbi Barney Kasdan

Explains how biblical customs are often the missing key to unlocking the depths of Scripture. Discusses circumcision, the Jewish wedding, and many more customs mentioned in the New Testament. Companion to *God's Appointed Times*. 170 pages.

English	978-1880226636	**LB26**	$12.99
Spanish	978-1880226551	**LB60**	$12.99

Celebrations of the Bible *A Messianic Children's Curriculum*

Did you know that each Old Testament feast or festival finds its fulfillment in the New? They enrich the lives of people who experience and enjoy them. Our popular curriculum for children is in a brand new, user-friendly format. The lay-flat at binding allows you to easily reproduce handouts and worksheets. Celebrations of the Bible has been used by congregations, Sunday schools, ministries, homeschoolers, and individuals to teach children about the biblical festivals. Each of these holidays are presented for Preschool (2-K), Primary (Grades 1-3), Junior (Grades 4-6), and Children's Worship/Special Services. 208 pages.

978-1880226261	**LB55**	$24.99

Passover: *The Key That Unlocks the Book of Revelation*
—Daniel C. Juster, Th.D.

Is there any more enigmatic book of the Bible than Revelation? Controversy concerning its meaning has surrounded it back to the first century. Today, the arguments continue. Yet, Dan Juster has given us the key that unlocks the entire book—the events and circumstances of the Passover/Exodus. By interpreting Revelation through the lens of Exodus, Dan Juster provides a unified overview that helps us read Revelation as it was always meant to be read, as a drama of spiritual conflict, deliverance, and above all, worship. He also shows how this final drama, fulfilled in Messiah, resonates with the Torah and all of God's Word. — Russ Resnik, Executive Director, Union of Messianic Jewish Congregations.

978-1936716210	**LB74**	$10.99

The Messianic Passover Haggadah
Revised and Updated
—Rabbi Barry Rubin and Steffi Rubin.

Guides you through the traditional Passover seder dinner, step-by-step. Not only does this observance remind us of our rescue from Egyptian bondage, but, we remember Messiah's last supper, a Passover seder. The theme of redemption is seen throughout the evening. What's so unique about our Haggadah is the focus on Yeshua (Jesus) the Messiah and his teaching, especially on his last night in the upper room. 36 pages.

English	978-1880226292	**LB57**	$4.99
Spanish	978-1880226599	**LBSP01**	$4.99

The Messianic Passover Seder Preparation Guide
Includes recipes, blessings and songs. 19 pages.

English	978-1880226247	**LB10**	$2.99
Spanish	978-1880226728	**LBSP02**	$2.99

The Sabbath *Entering God's Rest*
—Barry Rubin & Steffi Rubin

Even if you've never celebrated Shabbat before, this book will guide you into the rest God has for all who would enter in—Jews and non-Jews. Contains prayers, music, recipes; in short, everything you need to enjoy the Sabbath, even how to observe havdalah, the closing ceremony of the Sabbath. Also discusses the Saturday or Sunday controversy. 48 pages.

978-1880226742   LB32 $6.99

Havdalah *The Ceremony that Completes the Sabbath*
—Dr. Neal & Jamie Lash

The Sabbath ends with this short, yet equally sweet ceremony called havdalah (separation). This ceremony reminds us to be a light and a sweet fragrance in this world of darkness as we carry the peace, rest, joy and love of the Sabbath into the work week. 28 pages.

978-1880226605   LB69 $4.99

Dedicate and Celebrate!
A Messianic Jewish Guide to Hanukkah
—Barry Rubin & Family

Hanukkah means "dedication" — a theme of significance for Jews and Christians. Discussing its historical background, its modern-day customs, deep meaning for all of God's people, this little book covers all the how-tos! Recipes, music, and prayers for lighting the menorah, all included! 32 pages.

978-1880226834   LB36 $4.99

The Conversation

An Intimate Journal of the Emmaus Encounter
—Judy Salisbury

"Then beginning with Moses and with all the prophets, He explained to them the things concerning Himself in all the Scriptures." Luke 24:27
If you've ever wondered what that conversation must have been like, this captivating book takes you there.

"The Conversation brings to life that famous encounter between the two disciples and our Lord Jesus on the road to Emmaus. While it is based in part on an imaginative reconstruction, it is filled with the throbbing pulse of the excitement of the sensational impact that our Lord's resurrection should have on all of our lives." ~ Dr. Walter Kaiser President Emeritus Gordon-Conwell Theological Seminary. Hardcover 120 pages.

Hardcover	978-1936716173	**LB73**	$14.99
Paperback	978-1936716364	**LB77**	$9.99

Growing to Maturity

A Messianic Jewish Discipleship Guide
—Daniel C. Juster, Th.D.

This discipleship series presents first steps of understanding and spiritual practice, tailored for the Jewish believer. It's purpose is to aid the believer in living according to Yeshua's will as a disciple, one who has learned the example of his teacher. The course is structured according to recent advances in individualized educational instruction. Discipleship is serious business and the material is geared for serious study and reflection. Each chapter is divided into short sections followed by study questions. 256 pages.

978-1936716227   LB75 $19.99

Growing to Maturity Primer: *A Messianic Jewish Discipleship Workbook*
—Daniel C. Juster, Th.D.

A basic book of material in question and answer form. Usable by everyone. 60 pages.

978-0961455507   TB16 $7.99

Conveying Our Heritage A Messianic Jewish Guide to Home Practice
—Daniel C. Juster, Th.D. Patricia A. Juster

Throughout history the heritage of faith has been conveyed within the family and the congregation. The first institution in the Bible is the family and only the family can raise children with an adequate appreciation of our faith and heritage. This guide exists to help families learn how to pass on the heritage of spiritual Messianic Jewish life. Softcover, 86 pages

978-1936716739   LB93 $8.99

That They May Be One *A Brief Review of Church Restoration Movements and Their Connection to the Jewish People*
—Daniel Juster, Th.D

Something prophetic and momentous is happening. The Church is finally fully grasping its relationship to Israel and the Jewish people. Author describes the restoration movements in Church history and how they connected to Israel and the Jewish people. Each one contributed in some way—some more, some less—toward the ultimate unity between Jews and Gentiles. Predicted in the Old Testament and fulfilled in the New, Juster believes this plan of God finds its full expression in Messianic Judaism. He may be right. See what you think as you read *That They May Be One*. 100 pages.

| | 978-1880226711 | **LB71** | $9.99 |

The Greatest Commandment
How the Sh'ma Leads to More Love in Your Life
—Irene Lipson

"What is the greatest commandment?" Yeshua was asked. His reply—"Hear, O Israel, the Lord our God, the Lord is one, and you are to love Adonai your God with all your heart, with all your soul, with all your understanding, and all your strength." A superb book explaining each word so the meaning can be fully grasped and lived. Endorsed by Elliot Klayman, Susan Perlman, & Robert Stearns. 175 pages.

| | 978-1880226360 | **LB65** | $12.99 |

Blessing the King of the Universe
Transforming Your Life Through the Practice of Biblical Praise
—Irene Lipson

Insights into the ancient biblical practice of blessing God are offered clearly and practically. With examples from Scripture and Jewish tradition, this book teaches the biblical formula used by men and women of the Bible, including the Messiah; points to new ways and reasons to praise the Lord; and explains more about the Jewish roots of the faith. Endorsed by Rabbi Barney Kasdan, Dr. Mitch Glaser, & Rabbi Dr. Dan Cohn-Sherbok. 144 pages.

| | 978-1880226797 | **LB53** | $11.99 |

You Bring the Bagels, I'll Bring the Gospel
Sharing the Messiah with Your Jewish Neighbor
Revised Edition—Now with Study Questions
—Rabbi Barry Rubin

This "how-to-witness-to-Jewish-people" book is an orderly presentation of everything you need to share the Messiah with a Jewish friend. Includes Messianic prophecies, Jewish objections to believing, sensitivities in your witness, words to avoid. A "must read" for all who care about the Jewish people. Good for individual or group study. Used in Bible schools. Endorsed by Harold A. Sevener, Dr. Walter C. Kaiser, Dr. Erwin J. Kolb and Dr. Arthur F. Glasser. 253 pages.

| English | 978-1880226650 | **LB13** | $12.99 |
| Te Tengo Buenas Noticias | 978-0829724103 | **OBSP02** | $14.99 |

Making Eye Contact With God
A Weekly Devotional for Women
—Terri Gillespie

What kind of eyes do you have? Are they downcast and sad? Are they full of God's joy and passion? See yourself through the eyes of God. Using real life anecdotes, combined with scripture, the author reveals God's heart for women everywhere, as she softly speaks of the ways in which women see God. Endorsed by prominent authors: Dr. Angela Hunt, Wanda Dyson and Kathryn Mackel. 247 pages, hardcover.

978-1880226513   **LB68** $19.99

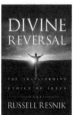

Divine Reversal
The Transforming Ethics of Jesus
—Rabbi Russell Resnik

In the Old Testament, God often reversed the plans of man. Yeshua's ethics continue this theme. Following his path transforms one's life from within, revealing the source of true happiness, forgiveness, reconciliation, fidelity and love. From the introduction, "As a Jewish teacher, Jesus doesn't separate matters of theology from practice. His teaching is consistently practical, ethical, and applicable to real life, even two thousand years after it was originally given." Endorsed by Jonathan Bernis, Dr. Daniel C. Juster, Dr. Jeffrey L. Seif, and Dr Darrell Bock. 206 pages

978-1880226803   **LB72** $12.99

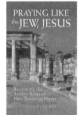

Praying Like the Jew, Jesus
Recovering the Ancient Roots of New Testament Prayer
—Dr. Timothy P. Jones

This eye-opening book reveals the Jewish background of many of Yeshua's prayers. Historical vignettes "transport" you to the times of Yeshua so you can grasp the full meaning of Messiah's prayers. Unique devotional thoughts and meditations, presented in down-to-earth language, provide inspiration for a more meaningful prayer life and help you draw closer to God. Endorsed by Mark Galli, James W. Goll, Rev. Robert Stearns, James F. Strange, and Dr. John Fischer. 144 pages.

978-1880226285   **LB56** $9.99

Growing Your Olive Tree Marriage *A Guide for Couples from Two Traditions*
—David J. Rudolph

One partner is Jewish; the other is Christian. Do they celebrate Hanukkah, Christmas or both? Do they worship in a church or a synagogue? How will the children be raised? This is the first book from a biblical perspective that addresses the concerns of intermarried couples, offering a godly solution. Includes highlights of interviews with intermarried couples. Endorsed by Walter C. Kaiser, Jr., Rabbi Dan Cohn-Sherbok, Jonathan Settel, Dr. Mitchell Glaser & Natalie Sirota. 224 pages.

978-1880226179   **LB50** $12.99

In Search of the Silver Lining *Where is God in the Midst of Life's Storms?*
—Jerry Gramckow

When faced with suffering, what are your choices? Storms have always raged. And people have either perished in their wake or risen above the tempests, shaping history by their responses…new storms are on the horizon. How will we deal with them? How will we shape history or those who follow us? The answer lies in how we view God in the midst of the storms. Endorsed by Joseph C. Aldrich, Ray Beeson, Dr. Daniel Juster. 176 pages.

978-1880226865 **LB39** $10.99

The Voice of the Lord *Messianic Jewish Daily Devotional*
—Edited by David J. Rudolph

Brings insight into the Jewish Scriptures—both Old and New Testaments. Twenty-two prominent Messianic contributors provide practical ways to apply biblical truth. Start your day with this unique resource. Explanatory notes. Perfect companion to the Complete Jewish Bible (see page 2). Endorsed by Edith Schaeffer, Dr. Arthur F. Glaser, Dr. Michael L. Brown, Mitch Glaser and Moishe Rosen. 416 pages.

9781880226704 **LB31** $19.99

Kingdom Relationships *God's Laws for the Community of Faith*
—Dr. Ron Moseley

Dr. Ron Moseley`s Yeshua: A Guide to the Real Jesus and the Original Church has taught thousands of people about the Jewishness of not only Yeshua, but of the first followers of the Messiah.

In this work, Moseley focuses on the teaching of Torah -- the Five Books of Moses -- tapping into truths that greatly help modern-day members of the community of faith. 64 pages.

978-1880226841 **LB37** $8.99

Mutual Blessing *Discovering the Ultimate Destiny of Creation*
—Daniel C. Juster

To truly love as God loves is to see the wonder and richness of the distinct differences in all of creation and his natural order of interdependence. This is the way to mutual blessing and the discovery of the ultimate destiny of creation. Learn how to become enriched and blessed as you enrich and bless others and all that is around you! Softcover, 135 pages.

978-1936716746 **LB94** $9.99

Train Up A Child *Successful Parenting For The Next Generation*
—Dr. Daniel L. Switzer

The author, former principal of Ets Chaiyim Messianic Jewish Day School, and father of four, combines solid biblical teaching with Jewish sources on child raising, focusing on the biblical holy days, giving fresh insight into fulfilling the role of parent. 188 pages. Endorsed by Dr. David J. Rudolph, Paul Lieberman, and Dr. David H. Stern.

978-1880226377 **LB64** $12.99

Fire on the Mountain - *Past Renewals, Present Revivals and the Coming Return of Israel*
—Dr. Louis Goldberg

The term "revival" is often used to describe a person or congregation turning to God. Is this something that "just happens," or can it be brought about? Dr. Louis Goldberg, author and former professor of Hebrew and Jewish Studies at Moody Bible Institute, examines real revivals that took place in Bible times and applies them to today. 268 pages.

978-1880226858   **LB38** $15.99

Voices of Messianic Judaism *Confronting Critical Issues Facing a Maturing Movement*
—General Editor Rabbi Dan Cohn-Sherbok

Many of the best minds of the Messianic Jewish movement contributed their thoughts to this collection of 29 substantive articles. Challenging questions are debated: The involvement of Gentiles in Messianic Judaism? How should outreach be accomplished? Liturgy or not? Intermarriage? 256 pages.

978-1880226933   **LB46** $15.99

The Enduring Paradox *Exploratory Essays in Messianic Judaism*
—General Editor Dr. John Fischer

Yeshua and his Jewish followers began a new movement—Messianic Judaism—2,000 years ago. In the 20th century, it was reborn. Now, at the beginning of the 21st century, it is maturing. Twelve essays from top contributors to the theology of this vital movement of God, including: Dr. Walter C. Kaiser, Dr. David H. Stern, and Dr. John Fischer. 196 pages.

978-1880226902   **LB43** $13.99

The World To Come *A Portal to Heaven on Earth*
—Derek Leman

An insightful book, exposing fallacies and false teachings surrounding this extremely important subject... paints a hopeful picture of the future and dispels many non-biblical notions. Intriguing chapters: Magic and Desire, The Vision of the Prophets, Hints of Heaven, Horrors of Hell, The Drama of the Coming Ages. Offers a fresh, but old, perspective on the world to come, as it interacts with the prophets of Israel and the Bible. 110 pages.

978-1880226049   **LB67**   .$9.99

Hebrews Through a Hebrew's Eyes
—Dr. Stuart Sacks

Written to first-century Messianic Jews, this epistle, understood through Jewish eyes, edifies and encourages all. 119 pages. Endorsed by Dr. R.C. Sproul and James M. Boice.

978-1880226612   **LB23** $10.99

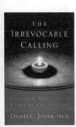

The Irrevocable Calling *Israel's Role As A Light To The Nations*
—Daniel C. Juster, Th.D.

Referring to the chosen-ness of the Jewish people, Paul, the Apostle, wrote "For God's free gifts and his calling are irrevocable" (Rom. 11:29). This messenger to the Gentiles understood the unique calling of his people, Israel. So does Dr. Daniel Juster, President of Tikkun Ministries Int'l. In *The Irrevocable Calling*, he expands Paul's words, showing how Israel was uniquely chosen to bless the world and how these blessings can be enjoyed today. Endorsed by Dr. Jack Hayford, Mike Bickle and Don Finto. 64 pages.

978-1880226346	**LB66**	$8.99

Are There Two Ways of Atonement?
—Dr. Louis Goldberg

Here Dr. Louis Goldberg, long-time professor of Jewish Studies at Moody Bible Institute, exposes the dangerous doctrine of Two-Covenant Theology. 32 pages.

978-1880226056	**LB12**	$ 4.99

Awakening *Articles and Stories About Jews and Yeshua*
—Arranged by Anna Portnov

Articles, testimonies, and stories about Jewish people and their relationship with God, Israel, and the Messiah. Includes the effective tract, "The Most Famous Jew of All." One of our best anthologies for witnessing to Jewish people. Let this book witness for you! Russian version also available. 110 pages.

English	978-1880226094	**LB15**	$ 6.99
Russian	978-1880226018	**LB14**	$ 6.99

The Unpromised Land *The Struggle of Messianic Jews Gary and Shirley Beresford*
—Linda Alexander

They felt God calling them to live in Israel, the Promised Land. Wanting nothing more than to live quietly and grow old together in the country of refuge for all Jewish people, little did they suspect what events would follow to try their faith. The fight to make *aliyah*, to claim their rightful inheritance in the Promised Land, became a battle waged not only for themselves, but also for Messianic Jews all over the world that wish to return to the Jewish homeland. Here is the true saga of the Beresford's journey to the land of their forefathers. 216 pages.

978-1880226568	**LB19**	$ 9.99

Death of Messiah *Twenty fascinating articles that address a subject of grief, hope, and ultimate triumph.*
—Edited by Kai Kjaer-Hansen

This compilation, written by well-known Jewish believers, addresses the issue of Messiah and offers proof that Yeshua—the true Messiah—not only died, but also was resurrected! 160 pages.

978-1880226582   **LB20** $ 8.99

Beloved Dissident *(A Novel)*
—Laurel West

A gripping story of human relationships, passionate love, faith, and spiritual testing. Set in the world of high finance, intrigue, and international terrorism, the lives of David, Jonathan, and Leah intermingle on many levels--especially their relationships with one another and with God. As the two men tangle with each other in a rising whirlwind of excitement and danger, each hopes to win the fight for Leah's love. One of these rivals will move Leah to a level of commitment and love she has never imagined--or dared to dream. Whom will she choose? 256 pages.

978-1880226766   **LB33** $ 9.99

Sudden Terror
—Dr. David Friedman

Exposes the hidden agenda of militant Islam. The author, a former member of the Israel Defense Forces, provides eye-opening information needed in today's dangerous world.

Dr. David Friedman recounts his experiences confronting terrorism; analyzes the biblical roots of the conflict between Israel and Islam; provides an overview of early Islam; demonstrates how the United States and Israel are bound together by a common enemy; and shows how to cope with terrorism and conquer fear. The culmination of many years of research and personal experiences. This expose will prepare you for what's to come! 160 pages.

978-1880226155   **LB49** $ 9.99

It is Good! *Growing Up in a Messianic Family*
—Steffi Rubin

Growing up in a Messianic Jewish family. Meet Tovah! Tovah (Hebrew for "Good") is growing up in a Messianic Jewish home, learning the meaning of God`s special days. Ideal for young children, it teaches the biblical holidays and celebrates faith in Yeshua. 32 pages to read & color.

978-1880226063   **LB11** $ 4.99